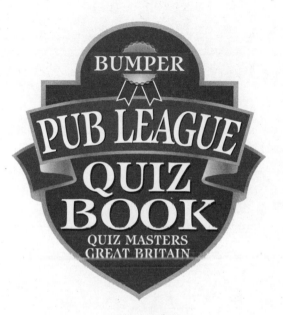

BUMPER

PUB LEAGUE

QUIZ
BOOK

QUIZ MASTERS
GREAT BRITAIN

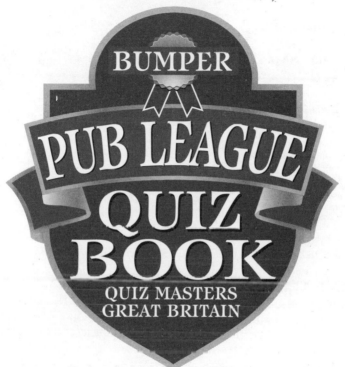

BUMPER

PUB LEAGUE

QUIZ
BOOK

QUIZ MASTERS
GREAT BRITAIN

foulsham
LONDON • NEW YORK • TORONTO • SYDNEY

foulsham

The Oriel, Thames Valley Court, 183–187 Bath Road, Slough,
Berkshire, SL1 4AA, England

Foulsham books can be found in all good bookshops and direct from
www.foulsham.com

ISBN: 978-0-572-03538-9

Copyright © 2010 W. Foulsham & Co. Ltd

Cover photographs © Press Association (left to right, images 1, 2 and 4)
and Superstock (image 3).

Beer pump © Alamy

A CIP record for this book is available from the British Library

Printed in Great Britain by Thomson Litho, East Kilbride

Contents

Introduction   7

Part 1   Pub League Quizzes   9

Rules of the Game   11

Pub League Quiz Score Sheet   13

Pub League Quizzes 1–51   15

Part 2   Quick-fire Questions   271

Quick-fire Quiz Score Sheet   274

Quick-fire Quizzes 1–5   275

Pub League Quiz Answers   325

Quick-fire Quiz Answers   481

Score Sheets   503

Introduction

Quizzes are a popular pastime both in the pub and home. It is great fun to test your knowledge, to tease your memory and to see how much you know about a range of subjects – and to discover what you don't know! This book includes questions on a vast range of topics, and they are pitched at varying levels of difficulty, so everyone has a fair shot at achieving a reasonable score. Even the hard questions, though more demanding, should be well within the scope of anyone with a fair spread of knowledge who takes an interest in the world at large.

Part 1 is made up of 51 exciting quizzes taken from the Quiz Masters Pub League quizzes. They are great fun to play at home with any number of team members, or you can use the correct pub league rules and try out the quizzes at your local.

In Part 2, there is a series of questions that can be used for a quick-fire round during which anyone can buzz in with the answer. However, they are also ideal for a more informal quiz that is not part of an organised league – or can even be used at home, just for fun.

Finally, dotted about through the book you will also find some fascinating questions with longer-than-usual answers. These are included mainly for interest, but if you can manage some correct answers, you are definitely in the master brain class!

So, pens at the ready: let's get started!

PART 1

Pub League Quizzes

Rules of the Game

When you play in a league, all the games are played on the same day at the same time. Questions are supplied in a sealed envelope to be opened by the question master in the presence of both teams at the beginning of the match. The questions and answers are normally listed together on a single sheet that is only seen by the question master. However, in this book the answers have been separated from the questions so that you do not need a separate question master.

In a formal setting, each team consists of four playing members. In addition, a question master/timekeeper is provided by the home team, and both teams supply a scorer (or the team captains can keep score).

The match is played in two halves. The question master tosses a coin to see who plays first.

The first four rounds in each half are team rounds. There are five questions for each team, which are asked to each team alternately. Conferring is allowed. If the team cannot answer or answers incorrectly, the question is passed over to the other team for a bonus point.

The final round in each half is a round of individual questions. The team that goes first answers the individual questions in the first half, and the opposing team answers the individual questions in the second half. At the beginning of the match, each team member chooses his or her subject for the individual round from the five categories provided. Conferring is not allowed on these questions. If the team member cannot answer the question or answers incorrectly, the question can be passed over to the other team for a bonus point, and the opposing team can confer.

All answers to the team questions and to bonus questions must be given by the team captains.

Thirty seconds are allowed for each answer, which starts after the question has been read out. An additional 15 seconds are allowed if the question is passed over for a bonus.

Scoring is as follows:

- All correct team questions: two points

- All correct individual questions: three points

- All correct bonus questions: one point

The question master acts as the adjudicator and his or her decision is final. In the case of any dispute, some reserve questions are supplied, which can be substituted if required.

A sample score sheet is given at the end of the questions. The scorers check and agree the points after each round. You can also use the score sheet is you are having a quiz at home, of course.

Questions are also provided for a drinks round. These are not counted as part of the match, but can be used as reserve questions if necessary. There are ten questions for each team, which are asked alternately.

Pub League Quiz Score Sheet

1st HALF	HOME		AWAY	
ROUND 1	SCORE	BONUS	SCORE	BONUS
Q1				
Q2				
Q3				
Q4				
Q5				
TOTAL				
ROUND 2				
Q1				
Q2				
Q3				
Q4				
Q5				
TOTAL				
ROUND 3				
Q1				
Q2				
Q3				
Q4				
Q5				
TOTAL				
ROUND 4				
Q1				
Q2				
Q3				
Q4				
Q5				
TOTAL				
ROUND 5				
Q1				
Q2				
Q3				
Q4				
Q5				
TOTAL				
1st HALF	HOME		AWAY	
TOTAL				

FINAL SCORE:

Home Team   Away Team

2nd HALF	HOME		AWAY	
ROUND 6	SCORE	BONUS	SCORE	BONUS
Q1				
Q2				
Q3				
Q4				
Q5				
TOTAL				
ROUND 7				
Q1				
Q2				
Q3				
Q4				
Q5				
TOTAL				
ROUND 8				
Q1				
Q2				
Q3				
Q4				
Q5				
TOTAL				
ROUND 9				
Q1				
Q2				
Q3				
Q4				
Q5				
TOTAL				
ROUND 10				
Q1				
Q2				
Q3				
Q4				
Q5				
TOTAL				
2nd HALF	HOME		AWAY	
TOTAL				

Pub League Quiz 1

The individual questions are in Rounds 5 and 10 and are on sport, classical music, TV and radio, science and law.

Round 1

Team 1

1 What is the capital of Cyprus?
2 Which actor starred in the film *Barefoot in the Park*?
3 Which boxer was the 'Ambling Alp'?
4 In what year was Gandhi assassinated?
5 Which film star's real surname is Mapother IV?

Team 2

1 What is the capital of Nigeria?
2 Which actor starred in the film *The Hustler*?
3 Who lost his heavyweight crown to 'Buster' Douglas in 1990?
4 In what year did General de Gaulle die?
5 Who was born Vivien Hartley?

Round 2

Team 1

1 Who succeeded King George III to the throne?
2 Which war took place between 1950 and 1953?
3 What does RNR stand for?
4 Which Kipling novel tells the story of Kimball O'Hara?
5 On which river is Leeds?

Team 2

1 Who succeeded Queen Anne to the throne?
2 Which war took place between 1337 and 1453?
3 What does RNIB stand for?
4 In which Dickens novel would you find Little Nell?
5 On which river is Barnstaple?

Round 3

Team 1

1 In which London botanical garden would you find a pagoda?
2 What is the science of projectiles and their propulsion?
3 Who invented bakelite?
4 Who composed the music for the opera *The Tales of Hoffman*?
5 What instrument did Cannonball Adderly play?

Team 2

1 Where in London is the residence of the Archbishop of Canterbury?
2 What is the biological study of relationships between living things?
3 Who invented the modern clarinet?
4 Who composed the music for the opera *The Flying Dutchman*?
5 What instrument did Dizzy Gillespie play?

Round 4

Team 1

1 Who shot Achilles in the heel?

2 What was the former name of Ethiopia?

3 In which month is Thanksgiving Day in the US?

4 What sort of animal is a karakul?

5 What is the first day of Lent called?

Team 2

1 In Greek mythology, who flew too close to the sun?

2 What is the capital of Ethiopia?

3 In which month is Burns Night?

4 What sort of animal is a takin?

5 What in the Christian liturgical year follows Lent?

Round 5   Individual questions for Team 1

Sport

Who was the Italian motorcyclist who won the 500cc World Championship seven times between 1966 and 1972?

Classical music

Who composed the music for the opera *Daphnis and Chloe*?

TV and radio

In *Star Trek*, which planet was home to Mr Spock?

Science

In what state of matter is krypton usually found?

Law

Name the four legal societies known as the Inns of Court.

Round 6

Team 2

1 In which village is *The Archers* set?

2 Who led the Charge of the Light Brigade?

3 Who wrote *Moll Flanders*?

4 Where is the Kariba dam?

5 In sport, what does LTA stand for?

Team 1

1 In which city was *Brookside* set?

2 Who was ousted in Nasser's 1954 coup?

3 Who wrote *Finnegan's Wake*?

4 Which Northern Irish county has the county town of Enniskillen?

5 In sport, what does MCC stand for?

Round 7
Team 2

1 Who was the eldest son of Queen Victoria?
2 What is abalone?
3 Who designed St Paul's Cathedral?
4 Which painter's first major work was 'Crucifixion '33'?
5 Whose films included *Rio Rita* and *The Wistful Widow of Wagon Gap*?

Team 1

1 Which king was thought to be afflicted by 'madness' in 1811?
2 What is a jacaranda?
3 Who designed Blenheim Palace?
4 Which artist is famous for his depiction of Cookham Regatta?
5 Who starred in the films *The Dawn Patrol*, *The Prisoner of Zenda* and *Gunga Din*?

Round 8
Team 2

1 Which Prime Minister involved Britain in the Crimean War?

2 Where was Thomas à Becket killed?
3 Who wrote *A History of Misfortunes*?
4 What name is given to an irrational fear of high places?
5 What product made the town of Axminster famous?

Team 1

1 What name was given to the rebellion by Irish nationalists against British rule on 24 April 1916?
2 Where was the Magna Carta signed?
3 Who wrote *Metamorphosis* and *The Trial*?
4 What is aesthetics the study of?
5 What fabric is the town of Honiton famous for?

Round 9
Team 2

1 What is royal assent?
2 At its greatest extent, which is Africa's largest lake?
3 Which river flowers through the Grand Canyon?
4 What is the capital of Sicily?
5 In the kitchen, what is sodium bicarbonate also known as?

Team 1

1 Who was the first woman to sit in the House of Commons?
2 Which is America's largest lake?
3 On which river is the Aswan Dam?
4 What is the capital of Majorca?
5 What is sodium chloride better known as?

Round 10   Individual questions for Team 2
Sport
What year saw the inauguration of the FA cup?
Classical music
Which Puccini opera was unfinished when he died?
TV and radio
Medavoy and Martinez appear in which TV show?
Science
What term describes -273.16° on the Centrigrade scale?
Law
In English law, who or what has priority of payment from a deceased person's estate?

Drinks round
Team 1

1 Which rock band do you associate with Noel and Liam Gallagher?
2 Where is the *La Scala* opera house?
3 Which US comedian starred in the film *Never Give a Sucker an Even Break*?
4 Who was the fourth wife of Henry VIII?
5 Who wrote *The Name of the Rose*?
6 When is Lady Day?
7 What is the third letter of the Greek alphabet?
8 What is the capital of Ghana?
9 In business, what does IMF stand for?
10 Who wrote *Madame Bovary*?

Team 2

1 With which group was Frederick Bulsara lead vocalist?
2 Which city is home to the Metropolitan Opera Company?
3 Which actress played Blanche du Bois in *A Streetcar Named Desire*?
4 Who was the second wife of Henry VIII?
5 Who wrote *Keep the Aspidistra Flying*?
6 When is St David's Day?
7 What is the last letter of the Greek alphabet?
8 What is the capital of Morocco?
9 What does ISBN stand for?
10 Who wrote *The Last of the Mohicans*?

Reserve questions
1 Apart from Geoff Hurst, who scored for England in the 1966 soccer World Cup final?
2 What sort of animal is a mandrill?
3 What was the name of the *Titanic*'s sister ship?

Pub League Quiz 2

The individual questions are in Rounds 5 and 10 and are on animals, pop music, transport, kings and queens, geography.

Round 1

Team 1
1 When is All Saints' Day?
2 Name the first bridge built across the Thames at London.
3 What name is given to a design or decoration made up of small pieces of glass or stone, etc?

4 Which was the only film to earn John Wayne an Oscar?
5 What was the date of D-day?

Team 2
1 When is All Souls' Day?
2 Name the second bridge built across the Thames at London.
3 In which art form are compositions made up of objects juxtaposed and pasted on a dry ground?
4 What was John Wayne's real name?
5 What was the date of VE day?

Round 2

Team 1
1 Who composed 'The Flight of the Bumble Bee'?
2 What was the name of the oil tanker that ran aground off Land's End in 1967?
3 Who had a hit with 'Sylvia's Mother'?
4 Who was the queen of the fairies in *A Midsummer Night's Dream*?
5 Which marine creature's skin used to be used as sandpaper?

Team 2
1 Who composed the 'Sabre Dance'?
2 What ship sank in the Solent in 1545 and was refloated in the 1980s?
3 Who had a hit with 'Chain Reaction'?
4 Who was king of the fairies in *A Midsummer Night's Dream*?
5 What part of a horse used to be used to make glue?

Round 3

Team 1

1 What is the maximum number of men in a tug of war team?
2 Which American state is nicknamed 'Heart of Dixie'?
3 Who painted 'The Rake's Progress'?
4 Who was executed at Fotheringay on 8 February 1587?
5 What is the name of the postmistress in the Postman Pat stories?

Team 2

1 How many players are there in a netball team?
2 Which American state is known as the 'Sunshine State'?
3 Who composed 'The Rake's Progress'?
4 Who was crowned King of all England at Bath in 973CE?
5 What is the name of the dim hunter who never catches the rabbit in Bugs Bunny cartoons?

Round 4

Team 1

1 Name the designer of the Volkswagen Beetle motor car.
2 In which European city is the Prado art gallery?
3 Pietro Mennea, Donald Quarrie and Joe Deloach were all Olympic champions in what event?
4 Which piece of medical equipment was invented by Rene Laenne in 1816?
5 Who wrote *The Importance of Being Earnest*?

Team 2

1 Who commissioned Porsche to design the Volkswagen Beetle?
2 For which king was the Palace of Versailles built?
3 In which women's event did Great Britain take silver medals at every Olympics from 1936–60?
4 What were the four elements from which Aristotle believed all matter to be composed of?
5 Who wrote *The Strange Case of Dr Jekyll and Mr Hyde*?

Round 5   Individual questions for Team 1

Animals
What type of animal is a basenji?
Pop music
Who recorded the song 'They Shoot Horses Don't They?'?
Transport
Where is there a heliport in Cornwall?
Kings and queens
Who was the only representative of the House of Saxe-Coburg and Gotha on the British throne?
Geography
Which is the second largest island in the Mediterranean?

Round 6

Team 2

1 Who was the 17th-century founder of the Quakers?

2 Which island was ceded to Britain by the Treaty of Nanking?

3 What is a cantrip?

4 Where were *The Killing Fields* of the 1984 hit film?

5 Where were the Winter Olympics of 1994 held?

Team 1

1 Who was the 19th-century founder of the Jehovah's Witnesses?

2 Which Nobel Prize winner was assassinated in 1968 in Memphis, Tennessee?

3 What is a parbuckle?

4 In which war-torn country was the 1982 film *The Year of Living Dangerously* set?

5 Which sport has been included in the Winter Olympics since 1920?

Round 7

Team 2

1 Which was the first planet discovered by telescope?

2 By what name is the Collegiate Church of St Peter better known?

3 What was Robert Adam famous for?

4 Who starred in TV's *Budgie* and *Love Hurts*?

5 What was the predecessor of the RAF?

Team 1

1 Who first sighted Uranus in 1781?

2 Who wears the Fisherman's Ring?

3 What was John Cabot famous for?

4 Who accompanied Oz Clarke on his *Big Wine Adventure*?

5 In what year was the RAF formed?

Round 8

Team 2

1 What is the devil's picture book?

2 Who wrote *Love in a Cold Climate*?

3 What does ESA stand for?

4 What name is given to the killing of one's brother?

5 What are grissini?

Team 1

1 What are the devil's bones?

2 Who wrote *A Kind of Loving*?

3 What does NVQ stand for?

4 What is the legal term for sea beyond the territorial waters of a nation?

5 What is pastrami?

Round 9

Team 2

1 What name is given to a person who makes barrels and casks?
2 What is the formula for finding the surface area of a sphere?
3 How many Tolpuddle Martyrs were there?
4 Which heavyweight boxer retired in 1956 as the undefeated world champion?
5 Which long-running gentle rural show was presented by Phil Drabble?

Team 1

1 What is a cordwainer?
2 What is the formula for finding the volume of a sphere?
3 Which President of Eire had an Irish mother, a Spanish father and was born in New York?
4 Which heavyweight boxing world champion held the title longest?
5 Who did not become host of *Question Time* but did become quiz master of *University Challenge*?

Round 10   Individual questions for Team 2

Animals
What is Britain's smallest bird?
Pop music
What town is home to heavy metal band Def Leppard?
Transport
What is a phaeton?
Kings and queens
Which British monarch was nicknamed 'Silly Billy'?
Geography
Where is the Sicilian Channel?

Drinks round

Team 1

1 Why are horses exempt from UK quarantine?

2 Which Commandment forbids the making of 'any graven image'?

3 Whose real name is Robert Zimmerman?

4 What was Percy Shaw's contribution to road safety?

5 Originating in Peru, what is the domestic cavy better known as?

6 What is the US name for a bowler hat?

7 What is the eighth sign of the zodiac?

8 What is the habitat of arboreal animals?

9 Who in politics became 'The Beast of Bolsover'?

10 In which TV comedy did Edina and Patsy feature?

Team 2

1 Why is Bridego Bridge in Bucks notorious in the annals of British crime?

2 What is an imam?

3 Whose real name is Steveland Morris Hardaway?

4 What was Christopher Cockerell's contribution to modern transport?

5 Most species of birds of paradise are found on which island?

6 What is a yarmulka?

7 What is the twelfth sign of the zodiac?

8 Fell, Dale, Exmoor and Welsh Mountain are examples of what?

9 Who in politics became 'The Chingford Skinhead'?

10 In what part did Betty Driver find fame in *Coronation Street*?

Reserve questions

1 What city is believed to have been the capital of the Inca Empire?

2 What part have both Lois Maxwell and Caroline Bliss played in the James Bond films?

3 Who wrote about 140 kinds of tobacco ash?

Pub League Quiz 3

The individual questions are in Rounds 5 and 10 and are on history, TV and radio, science, literature and poetry, discoverers and explorers.

Round 1

Team 1

1 The novel *The Day of the Jackal* was about the attempted assassination of whom?
2 What does FRAS stand for?
3 Who designed the mini skirt?
4 In which county is Castle Howard?
5 Which sea separates Australia from New Zealand?

Team 2

1 In the novel *Animal Farm*, which animals took over the farm?
2 What does FRCVS stand for?
3 Who designed the New Look in 1947?
4 In which county is Cadbury Castle?
5 Which stretch of water separates North and South Island, New Zealand?

Round 2

Team 1

1 In which month is the Cheltenham Gold Cup run?
2 Which A road connects London and Dover?
3 Who manufactured the DC10 aircraft?
4 Who wrote *The French Lieutenant's Woman*?
5 What date is American Independence Day?

Team 2

1 In which month is the St Leger run?
2 Which A road connects London and Brighton?
3 Who manufactured the TriStar aircraft?
4 Who wrote *Bhowani Junction*?
5 What day was Armistice Day in the First World War?

Round 3

Team 1

1 Where is Sugar Loaf Mountain?
2 What year was the St Valentine's Day Massacre?
3 Which actor starred in *Tom Jones* and *Gumshoe*?
4 How many humps has a Bactrian camel?
5 In the Bible, who was Solomon's father?

Team 2

1 What is the second highest peak in the world?
2 Where in America were the witch trials of 1692 held?
3 Who produced the films *High Noon* and *The Caine Mutiny*?
4 What is a one-humped camel called?
5 Who in the Bible were the first farmers?

Round 4

Team 1

1 Who wrote the music for *West Side Story*?
2 Who was taller – James Callaghan or Harold Wilson?
3 What was Beethoven's only opera?
4 How many strings has a violin?
5 Against whom did Oscar Wilde bring a libel action that led to his imprisonment?

Team 2

1 Who wrote the lyrics for *West Side Story*?
2 Which politician caused a stir by appearing at the Cenotaph in a duffle coat?
3 Who composed the ballets *Rodeo* and *Billy the Kid*?
4 What is the smallest member of the flute family?
5 About which prison did Oscar Wilde write?

Round 5   Individual questions for Team 1

History
Who was the first Welsh-born king to occupy the throne of England?

TV and radio
What was the first name of the younger Steptoe in *Steptoe and Son*?

Science
Of what is dendrology the study?

Literature and poetry
Which play, first performed in 1808, was Johann von Goethe's most famous work?

Discoverers and explorers
Which British mountaineer was the first person to scale the Matterhorn?

Round 6

Team 2

1 Which is the hottest planet?
2 What is alluvium?
3 What measure is equal to a quarter of an imperial pint?
4 What is an Australian kelpie?
5 On which river does Prague stand?

Team 1

1 Which is the coldest planet?
2 What type of rock is formed by the cooling and recrystallisation of molten magma?
3 What is measured in ohms?
4 What is a Dandie Dinmont?
5 On which river does Warsaw stand?

Round 7

Team 2

1 What is the chemical symbol for lead?
2 Who was the Greek goddess of hearth and family?
3 Which actress starred in *A Touch of Class*?
4 Which country won the Davis Cup five years in succession from 1968 to 1972?

5 What was Hitler's Final Solution?

Team 1

1 What is the chemical symbol for aluminium?
2 Who was the Greek god of war?
3 Which actor starred in *A Man Called Horse*?
4 Which soccer team won the European Champions' Cup three consecutive times from 1974 onwards?
5 Which Czech village was destroyed in 1942 by the Nazis in retaliation for the assassination of Reinhard Heydrich?

Round 8

Team 2

1 What does KCMG stand for?
2 Who wrote *The Railway Children*?
3 Which is the smallest of the North American Great Lakes?
4 What sort of game is bezique?

5 Apart from their surnames, what did Frederick and William Temple have in common?

Team 1

1 What does KT stand for?
2 Who wrote *Sons and Lovers*?
3 In which country are the 'Mountains of the Moon'?
4 In Monopoly, what completes the set with Trafalgar Square?
5 What do Sweden, Switzerland, Portugal, Spain and Ireland have in common?

Round 9

Team 2

1 What name is given to the study of bells and bell ringing?
2 What is the square root of 361?
3 What is the 12th letter of the Greek alphabet?
4 Which artist is famous for his portraits of Lord Nelson and the poet Cowper?
5 Who was the political leader of the Muslims in Kashmir and also served as Prime Minister of Jammu and Kashmir after India's independence in 1947?

Team 1

1 Of what is otology the study?

2 What is the square root of 441?
3 What is the 15th letter of the Greek alphabet?
4 Who painted *The Gross Clinic* and *The Swimming Hole*?

5 Name the Carthaginian general who marched against Rome in the second Punic war.

Round 10 Individual questions for Team 2

History
Name the 14th-century Bishop and Chancellor of England who chiefly remodelled Winchester Cathedral.

TV and radio
Who played Selwyn Froggit?

Science
What is a contusion?

Literature and poetry
Which winner of the Nobel Prize for Literature published *The Spirit Level* in 1996?

Discoverers and explorers
Who discovered the Niagara Falls?

Drinks round

Team 1

1 What is a katydid?
2 Name Noah's second son.

3 Who starred as *Shane* in the 1953 film of the same name?
4 Where was Henry V's victory over the French in 1415?
5 Who wrote *The Alchemist*?
6 Where are the Kaikoura Mountains?
7 Which acid is present in vinegar?

8 Who was the Greek god of sleep?

9 Who wrote 'Honeysuckle Blues'?
10 Between which two places does the Northern Irish M1 run?

Team 2

1 How many legs has a lobster?
2 Name the elder brother of Moses who made the golden calf.

3 Which actress starred in *A Star is Born* in 1954?
4 Who was the last Kaiser?

5 Who wrote *Look Back in Anger*?
6 What is the highest peak in North America?
7 Which acid can be formed by bacterial action in milk?
8 Who was the Roman god of wine?

9 Who wrote 'One O'clock Jump'?
10 Between which two places does the Northern Irish M2 run?

Reserve questions

1 Which European monarch was deliberately absent from the wedding of Prince Charles and Lady Diana Spencer?
2 Who invented frozen food?
3 To the nearest five years, when was the first complete sentence transmitted over the telephone?

Pub League Quiz 4

The individual questions are in Rounds 5 and 10 and are on classical music, geology, inventors, famous men, words.

Round 1

Team 1
1 Who is the mother of actress Joely Richardson?
2 Which countries are connected by the Brenner Pass?
3 How many Marx brothers were there?
4 What was *Dirty Harry*'s surname in the series of films starring Clint Eastwood?
5 Which queen married William of Orange?

Team 2
1 What TV role is associated with Sian Lloyd?
2 Name the three South American countries on the Equator.
3 Name the five Marx brothers.
4 What do Maggie Johnson and Dina Ruiz have in common?
5 Which king married Mary of Teck?

Round 2

Team 1
1 What was the nationality of the astronomer Copernicus?
2 How many even numbers above zero are there on a roulette wheel?
3 Who wrote *20,000 Leagues Under the Sea*?
4 Who directed the classic 1941 version of the film *The Maltese Falcon*?
5 What name is given to a wine bottle 8–12 times ordinary size?

Team 2
1 What was the nationality of the astronomer Tycho Brahe?
2 What number is directly opposite 19 on a dart board?
3 Who was the captain of the Nautilus in *20,000 Leagues Under the Sea*?
4 Name the Polish film director with a taste for the macabre as in *Rosemary's Baby*.
5 What is made only from pinot, meunier and chardonnay grapes?

Round 3

Team 1

1 What kind of animal is a margay?
2 Who designed the Queen's House at Greenwich?
3 Who painted 'The Light of the World'?
4 Where is home to Noddy?
5 What is the capital of Trinidad?

Team 2

1 What is the largest living lizard?
2 Who was responsible for building the Crystal Palace?
3 Who painted 'Olympia'?
4 Where is home to the Flintstones?
5 What is the capital of Hawaii?

Round 4

Team 1

1 What is also known as Hansen's disease?
2 Which A road links Oxford and Winchester?
3 Which Defence Secretary resigned over the Westland affair in 1986?
4 What part did Sir Alex Guinness play in TV's *Tinker, Tailor, Soldier, Spy*?
5 In which London borough is the Royal Albert Hall?

Team 2

1 What is the common name for tetanus?
2 Which A road runs from London to Fishguard?
3 Which American Vice-President resigned after being accused of tax evasion and fraud?
4 What part did Sir Alec Guinness play in the film *The Bridge on the River Kwai*?
5 In which London street is the Cenotaph?

Round 5   Individual questions for Team 1

Classical music
Name the English composer whose works include the 'Enigma' variations.
Geology
What substance forms an atoll?
Inventors
Who made the first dynamo?
Famous men
Who was the first Astronomer Royal in England?
Words
What is Spanish for black?

Round 6
Team 2
1 What does 'rabbi' actually mean?

2 Who discovered Brazil?

3 Who refused to accept an Oscar in 1972?

4 What were Liberty Ships?

5 Who made the first non-stop, solo flight from America to Europe?

Team 1
1 What does 'messiah' actually mean?

2 Who first sighted the Orinoco river?

3 Who was the Oscar-winning actress of the film *Mrs Miniver*?

4 Which historic US monument is housed in Independence Hall, Philadelphia?

5 What was the name of the aircraft in which Lindbergh made his non-stop Atlantic flight?

Round 7
Team 2
1 Who recorded 'Tusk'?

2 Who was born Goldie Mabovitch?

3 Which poet wrote *Arms and the Boy*?

4 What is a megapode?

5 How many players are there in a baseball team?

Team 1
1 Robert Smith is lead vocalist with which band?

2 By what name was Margaretha Geertruida Zelle better known?

3 Which poet wrote *The Highwayman*?

4 What is a boomslang?

5 How many players are there in a basketball team?

Round 8
Team 2
1 Which Scottish loch has the largest surface area?

2 Name the two bones of the forearm.

3 Name the Roman god of the sea.

4 Who was the first woman to be proclaimed Queen of England?

5 Who was the first presenter of TV's *The National Lottery Live*?

Team 1
1 Which is the largest freshwater lake in the British Isles?

2 Name the two bones of the lower leg.

3 Who was the Greek god of the sea?

4 Who was on the British throne at the outbreak of the First World War?

5 Which animator created *Wallace and Gromit*?

Round 9

Team 2

1 What is calcium oxide also known as?
2 What is the capital of Bangladesh?
3 Which political leaders brought about the Atlantic Charter?
4 What in art is a nimbus?
5 Where is Carisbrooke Castle?

Team 1

1 What is marsh gas?
2 Which is the largest of the United Arab Emirates?
3 In which year was the Atlantic Charter declared?
4 What in art is intaglio?
5 In which county is Maiden Castle?

Round 10   Individual questions for Team 2

Classical music

Which famous violinist of Russian Jewish parentage was born in New York in 1916?

Geology

What type of coal is formed from organic matter rich in spores and algae, and has no characteristic visible structure?

Inventors

What did L. E. Waterman invent?

Famous men

What was the name of the London landlord exposed in 1963 for charging extortionate rent and using violence against his tenants?

Words

What is palynology?

Just for fun

Which famous poet was a skilled boxer?

Lord George Byron. Despite a physical infirmity, he was a noted pugilist in his youth and took lessons from 'Gentleman' Jackson, the champion of England from 1795 to 1800. Censured by the university authorities for consorting with a prizefighter, Byron replied loftily that Jackson's manners were 'infinitely superior' to those of the fellows of his college at their high table.

Drinks round

Team 1

1 Who wrote the song 'White Christmas'?
2 In which novel would you find the Thought Police?
3 What is the state capital of Arkansas?
4 Who starred opposite Jeremy Irons in *The French Lieutenant's Woman*?
5 Who won the tennis gold medal in the Women's Singles at the 1992 Olympics?
6 What is a somnambulist?
7 Which British general won the Battle of Malplaquet?
8 What does NFU stand for?
9 What is the capital of Bolivia?
10 What is the essential flavour in mornay sauce?

Team 2

1 Who wrote the songs for *Gigi*?
2 Who wrote the novel *1984*?
3 Baton Rouge is the capital of which American state?
4 Who played opposite Meryl Streep in *Ironweed*?
5 Who won the tennis gold medal in the Men's Singles at the 1992 Olympics?
6 What is a fifth columnist?
7 Which British general won the Battle of Vimeiro?
8 In world politics, what does OAU stand for?
9 What is the capital of Nicaragua?
10 Name the main ingredient of mead.

Reserve questions

1 Who wrote *The Mystery of Edwin Drood*?
2 What is another name for the caribou?
3 What is kaolin?

Pub League Quiz 5

The individual questions are in Rounds 5 and 10 and are on pop music, politics, general knowledge, words and films.

Round 1

Team 1

1 What colour are the flowers of the hop plant?
2 Between which two places does the M6 run?
3 Which river runs through Lincoln?
4 Which George Bernard Shaw play inspired *My Fair Lady*?
5 What is the latest date on which Easter Sunday may fall?

Team 2

1 What colour are the flowers of the marjoram plant?
2 Between which two places does the M5 run?
3 Which river runs through Colchester?
4 Who solves the crime in *Death on the Nile*?
5 Which Sunday is Low Sunday or Quasimodo Sunday?

Round 2

Team 1

1 What does IAEA stand for?
2 Which UK coins are still regularly struck in standard silver?
3 What is the legislative capital of South Africa?
4 Who composed the opera *Prince Igor*?
5 Which sporting event did Italy win in 1995 with 112.958 points?

Team 2

1 In which city are the IAEA's headquarters?
2 Easter eggs that were jewels were customarily given by the last Tsar of Russia to the Tsarina. Who made them?
3 What is the administrative capital of South Africa?
4 Which Verdi opera was written for the Khedive of Egypt?
5 Who was world cross-country champion on four successive occasions from 1986?

Round 3

Team 1

1 How many gallons of beer in a firkin?
2 Which two elements are combined to make common salt?
3 What are marmosets?
4 In which country is the Mekong river delta?
5 For his part in which TV programme did Rowan Atkinson win the Golden Rose of Montreaux?

Team 2

1 What is the square root of a gross?
2 What element is added to steel to make it stainless?
3 What are marmots?
4 Which river flows into a vast swamp called the Sudd?
5 Which late British comedian was born in Southampton in 1925?

Round 4

Team 1

1 What nationality was Christopher Columbus?
2 Nowadays, who would regularly wear a wimple?
3 Whose first novel had the title *Crome Yellow*?
4 Who designed the Houses of Parliament?
5 Who, according to Greek mythology, was the first woman?

Team 2

1 What nationality was Irving Berlin?
2 Which famous men's outfitters started as a second-hand clothes shop in Covent Garden?
3 Who wrote *The Ambassadors*?
4 Who designed Covent Garden?
5 What remained in Pandora's box?

Round 5   Individual questions for Team 1

Pop music
Men and Women and *Picture Book* were hit albums for which pop group?
Politics
Who is the mother of Emperor Akihito of Japan?
General knowledge
On which London Underground line are Edgware and Morden?
Words
Sawney is a derogatory name for which kind of Briton?
Films
For their parts in which film about Helen Keller did both Anne Bancroft and Patty Duke win Oscars?

Round 6

Team 2

1 Who were the Lord Protectors of England?
2 What are people from Cambridge called?
3 Between which two rivers was Mesopotamia?

4 Whose real name is Priscilla White?

5 What was the pen name of Frederic Dannay?

Team 1

1 Who was the last King of Egypt?

2 What are people from Manchester called?
3 What was the ancient name of Iraq when it was part of Mesopotamia?
4 What was naturalist and broadcaster Joy Adamson's country of origin?
5 Who was the fictional detective created by Dashiell Hammett?

Round 7

Team 2

1 What did Samuel Johnson describe as 'the triumph of hope over experience'?
2 Who directed the 1962 film *Lolita*?
3 Where is Ronaldsway airport?

4 What sort of aircraft was the pioneering Heinkel 168?
5 'Dwarf dog' is the literal Welsh meaning of which breed of dog?

Team 1

1 Who said, 'Let them eat cake'?

2 Which Williams swam to fame in the film *Bathing Beauty*?
3 Which airport serves Amsterdam?
4 Who designed the Luftwaffe's Bf-109 fighter plane?
5 Why do lemmings rush over cliffs?

Round 8

Team 2

1 What is the administrative capital of the Palestinian Autonomous Areas?
2 What is the capital of Paraguay?
3 What dye is used for testing for the presence of acid?
4 What was the food of Roman and Greek gods?
5 What is the anatomical name for the kneecap?

Team 1

1 Where was the World Fair held in 1904?

2 What is the capital of Ecuador?
3 Invar is an alloy of which two metals?
4 What was the drink of Roman and Greek gods?
5 What is the shoulder blade called?

Round 9

Team 2

1 Who was the first person to sail non-stop single-handed around the world?
2 At which royal palace was Henry VIII born?
3 To what family of instruments does the fife belong?
4 What in English law are relations on the father's side called?
5 Which President was responsible for making France a nuclear power?

Team 1

1 Who led the Commonwealth Trans-Antarctic Expedition of 1957–58?
2 Which is the oldest of London's royal parks?
3 How many pistons has a cornet?
4 What in English law are relations on the mother's side called?
5 Which US President abolished slavery?

Round 10   Individual questions for Team 2

Pop music
Who had hits with 'Run to You' and 'Summer of '69'?
Politics
Who was the last Liberal Prime Minister of Britain?
General knowledge
When is Michaelmas Day?
Words
What does callisthenics pertain to?
Films
What does Billy Wilder have in common with Andrew Lloyd Webber, professionally?

Drinks round

Team 1

1 Who recorded 'Suicide Blonde'?

2 What was the former name of Malawi?

3 Where would you find the kangaroo rat?

4 Who founded the first Sunday school?

5 In which town did Lowry paint his landscapes?

6 Who was appointed Master of the Queen's Music in March 2004?

7 What did Joseph of Arimathea beg from Pontius Pilate?

8 By what name is spirit of hartshorn better known?

9 With which sport would you associate Peter Gilchrist?

10 Who is fifth in line to the British throne?

Team 2

1 Who recorded 'Cigarettes and Alcohol'?

2 What was the former name of Botswana?

3 To what bird family does the yellowhammer belong?

4 What religious organisation was founded by Charles and John Wesley?

5 Who painted 'Mr and Mrs Clark and Percy' in 1971?

6 Who succeeded John Betjeman as Poet Laureate in 1984?

7 Which two books in the Bible recount the histories of Judah and Israel from the beginning of Solomon's reign to the fall of Judah and destruction of Jerusalem?

8 By what name is ethylene glycol better known?

9 With which sport would you associate the Swaythling Cup?

10 What was Princess Margaret's middle name?

Reserve questions

1 Who wrote *Waiting for Godot*?

2 Which sporting games were held at Buffalo in 1993?

3 Which Gospel records Jesus' last words as 'It is finished'?

Pub League Quiz 6

The individual questions are in Rounds 5 and 10 and are on law, geology, London, horse racing, TV and radio.

Round 1

Team 1

1 Name the Supreme Commander of the Allied Forces in the Second World War.
2 Which England Test Cricketer began his playing career in Zimbabwe?
3 Which *Mikado* character was Lord High Everything Else?
4 Which two actors starred in the *Road to . . .* films?
5 Who was the first man to orbit the earth?

Team 2

1 Where was the second atomic bomb dropped in the Second World War?
2 With what type of bowling is Abdul Qadir associated?
3 What were Gilbert and Sullivan's forenames?
4 Of the *Road to . . .* films, where did the first road lead?
5 Who was the first man on the moon?

Round 2

Team 1

1 In which year did Neil Kinnock become leader of the Labour Party?
2 In which month is the Henley Royal Regatta held?
3 What do the Americans call a tramp?
4 Whom did Alan Dukes replace as leader of Fine Gael?
5 How long does the pregnancy of a cat last?

Team 2

1 In which year did James Callaghan resign as leader of the Labour Party?
2 In which month is the Crufts Dog Show held?
3 What do Americans call potato crisps?
4 Who founded Fianna Fail?
5 How long does the pregnancy of a dog last?

Round 3

Team 1

1 Who instigated the building of Hampton Court Palace?
2 Which statesman and general founded British India?
3 Which painter had a 'blue period'?
4 What is alopecia?

5 In which sport are the leading exponents called 10th dans?

Team 2

1 To whom did Cardinal Wolsey give Hampton Court Palace?
2 Who acquired Singapore for Britain?
3 Which city is Canaletto famous for painting?
4 What would you have if you suffered from microcephaly?
5 Which martial art is judo a form of?

Round 4

Team 1

1 Who built the first British motor car?
2 On which river is the town and port of Bordeaux?
3 What is the French for eight?
4 Which actor starred in *Some Like it Hot* and *The Apartment*?
5 What was Sonny Ramadhin's sport?

Team 2

1 What did the Rover company build before it built cars?
2 On which river does Baghdad stand?
3 What is the French for nine?
4 Which actor won an Oscar for his role in *Ryan's Daughter*?
5 To the nearest 10 years, when was the first test match held in England?

Round 5   Individual questions for Team 1

Law

What is the legal term for a right over the property of another person, pending settlement of a claim?

Geology

What is the snow white variety of gypsum (calcium sulphate) better known as?

London

Where can you see a slab of marble inscribed 'Remember Winston Churchill'?

Horse racing

Which are the three classic horse races that make up racing's triple crown?

TV and radio

What is Radio 4's lunchtime news and current affairs programme called?

Round 6

Team 2

1 Which explorer wrote a book entitled *Aku-Aku*?

2 Who won the 1979 best actor Oscar for his part in *Kramer vs Kramer*?

3 How many children did Queen Victoria have?

4 Which is the only country in whose forests the aye-aye may be found?

5 What is the name for a young pilchard?

Team 1

1 Which book begins: 'It was a bright cold day in April, and the clocks were striking thirteen.'?

2 Which mixture of champagne and orange juice won the 1981 Eurovision Song Contest?

3 In which country did the Mau-Mau revolt against British colonial rule in the 1950s?

4 What is the capital of the Australian state of Victoria?

5 What is the name for a young eel?

Round 7

Team 2

1 Who was voted Young Cricketer of the Year in 1963?

2 Which game used to be known as Housey-Housey?

3 Beriberi is cause by the deficiency of which vitamin?

4 Who in literature was Sir Percy Blakeney?

5 Which Greek mathematician discovered that altering the length and tension of a string altered the pitch of the sound emitted?

Team 1

1 Who won the men's long jump at the Tokyo Olympics in 1964?

2 How many does an ace count in the game of pontoon?

3 What part of the body does Menière's Disease affect, giving rise to vertigo?

4 In Kipling's *The Jungle Book*, what kind of creature is Ka?

5 Which American industrialist pioneered mass production techniques for watches and produced a $1 watch in 1892?

Round 8
Team 2

1 Whose hat and cane were auctioned at Christie's in 1986?
2 Who formed his drab 'Commonwealth Government' in London?

3 What is a female badger called?

4 Where in England was the first iron bridge built?
5 Which son of Jacob and Rachel was skilful at interpreting dreams?

Team 1

1 Which pop star's guitar was sold at auction for £198,000 in 1990?
2 What stone, taken to Westminster Abbey in 1296, has now been returned to its original home in Scotland?
3 Halcyon is a poetic name for which animal?
4 Which river does the Huey P. Long Bridge in the USA span?
5 Why was Lot's wife turned into a pillar of salt?

Round 9
Team 2

1 The ancient Phoenician cities of Tyre and Sidon are on the coast of which modern country?

2 What does ROC stand for?
3 Who was the first woman Prime Minister of Turkey?

4 Who wrote *Clayhanger*?
5 At which sport did Lazlo Papp win three Olympic gold medals?

Team 1

1 In classical mythology, one of Amalthea's horns broke off as a she-goat suckled Zeus. What did it become?
2 What does RAOC stand for?
3 Who born at Ulm, Germany, became a scientist and declined an invitation to be President of Israel?
4 Who wrote *The Female Eunuch*?
5 In which county was the boxer Bob Fitzsimmons born?

Round 10 Individual questions for Team 2
Law
According to the letter of the law, what crime is still punishable by death in Britain?
Geology
What is lignite?
London
In which London street is the Bank of England?
Horse racing
Which horse won the Derby, the Irish Derby, the 2000 Guineas, the King George VI and Queen Elizabeth Diamond Stakes in 1975?
TV and radio
Which real village was the TV setting for *Last of the Summer Wine*?

41

Drinks round

Team 1

1 Name the first manned spacecraft.
2 Which American singer and dancer has the surname Ciccone?
3 Who wrote *Oedipus Rex*?
4 Of what fossilised material does the semi-precious gem amber consist of?
5 Who directed the films *Brewster McCloud* and *M*A*S*H*?
6 What is the longest running current affairs programme on British television?
7 Which country led the Medway Raid in 1667?
8 What is the name for a male giraffe?
9 What is the capital of Nepal?
10 Which area does the wine Macon come from?

Team 2

1 Name the first spacecraft to land on the moon.
2 Which singer was born Robert David Jones in 1947?
3 Who wrote *Quo Vadis?*?
4 Which geological period is known as the Age of Coal?
5 Who directed the film *A Bridge Too Far*?
6 Which TV soap ran for 24 years and ended in 1988?
7 Which English king was involved in the Barons' War?
8 What is an ungulate?
9 What is the capital of Cuba?
10 Which area does the wine Barsac come from?

Reserve questions

1 Whose cartoon bore the legend: 'It's a naive domestic Burgundy without any breeding, but I think you'll be amused by its presumption'?
2 What is a skerry?
3 For what constituent of drinks is spirits of wine another name?

Pub League Quiz 7

The individual questions are in Rounds 5 and 10 and are on boxing,
biology, literature, wars and pot luck.

Round 1

Team 1

1 Which famous explorer located
   the magnetic South Pole and
   climbed Mount Erebus?
2 Who composed the 'St Anthony
   Variations' and the 'Academic
   Festival Overture'?
3 Of which country is the lemur a
   native?
4 Which record company refused
   to give a recording contract to
   the Beatles?
5 How many old pennies were
   there in half a guinea?

Team 2

1 What was the name of
   Shackleton's ship that sank in the
   Weddell Sea?
2 Who composed 'The
   Harmonious Blacksmith'?
3 What is a mamba?
4 Which American record label
   was bought by Polygram in
   August 1993?
5 How many old pennies made up
   17/6d?

Round 2

Team 1

1 Who played the Prime Minister
   in *Yes, Prime Minister*?
2 Who painted 'The Harlot's
   Progress'?
3 What was the first major film to
   use a sound?
4 Who was Lord Horatio Nelson's
   mistress?
5 Who wrote the novel *Tobacco
   Road*?

Team 2

1 Name the two stars of *Cagney and
   Lacey*.
2 Who painted 'La Femme au
   Chapeau'?
3 Who starred in *The Jazz Singer* in
   1927?
4 Who was the mother of James I
   of England?
5 Who wrote the novel *That
   Uncertain Feeling*?

Round 3

Team 1

1 What is the state capital of Georgia, USA?
2 Which chemist first described colour blindness?
3 Who was the malicious companion of Thor and Odin?
4 Who wrote the musical score *The Entertainer*?
5 By what other name is the skull bone known?

Team 2

1 What is the state capital of South Australia?
2 Who first discovered the atomic nucleus?
3 Which god of victory gives its name to a popular brand of sportswear?
4 *The Entertainer* was the theme tune for which film?
5 What substance makes human hair and skin dark?

Round 4

Team 1

1 Where is the Irish Grand National run?
2 Which spacecraft accomplished the first approach to Mars?
3 Who made the first reliable ballpoint pen?
4 Name two of the Balearic Islands.
5 What does *ad int* stand for?

Team 2

1 Where was the Scottish Grand National run until 1966?
2 From which spacecraft were the first ever close-up TV pictures of the moon taken?
3 Who invented the yale lock?
4 Off the coast of which country are the Galapagos Islands?
5 What does *ad mod* stand for?

Round 5   Individual questions for Team 1

Boxing
What was Floyd Patterson's special style of boxing called?
Biology
What is the outer layer of a cell called?
Literature
Who was Bathsheba's second husband in *Far From the Madding Crowd*?
Wars
Which battle took place on 23 October 1642 and was the first encounter of the English Civil War?
Pot luck
What is Auld Reekie?

Round 6

Team 2

1 What is an isobath?
2 In which Disney film does a pedigree spaniel come into conflict with two Siamese cats?
3 Where was the world's first underground railway?

4 What is a schnitzel?

5 What 8th-century barrier runs from Prestatyn to Sedbury near Chepstow?

Team 1

1 What causes a tsunami?
2 Which Walt Disney character had alcoholic hallucinations of pink elephants?
3 Which express company first operated between New York and San Francisco?
4 What colour is the Italian liqueur galliano?
5 What is the name given to the area around the Wash that is below the sea level?

Round 7

Team 2

1 In which region of Italy is Genoa?
2 Who wrote *Cider with Rosie*?
3 What does BCL stand for?
4 Which king succeeded Edward IV?
5 In which London street does the Post Office have its headquarters?

Team 1

1 In which region of Italy is Naples?
2 Who wrote *The Seven Pillars of Wisdom*?
3 What does LLB stand for?
4 Who first awarded the George Cross?
5 In which London street is the National Portrait Gallery?

Round 8

Team 2

1 What nationality is Helena Sukova?
2 Which English king stood for election as Holy Roman Emperor?
3 What was the year of the first Live Aid concert at Wembley?
4 Who directed the film *Murder on the Orient Express*?
5 What is the name of the small independent state between Austria and Switzerland?

Team 1

1 What is Ian Botham's middle name?
2 For what is Elizabeth Fry best remembered?
3 With which record company did George Michael enter into legal dispute?
4 Who directed the Beatles' *Help* and *A Hard Day's Night*?
5 What is the capital of Liechtenstein?

Round 9

Team 2

1 What was first celebrated in 776BCE?

2 How many operas did Beethoven write?

3 In which two years was bubonic plague rampant in London?

4 Who wrote *Lucky Jim*?

5 What is the second sign of the zodiac?

Team 1

1 In which decade was the first LP produced?

2 How many violin concertos did Beethoven write?

3 What halted the plague in London?

4 Who wrote the book *Mary Poppins*?

5 What is the seventh sign of the zodiac?

Round 10   Individual questions for Team 2

Boxing
Who did Cassius Clay beat to become world champion for the first time?
Biology
Where in your body would you find keratin?
Literature
In Our Mutual Friend, who married John Harmon, alias John Rokesmith?
Wars
Who was the Admiral of the British Fleet at the battle of Jutland in 1916?
Pot luck
What in Oman is the Khareef?

Just for fun

Have rhinoceroses ever inhabited the British Isles?
Yes. Rhinos were in these islands from the onset of the Pleistocene period about a million years ago. More recently, the woolly rhinoceros flourished all over Europe, including Britain. It is the largest known land mammal and stood about five metres high, with its front legs longer than the back and a skull about a metre long. It died out during the last glacial period of the Ice Age 10,000 years ago. Other mammals that used to live in Britain include the elephant, zebra, bison, hyena and hippopotamus.

Drinks round

Team 1

1 'I come from haunts of coot and hern' is from which poem?
2 What is an avocet?
3 Who beat Steve Davis to win the 1986 World Snooker Championship?
4 What is a creel?
5 Which of the McGann brothers played *Dr Who* in the 1996 television revival?
6 Between which two towns did the first public railway run?
7 What does an oscillograph record?
8 What is the capital of Burkina Faso?
9 Who wrote *The Winslow Boy*?

10 What name was given to the mutiny in 1931 of the British sailors of the Atlantic Fleet?

Team 2

1 Who wrote *The Brook*?
2 What is a basilisk?
3 Who beat Steve Davis to win the 1985 World Snooker Championship?
4 What is a cabal?
5 What was the answer to the ultimate question in *The Hitch Hikers' Guide to the Galaxy*?
6 Between which two cities does the Orient Express run?
7 What is recorded on a seismograph?
8 In which country are the Owen Falls?
9 Who wrote *Swallows and Amazons*?

10 What is the name of the army formed in 1645 that won the English Civil War for Cromwell?

Reserve questions

1 What colours are the vertical stripes in the Italian flag?
2 What was the name given to the 1896 goldrush in the Yukon?
3 What is the scientific name for an exploding star?

Pub League Quiz 8

The individual questions are in Rounds 5 and 10 and are on athletics, geography, pot luck, famous women and Britain.

Round 1

Team 1

1 Who wrote the music for *Hair*?
2 What is army slang for a psychiatrist?
3 What nationality is singer Celine Dion?
4 Which country has the bolivar as its currency?
5 How many points are there on a compass?

Team 2

1 Who wrote the lyrics for *Hair*?
2 What is navy slang for a severe reprimand?
3 Which country is home to 1990s pop group Real McCoy?
4 What currency is used in the Philippines?
5 What is the square root of 256?

Round 2

Team 1

1 Which religious system and teaching was founded by Mary Baker Eddy?
2 Where was the *Mary Celeste* bound on her ill-fated voyage of 1872?
3 Who was the famous husband of the actress Elsa Lanchester?
4 Name the US navy officer who was first to reach the North Pole in 1909?
5 Which actor played himself in the film *To Hell and Back*?

Team 2

1 What are members of various Muslim orders, noted for their frenzied whirling dancing, called?
2 Where did the *Mary Rose* sink?
3 Who was Liza Minnelli's mother?
4 Who discovered Lake Edward in Africa?
5 Which Hollywood star made his final film appearance in *Guess Who's Coming to Dinner*?

Round 3

Team 1

1 Which country produced the Edsel motor car?
2 What type of animal is a lhasa apso?
3 Which Christian saint has the emblem of a winged lion?
4 Who killed herself when Oedipus gave the right answer to her riddle?
5 Who wrote *Exodus*?

Team 2

1 Which country did the Lloyd motor car come from?
2 What type of animal is a guanaco?
3 In which religion are drawings of humans and animal forms forbidden?
4 Who in ancient Greece 'looked all his life for an honest man'?
5 Who wrote *The Thirty-nine Steps*?

Round 4

Team 1

1 In what fictional city hospital is *Casualty* set?
2 Which horse won the 1996 Grand National?
3 Which boxer was known as Bombardier?
4 In which county is Longleat?
5 What were Lenin's first names?

Team 2

1 In which TV series did WPC Polly Page appear?
2 Which horse won the 1996 Cheltenham Gold Cup?
3 Who did Robert De Niro portray in the film *Raging Bull*?
4 In which county is Mereworth Castle?
5 What was Lenin's original surname?

Round 5 Individual questions for Team 1

Athletics

How many track events are there in a decathalon?

Geography

What is the most southerly town in Portugal?

Pot luck

Noted for his large nose and as a duellist, what was the more peaceful profession of Cyrano de Bergerac?

Famous women

Who was married to both Henry V and Owen Tudor?

Britain

What do Harlow and Telford have in common?

Round 6
Team 2
1 What kinds of creatures are crakes and rails?
2 Who recorded 'Apocalypse '91'?
3 Who was the Greek god of dreams?
4 What name is given to the scientific study of light?
5 What element has the symbol Na?

Team 1
1 The capercaillie is the largest of which kind of European bird?
2 Who recorded 'Diamonds and Pearls' in 1991?
3 Who killed the minotaur?
4 What name is given to the study of the functional and structural changes caused by disease?
5 What element has the symbol Zr?

Round 7
Team 2
1 The white cliffs of Dover are a part of which hill range?
2 What is a coluber?
3 Who wrote *The Call of the Wild*?
4 What branch of science studies the structure of an organism?
5 To which royal house did Queen Victoria belong?

Team 1
1 Which river enters the Thames estuary at Sheerness?
2 What is a colobus?
3 Who wrote *The Moon's a Balloon*?
4 What is the name for the scientific study of human beings?
5 To which royal house did Queen Elizabeth I belong?

Round 8
Team 2
1 What is the Imperial equivalent to 28.35 grams?
2 Which actress starred in the films *Grand Hotel* and *Camille*?
3 Who wrote *Das Kapital*?
4 By what name do Argentineans know the Falkland Islands?
5 What do the capital cities Belgrade, Vienna and Budapest all have in common?

Team 1
1 What fraction of a cubic yard is a cubic foot?
2 Which actress starred in the 1942 film *I Married a Witch*?
3 Who was the Maid of Orleans?
4 Where do Falashas come from?
5 Which Chinese river rises as the Za Qu in Tibet?

Round 9

Team 2

1 Who wrote the tune 'Maple Leaf Rag'?
2 What is a caravel?

3 What was Andrea Palladio famous for?
4 In which country are the High Atlas Mountains?
5 Who taught the Four Noble Truths?

Team 1

1 What was Glenn Miller's signature tune?
2 Which horse-drawn vehicle was open at the front and had the driver at the back seated above the passengers?
3 What was Nostradamus famous for?
4 Iceland is part of which continent?
5 What divine revelation contains 114 Saras?

Round 10   Individual questions for Team 2

Athletics
Who won a gold medal for the men's long jump in the 1968 Olympics?
Geography
With which country does Saudi Arabia have its longest northern frontier?
Pot luck
The Evening Star and the Morning Star are the same body. What is it?
Famous women
Who was born Helen Porter Mitchell in Australia in 1861?
Britain
What does the word *mull* mean in a Scottish place name?

Just for fun

Has a British Prime Minister ever been assassinated?
Yes. Spencer Perceval, Tory Prime Minister from 1809 to 1812. He was shot dead in the lobby of the House of Commons. By contrast, in a much shorter history four Presidents of the United States have been struck down by assassins.

Drinks round

Team 1

1 Which Dickens character said, 'If the law supposes that . . . the law is a ass – a idiot'?
2 What was Elvis Presley's middle name?
3 Who wrote the poem 'Dover Beach'?
4 What year saw the Bay of Pigs invasion?
5 What is a Havana brown?
6 When is Maundy Thursday?
7 What unit of capacity is the volume of 1kg of pure, air-free water at 4° C and 760 mm of pressure?
8 What is insomnia?

9 Who played TV's *Boon*?
10 Where is the Malabar Coast?

Team 2

1 In which Dickens novel does Mr Bumble appear?
2 What was Elvis Presley's brother's forename?
3 Who wrote the poem 'Reynard the Fox'?
4 What year did Prince Rainier marry Princess Grace?
5 What is an Alaskan malamute?
6 When is Mardi Gras held?
7 With which unit is heat measured?

8 What is the meaning of the term *caveat emptor*?
9 Who played T. J. Hooker?
10 What divides Niagara Falls between Canada and the United States?

Reserve questions

1 In what would a lapidary be skilled?
2 Which cereal is obtained from the root of the cassava plant?
3 The Camorra was the forerunner of which organisation in the United States?

Pub League Quiz 9

The individual questions are in Rounds 5 and 10 and are on soap operas, space travel, buildings, art and Rugby Union.

Round 1

Team 1

1 Where was William Wordsworth's most famous London sonnet composed?
2 The rebellion known as 'the Forty-five' ended at which battle in 1746?
3 Who composed the tune 'Keep the Home Fires Burning'?
4 Which former Foreign Secretary, who died in 1951, was once general secretary of the TUC?
5 In which country is a mulled red wine called glogg served, especially at Christmas?

Team 2

1 What hit musical show includes 'The Lambeth Walk'?
2 By whom and where was the King of the Franks, Charles the Great (Charlemagne), crowned Emperor?
3 Who wrote the musical *Oklahoma*?
4 Who was the first British socialist MP?
5 Where does the sweet wine Marsala come from?

Round 2

Team 1

1 What Imperial title did the British sovereign relinquish in 1947?
2 Where would you find autographs of British monarchs from Richard II onwards?
3 Whom did the Roman soldiers compel to carry Christ's cross?
4 Of which element is silica an oxide?
5 Why is 21 April a day for hoisting the Union flag on government buildings?

Team 2

1 Which are the two Crown dependencies of the British Isles?
2 Which explorer's last recorded message can be seen in British Museum?
3 Who was the Roman Emperor at the time of Crucifixion?
4 What type of element is niobium?
5 What is the popular name for the headgear worn by sentries outside Buckingham Palace?

Round 3

Team 1

1 Whose successful first novel was entitled *No Orchids for Miss Blandish*?
2 How does a boxer get to keep a Lonsdale Belt?
3 What did the ancient Romans call the Mediterranean Sea?
4 Name the ferry that capsized at Zeebrugge in 1987.
5 A spa in England derives its name from a town called Spa. In which country is Spa?

Team 2

1 What state prison was immortalised in Dumas' *The Count of Monte Christo*?
2 In which sport is a stimpmeter used?
3 What was the old Roman name for Britain?
4 In what month did the Zeebrugge ferry disaster occur?
5 Which country gives London an arboreal appreciation of its wartime support every year?

Round 4

Team 1

1 In which epistle did Paul write, 'And now abideth faith, hope, charity, these three; but the greatest of these is charity'?
2 Who played TV's *Bergerac*?
3 Who said, 'You're only as old as the woman you feel'?
4 Who played the leading role in *Stardust*?
5 What does consanguineous mean?

Team 2

1 At which council in 325 was it laid down that Easter Day should be the first Sunday following the paschal full moon?
2 Who played TV's *Magnum PI*?
3 Who asked, 'What contemptible scoundrel stole the cork from my lunch?'?
4 Whose first film was *Fourteen Hours*?
5 What is confraternity?

Round 5 Individual questions for Team 1

Soap operas

In which city is *Neighbours* set?

Space travel

What was the name of the first space shuttle?

Buildings

Which famous 19th-century theatre started life as the Royal Coburg?

Art

Which gallery has the largest number of Goya's works on view?

Rugby Union

Which Rugby Union trophy is made from melted down rupees?

Round 6

Team 2

1 Which group has had 18 consecutive top 10 hits in the UK?
2 What did the blowing up of the Gamboa Dyke effectively open in 1913?
3 Name the 17th-century Poet Laureate whose poem *Annus Mirabilis* was about war with the Dutch and the Great Fire of London.
4 To whom did the risen Jesus say, 'Touch me not'?
5 Who played the female lead in the 1991 hit film *Sleeping with the Enemy*?

Team 1

1 How did Otis Redding die?
2 K. C. Gillette invented the safety razor. What do the initials K. C. stand for?
3 Complete the following verse, 'Drink to me only with thine eyes, And I will pledge with mine, Or leave a kiss but in the cup...'
4 Who in the Old Testament is the guardian of Israel?
5 Who did Jackie Coogan play in 1931 and Mickey Rooney in 1939?

Round 7

Team 2

1 Where did Dick Whittington originally come from?
2 What zodiac sign covers the period from 21 March to 20 April?
3 Who won a match 6-0, 6-0, 6-0 at Wimbledon in 1987?
4 Which Second World War general was known as 'Blood and Guts'?
5 Who designed the Menai Suspension Bridge?

Team 1

1 Whom did Dick Whittington marry?
2 What zodiac sign covers the period from 22 May to 21 June?
3 Whose real name is Edson Arantes do Nascimento?
4 Which King of the Belgians surrendered to Germany in the Second World War?
5 Who designed the Menai Railway Bridge?

Round 8

Team 2

1 Who won an Academy Award in 1971 for his role in *The French Connection*?
2 What is the capital of Peru?
3 What word means to strip the blubber of a whale?
4 Where was Mother Teresa born?
5 What year saw the Festival of Britain?

Team 1

1 Who won an Oscar for writing the screenplay for the film *Tom Jones*?
2 What is the capital of Angola?
3 What word means occurring in winter?
4 Where was Florence Nightingale born?
5 What year saw the General Strike in Britain?

Round 9

Team 2

1 What does *mahatma* mean?
2 Who won the World Driver's Championship in 1975 and 1977?
3 Who wrote *Out of Africa*?
4 What is the American equivalent of the Victoria Cross?
5 What does isochromatic mean?

Team 1

1 What does *kismet* mean?
2 Who won the 1994 German Grand Prix driving a Ferrari?
3 Who was the writer Baron Tweedsmuir?
4 Who in the British navy would wear two gold rings?
5 What is an Ishmaelite?

Round 10   Individual questions for Team 2

Soap operas
What was the name of the pub in *Brookside*?
Space travel
Name the first artificial space satellite.
Buildings
Who designed Marble Arch and planned Regent Street?
Art
What colour is artist's burnt sienna?
Rugby Union
Who won the World Cup in 1991?

Drinks round

Team 1

1 Who began his first British premiership in 1940?

2 What is the name of the village in New York?

3 By what name was William H. Bonney better known?

4 Who wrote *Our Man In Havana*?

5 Who was married to Lotte Lenya?

6 Who recorded 'Wherever I Lay my Hat' in 1983?

7 What does ANC stand for?

8 To what animal group do caracals belong?

9 In which country is the river Aude?

10 What is the average normal body temperature?

Team 2

1 Which British Prime Minister's memoirs are entitled *Time and Chancel*?

2 Where is Rotten Row?

3 By what name was William F. Cody better known?

4 Who wrote *The Forsyte Saga*?

5 What was Kurt Weill's most famous work?

6 Who recorded 'Love in an Elevator'?

7 What does BFI stand for?

8 To what animal group do capybaras belong?

9 In which country is the Kennebec river?

10 How many vertebrae are in your neck?

Reserve questions

1 What do Ethiopians celebrate on 7 January?

2 By what name is the Lenten lily usually known?

3 What is the difference between a Greek cross and a Latin cross?

Pub League Quiz 10

The individual questions are in Rounds 5 and 10 and are on films, sport, science, pot luck and geography.

Round 1

Team 1

1 Who led the Ra expeditions?

2 Who, in 1875, composed the Symphonie Espagnole?
3 In which continent would you find the Apennines?
4 Who wrote the poem *The Lady of the Lake*?
5 Whom did the Jacobites support?

Team 2

1 What was the purpose of the Ra expeditions?
2 Who wrote the opera *Carmen*?
3 In which continent would you find the Atlas Mountains?
4 Who wrote the poem *The Lady of Shalott*?
5 Who was the father of James II?

Round 2

Team 1

1 What symbol represents the sign of Cancer in the zodiac?
2 What was Britain's first winning entry in the Eurovision Song Contest?
3 What is the largest living antelope?
4 Which castle is the home of the Dukes of Argyll?
5 To which royal house did George II belong?

Team 2

1 What zodiac sign is represented by a goat?
2 On which writer's books was the TV series *The Darling Buds of May* based?
3 What type of animal is a lamprey?
4 Where in England is Barnard Castle?
5 Who was the wife of François II of France?

Round 3

Team 1
1 What does RADAR stand for?
2 Which is the fourth planet from the sun?
3 Which US chemist discovered nylon?
4 What does the legal term *de jure* mean?
5 Who had his first number one hit as a solo singer two years after his death with 'Living On My Own'?

Team 2
1 What did OAS stand for?
2 Which is the second planet from the sun?
3 Who, in 1837, invented the steel plough?
4 In which year was Legal Aid introduced in the UK?
5 From which album did Michael Jackson take his hit single 'Black or White'?

Round 4

Team 1
1 Who was the world's first woman Prime Minister?
2 What is the common name for the clavicle?
3 Which jockey rode Grundy to win the Derby in 1975?

4 Which Canadian city used to be called Bytown?
5 Who wrote *The Cruel Sea*?

Team 2
1 Who murdered Jean-Paul Marat?
2 Where would you find your deltoid muscle?
3 Which US swimmer won four gold medals in the 1976 Olympics, all in world record times?
4 Which city in Australia took its name from William IV's wife?
5 Who wrote *Utopia*?

Round 5   Individual questions for Team 1

Films
On which classical work was the film *Kiss Me Kate* based?
Sport
Who in baseball was the Georgia Peach?
Science
What is described by c in scientific texts and was considered by Einstein to be the only absolute in the universe?
Pot luck
What is the male singing voice next above baritone?
Geography
What is the tundra?

Round 6
Team 2
1 What substance makes plants green?
2 What type of fish is a char?
3 Who wrote *An American Dream*?
4 Which Irish political party was founded in 1933 as a successor to the party led by William Cosgrave?
5 Who is the patron saint of sailors?

Team 1
1 What is another name for tungsten?
2 What is a male pike called?
3 Who wrote *A Small Town in Germany*?
4 When was the first National Insurance Act passed in Great Britain?
5 Who is the patron saint of France?

Round 7
Team 2
1 What relation was Queen Victoria to George III?
2 Which member of the Rolling Stones drowned in a swimming pool?
3 How many square yards to an acre?
4 Who invented the lightning rod?
5 Who played Bluebottle in *The Goon Show*?

Team 1
1 What relation was Louis XV of France to Louis XIV?
2 Which composer died of typhoid fever, aged 31?
3 How many acres to a square mile?
4 Who invented the power-loom?
5 Who played Seagoon in *The Goon Show*?

Round 8
Team 2
1 Whose novels are set in the Potteries?
2 What type of animal is a loon?
3 Who composed the opera *Don Giovanni*?
4 Whose vital statistics were 19-19-19?
5 How many 'pillars of Islam' are there?

Team 1
1 Whose novels are set in Wessex?
2 What type of animal is a lumpsucker?
3 How many operas make up the Ring Cycle of Wagner?
4 In fiction, who owned the dog Gnasher?
5 What name is given to the trinity of Hindu gods, Brahma, Siva and Vishnu?

Round 9

Team 2

1 Who composed the music for the ballet *Giselle*?
2 What is the name of the place where Jesus was crucified?
3 Which famous comedian sent his Christmas cards in July?
4 Who in the 1830s and 1840s was nicknamed the 'Factory King'?
5 Who was the Greek herald who could shout as loudly as 50 ordinary men?

Team 1

1 From which piece of music does 'Fingal's Cave' come?
2 What is the name of the place where Jesus was arrested?
3 What was W. C. Fields' real name?
4 Who was the leader of the Peasants' Revolt?
5 Who in Arthurian legend found the Holy Grail?

Round 10   Individual questions for Team 2

Films

Who portrayed the US showman George M. Cohan on film?

Sport

Which American tennis player was nicknamed 'Little Mo'?

Science

Samuel Hahnemann is generally credited with the founding of which medical science?

Pot luck

Name the curate who wrote the classic *Natural History and Antiquities of Selborne*, published in 1789.

Geography

What sea in the Atlantic Ocean doesn't have a coast?

Drinks round

Team 1

1 Who wrote a story about Melibee?

2 What does RAPC stand for?

3 What is the capital of the Philippines?

4 What type of fruit is a nectarine?

5 Which great Florentine painter is known by his Christian name rather than his surname, Buonaroti?

6 In which post-war year was the Morris Minor produced?

7 Who recorded the song 'Think' in 1968?

8 How many countries were originally in the EC?

9 In computer terminology, what does RAM stand for?

10 What is the other common name given to the plant delphinium?

Team 2

1 Who wrote *Moby Dick*?

2 What does RLC stand for?

3 What is the capital of Venezuela?

4 What is the common name of the fruit *citrus sinensis*?

5 Which great painter, born Michelangelo Merisi, took the name of the small town in northern Italy where he grew up?

6 Who designed the Kodak camera?

7 Who recorded the song 'Man of the World' in 1969?

8 Name four of the original EC countries.

9 In computer terminology, what does ROM stand for?

10 What is the other name for the plant Nicotiana?

Reserve questions

1 Which fictional detective first appeared in 1920 in *The Mysterious Affair at Styles*?

2 What was the name of the island prison in San Francisco Bay?

3 Which American sprinter, an Olympic gold medallist in 1904 and 1906, was nicknamed the 'Milwaukee Meteor'?

Pub League Quiz 11

The individual questions are in Rounds 5 and 10 and are on films, the arts, Paris, who said? and world leaders.

Round 1

Team 1

1 In heraldry, what colour is murrey?
2 What musical instrument would you associate with Reginald Dixon?
3 What is the monetary unit of Senegal?
4 What three colours make up the flag of Iran?
5 Which stretch of water lies between the Bosphorus and the Dardanelles?

Team 2

1 In heraldry, what colour is vert?
2 What musical instrument would you associate with Harry James?
3 What is the monetary unit of Guatemala?
4 What three colours along with three green stars in the centre make up the flag of Iraq?
5 In which country is Ravenna?

Round 2

Team 1

1 What historic event took place at Runnymede?
2 What is a glockenspiel?
3 What is measured on the Beaufort Scale?
4 How many paintings did Van Gogh sell during his lifetime?
5 Who wrote *For Whom the Bell Tolls*?

Team 2

1 Where was Napoleon's final place of exile?
2 From where is the word 'bedlam' derived?
3 What is a pitot tube?
4 Which Belgian is famous for the painting 'Ceci n'est pas une pipe'?
5 Who wrote *Pride and Prejudice*?

Round 3

Team 1

1 Which Motown star was killed by his father in 1984?
2 What was different about the 1970 FA Cup between Leeds United and Chelsea?
3 In which novel by George Eliot does Dr Lydgate appear?
4 What is East Pakistan now known as?
5 Which statesman's slogan was 'You've never had it so good'?

Team 2

1 Which pop star was knighted in 1995?
2 Name the white boxer who won the world heavyweight crown by beating Floyd Patterson.
3 Name the Anthony Burgess book about London terrorised by teenage gangs.
4 Monte Marmolada is the highest peak in which mountain range?
5 Which statesman won the Nobel Prize for Literature in 1953?

Round 4

Team 1

1 Who was commander-in-chief of the Spanish Armada?
2 What, according to its advertising slogan, is 'the nation's favourite airline'?
3 Name the lighthouse immediately due west of Land's End.
4 Which prominent member of the New York Dadaists moved to Paris in 1921?
5 In which year did the German forces surrender in Italy?

Team 2

1 Who commanded the English fleet that defeated the Spanish Armada?
2 What drink was advertised as 'the bright one, the right one'?
3 Name the lighthouse 23 km south-west of Plymouth.
4 Which Dutch painter's masterpiece is 'The Third Marquess of Hamilton'?
5 Where did Field Marshal von Paulus surrender to the Russians in February 1943?

Round 5   Individual questions for Team 1
Films
Who won Best Actress Oscars for her performances in *To Each His Own* in 1946 and *The Heiress in* 1949?
The arts
In 1913, Diaghilev's Ballet Russe performed a work at the Théatre des Champs Elysées in Paris, which caused a riot. What was the work and who wrote it?
Paris
Which is the oldest bridge over the Seine in Paris?
Who said?
Who promised to 'make Britain a fit place for heroes to live in'?
World leaders
John F. Kennedy was the 35th president of the United States. What did the 'F' represent?

Round 6
Team 2

1   Who were Gog and Magog?

2   What does the musical term *largo* mean?

3   From which tower of the Palace of Westminster does the Union Jack fly by day when Parliament is sitting?
4   What was printed for the first time in 1455?
5   Through which country does the river Flinders flow?

Team 1

1   Who slew Grendel and Grendel's mother?

2   What musical instruction means to be played in a sustained or prolonged manner?

3   In which English town would you find the Holst Birthplace Museum?

4   How many books of John are there in the New Testament?
5   In which country does the river Po flow?

Round 7
Team 2
1   Which country's civil aircraft markings are OY?
2   Who wrote the poem that begins, 'When I consider how my light is spent'?
3   In which country is Mount Logan?
4   What is 20 in German?
5   Of which country was Jomo Kenyatta president?

Team 1
1   Which country's civil aircraft have TF markings?
2   Which poem has the first lines, 'Not a drum was heard, not a funeral note'?
3   In which American state is the Great Salt Lake?
4   What is eight in Italian?
5   Of which country was James K. Polk president?

Round 8

Team 2

1 In law, what are the rights of estovers?
2 What did Christian Friedrich Schönbein discover?
3 Who played Emma Peel in *The Avengers*?
4 What is a gazebo?
5 What does RCVS stand for?

Team 1

1 In law, what is a wayleave?
2 What did Nicholas-Louis Vauquelin discover?
3 Who played Cathy Gale in *The Avengers*?
4 What is the architectural term for a bell-tower?
5 What does EFTA stand for?

Round 9

Team 2

1 Of which disease did D. H. Lawrence die in 1930?
2 Who crowned Napoleon Bonaparte Emperor of the French?
3 Who or what would compete in the Golden Jacket?
4 Give another name for the Tonga Islands.

5 Pica pica is another name for which bird?

Team 1

1 How did Lawrence of Arabia die?
2 Which emperor's horse was called Bucephalus?

3 Why can a horse not win the Derby in successive years?
4 Name the island separated from the mainland by the Juan de Fuca, Georgia and Queen Charlotte Straits.
5 What is a ha-ha?

Round 10   Individual questions for Team 2

Films

Who played Abraham Lincoln in the 1940 film *Abe Lincoln in Illinois*?

The arts

What were the three favourite subjects of the artist Degas?

Paris

Where in Paris is the basilica of Sacré Coeur?

Who said?

Who described Russian policy as 'a riddle wrapped in a mystery inside an enigma'?

World leaders

Who was elected president of Cyprus in 1959?

Drinks round

Team 1

1 What did the owl and the pussy cat take to sea with them?

2 In which Shakespeare play is the famous line, 'Woman, thy name is frailty'?

3 What is the meaning of the Latin phrase *deo volente*?

4 In which art gallery is the Venus de Milo?

5 What is the name of the Islamic holy month?

6 In which country was Che Guevara born?

7 Which former head of state was found guilty of drugs offences in a US court in 1992?

8 What is a pelerine?

9 What instrument did jazz musician Stan Getz play?

10 Who played Clegg, the former Co-op assistant in *Last of the Summer Wine*?

Team 2

1 Solomon Grundy, born on Monday, christened on Tuesday, what did he do on Wednesday?

2 Which Dickens character repeatedly said, 'We are so very 'umble'?

3 What is the meaning of the Latin phrase *compos mentis*?

4 Where in Belgium is the former house of the painter Rubens?

5 What is the name given to the final battle between God and Satan that is foretold in the Bible?

6 From what country did Cleopatra's ancestors come?

7 Name the Swedish prime minister who was assassinated in 1986.

8 What is a toque?

9 Who in jazz was nicknamed 'Bird'?

10 Who was 'a man called Ironside' on TV?

Reserve questions

1 Name the explorer born in 1728 at Marton-in-Cleveland who charted Australia's east coast?

2 What is the name for the point on the surface of the earth from which the shockwaves of an earthquake proceed?

3 Who was the British prime minister in the reign of Edward VIII?

Pub League Quiz 12

The individual questions are in Rounds 5 and 10 and are on pot luck, history, politics, biology and art.

Round 1

Team 1

1 Who wrote the song 'White Christmas'?
2 Scurvy is caused by a deficiency of which vitamin?
3 Why is a white elephant so called?
4 When, legally, is 'time immemorial'?

5 Who was the British prime minister when India was granted independence?

Team 2

1 Who wrote the song 'Do They Know It's Christmas'?
2 Which letter is at the left of the top row of a typewriter keyboard?
3 Where would you find firedamp?
4 Within what period must a victim's death occur for the crime to be murder?
5 Who became leader of the British Labour Party in 1955?

Round 2

Team 1

1 What kind of creature is a taipan?

2 What do the letters FRGS stand for?
3 Where in Britain is the Martyrs' Memorial to Cranmer, Ridley and Latimer?
4 Who painted 'The Fighting Téméraire'?
5 Within 20 ft, how tall is the Blackpool Tower?

Team 2

1 What breed of dog has the same name as a mythological creature with the head and wings of an eagle and the body of a lion?
2 What do the letters NUS stand for?
3 Where in Britain is Cabot Tower?

4 Who sculpted Eros in Piccadilly?

5 To within 30 ft, how tall is the Eiffel Tower?

Round 3

Team 1

1 In which country is the city of Delft?
2 In which year was the first women's marathon run in the Olympics?
3 What does a speleologist study?
4 Which country's international car registration letters are SF?
5 Who discovered Tristan da Cunha?

Team 2

1 Which town in Spain was noted for its sword blades?
2 In which sport would you use the term 'catching a crab'?
3 What is a *locum tenens*?
4 Which country's international car registration letters are PL?
5 Who discovered Spitsbergen?

Round 4

Team 1

1 Where was the first football World Cup held?
2 Which English monarch was killed while out hunting in the New Forest?
3 Who composed the opera *War and Peace*?
4 In which ocean are the Seychelles?
5 Who in pop music were Tania Evans and Jay Supreme?

Team 2

1 Who won the first football World Cup?
2 Which ancient body controls the grazing rights in the New Forest?
3 What nationality was Frederick Delius?
4 Name the largest of the Seychelle Islands.
5 Who was successively part of Depeche Mode, Yazoo and Erasure?

Round 5   Individual questions for Team 1

Pot luck

What is a flpple?

History

Which buccaneer was made Lieutenant-Governor of Jamaica in 1674?

Politics

Who led the parliamentary campaign in Britain against the slave trade in the 1800s?

Biology

What is the average heart rate for a normal, healthy human being?

Art

Who was commissioned by the city of Florence to create the sculpture of David?

Round 6

Team 2

1 What is the last word in the New Testament?
2 How many pawns are there in a chess game?
3 Name two of Lebanon's three main languages.
4 Which city did Scot McKenzie sing about?
5 Which American city is known as 'motor city'?

Team 1

1 Name the first three books of the Old Testament.
2 How many people take part in the Oxford/Cambridge boat race?
3 Name two of Lebanon's three principal religious denominations.
4 In the Perry Como song, what did Delaware?
5 What colour sari is worn by an Indian bride?

Round 7

Team 2

1 Which bird is sometimes known as Mother Carey's chicken?
2 How many parts of speech are there?
3 Which English king was called 'the hammer of the Scots'?
4 In which capital city is Hradcany Castle?
5 In which sport is the Stanley Cup competed for?

Team 1

1 Which thrush is also called the storm cock?
2 Name six of the parts of speech.
3 Which king of England was nicknamed 'Longshanks'?
4 Where is Shah Jahan's Red Fort?
5 In which sport is the Grand Challenge Cup competed for?

Round 8

Team 2

1 Who in a poem by Coleridge decreed a stately pleasure dome in Xanadu?
2 What do the French call the English Channel?
3 What are the Christian names of the heir apparent to the British throne?
4 Which actor played *The Fugitive* on television?
5 Which metal is alloyed with copper to make brass?

Team 1

1 Which poem begins, 'He did not wear his scarlet coat'?
2 What is decompression sickness often known as?
3 Where was Princess Elizabeth when her father died in 1952?
4 Who was *The Fugitive* looking for?
5 From which ore does chromium come?

Round 9

Team 2

1 What is the capital of Bolivia?

2 Who kissed the girls and made them cry?

3 In which country is the volcano Popocatepetl?

4 What monetary unit is used in Afghanistan?

5 In what year did an IRA bomb explode outside Harrods?

Team 1

1 What is the capital of Trinidad and Tobago?

2 'Ring a Ring o' Roses' is about what event?

3 On which island is Fingal's Cave?

4 What monetary unit is used in Iceland?

5 Where were 35 people killed in a crash on the London Underground in 1975?

Round 10   Individual questions for Team 2

Pot luck

The town of Dum-Dum gives its name to a bullet and an airport. To which large city is it close?

History

Which French Jewish soldier was imprisoned on Devil's Island for alleged espionage?

Politics

What was President Tito's original name?

Biology

What name is given to the study of population control by selective breeding?

Art

'Vision of a Knight' was the work of which Italian painter?

Drinks round

Team 1

1 What are the large plains of South America called?

2 Who wrote the novel *The Moonstone*?

3 What is the state capital of Montana?

4 How many Laws of Motion did Newton propose?

5 What was the name of the B-29 aircraft that dropped the atomic bomb on Hiroshima?

6 In which country is Lund Cathedral?

7 Name the spice that comes from the outer covering of nutmeg.

8 In which country is Rennes?

9 Who was the Philistine giant slain by David?

10 In Rugby League, how many points are given for a try?

Team 2

1 Which wind sweeps down from the north along the lower Rhône valley?

2 Who wrote *The Pursuit of Love*?

3 What is the highest peak in the Alps?

4 What kind of acid is normally used in a car battery?

5 Name the last steam locomotive to be built in the UK for express passenger service.

6 In which country is Ulm Cathedral?

7 From what is laver bread made?

8 In which country is Omdurman?

9 What is the music of Rastafarians called?

10 In Rugby League, how many points are given for a conversion goal or penalty goal?

Reserve questions

1 From west to east, which countries of the Europe/Asia land mass extend northwards into the Arctic Circle?

2 Where was Archduke Ferdinand assassinated?

3 Name two of the three kinds of artichoke.

Pub League Quiz 13

The individual questions are in Rounds 5 and 10 and are on kings and queens, famous men, sport, places and general knowledge.

Round 1

Team 1

1 Which actor directed the film *The Outlaw Josey Wales*?
2 Who created the Native American Indians Chingachgook and Uncas?
3 Name the artificial European language invented by Dr L. L. Zamenhof.
4 What series of races began in 1907 in the Isle of Man?
5 The president of which republic has his office in the Quirinal Palace?

Team 2

1 Which actor directed *Reds*?
2 What was the name of *Othello*'s malignant 'ancient'?
3 To within 30 years, when was Esperanto invented?
4 In motorcycling, what does TT stand for?
5 Give another name for the French ministry of foreign affairs derived from the Paris street on which it is situated.

Round 2

Team 1

1 Who, in *The Tempest*, sings to Ferdinand, 'Full fathom five thy father lies'?
2 From which spacecraft was the first moon landing made?
3 What name is given to the fruit of the wild rose?

4. What does FIA stand for?
5 What type of TV programme was *Gideon's Way*?

Team 2

1 What was the name of *Hamlet*'s mother?
2 What was the name of the dog carried into space with *Sputnik 2*?
3 Which plant of the same family as the buttercup is also known as traveller's joy and old man's beard?
4 What does FCIB stand for?
5 Which detective thriller had the theme music entitled 'Eye Level'?

Round 3

Team 1

1 What is navarin of lamb?
2 What is the religious denomination of the majority in Germany?
3 Whose last novel was *Endymion*?
4 Who was the first British golfer to win the US Open after the Second World War?
5 Who was sold to Potiphar, an officer of Pharoah and Captain of the Guard?

Team 2

1 What is a syllabub?
2 What is the religious denomination of the majority in Switzerland?
3 What was Disraeli's first novel called?
4 What animal phrase describes a particularly rough area on a golf course?
5 Name the son of Nun who became leader of the Israelites after the death of Moses.

Round 4

Team 1

1 Whose first British hit was 'Space Oddity'?
2 What new state in the Middle East was proclaimed in 1948?
3 How many sixpences made up half a crown?
4 Name the wizard in the court of the legendary King Arthur.
5 What name is given to a geographical index or dictionary?

Team 2

1 How were the Moody Blues attired at night in a hit record?
2 Which country overthrew its Communist dictator at Christmas in 1989?
3 What is today's equivalent value to a florin?
4 What was King Arthur's castle called?
5 What name is given to the science or study of fungi?

Round 5   Individual questions for Team 1

Kings and queens
Which king was married to Marie-Antoinette?
Famous men
Which American president wrote the book *Profiles in Courage*?
Sport
What colour is the lowest rank judo belt?
Places
For what is the town of Coalport famous?
General knowledge
What were Martello towers originally built for?

Round 6

Team 2

1 Name one of the planets that shows lunar-type phases as seen from the earth.
2 Who wrote the nursery rhyme *Old Mother Hubbard*?
3 What is the Norwegian parliament called?
4 Who directed the musical film *Meet Me in St Louis*?
5 Who wrote the novel *Les Misérables*?

Team 1

1 Name the other planet that shows lunar-type phases as seen from earth.
2 Who wrote *Ivor the Engine*?
3 Of what university is the Sorbonne a part?
4 Who wrote the musical *Jesus Christ Superstar*?
5 Who wrote the novel *Dr Zhivago*?

Round 7

Team 2

1 In which country is Monterrey?
2 Which kind of wood was Noah told to use to build his ark?
3 The term ordnance embraces what kind of weapons?
4 Who was the 18th-century writer of *The Beggar's Opera*?
5 What was Paddington Bear's country of origin?

Team 1

1 Which river flows from Colorado to the Gulf of Mexico?
2 What was the name of the manuscripts found in caves at Qumran, Palestine, in 1947?
3 Which countries were the British fleet fighting at the Battle of Navarino?
4 The Septuagint was the principal Greek version of what?
5 Who was the swashbuckling hero created by novelist Baroness Orczy?

Round 8

Team 2

1 Which poet wrote the line, 'The Paths of Glory lead but to the Grave'?
2 What is the familiar name of the obelisk erected in 1878 on the Victoria Embankment in London?
3 Who played *Worzel Gummidge* in the television series?
4 Where is the Orange river?
5 What was John Loudon MacAdam's contribution to road transport?

Team 1

1 Who wrote *Ode to the West Wind*?
2 Did Eton College receive its first charter in 1240, 1340, 1440, 1540 or 1640?
3 In *Worzel Gummidge*, who played Aunt Sally?
4 In which European country is Mount Ossa?
5 Which well-known motor vehicle was launched in 1959 by Alec Issigonis?

Round 9

Team 2

1 What is an animal's pug?
2 Who said, 'England is a nation of shopkeepers'?

3 Which group of instruments are positioned closest to the conductor in an orchestra?
4 Who in the Bible wore a coat of many colours?
5 Of which country was Douglas Hyde president?

Team 1

1 What is simony?
2 Who wrote, 'If God did not exist it would be necessary to invent him'?

3 What sort of instrument was a flageolet?

4 Who in the Bible was rid of seven demons by Jesus?
5 What nationality was the father of Eamon de Valera?

Round 10   Individual questions for Team 2

Kings and queens
Which king died near Rouen in 1087 and is buried at Caen?
Famous men
How did Ernest Hemingway die?
Sport
In what year did Britain last win an Olympic Gold for football?
Places
In which town is Brunel University?
General knowledge
Who, but for disclaiming the peerage, would be Viscount Stansgate?

Just for fun
Which great poetic work was sold for £5?
Paradise Lost by John Milton. Although the work had taken seven years to write, the blind poet sold the copyright for a mere £5. He was to receive a further £5 if and when the first edition of 1,300 copies was sold out. Subsequent editions would attract a further £5 each for the author. The 17th-century masterpiece is now acknowledged to be one of the greatest long poems in the world and has been reprinted countless times.

Drinks round

Team 1

1 Which saint's day is 25 April?
2 Which prelate was killed on the orders of Henry II, which Henry said had been misinterpreted?
3 What is the British Army equivalent of the rank of rear-admiral in the Navy?
4 What is the monetary unit of Peru?
5 Who wrote the novel *Le Rouge et le Noir*?
6 Which famous film star was born William Henry Pratt?

7 In which country is the Irrawaddy Delta?
8 How many faces has a prism?
9 Where is Great Slave Lake?
10 Who played Superintendent Tyburn in TV's *Heat of the Sun*?

Team 2

1 Which saint's day is 25 July?
2 Which Bolshevik leader was killed in Mexico City by a Stalinist agent?
3 What is the naval equivalent of the rank of brigadier in the British Army?
4 What is the monetary unit of Nepal?
5 Who wrote the novel *Cousin Bette*?
6 Who starred in *Spartacus*, *The Boston Strangler* and *The Last Tycoon*?
7 In which country is the river Test?
8 How many sides has a rhombus?
9 Where is Bala Lake?
10 On TV, who played the narrator in *Brideshead Revisited*?

Reserve questions

1 The Americans call it a tuxedo. What do the British call it?
2 A food that is 'butyraceous' contains or resembles what?
3 What would a sailor do with a scuttlebut?

Pub League Quiz 14

The individual questions are in Rounds 5 and 10 and are on mythology and legend, Africa, entertainment, people and places, and numbers.

Round 1
Team 1
1 What type of animal is an ortolan?
2 Which footballer won 108 caps for England and finished his playing career with Fulham?
3 Where do the Expos play baseball?
4 What is the largest of the four provinces of the Republic of Ireland?
5 Whose first book of poems was *A Twin Cloud*?

Team 2
1 What predatory animal is also call a prairie wolf?
2 Name the German who was footballer of the year in 1970.
3 What soccer team plays at Edgar Street?
4 Name four of the counties that make up Munster.
5 Who wrote *Mr Midshipman Easy*?

Round 2
Team 1
1 Who composed oratorios entitled *St Paul* and *Elijah*?
2 Which British biologist founded and named the science of genetics?
3 What does FRCS stand for?
4 Which actor played the title role in the 1963 spoof horror film *The Raven*?
5 Of which river is the river Drava a tributary?

Team 2
1 At what age did Yehudi Menuhin make his concert debut?
2 At which London teaching hospital did Alexander Fleming discover penicillin?
3 What does FRHS stand for?
4 In which country was Peter Lorre born?
5 In which country does the Rhine rise?

Round 3

Team 1

1 Indigenous covered five furlongs in world record time for the distance at Epsom in 1960. What was his speed: a little over 35 mph, 40 mph, 45 mph or 50 mph?
2 Who sang 'Help Me Make It Through the Night' in 1972?
3 Which comedian was christened Eric Bartholomew?

4 A very large armadillo is called a giant. What is the smallest type of armadillo called?
5 By what name is Peter Sutcliffe better known?

Team 2

1 Red Rum recorded the fastest time ever for the Grand National in 1973. Was his time a little over seven, eight, nine or 10 minutes?

2 Who sang 'Autumn Almanac' in 1967?
3 Who, according to Benny Hill, 'drove the fastest milk cart in the West'?
4 Of which continent is the aardvark a native?

5 Which African leader gave himself the title 'Conqueror of the British Empire'?

Round 4

Team 1

1 Which mollusc protects itself by ejecting a cloud of inky fluid called sepia?
2 Whose assassination in 1924 led to anti-Fascist demonstrations in the Italian parliament?
3 What were the several thousand projectiles used in Laurel and Hardy's *Battle of the Century*?
4 Which Roman emperor instigated the second invasion of England?
5 Who played Basil Fawlty on TV?

Team 2

1 How many tentacles has a cuttlefish?

2 What position did Hendrik Verwoerd hold at the time of his assassination?
3 Who was reputed to be the fastest mouse in all of Mexico?

4 In whose reign was the 'Wonderful Parliament' of 1388?

5 Who played Sybil Fawlty on TV?

Round 5   Individual questions for Team 1
Mythology and legend
Whose temple was the Parthenon?
Africa
Which country lies between Ghana and Benin?
Entertainment
Which famous dance hall was opened in Paris in 1900?
People and places
Where was the Minoan civilisation?
Numbers
Divide £66 amongst A, B and C, so that B has £8 more than A, and C £14 more than B.

Round 6
Team 2

1 Who was the first woman mayor in Britain?
2 Who in music was 'Flash Harry'?
3 What British medal is given for saving life at sea or on land?
4 Who wrote *Cakes and Ale*?
5 Which sign comes after Cancer in the zodiac?

Team 1

1 Who was the first Archbishop of Canterbury?
2 For what was Emmeline Pankhurst famous?
3 What is the highest military decoration awarded in the USA?
4 Who wrote *Love's Labour's Lost*?
5 Which sign comes after Scorpio in the zodiac?

Round 7
Team 2

1 Who said, 'Now I am on the side of the angels'?
2 Which Pope reigned from 1958 to 1963?
3 Name the mountain range in County Down, Northern Ireland.
4 From which album did George Michael take four number one hits?
5 What is a gravimeter?

Team 1

1 Who said, 'An army marches on its stomach'?
2 Who in the 20th Century was Pope for only 33 days?
3 Name the highest peak in Northern Ireland.
4 Who had a hit album called *Gracelands*?
5 What is a magnetometer?

Round 8

Team 2

1 Which European country claims to have the oldest parliament?
2 Which is the brightest of the five planets visible to the naked eye?
3 Which writer created the Toff?

4 Which actress starred as Julie in the film *Showboat* in 1951?

5 What is a perfect score in a gymnastics exercise?

Team 1

1 What nationality were Karl Marx and Friedrich Engels?
2 Which is the hottest of the planets in the solar system?
3 Which writer created Father Brown?

4 Which actress's story was portrayed in the 1981 film *Mommie Dearest*?

5 In athletics, what is the hop, step and jump officially called?

Round 9

Team 2

1 In which county is the New Forest?
2 The Queen's Cup and the Prince Philip Cup are competed for in which sport?

3 Who in the Bible was famous for his wisdom?
4 Who composed the music for the film *High Society*?
5 Who was the chief commentator for the BBC on the coronation of Elizabeth II?

Team 1

1 The Forest of Dean is almost wholly in one county – which?
2 In which sport are the King George V Gold Cup and the Queen Elizabeth II Cup contested?

3 According to Exodus, what was the first commandment?
4 What is the American equivalent of the British music hall?
5 What were the names of the three radio programmes before Radios 1, 2, 3 and 4?

Round 10   Individual questions for Team 2

Mythology and legend
What is another name for the Roman god Amor?
Africa
In which country is Timbuktu?
Entertainment
Who played the green monster in *The Incredible Hulk* in the 1970s TV series?
People and places
For what is George Horace Gallup remembered?
Numbers
Divide the number 16 into two, so that the sum of the squares of the two parts is 130.

Drinks round

Team 1

1 What is a steak called that has been cut from between two ribs?

2 Who is buried in 'some corner of a foreign field that is for ever England'?

3 What is the simplest compound of hydrogen and oxygen?

4 Who was the Oscar-winning star in the 1939 film of *Goodbye Mr Chips*?

5 What colour is the gemstone malachite?

6 How long did Jonah spend inside the whale?

7 Who wrote the play *Cat on a Hot Tin Roof*?

8 Which cartoonist created the character Maudie Littlehampton?

9 In which year did Samuel Pepys begin his famous diary?

10 Name the character who sucks his thumb in the strip cartoon *Peanuts*.

Team 2

1 What is the main ingredient of taramasalata?

2 The word 'cenotaph' comes from two Greek words. What does it actually mean?

3 What gas is most plentiful in the air that we breathe?

4 Who was the Oscar-winning star of the films *Gaslight* and *Anastasia*?

5 What colour is the gemstone citrine?

6 Who was Herodias's famous daughter?

7 Who wrote *The Corn is Green*?

8 Name the cartoonist who drew absurdly complicated and fantastic machines.

9 In which year were the lions added to the foot of Nelson's Column?

10 Name Mickey Mouse's girlfriend.

Reserve questions

1 What is an amadavat?

2 St Andrew is the patron saint of which country other than Scotland?

3 What is the capital of New York State?

Pub League Quiz 15

The individual questions are in Rounds 5 and 10 and are on classical music, motoring, history, television and chance.

Round 1

Team 1
1 What is a tazza?
2 Who said, 'Genius is one per cent inspiration and 99 per cent perspiration'?
3 Which of these composers set the story of *Romeo and Juliet* to music? Tchaikovsky, Prokofiev, Berlioz, Bernstein?
4 Who wrote the play *Up the Junction*?
5 Who became prime minister as MP for Sedgefield?

Team 2
1 What is a megalith?
2 Who said, 'War is much too serious a thing to be left to the military'?
3 Which Verdi opera is based on Shakespeare's *The Merry Wives of Windsor*?
4 Who wrote *The Jewel in the Crown*?
5 What title did Margaret Thatcher take in the House of Lords?

Round 2

Team 1
1 Which drug is obtained from the cinchona tree?
2 What was the former name of Thailand?
3 What do the Jewish people call the Day of Atonement?
4 Who twice succeeded Ramsay MacDonald as British prime minister?
5 What is a spectrograph?

Team 2
1 What is novocaine widely used as?
2 What is an inhabitant of Oxford called?
3 What is a bar mitzvah?
4 Who succeeded F. D. Roosevelt as American president?
5 What is a heliograph?

Round 3

Team 1

1 Which mountains form the boundary between European Russia and Siberia?
2 Which Scottish football team plays at Hampden Park?
3 In Mecca, what is the name of the Holy of Holies?
4 What does NAAFI stand for?
5 Who played King Arthur in the 1967 film *Camelot*?

Team 2

1 Give another name for the river Hwango-Ho.
2 How long is a cricket pitch from stumps to stumps?
3 Diwali, or Festival of Light, is an important celebration in which religion?
4 What does OPEC stand for?
5 Who played *The Wicked Lady* in the 1945 version of the film of the same name?

Round 4

Team 1

1 Which monarch was the son of Henry VIII and Jane Seymour?
2 By what name is the figure, design or device FYLFOT better known?
3 Who wrote, 'O my love's like a red, red rose that's newly sprung in June'?
4 Who said, 'The only thing I mind about going to prison is the thought of Lord Longford coming to visit me'?
5 Which film studio had a roaring lion as its trade mark?

Team 2

1 How many complaints did Luther list and nail on the church door at Wittenberg?
2 Which political movement had an emblem comprised of a bundle of rods tied with an axe in the middle?
3 Who wrote, 'Laugh, and the world laughs with you; weep, and you weep alone'?
4 Who said, 'Those in the cheap seats, clap; the rest of you, rattle your jewellery'?
5 Which film studio had a radio station mast as its trade mark?

Round 5   Individual questions for Team 1
Classical music
The *Symphonie Fantastique* is a popular work by which French composer?
Motoring
When was the AA founded?
History
Who shot the British prime minister Spencer Perceval?
Television
Which TV programme opened with a naked light bulb swinging to and fro?
Chance
Which two countries are separated by the Palk Strait?

Round 6
Team 2

1   In which country is the Murray river?
2   Whose only novel was *Gone with the Wind*?
3   What do the Muslims call their god?
4   What does FRSL stand for?
5   Name the dry brown brandy distilled in the French district of Gers.

Team 1

1   In which American state is the Mojave Desert?
2   Whose first successful novel was entitled *Decline and Fall*?
3   What did Salome receive as a reward from Herod for her dancing?
4   What does NOIC stand for?
5   If you saw 'fino' on a bottle, what would you expect to find in it?

Round 7
Team 2

1   Off the coast of which country was the Second World War Battle of Matapan?
2   What sport's name means literally 'empty hand'?
3   Of what is nephology the study?
4   'Much have I travell'd in the realms of gold', is the opening line of a poem by whom?
5   Who was the last 20th-century prime minister educated at Eton?

Team 1

1   Who commanded the British fleet at the Battle of the Nile?
2   What sport's name means literally 'gentle way'?
3   What is the opposite of Utopia?
4   'Earth has not anything to show more fair', is the opening line of a poem by whom?
5   Who was the conductor at the opening of the Carnegie Hall, New York?

85

Round 8

Team 2

1 Which famous character was created by Richard Herne?
2 Which building in London is associated with looking after English lighthouses?
3 For which sport is the town of Klosters famous?
4 What German word, often used in art criticism, means 'work in bad taste'?
5 Who had a historic meeting in Ujiji in 1871?

Team 1

1 Name two of the Beatles' five films.
2 Where is HMS *Victory* moored?
3 Where is a mountain called Kosciusko?
4 By what name was US painter Anna Robertson better known?
5 Which two fictional characters met supposedly for the last time on a precipice over the Reichenbach Falls?

Round 9

Team 2

1 What name is given to the stem of a plant from which the leaves, buds and side shoots spring?
2 Who played Stewart McMillan in *McMillan and Wife*?
3 What is the medical term for the back part of the neck?
4 What do the letters DC mean, as in Washington DC?
5 Which burglar, hanged in 1879, carried his tools in a violin case?

Team 1

1 What name is given to the main root of a dandelion?
2 Who played *The Charmer* on TV?
3 What is the more usual name for coryza?
4 What does AWACS stand for?
5 To which piece of clothing did Sir Anthony Eden give his name?

Round 10 Individual questions for Team 2

Classical music

Who composed *The Creation* and *The Seasons*?

Motoring

What major contribution to road safety did Leslie Hore-Belisha make?

History

Which wife of Henry VIII was the mother of Queen Elizabeth I?

Television

What programme has appeared since 1956 on three different channels and provides a review of recent events in the light of newspaper coverage?

Chance

What do the letters MS after a doctor's name mean?

Drinks round

Team 1

1 Gerardus Mercator was famous for what skill?
2 The Yom Kippur War is also known as the Six-Day War. Is that true or false?
3 In Greek mythology, who were the twins who were turned into stars?
4 What is the white ring on an archery target called?
5 With which sport would you associate Babe Ruth?
6 What theory starts with the formula $e=mc^2$?
7 Who wrote *The Hunchback of Notre Dame*?
8 What is a palomino?
9 In computer terminology, what does GIGO mean?
10 Which is the largest of the Inner Hebrides?

Team 2

1 Queen Salote reigned over which island kingdom?
2 The Duchess of Windsor was married three times. Is this true or false?
3 What is the connection between the Greek mythological character Procrustes and a bed?
4 What is the central division on a backgammon board called?
5 With which sport would you associate the Jules Rimet Cup?
6 Who developed the Special Theory of Relativity?
7 Who wrote *The Road Past Mandalay*?
8 What is a motmot?
9 What chemical element has the symbol Sb?
10 What is Scotland's longest loch?

Reserve questions

1 Who created Colonel Blimp?
2 In which city did the St Valentine's Day Massacre take place?
3 Who recorded 'Like a Virgin' in 1984?

Pub League Quiz 16

The individual questions are in Rounds 5 and 10 and are on holiday and travel, food and drink, music, the Bible and history.

Round 1

Team 1

1 Who succeeded Charles de Gaulle as French president in 1969?
2 Who wrote *The Napoleon of Notting Hill*?
3 What is the SI unit of time?
4 Who wrote the music for 'Rule, Britannia'?
5 How many times did Rod Laver win the men's singles at Wimbledon?

Team 2

1 Which British prime minister was born in Canada in 1858?
2 Which dramatist invented the character of Mrs Malaprop?
3 What was once known as brimstone?
4 Who wrote the anthem 'Zadok the Priest', performed at all British coronations since that of George II?
5 In which athletics event was Dick Fosbury an Olympic record holder?

Round 2

Team 1

1 What is Greek for the letter K?
2 Who sculpted *The Thinker* and *The Kiss*?
3 Which cinematographic mob was led by Alec Guinness?
4 In which country is Cape Trafalgar?
5 Which rock did Sir George Rooke take for Queen Anne in 1704?

Team 2

1 What is the fourth letter of the Greek alphabet?
2 With what kind of paintings do you associate with the names of Nicholas Hilliard, Richard Cosway and George Engleheart?
3 Who played Napoleon in the 1970 film of *Waterloo*?
4 On which river does Ottawa stand?
5 Who was the 17th-century adventurer who almost succeeded in stealing the crown jewels?

Round 3

Team 1

1 What does WCC stand for?
2 Who wrote the novel *Brighton Rock*?
3 What is the country of origin of the Proton motor car?

4 Which branch of mathematics takes its name from the Latin word for pebble?
5 Who wrote the music for *Kiss Me Kate*?

Team 2

1 What does CBI stand for?
2 Who wrote *The Green Hills of Africa*?
3 Which motor manufacturer made the Plus 4, Plus 8 and SS models?

4 How did the word 'salary' originate?

5 Who wrote the music for the operetta *Showboat*?

Round 4

Team 1

1 What kind of animal is an eider?
2 When in the church calendar is Advent?
3 Who designed the Horse Guards building in Whitehall and the Royal Mews?
4 Which famous film was based on the life of William Randolph Hearst?
5 In which ocean would you find Ascension Island?

Team 2

1 What kind of animal is a gecko?
2 What is the literal meaning of 'Advent'?
3 Who designed Regent's Park, Regent Street and the Royal Pavilion, Brighton?
4 What was captured in the film *The Taking of Pelham 123*?
5 In which ocean would you find Ashmore Reef and Cartier Island?

Round 5   *Individual questions for Team 1*

Holiday and travel
If you were on Mona, where would you be?
Food and drink
What name is given to the thin type of pancake eaten throughout Mexico?
Music
Which composer would you associate with the *Brandenburg Concertos*?
The Bible
Who were the parents of John the Baptist?
History
What relation was King Haakon VII of Norway to King Edward VII of Britain?

Round 6

Team 2

1 What is marl a mixture of?
2 Which organ produces insulin?
3 What sporting event did Dionicio Ceron of Mexico win in April 1995?
4 Which family lives at Brookfield Farm?
5 What name is given to a bishop's headdress?

Team 1

1 From which ore is aluminium extracted?
2 Which organ is concerned with balance?
3 Ellery Hanley was captain of which Rugby League team?
4 In *EastEnders*, who was the father of Michelle Fowler's baby?
5 What is the skirt-like garment worn by Malaysians called?

Round 7

Team 2

1 What is an infanta?
2 What is the capital of Pakistan?
3 Who wrote *Women in Love*?
4 What RNVR stand for?
5 Who was the British chancellor of the exchequer in 1974–79?

Team 1

1 What is a mazurka?
2 What is the capital of Nova Scotia?
3 What did the D. H. in D. H. Lawrence stand for?
4 What does RCMP stand for?
5 Who was the British prime minister during 1970–74?

Round 8

Team 2

1 What type of tree is the lemon tree?
2 Which battle was fought on 21 October 1805?
3 Who was the oldest holder of the world heavyweight boxing crown?
4 In a suit of medieval armour, what part of the body is covered by greaves?
5 On which river is Winchester?

Team 1

1 Give another name for the wellingtonia.
2 At which 1746 battle were the Jacobites defeated?
3 Who was the lightest world heavyweight boxing champion ever?
4 What was Louis IX the last to lead?
5 The confluence of which two rivers forms the Humber?

Round 9

Team 2

1 Which country has the international vehicle registration letter CH?
2 Who summoned the Model Parliament?
3 What do football, Woolworth, Heinz and Dr Pepper have in common?
4 To which subsequent Poet Laureate was Sylvia Plath married?
5 In which country is the city of Chihuahua?

Team 1

1 What is the international vehicle registration letter for Germany?
2 Which famous battle took place in July 1690?
3 How many cards are there in a Tarot pack with the Greater and Lesser Arcana?
4 Which Poet Laureate declared, 'I must go down to the seas again, to the lonely sea and the sky'?
5 In which countries is the region of Patagonia?

Round 10   Individual questions for Team 2

Holiday and travel
Who exactly requests and requires free passage for the bearer of a British passport?
Food and drink
What are Desirées, Majestics and Vanessas?
Music
Which composer's sixth symphony is known as the 'Pastoral'?
The Bible
What did Solomon begin to build 'in the second day of the second month, in the fourth year of his reign'?
History
Who was the Confederate president at the time of the American Civil War?

Drinks round

Team 1

1 What is the former name of Malawi?
2 Which fictional character did Reg Smythe create?
3 What organisation, formed in 1863, has its headquarters in Geneva?
4 What liqueur is made from high-proof brandy, wormwood and other aromatics?
5 Who choreographed the musical film *42nd Street*?
6 Name one of the official languages of Afghanistan.

7 Which writer and peer bought London's Playhouse Theatre in 1992?
8 What is the capital of Uruguay?
9 Name the year that Idi Amin ordered the expulsion of British Asians from Uganda, Maurice Chevalier died and Sir John Betjeman became Poet Laureate.
10 Who starred in the silent western *Destry Rides Again*?

Team 2

1 Which country has the Malabar Coast?
2 Whose arch enemy is Ming the Merciless?
3 By what name is the equivalent of the Red Cross known in Muslim countries?
4 What liqueur is made from Dalmatian cherries?
5 Who co-directed and starred in the film *Singing in the Rain*?
6 Which country's language has two major dialects, Gheg and Tosk?
7 Who succeeded Sir Peter Hall as director of the National Theatre?
8 What is the capital of Mongolia?
9 Name the year breakfast TV began in Britain, the Franks Report on the Falklands was published and Derby winner Shergar was stolen.
10 Who wrote the story *Destry Rides Again*?

Reserve questions

1 The Melling Road crosses which racecourse?
2 How many eyes has the wolf spider?
3 Which Scottish chemist perpetuated his name with an invention of a waterproof fabric for garments in 1823?

Pub League Quiz 17

The individual questions are in Rounds 5 and 10 and are on dress and fashion, law, inventors and inventions, famous men and words.

Round 1

Team 1

1 What is the chief port of Iraq?

2 What name is given to animals that eat both vegetable and animal foods?

3 Name Noah's three sons.

4 What type of material is guipure?

5 Who first manufactured basaltes crockery?

Team 2

1 Which is the second city and port of Algeria?

2 What name is given to an animal with no backbone?

3 Who was the prostitute who aided Joshua during the siege of Jericho?

4 What in architecture is a lancet?

5 Which potter was the first to produce the famous willow pattern ware in Britain?

Round 2

Team 1

1 Name two of the founder members of the United Artists film company.

2 Who defeated Prince Rupert at Marston Moor?

3 Who wrote *Ending Up*?

4 What are igneous rocks?

5 What is the fat-like substance derived from sheep's wool and used with water as a base for ointments and cosmetics?

Team 2

1 Which film star's body was stolen by grave robbers in Switzerland?

2 Who was the father of the first Prince of Wales?

3 Who wrote *The Little Match Girl*?

4 What is the geological name for the outer rocky shell of the earth?

5 Name the form of oxygen in which three atoms form one molecule, found most abundantly in the upper atmosphere.

Round 3

Team 1

1 Who removed a thorn from a lion's foot and later faced the same lion in a Roman arena?
2 Who was Pearl Bailey?
3 Where in your body would you find aqueous humour?
4 Who was the first black American tennis player to win the Wimbledon men's singles title?
5 Who wrote the opera *Madame Butterfly*?

Team 2

1 Who constructed the labyrinth for King Minos of Crete?
2 Which jazz composer and saxophonist married Cleo Laine?
3 Where in your body is your olfactory organ?
4 How many goals did England score in the 1966 World Cup final?
5 Which Verdi opera was about the son of Phillip II of Spain?

Round 4

Team 1

1 What did Clyde Tombaugh discover?
2 Who had a hit with 'My Guy'?
3 Who first patented the phonograph?
4 What does ECG stand for?
5 Who lived at 23 Railway Cuttings, Cheam?

Team 2

1 What name is given to a luminous concentration of gas and dust in space?
2 Who in a pop song was 'wearing the face that she keeps in a jar by the door'?
3 Who invented the spinning-jenny?
4 What does MRC stand for?
5 Who played Alf Garnett's daughter in *Till Death Us Do Part*?

Round 5   Individual questions for Team 1

Dress and fashion

Which fashion designer was responsible for Biba fashion?

Law

What is the name given to the prosecution of a public official by the legislature of the state?

Inventors and inventions

Who invented the vacuum flask?

Famous men

He was born in 1856 and died in 1939. He was Austrian by birth and specialised in psycho-analysis. Who was he?

Words

What is the first meaning of didactic?

Round 6

Team 2

1 Excluding Oxford and Cambridge, which is the oldest university in England?
2 Which fruit is a cross between a grapefruit and a tangerine?
3 Where is the home of Radio Hallam?
4 Arthur Koestler wrote a history of cosmology. What is it called?
5 Where did Nelson lose the sight of his right eye?

Team 1

1 Which is the oldest college in the USA?
2 Which fruit is a cross between a blackberry and a raspberry?
3 Where are the headquarters of Radio Piccadilly?
4 Where was Arthur Koestler born?
5 Where did Nelson lose his right arm?

Round 7

Team 2

1 Who was the king of Iraq who fought against the Turks with T. E. Lawrence in the First World War?
2 Name the two stars of *A Midsummer Night's Sex Comedy*?
3 Who played Hannibal Smith in *The A-Team*?
4 Who wrote *The Honourable Schoolboy*?
5 What was Derek Trotter's nickname in *Only Fools and Horses*?

Team 1

1 What is the family name of the ruling house of Saudi Arabia?
2 Which actress co-starred with Clint Eastwood in *The Enforcer*?
3 Who played Faceman in *The A-Team*?
4 Who wrote *Lorna Doone*?
5 What was different about Harpo Marx's character?

Round 8

Team 2

1 According to Shakespeare, how many daughters did King Lear have?
2 What are the colours of the flag of the United Nations?
3 The first of the Great Western Railway's main lines was completed in 1841. Between which two places did it run?
4 Who topped the charts for 10 weeks in 1992 with 'I Will Always Love You'?
5 What type of dog is a Bedlington?

Team 1

1 What was *Mrs Warren's Profession* in the play by George Bernard Shaw?
2 What is the American national anthem called?
3 Within three years, when was the Stockton and Darlington Railway opened?
4 In which city were Wet Wet Wet formed?
5 Name one of the two main types of Welsh corgi.

Round 9

Team 2

1 Which is the largest of the national parks in Great Britain?
2 What is the Apple Isle to Australians?
3 What nationality was Marie-Antoinette?
4 Where in football is the Stretford End?
5 In awards, what does MM stand for?

Team 1

1 Name one of the three people who set up the National Trust.
2 Which is the largest city in Australia?
3 What nationality was Marie Curie?
4 In which sport is a sand wedge used?
5 In finance, what does MLR stand for?

Round 10   Individual questions for Team 2

Dress and fashion
Which French fashion designer was responsible for the little black dress?
Law
What word describes a person who dies without leaving a will?
Inventors and inventions
Who planned a mechanical calculator, the forerunner to the modern computer?
Famous men
Which surgeon first performed the human heart transplant operation?
Words
What is hypermetropia?

Drinks round

Team 1

1 Who wrote *The Egoist*?

2 What piece of furniture was always featured on *The Val Doonican Show*?

3 What nationality was speedway star Ivan Maugher?

4 What are marlin?

5 Who painted 'The Reapers' and 'The Gleaners'?

6 What were the female fans of Frank Sinatra called?

7 What is the chemical symbol for mercury?

8 What name is given to second-year students at American universities?

9 What is processed germinated barley called?

10 Name one of the independent kingdoms between India and China.

Team 2

1 Who wrote *The Tailor of Gloucester*?

2 Who was the first presenter of *Tomorrow's World*?

3 When did women first compete in the Olympics?

4 What is a baby hare called?

5 What is 'La Giaconda' better known as?

6 What instrument did King Oliver play?

7 What is the chemical symbol for magnesium?

8 What school of Greek philosophy gave its name to reasoning that is plausible but false?

9 Of what cereal is sweetcorn a type?

10 What is the old name for the South African province of Kwa Zulu?

Reserve questions

1 Charles Wesley was a prodigious writer of hymns. Did he write over 2,500, 3,500, 4,500 or 5,500?

2 Roger Bannister ran the first sub-four-minute mile in 1954; by how much less than four minutes?

3 From which fruit is slivovitz made?

Pub League Quiz 18

The individual questions are in Rounds 5 and 10 and are on water life, television, organisations, games and flight.

Round 1

Team 1

1 'Empty Garden' was a tribute by Elton John to whom?
2 Where might you find a finial, a chevet and a slype?
3 Who wrote *Fear of Flying*?
4 Which country was the first to grant women the vote?
5 By what name is K'ung tsu better known?

Team 2

1 Which Dire Straits album became the first million-selling CD?
2 In medieval times, where would you have found loopholes?
3 Which novel by Jane Austen was originally called *First Impressions*?
4 Which Middle Ages heroine was born at Domrémy?
5 Which Church of England bishop would sign himself Sarum?

Round 2

Team 1

1 What colour is the three ball in pool?
2 What does AWOL stand for?
3 What made the Lascaux Cave in south-west France famous?
4 Which enemy of Batman usually carries an umbrella?
5 Which Washington edifice has 898 steps?

Team 2

1 In croquet singles, what other colour ball does the player with blue have?
2 What do Mc and Mac mean in surnames?
3 Which modern animal is descended from the eohippus?
4 On which planet was Superman born?
5 Which Rome tourist attraction has 137 steps?

Round 3

Team 1

1 In which country was Maria Bueno born?
2 On the London Underground map, what colour represents the Bakerloo Line?
3 In which country did Antony and Cleopatra end their lives?
4 What was the code name for the German invasion of Russia?
5 Which actress played Judy opposite James Dean's Jim in *Rebel Without a Cause*?

Team 2

1 Who defected at the 1975 American Tennis Open?
2 What is the national, long-distance railroad system in the USA called?
3 Who is Jessica's father in *The Merchant of Venice*?
4 What was the code name for the allied invasion of Normandy?
5 Who played the girl in *The Girl Can't Help It*?

Round 4

Team 1

1 Which Caribbean island was invaded by US forces in 1983?
2 What is majolica?
3 Which constellation is the water bearer?
4 What is the sequel to D. H. Lawrence's *The Rainbow*?
5 Who was known as 'the flying Finn'?

Team 2

1 Where do you pass through the Pedro Miguel locks?
2 What is bruschetta?
3 Which star is known as the Dog Star?
4 Who wrote *Ivanhoe*?
5 Which Olympic gold medallist was banned from athletics in 1913 when it was discovered he had played minor league baseball for money?

Round 5   *Individual questions for Team 1*

Water life
What is an infant whale called?

Television
Which Glasgow comedian is known as The Big Yin?

Organisations
Which organisation works for human rights all over the world?

Games
At what game are points scored 'below the line'?

Flight
Who manufactured the Comet airliner?

Round 6

Team 2

1 How long did Sleeping Beauty sleep?
2 Which part did Judy Garland play in the film *The Wizard of Oz*?
3 What is Bolivia's chief export?
4 What was the nickname of Rolls-Royce's experimental vertical take-off aircraft?
5 Which famous landmark was designed by Auguste Bartholdi?

Team 1

1 Who owned a chocolate factory in the film of Roald Dahl's story?
2 Who created Kermit the frog?
3 Which country has the world's largest sheep population?
4 What was the nickname of the Model T Ford?
5 For what event did Gustave Eiffel build the Eiffel Tower?

Round 7

Team 2

1 What class is categorised as the bourgeoisie?
2 Which musical was based on T. H. White's novel *The Once and Future King*?
3 Which bird is on Australia's coat of arms?
4 What was the name of Edward Heath's yacht?
5 How often is golf's Ryder Cup played?

Team 1

1 What is the only house in England that the Queen may not legally enter?
2 Which musical horror was first staged in 1974?
3 Which famous Sydney landmark was opened in March 1932?
4 Which famous explorer sailed in the *Theodore Roosevelt*?
5 In boxing what weight division comes between heavyweight and light-heavyweight?

Round 8

Team 2

1 The Hawaiian flag carries the flag of which country in its upper left-hand corner?
2 What does UDR stand for?
3 Who was the first woman to fly the Atlantic solo in 1932?
4 Which country is the setting for Edgar Allan Poe's *The Pit and the Pendulum*?
5 What country's flag is red with a white crescent and star?

Team 1

1 Which nation's flag flies over Easter Island?
2 Which sport's ruling body is the FIBA?
3 Where did Phineas Fogg begin and end his trip around the world?
4 Which English county provided the setting for most of L. S. Lowry's work?
5 What single colour constitutes the flag of Libya?

Round 9

Team 2

1 Which liqueur is the base for a Copenhagen Mary?

2 What was the prequel to *Gentlemen Marry Brunettes*?
3 Which leader was known as the Lion of Judah?
4 To the nearest 5 per cent, what is the approximate percentage of the world covered by oceans?
5 Which insect transmits yellow fever?

Team 1

1 Which spirit was known in 18th-century England as Cuckold's Comfort, Make Shift and Ladies' Delight?

2 Who created Charlie Chan?

3 Who was the only English pope?

4 Where is the Beaufort Sea?

5 What is rubella better known as?

Round 10   Individual questions for Team 2

Water life
What is an orc?
Television
Which *Peyton Place* star married Frank Sinatra?
Organisations
What organisation did Pol Pot lead?
Games
How many different colours are the spaces on a Scrabble board?
Flight
Where was London's first airport?

Drinks round

Team 1

1 What was John Steinbeck's travelling companion Charley?
2 Where did the gunfight at the OK Corral take place?

3 By what Indian name is Mount McKinley also known?
4 What do gall wasps cause in oak trees?
5 Who was the first woman to produce, write, direct and star in a major Hollywood film?

6 In which country is Casablanca?

7 From what game do we get the phrase 'stand pat'?
8 Which is the only female animal that has antlers?
9 Which English artist drew 'The Anatomy of the Horse'?
10 In which county would you find the prehistoric monuments of Stonehenge?

Team 2

1 Which books tell the stories of Brer Fox and Brer Rabbit?
2 Which film had gunslinger Frank Miller arriving on the midday train?
3 In which US state is Mount McKinley?
4 Which trees are commonly found in English churchyards?
5 Which of the film title characters played by Charlton Heston was known in real life as Rodrigo Diaz de Vivar?
6 The Owen Falls are below the point at which the White Nile leaves which lake?
7 Which game is fatal to anyone over 21?
8 To which family of animals does the gnu belong?
9 Which artist painted 'The Leaping Horse'?
10 Which museum houses the Elgin Marbles and the Rosetta Stone?

Reserve questions

1 How many land miles are there in a league?
2 Which Australian city is served by Tullamarine airport?
3 Who wrote the score for *A Funny Thing Happened on the Way to the Forum*?

Pub League Quiz 19

The individual questions are in Rounds 5 and 10 and are on cathedrals, heraldry, numbers, who said? and soap operas.

Round 1

Team 1

1 What is the state capital of Tennessee?
2 Who wrote the play *Major Barbara*?
3 In awards, what does KP stand for?
4 What is the name of the leading horse racing course of Paris?
5 Who was the first president of the United Arab Republic?

Team 2

1 What is the state capital of Maine?
2 Which dramatist wrote *The Caretaker*?
3 What does MVO stand for?
4 What is the most famous race held at Longchamp?
5 Who became the first chairman of the People's Republic of China?

Round 2

Team 1

1 What name is given to a positive electrode?
2 Motor racing's worst accident was in 1955; over 80 spectators were killed. Where was it?
3 Who starred in the films *Bus Stop* and *The Misfits*?
4 What is the longest river in France?
5 *Eliminator* was in the album charts for over two years. Who recorded it?

Team 2

1 What name is given to a negative electrode?
2 Who won the Le Mans 24-Hour Race in 1955 and the World Driver's Championship in 1958?
3 What was Marilyn Monroe's real name?
4 In which continent is the Limpopo river?
5 What group did Paul McCartney form after the break-up of the Beatles?

Round 3
Team 1

1 Which TV presenter wrote a book called *Men: A Documentary*?

2 Who founded the world's first Fascist Party?

3 What Russian did both Greta Garbo and Vivien Leigh play on screen?

4 What is an onager?

5 Before Tony Blair, how many Labour prime ministers had there been?

Team 2

1 Who played Bella in *Our Mutual Friend*, Mrs Lisa Leeson in *Rogue Trader* and got married to an airman in *Land Girls*?

2 What was Mussolini also known as?

3 Who wrote *Letters from the Underworld*?

4 What is a merino?

5 Name three Labour prime ministers before Tony Blair.

Round 4
Team 1

1 In which county is Alton Towers?

2 From which film is the song 'Moon River'?

3 What do you get from the product of the length of one side, and its perpendicular distance from the opposite side?

4 What is oology the study of?

5 Juneau is the capital of which American state?

Team 2

1 Which family lives at Hatfield House?

2 Who won an Oscar for the song 'Moon River'?

3 Mass times acceleration equals what?

4 What is etymology?

5 Which is the 'Keystone State' of the US?

Round 5   *Individual questions for Team 1*
Cathedrals
In which French cathedral was Charles VII crowned in 1429? ·
Heraldry
What in heraldry is tincture?
Numbers
Find a number that is less 72 than its square.
Who said?
Who said, 'A week is a long time in politics'?
Soap operas
Which soap did Phil Redmond, formerly of *Grange Hill*, create?

Round 6

Team 2

1 Which famous writer was the son of the curator of the Central Museum at Lahore?

2 Who built the first steam locomotive to run on a railway?

3 Which French province does Camembert cheese come from?

4 What was the name of the minstrel in Robin Hood's gang?

5 In which country is Salamanca?

Team 1

1 Who was born in Bedford, the son of a tinker, and wrote a large part of his most famous book in jail?

2 In which British city are there railway stations called Foregate Street and Shrub Hill?

3 Of what is marzipan made?

4 How did Robin Hood help the minstrel's bride?

5 In which country is Topeka?

Round 7

Team 2

1 To which part of the body does the prefix 'derm' refer?

2 What in heraldry is gold?

3 Who was the winning commander at the naval Battle of the Falklands?

4 What park lies between Buckingham Palace and Piccadilly?

5 What nationality was Pocahontas?

Team 1

1 To which part of the body does the prefix 'cerebro' refer?

2 What in heraldry is silver?

3 Who was the winning commander at Omdurman?

4 Where in Piccadilly is the home of the Royal Academy?

5 What nationality was Count Cavour?

Round 8

Team 2

1 Which playwright wrote *The Master Builder*?

2 What is the name of the small independent state between France and Spain?

3 Give another name for potassium nitrate.

4 Who was the Greek goddess of love?

5 What name is given to a book of words and their synonyms?

Team 1

1 Which playwright wrote *An Ideal Husband*?

2 What is the southernmost province of Portugal?

3 Which gas is also known as laughing gas?

4 What name did the Romans give to Aphrodite?

5 What name is given to an index of the principal words in a book or in an author's works?

Round 9

Team 2

1 What is the name of the protein present in red blood cells that is scarlet when combined with oxygen?

2 What is the Bengali name for a small rowing boat, used as an auxiliary in yachting?

3 What nationality was the composer Friedrich Smetana?

4 Who was the second man on the moon?

5 What name is given to an abnormally bright star caused by a Crab nebula?

Team 1

1 What is haemophilia?

2 In what sport are Telemark and Christiana turns used?

3 Which composer wrote a suite entitled *Mother Goose* in English?

4 What was the first commercial communications satellite called?

5 Which planet is closest to the sun?

Round 10   Individual questions for Team 2

Cathedrals

In which cathedral was Charlemagne buried?

Heraldry

What in heraldry is a tabard?

Numbers

Divide 48 into two parts so that one is three-fifths of the other.

Who said?

Who said, 'The ballot is stronger than the bullet'?

Soap operas

Which character from *The Archers* died on the opening night of ITV?

Drinks round

Team 1

1 What does IAEA stand for?
2 Which European country has more than two-fifths of its land below sea level?
3 Who wrote *King Solomon's Mines*?
4 Who murdered Lee Harvey Oswald?
5 Who reigned in England between the years 871 and 899?
6 Which actress starred in the film *Boy on a Dolphin*?
7 What is the capital of New Zealand?
8 What was the name of the Lone Ranger's horse?
9 In eight hours, Fiona walks three miles more than Jean does in six hours, and in seven hours Jean walks nine miles more than Fiona does in six hours. How many miles does each walk per hour?
10 In which country is Kirkcaldy?

Team 2

1 What does ICAO stand for?
2 Name three of the six American states that make up New England.
3 Who wrote *The Water Babies*?
4 Who murdered Robert Kennedy?
5 Who reigned in Scotland between 1040 and 1057?
6 In which film did Glynis Johns play a mermaid?
7 What is the capital of Luxembourg?
8 Whose horse was Trigger in films and TV?
9 Half Edward's age exceeds a quarter of Cyril's by 12 months, and three-quarters of Cyril's age exceeds Edward's by 11 years. How old are they both?
10 In which country is Armagh?

Reserve questions

1 What was President Jimmy Carter's middle name?
2 How many noughts were there in a British billion?
3 Which game is mentioned in Shakespeare's *Antony and Cleopatra*, though it was not invented until the 15th Century?

Pub League Quiz 20

The individual questions are in Rounds 5 and 10 and are on films, the arts, literature, sport and proverbs.

Round 1

Team 1
1 In which English county would you find both Toronto and Pity Me?
2 Which European country used the escudo as its unit of currency?
3 In which sport would you hear of a roundhouse, knuckler and outcurve?
4 What is a badger's home called?
5 Which year was India given its independence?

Team 2
1 In which English county would you find Wookey Hole?
2 Which country uses the lev as its unit of currency?
3 Kip, crossgrasp and pike are movements in which sport?
4 What is a squirrel's home called?
5 Who was the last Viceroy of India?

Round 2

Team 1
1 Name the capital of Chile.
2 Who wrote the opera *The Fair Maid of Perth*?
3 What is xenophobia?
4 In Greek mythology, who stole fire from the gods and gave it to mankind?
5 Name the snail in *The Magic Roundabout*.

Team 2
1 Name the capital of Mexico.
2 Who wrote *A German Requiem* in memory of his mother?
3 Of which disease is hydrophobia a major symptom?
4 By what collective name are Stheno, Euryale and Medusa known?
5 Name the cow in *The Magic Roundabout*.

Round 3

Team 1

1 Charles Buchinski became a major film star. By what name do we know him?

2 Which famous author spent the last 10 years of his life at Gad's Hill?

3 What is a dhow?

4 How long does a game of hockey last?

5 Which pop group had a 1960s hit with 'When You Walk in the Room'?

Team 2

1 Which American director was famous for his westerns, such as *She Wore a Yellow Ribbon*?

2 Which fictional French detective always smoked a pipe?

3 What is an umiak?

4 How many active players are there in a water polo team?

5 Who had a 1983 hit with 'Total Eclipse of the Heart'?

Round 4

Team 1

1 Who, in Greek mythology, was the god of marriage?

2 What for William James was 'the bitch goddess'?

3 Where is Lake Koko-Nor?

4 In what art process would specimens be line engraved or lithographed?

5 What is the common name for the infectious fever variola?

Team 2

1 Who, in Greek mythology, was a surly ferryman?

2 Who, according to Dorothy Parker, 'ran the whole gamut of emotions from A to B'?

3 Where is Lake Como?

4 What would a lepidopterist collect?

5 Which organ of the body is affected by hepatitis?

Round 5   Individual questions for Team 1

Films

What was the title of the film in which Elvis Presley played a boxer?

The arts

What great French artist is associated with Polynesia?

Literature

Who, famed for his literary works, also invented the pillar box?

Sport

What type of race is run for horses over hunting country?

Proverbs

Complete the proverb, 'Marry in haste and...'

Round 6

Team 2

1 On whose life did Terence Rattigan base his play *Ross*?
2 Who sang, 'One Day I'll Fly Away'?
3 What is depicted on the reverse of an English 2p coin?
4 Who wrote The Secret Seven series?
5 Who starred in the films *Tom Jones*, *Charlie Bubbles* and *Annie*?

Team 1

1 Who wrote the play *Death of a Salesman*?
2 'Touch Me in the Morning' was a hit for which singer?
3 What is on the reverse of an English ten-pence piece?
4 Name Captain Pugwash's boat.
5 Who directed and starred in the silent movies *The Navigator* and *The General*?

Round 7

Team 2

1 What is a Camberwell Beauty?
2 What is LXX in Roman numerals?
3 What language is spoken in Brazil?
4 How many stars are on the Australian flag?
5 Which football team plays at Elland Road?

Team 1

1 What is a mastiff?
2 In geometry, what do we call a straight line that touches a curve at one point but does not cut it?
3 What is the official language of Cuba?
4 How many stars are on the American flag?
5 Which football team plays at Filbert Street?

Round 8

Team 2

1 How many faces has a dodecahedron?
2 Olympic Airways is the national airline of which country?
3 Which French artist was famed for his paintings of prostitutes?
4 What does BDA stand for?
5 What have David Jacobs, Noel Edmonds and Jools Holland all presented on TV?

Team 1

1 How many sides has a hendecagon?
2 Sabena Airways is the national airline of which country?
3 Who painted 'The Swing'?
4 What does ETD stand for?
5 Who played *Quincy* in the TV series of the same name?

Round 9

Team 2

1 The General Strike of 1926 was called in support of which union?

2 Which French monarch was known as the Sun King?

3 Which English city has the postcode LS?

4 Who in the Bible promoted Shadrach, Meshach and Abednego?

5 'Little White Bull' was a hit for which singer?

Team 1

1 What other title is held by the First Lord of the Treasury?

2 Charles Beauclerk was the illegitimate son of which English king?

3 What place is England uses the postcode SS?

4 Name the apostles of Christ whose Christian names begin with the letter 'P'.

5 Which artist sang 'Morning Has Broken'?

Round 10   Individual questions for Team 2

Films

In which film did Mae West say, 'Why don't you come up sometime, see me?'

The arts

Who worked as court painter to Ludovico il Moro of Milan from 1482 to 1499?

Literature

What word describes a break in a line of poetry, often to emphasise an antithesis or comparison?

Sport

Which London soccer club was founded in 1882 by boys from a Presbyterian school?

Proverbs

Complete the proverb, 'The road to hell is paved with...'.

Drinks round

Team 1

1 Name the capital of Ethiopia.

2 In which film did Danny Kaye sing 'Wonderful Copenhagen'?

3 In which opera is the character Lieutenant Pinkerton?

4 Which metal has the chemical symbol Pb?

5 Which invention began with experiments to aid the deaf?

6 Which country has won most World Curling Championships?

7 What type of creature was Riki Tiki Tavi?

8 Bideford is at the mouth of what river?

9 Which American rock group released 'Riders on the Storm' and 'Light My Fire'?

10 In which sport would the Minnesota Twins play the St Louis Cardinals?

Team 2

1 Name the chief town of the Shetland Islands.

2 Who wrote and directed *Star Wars*?

3 Who wrote *The Gondoliers*?

4 Which chemical element has the symbol Cu?

5 Which people reputedly invented paper money?

6 In which sport would you find the terms inner, outer and magpie?

7 What type of creatures live in a formicary?

8 On which river does Peterborough stand?

9 Which group had hits with 'Life is a Minestrone' and 'Donna'?

10 Which game is played with white, spot and red balls?

Reserve questions

1 Which planet's satellites are named after characters from Shakespeare?

2 Who is the patron saint of Poland?

3 In which country did the Pied Piper play?

Pub League Quiz 21

The individual questions are in Rounds 5 and 10 and are on Pop music, the Olympics, the Bible, what comes next? and where is it?

Round 1

Team 1

1 By what name is scorpion grass better known?

2 Where would you find the Dewey decimal system in use?

3 Cousins Manfred B. Lee and Frederic Dannay are better known as whom?

4 Where is the *Northern Echo* published?

5 The town of Moron is in which South American country?

Team 2

1 What flower has the same name as a reddish-orange mineral sometimes used as a gem?

2 What are and where would you find the Pleiades?

3 Which famous person left his wife his furniture and his second-best bed in his will?

4 In which town is the *Dorset Evening Echo* published?

5 The town of Ghent is in which country?

Round 2

Team 1

1 Which pop group sang 'Bits and Pieces'?

2 Who wrote, 'When a man is tired of London, he is tired of life; for there is in London all that life can afford'?

3 Which number in bingo is called half a crown?

4 What shipping forecast area lies between Faeroes and Viking?

5 Who opened the first British birth control clinic?

Team 2

1 Which singer was 'Watching the Detectives'?

2 Who invented the concept of 'doublethink'?

3 How many pieces does each player have in draughts?

4 What geological era follows the Jurassic?

5 Who founded the East End Mission for destitute children?

Round 3

Team 1

1 In what year did the voting age in Britain became 18?

2 What is the word for a woman's long, double-breasted outer garment, with skirts often cut away in front?

3 Who would use an étrier or a chockstone?

4 In mythology, which gift was given to Cassandra by Apollo?

5 What is the title of the highest ranking judge in the Court of Appeal?

Team 2

1 In which year did James Dean die?

2 Name the loose over-garment prescribed by law, the distinctive garment of the Jews in the Middle Ages?

3 In which sporting event do the winners only move backwards?

4 Which day of the week is named after a Roman god?

5 How should the Bishop of London be formally addressed?

Round 4

Team 1

1 Which river flows through Lisbon?

2 Name the highest commissioned rank of the Royal Air Force.

3 What ball game is peculiar to Eton College?

4 From which area of Spain was Don Quixote supposed to have come?

5 What was Bing Crosby's first baptismal Christian name?

Team 2

1 On what river does Moscow stand?

2 The RAF adopted the motto *Per ardua ad astra*. What does it mean?

3 Which is the first property on a Monopoly board after 'Go'?

4 In which book would you find the characters Winston Smith and Julia?

5 Which singer sold one million records of the song 'Who's Sorry Now' and called her autobiography by the same title?

Round 5   Individual questions for Team 1

Pop music

Which folk-rock group had a hit with the album *Angel Delight*?

The Olympics

How many gold medals were won by the USA in the 1980 Summer Olympics?

The Bible

Who in the Bible was asked to interpret the writing on the wall?

What comes next?

2, 17, 3, 19. What comes next?

Where is it?

Where is the Bay of Plenty?

Round 6

Team 2

1 What name is given to the study of the properties and distribution of water?
2 Where is your epiglottis?
3 Who was known as the Great Commoner?
4 Name the largest of the Greek islands.
5 Of which novel is Fanny Price the heroine?

Team 1

1 What name is given to the art of working metals?
2 What is the epidermis?
3 Who was named Supermac by the cartoonist Vicky in 1958?
4 Name the oldest city in Germany on the banks of the Rhine.
5 Who created Frankenstein?

Round 7

Team 2

1 Name the fifth book of the Old Testament.
2 The marrka is the currency of which country?
3 Spider, hermit and masked are all what?
4 What does CBS stand for?
5 What is a double bogey in golf?

Team 1

1 Which is the only miracle mentioned in all four gospels?
2 What is the unit of currency in Norway?
3 What kind of creature is a copperhead?
4 What does RADA stand for?
5 How many beds has a shove ha'penny board?

Round 8

Team 2

1 How many years is a coral anniversary?
2 Which literary character's favourite expression was, 'Off with his head'?
3 Henry Carey has been credited with the composition and singing of a famous musical work in about 1740. What was it?
4 What was the Christian name of Hardy of Laurel and Hardy fame?
5 Who headed the inquiry into the Brixton riots?

Team 1

1 What is celebrated on 7 January in the Russian Orthodox Church?
2 Which Thomas Hardy novel ends, 'As soon as they had strength they arose, joined hands again, and went on'?
3 'Strike Up the Band' was written by which American composer and pianist and his brother?
4 What was Stan Laurel's surname at birth?
5 Which MP started his political career in 1900 as the successful Tory candidate for Oldham?

Round 9

Team 2

1 Which Shakespeare play begins, 'When shall we three meet again...'?
2 What does a shoat grow up to be?
3 What did Kirkpatrick MacMillan invent in 1839?
4 What is the monetary unit of Singapore?
5 What kind of creature is a barbastelle?

Team 1

1 Which Shakespeare play begins, 'If music be the food of love ...'?
2 What is a female donkey called?
3 Who invented the hot air balloon?
4 What is the monetary unit of Tunisia?
5 What is a pochard?

Round 10   Individual questions for Team 2

Pop music
Which trio had a hit with 'Lily the Pink'?
The Olympics
Who won four gold medals in the 1936 Berlin Olympics?
The Bible
According to the Bible, who was the father of the Jews?
What comes next?
Who followed Lyndon B. Johnson as president of the USA?
Where is it?
Where is the Hall Napoléon below the Pyramid?

Just for fun
What fish cannot see, hear or feel?
Amblyopsis, a species of fish that inhabit the Mammoth Cave of Kentucky, one of the deepest caverns in the world. The fish live at such a depth and in such conditions that all their normal senses have atrophied.

Drinks round

Team 1

1 Which British king was styled 'the first gentleman of Europe'?

2 What type of food is Roquefort?

3 Which football team is nicknamed 'the Canaries'?

4 Which explorer discovered Newfoundland in 1497?

5 What is sodium hydroxide commonly known as?

6 In which countries is Lake Titicaca?

7 Of which country was Juan Peron president?

8 Which 1960s vocal group's singer claimed to be Kaiser Bill's batman?

9 Who was credited with the quotation, 'I never hated a man enough to give him his diamonds back'?

10 In the grounds of which royal residence is St George's Chapel?

Team 2

1 Which British king was described as 'the wisest fool in Christendom'?

2 For which delicacy are the towns of Whitstable and Colchester famous?

3 Which football team is nicknamed 'the Hatters'?

4 What nationality was the explorer Abel Tasman?

5 What is hydrated magnesium sulphate commonly known as?

6 Lake Manitoba is in which country?

7 Who was Israel's first president?

8 'Ride a White Swan' was a hit for which pop group?

9 Who said, 'The House of Lords is the British Outer Mongolia for retired politicians'?

10 On the outside wall of which building can you find Sir Jacob Epstein's bronze statue of St Michael slaying the Devil?

Reserve questions

1 Who composed the rock opera *Tommy*?
2 In which American state is Camp David?
3 What name is given to the dish consisting of oysters in bacon?

Pub League Quiz 22

The individual questions are in Rounds 5 and 10 and are on entertainment, words, industry, finance and music.

Round 1

Team 1
1 Name the capital of Syria.
2 Who wrote the lines, 'Theirs not to make reply, theirs not to reason why, theirs but to do and die'?
3 What does BAFTA stand for?
4 What spirit comes from the terebinth tree?
5 What is the smallest continent?

Team 2
1 Name the capital of Turkey.
2 Who wrote the play *Man and Superman*?
3 What does NUJ stand for?
4 What is the name of the solution of shellac in alcohol used by furniture makers?
5 Where in Kent are the Pantiles?

Round 2

Team 1
1 Which county cricket team plays at Trent Bridge?
2 Which part of the body may suffer from opthalmia?
3 Who composed 'Ode to Joy'?

4 St Johnstoun once held claim to be the capital of Scotland. By what name is it now known?
5 Which pop singer sang 'Dead Ringer for Love'?

Team 2
1 Which county cricket team plays at Edgbaston?
2 Which part of the body does something cutaneous affect?
3 Who composed the incidental music for *A Midsummer Night's Dream*?
4 Which town in Northern Ireland is the seat of both Protestant and Roman Catholic archbishops?
5 'Twenty-four Hours from Tulsa' was originally a hit for which singer?

Round 3

Team 1

1 Where was the abode of the gods in Greek mythology?
2 Three English kings were killed by arrows. Name two.

3 Which actor directed the film *Staying Alive*?
4 Which Englishman painted 'Resurrection', now in the Tate Gallery?
5 In what field did Igor Ivanovich Sikorsky, the Russian inventor, specialise?

Team 2

1 Name the Greek mountain consecrated to the Muses.
2 Which king quelled the Peasants' Revolt, had Gloucester murdered and was deposed after a rebellion led by Henry Bolingbroke?
3 Which actor directed the film *Ordinary People*?
4 'Woman Taken in Adultery' was the work of which Dutch artist?

5 In which field of invention was Sir Frank Whittle a pioneer?

Round 4

Team 1

1 The berry of which tree is used to flavour gin?
2 What is a topgallant?
3 What is mixed with nickel to make nickel silver?
4 Who sang 'North to Alaska' on record?
5 In which war was Britain engaged between 1899 and 1902?

Team 2

1 What spirit forms the main ingredient of daiquiri?
2 What is a bain-marie?
3 Which metal is derived from the mineral cinnabar?
4 Who wrote the novel *Northwest Passage*?
5 The Germans call a First World War sea battle the Battle of the Skagerrak. What do the British call it?

Round 5 Individual questions for Team 1

Entertainment
Who founded the Method school of acting?
Words
If you suffered from pyrophobia what would you fear?
Industry
What is processed in a ginnery?
Finance
What is the US equivalent of the FTSE Index?
Music
Name the bandleader who died in an air crash over the English Channel during the Second World War.

Round 6

Team 2

1 In which London street is the Garrick Club?

2 What is the name of the Vatican's army?

3 Which sport do you associate with the Los Angeles Lakers?

4 Which famous building would you find at Agra?

5 In which field of art was Barbara Hepworth famous?

Team 1

1 What post for travellers is kept for a limited period at a specified post office?

2 Which religious body was founded by George Fox?

3 Which sport would you associate with the Boston Red Sox?

4 Where in London is the Whispering Gallery?

5 In which of the arts did Joan Sutherland achieve fame?

Round 7

Team 2

1 Who discovered Brazil?

2 Which planet shares its name with a glass sponge called a flower-basket?

3 What was the Manhattan Project?

4 The name of which branch of mathematics means triangle measurement?

5 Which pop group sang 'He Ain't Heavy, He's My Brother'?

Team 1

1 Who first explored the river Amazon?

2 Which planet was discovered in 1846?

3 Why was the poppy chosen for Remembrance Sunday?

4 If a clock seen in a mirror is read as 2.40 what time is it?

5 Which soul singer was 'Sittin' on the Dock of the Bay'?

Round 8

Team 2

1 In which country are the ruins of Carthage?

2 In which English county is Hartland Point?

3 What was the maiden name of Jacqueline Kennedy-Onassis?

4 What perennial East Indian plant is used in curry powder and also as a chemical indicator of alkalis?

5 Name the science of correcting deformities of bones, joints, ligaments, muscles and tendons.

Team 1

1 Who was responsible for the Domesday Book?

2 Which new town in Shropshire was named after a local engineer?

3 Who was known as Madame Deficit?

4 What is another name for endive?

5 What name is given to the kind of mistakes in speech, in which a person mixes up the initial sounds of words.

Round 9

Team 2

1 If you were born on 1 October, what would your astrological sun sign be?
2 Which Egyptian leader was assassinated in 1981?
3 In which TV soap did the character Cliff Barnes appear?
4 What is the popular name for Tchaikovsky's Symphony No. 6 in B Minor?
5 What English word from the Greek for black means sadness?

Team 1

1 How many animals are used to denote years in Chinese astrology?
2 Which statesman was assassinated on 15 March 44BCE?
3 Who played Sable Colby in *Dynasty*?
4 What is the popular name for Beethoven's Symphony No. 9 in D Minor?
5 What English word from the Greek for black describes the pigment that makes human hair and skin dark?

Round 10   Individual questions for Team 2

Entertainment

Which city burned in *Gone With the Wind*?

Words

'Veni, vidi, vici' were famous words of Julius Caesar. What do they mean?

Industry

What is dried in oast houses?

Finance

What is GNP?

Music

Which American composed the ballet music for *On the Town*?

Drinks round

Team 1

1 Which phrase devised by Joseph Heller means a no-win situation?
2 What is a sphygmomanometer used for?
3 Balm, dill and sorrel are all what?
4 What sort of musical instrument was a timbal?
5 This Dutchman died in 1939. During the First World War he designed German aircraft. Who was he?
6 What is the name of the chief muscle used in breathing?
7 Which painter is credited with the development of pointillism?
8 Who succeeded Hoover as president of the USA?
9 Name the stretch of water that separates the Inner and Outer Hebrides.
10 Who was prime minister of Great Britain from 1955–57?

Team 2

1 What does the phrase *exempli gratia* mean in English?
2 What is tinnitus?
3 Foreman, Longman, Lechman, Little Man and Thuma are always found together. Why?
4 Long before it became a popular operatic piece, a barcarole used to be sung by whom?
5 Which German developed the V2 and later the Saturn rockets?
6 What is the other name for the scapula?
7 Which painter was shot by the actress Valeria Solarnis?
8 Which American president followed James Buchanan?
9 Puffin Island gets its name from the birds that breed there. Where is Puffin Island?
10 Who became Prime Minister of Israel in 1969?

Reserve questions

1 What did John Logie Baird invent?
2 What name is given to the sea route from the Atlantic round the north of Canada to the Pacific?
3 Name the Greek goddess of peace.

Pub League Quiz 23

The individual questions are in Rounds 5 and 10 and are on the Bible, opera, mythology, trees and plants, and games and pastimes.

Round 1

Team 1

1 Which English king was beheaded in 1649?
2 What is the correct title of the painting known as 'The Rokeby Venus'?
3 Within five, how many symphonies did Haydn write?
4 During which king's reign was the Bloody Assize held?
5 Which card is removed from the pack at the beginning of the game Pope Joan?

Team 2

1 What caused Prince Albert's death in 1861?
2 Which famous picture did Basil Hallward paint?
3 Within five, what is the atomic number for plutonium?
4 What were Charles I's supporters called in the Civil War?
5 Bamboos are one of three suits in which game?

Round 2

Team 1

1 'From the earth thou springest, Like a cloud of fire'. To what was Shelley referring?
2 Name the largest of the Society Islands, which was visited by Captain Cook and William Bligh.
3 In Greek mythology, by what was the sword of Damocles suspended?
4 What is Eva Herzigova famous for modelling?
5 Who composed the opera *Boris Godunov*?

Team 2

1 Which 20th-century English poet wrote about Rannoch by Glencoe?
2 In which Irish county are Ballymena and Ballymoney?
3 Who, in Greek mythology, was the equivalent of the Roman god Saturn?
4 Who was the first haute couture designer to show a collection for men?
5 Who composed the opera *Duke Bluebeard's Castle*?

Round 3
Team 1

1 Who wrote *A Farewell to Arms*?

2 Where is the San Andreas Fault?
3 Umbles can be made into a pie and gave rise to the expression to eat (H)umble pie. What are umbles?

4 Who succeeded Alf Ramsey as England's soccer manager?
5 What does ICBM stand for?

Team 2

1 Who wrote *The Mallens* trilogy of novels?
2 On which island is Adams Peak?
3 Gnocchi is a food from Italy. What is it?

4 Who was the first footballer to be knighted?
5 What does SALT stand for?

Round 4
Team 1

1 What is the capital of Sierra Leone?
2 What kind of plane was an Avro Lancaster?
3 Who was David Copperfield's nurse?
4 Which town did Slade come from?

5 What is the name of the House of Representatives of the national parliament of the Republic of Ireland?

Team 2

1 What is the capital of Jamaica?

2 Which country developed Mirage warplanes?
3 Who wrote the original bestseller about Provence?
4 Where did the Rolling Stones give a free concert in 1969, when 3,000 butterflies were released in memory of Brian Jones?
5 Which statesman who died in 1527 gave his name to a word meaning unscrupulous political cunning?

Round 5   Individual questions for Team 1
The Bible
In the New Testament, which book follows the four gospels?
Opera
In which of Mozart's operas does the statue of the murdered Commandant come to life?
Mythology
Who was the ancient Egyptian god of the sun?
Trees and plants
Scotch and wych are two species of which tree?
Games and pastimes
A game played with a small hour-glass-shaped object spun on a string fastened to two sticks was once known as Devil on Two Sticks. By what name is it now familiarly known?

Round 6

Team 2

1 How many chambers has the human heart?

2 On a three-masted vessel, which mast is the mizzen mast?

3 What was the official residence of the British sovereign between 1689 and 1837?

4 Which British doctor became famous for his concept of lateral thinking?

5 In which country is Lusaka?

Team 1

1 What is the part of the small intestine leading from the stomach in humans called?

2 How many masts has a yawl?

3 A tollbooth was used as a customs house or a town house. To what other use was it sometimes put?

4 Whose accurate observation of the moon helped Newton to formulate the laws of gravity?

5 Badwater is the western hemisphere's lowest point. Where is it?

Round 7

Team 2

1 *Henrietta Temple* was a novel by which statesman?

2 In which county are Mousehole and Indian Queens?

3 With which of the arts was Sergei Diaghilev associated?

4 In which year did George V become king?

5 From what is the liqueur calvados made?

Team 1

1 By what name is writer David John Moore Cornwell better known?

2 Queensferry is a royal burgh of which city?

3 Who designed the tapestry for the rebuilt Coventry Cathedral?

4 Who was king of England after Richard I?

5 With what is Grand Marnier flavoured?

Round 8

Team 2

1 How many grains go into a scruple?

2 What is a Suffolk Punch?

3 How many volleyball players are there on each side?

4 Who was the original presenter of television's *Question Time*?

5 What is the offspring of a male ass and a mare?

Team 1

1 How many psalms are in the Book of Psalms?

2 What is lexicography?

3 Who won the men's singles at Wimbledon in 1993, 1994 and 1998?

4 Who was the original host of the TV show *Call My Bluff*?

5 What dog of African origin cannot bark?

Round 9

Team 2

1 Which queen's divorce is one of the principal incidents of Shakespeare's Henry VIII?

2 Name the disease of the eye in which the lens becomes opaque.

3 What Hindi word means both 'curtain' and 'seclusion of women'?

4 Who wrote *A Tale of a Tub* in 1704?

5 In which year was the Aberfan disaster?

Team 1

1 In Hamlet, whose grave was being dug when Yorick's skull was unearthed?

2 Where is the jugular vein?

3 What is the Hindi word for 'holy war'?

4 Who wrote *Rich Man, Poor Man*?

5 Who in 1985 became the youngest world chess champion ever?

Round 10   Individual questions for Team 2

The Bible

Who was the wife of both Uriah the Hittite and David?

Opera

Which Gilbert and Sullivan opera is subtitled *A Merryman and His Maid*?

Mythology

Who was the nymph who was changed into a laurel bush to save her from Apollo?

Trees and plants

Give another name for the underground stem of a potato.

Games and pastimes

Which playing card is sometimes referred to as the Black Lady?

Drinks round

Team 1

1 Which post-war Prime Minister represented the constituencies of Stockton-on-Tees (1924–29 and 1931–45) and Bromley (1945–64)?
2 In which George Eliot book is Dorothea Brooke the heroine?
3 Who packed her trunk and said goodbye to the circus?
4 Abu Simbel is in which river valley?
5 What would the garnish be if something was à la Crécy?
6 What is a davenport?
7 On whose book was the film *Strangers on a Train* based?
8 What comedian sang about 'Careless Hands' in 1967 and 'Loneliness' in 1969?
9 What novel by M. M. Kaye ends, 'And it may even be that they found their Kingdom'?
10 What is the meaning of the abbreviation ASH?

Team 2

1 Which Prime Minister lived at Hughenden House, north of High Wycombe?
2 Who wrote *Erewhon*?
3 What was the name of Andy Pandy's girlfriend?
4 In which country is Agadir?
5 If something is dubarry, what will one of the ingredients be?
6 What is a matrass?
7 On whose play was the film *Witness for the Prosecution* based?
8 Who sang 'Tie Me Kangaroo Down, Sport'?
9 What book begins, 'The Mole had been working very hard all morning'?
10 What does ESP stand for?

Reserve questions

1 In which Dickens novel do Thomas Gradgrind and Josiah Bounderby appear?
2 What drug is named after an ancient god of dreams?
3 How many office holding cardinals are permanently resident in England?

Pub League Quiz 24

The individual questions are in Rounds 5 and 10 and are on soccer, famous women, name the year, nature and spelling.

Round 1

Team 1

1 Which formerly warlike tribes of central and southern Sudan are still famous for their powerful wrestlers?
2 Where is the Gulf of Carpentaria?
3 Of whose autobiography is *Snakes and Ladders* a part?

4 In what month is the Lord Mayor's procession and show held in London?
5 Where did Jesus turn water into wine at a marriage?

Team 2

1 The Watussi or Tutsi tribe come from Burundi in Africa. What is this tribe remarkable for?

2 What is the name of the gulf that separates Finland and Sweden?
3 Whose autobiographical books include *Confessions of a Hooker, My Lifelong Love Affair with Golf*?
4 When is St George's Day?

5 What bird did Noah first release after the rain abated?

Round 2

Team 1

1 What does a phillumenist collect?

2 The most powerful man in the Chinese Communist Party died in 1997. Who was he?
3 Which actress said, 'It is better to be looked over than overlooked'?
4 On what day of the week was the Grand National run in 1997?
5 What type of creature is a mugger?

Team 2

1 Which word describes all these animals: voles, mice, rats and hamsters?
2 Which ex-Tory minister became 'Fat Pang' during his time in the Far East?
3 Which actress wrote the book *You Can Get There From Here*?
4 Which horse won the 1998 Epsom Derby?
5 What type of insect is a devil's coach-horse?

Round 3

Team 1

1 What was the name of Don Quixote's squire?
2 What are the Northern Lights also known as?
3 Which Italian artist was responsible for a famous series of anatomical sketches?
4 On which part of the body would you have a tracheotomy?
5 What name is given to a sugar syrup gently heated until it browns?

Team 2

1 What did Don Quixote mistake for evil giants?
2 Name two planets that are much bigger than the earth.
3 The artist Stubbs was most famous for painting which subjects?
4 What are Ishihara tests used for?
5 Name the highly flavoured East Indian soup made with curry powder and hot seasoning.

Round 4

Team 1

1 From which type of aircraft were the Hiroshima and Nagasaki atom bombs dropped?
2 What does *mein kampf* mean in English?
3 Who wrote the musical composition 'La Mer'?
4 What is the monetary unit of Argentina?
5 In which country would you find the volcano Villarica?

Team 2

1 Which company built the Vimy and the Wellington?
2 What is the actual meaning of *cosa nostra*?
3 Who composed 'Brigg Fair'?
4 What is the monetary unit of Malta?
5 In which mountain range would you find the extinct volcano, Elbrus?

Round 5   Individual questions for Team 1

Soccer

Which station on the Piccadilly Line is the only one in Britain named after a football club?

Famous women

Who is both Chief-Commandant for Women in the Royal Navy and Colonel-in-Chief of the Royal Scots Regiment?

Name the year

In what year was the Panama Canal opened?

Nature

Which wild plant is associated with St Patrick's Day?

Spelling

Spell a word beginning with 'p' meaning nom de plume.

Round 6
Team 2

1 Who is the patron saint of Venice?
2 What is a sheep ked?
3 Which Spanish monarchs financed Christopher Columbus's first voyage to the New World?
4 What is the collective noun for a group of chickens?
5 What is the capital of Sudan?

Team 1

1 Which saint is the patron of travellers?
2 What is a lousewort?
3 Name the European country in which the Cortes is the parliament.
4 What is the collective noun for a group of angels?
5 What is the capital of Albania?

Round 7
Team 2

1 What does ANZAC stand for?
2 In which Jane Austen novel did Sir Thomas Bertram and Mrs Norris appear?
3 'Ring of Fire' and 'Jackson' were hits for which country singer?
4 Which Cornish castle is associated with Arthurian legend?
5 Which TV sit-com was based in Grace Brothers store?

Team 1

1 What does ERNIE stand for?
2 In Charlotte Bronte's *Jane Eyre*, whom does the heroine eventually marry?
3 'We All Stand Together' was a hit for which pop artist?
4 Which mythical hero is sometimes said to be buried in Glastonbury?
5 Which TV sitcom featured the Boswells?

Round 8
Team 2

1 Name the notch in the Appalachian Mountains near the juncture of Virginia, Tennessee, and Kentucky.
2 Who succeeded Lenin after his death in 1924?

3 What is a kaftan?
4 In which country would you hear the Frisian language?

5 What did Sir Rowland Hill introduce in Britain in 1840?

Team 1

1 Which rock needle overlooks Chamonix in the Mont Blanc massif?

2 What was Adolf Hitler's original family name, parodied by his opponents during and after his rise to power?
3 What is a puttee?
4 What language is spoken in Roussillon, Andorra, north-eastern Spain and the Balearic Isles?
5 Of what in sport were mufflers, invented by Jack Broughton in the second half of the 18th Century, the forerunner?

Round 9

Team 2

1 Which American city was almost destroyed by fire in 1871?
2 Who was MP for Peckham and in 1997 became a minister in the Labour government?
3 Who composed the music for the ballet *The Sleeping Beauty*?
4 What does MG stand for, as in the MG motor car?
5 What does NASA stand for?

Team 1

1 Of which US state is Salem the capital?
2 Who lives at Nelson Mandela House, Peckham?
3 *Children's Corner* is a suite of piano pieces by which composer?
4 Which instrument measures RPM in a motor car?
5 What does ESA stand for?

Round 10   Individual questions for Team 2

Soccer
Which manager guided Arsenal to the double in 1971?

Famous women
Who was a successful motor racing driver before inheriting the Windmill Theatre, which she was forced to close in 1964?

Name the year
In what year did Sir Francis Chichester win the first single-handed transatlantic yacht race?

Nature
Pink Pearl, Pink Drift and Pink Perfection are hybrids of which flowering shrub?

Spelling
Spell a word beginning with 'p' which means inflammation of the throat.

Drinks round

Team 1

1 What is a person who draws up maps called?
2 Which stretch of water separates Tasmania from Australia?
3 Which French artist is recognised as the co-founder of cubism?

4 Where in the USA does the football team the Cowboys come from?
5 In Spain whiteness of the skin used to be seen as a sign of nobility. What well-known expression did this give rise to?
6 In 1519 Trinidad, San Antonio, Concepcion, Vittoria and Santiago made up the fleet of which explorer?
7 Which actress starred in *The Millionairess* and *The Cassandra Crossing*?
8 Name the IRA hunger striker who died in May 1981 after 66 days' fasting.

9 What is the feminine of testator?
10 In what art form has Henri Cartier-Bresson achieved fame?

Team 2

1 What is a person who studies bird life called?
2 Where is the Bowery?

3 With which London district are the painters Walter Sickert and Frederick Spencer Gore associated?

4 Where in the USA do the football team the Dolphins come from?
5 Name the supposed city of gold which inspired the Spanish conquest of South and Central America.
6 In which war was the Battle of Inkerman fought?

7 Who was the female star of the film *Soldier Blue*?

8 Name the police constable who was awarded the George Medal for his part in the Iranian embassy siege of 1980.
9 What is the feminine of ogre?
10 Which photographer's books include *The Most Beautiful Women*?

Reserve questions

1 What single word describes a leg of mutton?
2 What type of fruit is a queening?
3 In which of Shakespeare's plays does Polonius appear?

Pub League Quiz 25

The individual questions are in Rounds 5 and 10 and are on books, also known as, characters, time and pot luck.

Round 1

Team 1

1 What was the circus name of Nikolai Poliakov?
2 What is Paddington Bear's favourite snack?

3 What was the name of Jacques Cousteau's famous research ship?
4 On what colour square does the white king start a chess game?

5 What does FAO stand for?

Team 2

1 Which violin-playing comedian was born Benjamin Kubelsky?
2 Which fairy story was turned into the film *The Slipper and the Rose*?
3 Name the great warship that sank off Portsmouth in 1545.

4 What is the British game of noughts and crosses called in America?
5 Where does the FAO have its headquarters?

Round 2

Team 1

1 Whose story was portrayed in *The Naked Civil Servant*?

2 In which Arab country did Idi Amin take refuge in 1979?
3 What sort of young fish is a smolt?
4 What in Germany is the Brockhaus?
5 Which unit of currency is used in Iraq, Jordan and Tunisia?

Team 2

1 Which former wife of Frank Sinatra later married Woody Allen?
2 Whose flight from Tibet made headlines in 1959?
3 What is a carabao?

4 What book was published for the first time in Edinburgh in 1768?
5 Where did the pirates expression 'pieces of eight' come from?

Round 3

Team 1

1 Who won an Oscar for playing a mentally handicapped pianist?
2 What did a Sybil utter in ancient Greece?
3 Who wrote *Little Women*?
4 How many moons has Mercury?
5 From which flower is saffron obtained?

Team 2

1 For her part in the film version of what play did Vivien Leigh win an Oscar in 1951?
2 What does the Bible call 'the beginning of wisdom'?
3 In which of Hardy's novels is Bathsheba Everdene the central character?
4 Which planet has two dwarf satellites called Phobos and Deimos?
5 Tied together, what do a sprig of parsley, thyme and a bay leaf comprise?

Round 4

Team 1

1 Which is the largest of the lakes in the USA?
2 In which film did Rod Steiger play the part of Police Chief Bill Gillespie?
3 Which country did the Allies invade in Operation Avalanche of the Second World War?
4 In which of his plays did Shakespeare write one scene entirely in French?
5 What was the Magnus Portus of Roman Britain?

Team 2

1 Which American city has the second largest number of ethnic Poles in the world after Warsaw?
2 Which 1930 film made Edward G. Robinson a star and featured the line, 'Is this the end of Rico?'
3 What was the name given to Hitler's Blitzkrieg offensive against the USSR in June 1941?
4 In which city did Shakespeare set the greater part of *Romeo and Juliet*?
5 What northern town in Britain was called Aquae by the Romans?

Round 5   Individual questions for Team 1

Books
Who created the stories of the detective called Maigret?
Also known as
What was the secret identity of Don Diego, the masked avenger?
Characters
Who was Lancelot's son in Arthurian legend?
Time
In which century was the first watch invented?
Pot luck
With which African river was Mungo Park most closely associated?

Round 6

Team 2

1 In which sport was Irina Rodnina a world champion?
2 Where would you step out to see the Giant's Causeway?
3 What did Queen Victoria specifically ban from her funeral?

4 What is the largest species of shark?
5 What was the first 'garden city' in Britain, begun in 1903?

Team 1

1 In which sport was Sonja Henie a world champion?
2 In which British city is the Royal Liver Building?
3 Which subsequent head of state was born a member of the royal family of the Tembu tribe in the Transkei?
4 Name both creatures of which there is a long-eared variety.
5 What building used to be the headquarters of the Commander-in-Chief of the British Army?

Round 7

Team 2

1 Which gas is represented by the chemical formula CO?
2 What were featheries, gutties and putties?
3 What type of creatures appear last in the fossil record?
4 Which fruit is impossible to eat, according to a Trini Lopez song?

5 Which Scottish hero travelled under the name of Betty Burke?

Team 1

1 What is the chemical symbol for neon?
2 Which sport uses granites?
3 How many ice ages were there in the Pliocene era?
4 Where did Ralph McTell offer to 'take you by the hand and lead you'?
5 Which country numbers William Tell among its national heroes?

Round 8

Team 2

1 Who created Prince Caspian and Aslan?

2 What is the French word for a dowry?

3 Which Swiss winter sports resort is the home of the Cresta Run?
4 What does the river Seine empty into?
5 Which operatic heroine commits suicide on her father's sword?

Team 1

1 Which novel by Grace Metalious, her first, was on the bestseller list for two years?
2 What is the word from French for a royal state reception attended only by males?
3 From which language did English adopt the word ski?
4 Which maritime country has the shortest coastline?
5 Which Mozart opera has associations with freemasonry?

Round 9

Team 2

1 Who created the fictional detective Philip Marlowe?

2 Which bird pursued the ship in *The Rime of the Ancient Mariner*?

3 Which football team plays its home matches at the Santiago Bernabéu Stadium?

4 In Britain, who was the first king of the Hanover line?

5 Which 1964 film, based on a novel by Nikos Kazantzakis, starred Anthony Quinn in the title role?

Team 1

1 In *The Return of the Saint* in the 1970s, who played Simon Templar?

2 How many points are awarded for potting the yellow ball in snooker?

3 Who scored the winning goal for England in the 1966 football World Cup final?

4 Which composer founded Aldeburgh Festival of Music and the Arts?

5 Who wrote *Murders in the Rue Morgue*?

Round 10   Individual questions for Team 2

Books

Who wrote the book on which the film *Camille* was based?

Also known as

Who is British actor Maurice Micklewhite better known as?

Characters

What kind of school did Pussy Galore run?

Time

Who introduced leap year?

Pot luck

What was the last port of call of the *Mayflower* before setting sail for America?

Drinks round

Team 1

1 What nationality was the painter Diego Rivera?

2 What sea separates West and East Malaysia?

3 On the life of which religious Scottish athlete was the film *Chariots of Fire* based?

4 'London. Michaelmas term lately over, and the Lord Chancellor sitting in Lincoln's Inn Hall.' These are the opening lines of which novel by Dickens?

5 In which Hitchcock film did Shirley MacLaine make her debut?

6 Which lord went missing when his luck ran out in 1974?

7 What precedes, 'And never the twain shall meet'?

8 How many pairs of chromosomes does a normal person have?

9 Who succeeded Uwe Seeler as Germany's soccer captain?

10 Which South American country's name means Little Venice?

Team 2

1 What nationality by birth was René Magritte?

2 What large island lies east of Africa and west of Australia?

3 Which British film grossed over £50 million in the UK alone from 1997 onwards?

4 Which classic novel opens with the dictum, 'Every man in possession of a fortune, must be in want of a wife'?

5 Which Hollywood producer said, 'A wide screen makes a bad film twice as bad'?

6 Who went for a swim in Miami and later emerged in Australia with two new names?

7 Which cartoonist said, 'A woman's place is in the wrong'?

8 How often are brain cells replaced?

9 Who captained the Dutch soccer side in the 1974 World Cup?

10 Name the highest waterfall in South America.

Reserve questions

1 Who was the first black performer to have a Number 1 hit in the UK with 'Let's Have Another Party'?

2 What was the name of the first sheep to be cloned in Britain?

3 What does hell have no fury like?

Pub League Quiz 26

The individual questions are in Rounds 5 and 10 and are on pop music, astronomy, drink, motor sports and land animals.

Round 1

Team 1

1 Name the author of *War and Remembrance*.
2 What is the date of Scotland's national day?
3 In which novel does the ship *Pequod* appear?
4 What was Thomas Crapper's claim to fame?
5 What in chess was 'Deep Blue'?

Team 2

1 Name the author of *The Thorn Birds*.
2 When is St Patrick's Day?
3 Which Shakespeare play has the alternative title *What You Will*?
4 Under which tree is the Buddha supposed to have sat when he attained enlightenment?
5 What is a natatorium?

Round 2

Team 1

1 Which Australian city was named after the father of the theory of evolution?
2 Which 1953 Broadway musical introduced the song 'Stranger in Paradise'?
3 What did the Tories give Tony Blair during the 1997 general election campaign to which the Advertising Standards Authority objected?
4 Who founded the Habitat design empire?
5 Which motorway links Coventry and Leicester?

Team 2

1 What was David Livingstone's calling when he began his travels in Africa?
2 Which successful film featured the Number 1 hit 'Love Is All Around'?
3 By what name is the Parliamentary Commissioner for Administration better known?
4 What did Capability Brown design?
5 Which Italian city is referred to by the 'T' in FIAT?

Round 3

Team 1

1 Who, when asked what his golf handicap was, replied, 'I'm a one-eyed Jewish negro'?

2 Who was the first Roman Catholic president of the USA?

3 What kind of animal was Pinocchio's pet Figaro?

4 Which ship of 1906 held the Blue Riband for 22 years?

5 Manque and passe are terms in what game?

Team 2

1 Which comedian quipped, 'President Johnson says a war isn't really a war without my jokes'?

2 After which American president is the capital of Liberia named?

3 What do Tiggers do best?

4 Which liner was the last holder of the Atlantic Blue Riband?

5 How many backgammon pieces does each player start with?

Round 4

Team 1

1 What is the name of the Addams family's butler?

2 How many strings has a cello?

3 Which European city has become famous for its gnomes?

4 Who wrote *Round the Bend*?

5 Which composer said of another, 'Wagner has lovely moments but awful quarters of an hour'?

Team 2

1 In which country was the TV series *Crane* set?

2 In music, what word means to displace beats or accents so that what was 'strong' becomes 'weak', and vice versa?

3 In which American state is Fort Knox?

4 Who wrote the poem 'The Rolling English Road'?

5 Who called religion 'the opium of the people'?

Round 5   Individual questions for Team 1

Pop music
Who sang 'Silver Lady'?

Astronomy
What is the disc or halo round the sun called?

Drink
What is known as the queen among drinks?

Motor sports
Who won the 1962 Grand Prix world championship in a BRM?

Land animals
Which venomous serpent is also known as the pit viper?

Round 6

Team 2

1 What do Ryan Giggs, Richard Burton and Augustus John have in common?
2 Who, by the age of 13, had composed concertos, symphonies, sonatas and operettas?
3 What was erected overnight in August 1961?
4 Who created Harry Lime?
5 Which bird lays the largest eggs?

Team 1

1 In which country does a true Bohemian live?
2 Which composer was the subject of the film *The Music Lovers*?
3 Something special happened to the Archbishop of Cracow in 1978. What was it?
4 Who was Dorothy L. Sayers' aristocratic sleuth?
5 Which bird lays the largest eggs in proportion to its size?

Round 7

Team 2

1 What are the initials of the governing body of world soccer?
2 Where did the last *Road to* film set off to in 1940?
3 Which Dustin Hoffman film took place in a Cornish village?
4 Which famous speech was described in the press as 'silly, flat and dishwatery'?
5 Who wrote *The Trial* and *The Castle*?

Team 1

1 After whom was the soccer World Cup trophy named?
2 Where was *A Bridge Too Far*?
3 In which film was Dustin Hoffman seen approaching a swimming pool in a wetsuit?
4 Which composer once said, 'Competitions are for horses, not artists'?
5 Who wrote *Death In Venice*?

Round 8

Team 2

1 By what name is Michael Dumble-Smith better known?
2 Who succeeded Stalin as USSR premier?
3 What nationality was Aladdin?
4 Which European capital is home to the world's most accurate mechanical clock?
5 The waters of which ocean wash against Copacobana beach?

Team 1

1 Who is Lesley Hornby better known as?
2 Who succeeded Lincoln as president of the USA?
3 What nationality was El Cid?
4 Which English cathedral has the oldest surviving working clock in the world?
5 Which tropical island paradise lies 400 miles south-west of Sri Lanka?

Round 9

Team 2

1 Who was emperor of China when Marco Polo visited his court?

2 To whom was Natalie Wood married when she died?

3 Who, with his twin Remus, was suckled by a wolf?

4 What is the study of fossils called?

5 Which is the smallest of the Great Lakes?

Team 1

1 What were Baffin, Frobisher and Franklin all searching for?

2 Who was Laurence Olivier's first wife?

3 Which day of the week is named after the Norse goddess of love?

4 What branch of science is called after the Greek for 'house'?

5 Which international border is crossed the most?

Round 10   Individual questions for Team 2

Pop music

Who sang 'When Will I See You Again'?

Astronomy

Which planet is farthest from the sun?

Drink

Name the blind Benedictine monk who invented the first true sparkling champagne.

Motor sports

Which world champion racing driver was born in Milton, Dunbartonshire?

Land animals

Which mammal is considered to be the tallest?

Just for fun

Whose presence on a battlefield 'made the difference of 40,000'?
Napoleon I, Emperor of the French, whose military genius held Europe in thrall for nearly 20 years. This remark is attributed to the Duke of Wellington, who finally took his measure at Waterloo.

Drinks round

Team 1

1 Who infuriated Mae West by calling her 'My Little Brood Mare'?
2 What is a dipsomaniac?
3 For which county cricket side did W. G. Grace play?
4 Which US state capital has the most Buddhist temples?
5 What did Doctor Bob S. and Bill W. found in June 1935?
6 Which poet popularised the limerick?
7 What term applies to space devoid of matter?
8 What is the name of the pre-match war dance performed by the New Zealand rugby team?
9 Which Asian country has the other name of Bharat?
10 What has to be produced in a writ of *habeas corpus*?

Team 2

1 In which film does Groucho Marx say, 'Either this guy's dead or my watch has stopped'?
2 Which part of the body is affected by cirrhosis?
3 Who was the first Australian cricketer to be knighted?
4 Which German directed the film *The Marriage of Maria Braun*?
5 How many gills in a pint?
6 Which American state borders only one other?
7 To what use was nitrous oxide first put in 1842?
8 Ninian Park is the home of which soccer club?
9 Which country is nicknamed 'the roof of the world'?
10 Whose law states, 'If anything can go wrong it will'?

Reserve questions

1 Who was King Zog?
2 What is the more usual name for the bird *Turdus merula*?
3 What type of salad ingredient is a cos?

Pub League Quiz 27

The individual questions are in Rounds 5 and 10 and are on TV and radio, ships, geography, classical music and kings and queens.

Round 1

Team 1

1 Into which sea does the river Nile empty?
2 What was the pseudonym of Henri Charrière, famous escaper?
3 What is the name of the governing body of the Roman Catholic Church?
4 In 1941, the British sank a German ship bearing the name of Germany's Iron Chancellor. What was it?
5 In which sport is yokozuna the rank of a grand champion?

Team 2

1 What country was known as the cockpit of Europe?
2 What was the assumed name of François-Marie Arouet, French poet and dramatist?
3 Who is the Vicar of Christ?
4 What was the main base for British submarines during the Second World War?
5 Who became world snooker champion, aged 21, in 1990?

Round 2

Team 1

1 Which architect designed the Cenotaph in Whitehall?
2 In the 1860s, Louis Dobermann developed a breed of dog to protect him at work. What was his profession?
3 In which book by Charles Dickens would you find Bill Sikes?
4 What is the knob at the front of a horse saddle called?
5 Who first reached the South Pole?

Team 2

1 Which great country house north of Leeds is the seat of the Lascelles family?
2 What is a miniature foxhound used for coursing hares called?
3 What was the actual name of the Artful Dodger?
4 Sayonara is 'goodbye' in which language?
5 Who found and opened Tutankhamen's tomb in 1922?

Round 3

Team 1

1 What is the name of the ceremony at which a prime minister accepts the seals of office from the Queen?
2 Who played Miss Jones in *Rising Damp*?

3 Who wrote *The Lord of the Rings*?
4 What does RNLI stand for?
5 Which US president had previously commanded the invasion of North Africa (1942) and the Allied invasion of Europe (1944)?

Team 2

1 What is the name of the hall in New York which is the headquarters of the Democratic Party?
2 Who played Detective Sergeant Harriet Makepeace in *Dempsey and Makepeace*?
3 Who wrote *Wuthering Heights*?
4 What does NATO stand for?
5 Who was the USSR premier at the time of the Cuban missile crisis?

Round 4

Team 1

1 Where would you find the Trevi Fountain?
2 To within five years, when was the BBC established?
3 Which royal personage said of another, 'After I am dead, the boy will ruin himself in 12 months'?
4 Which rank is below a colonel and above a major in the British Army?
5 Whose book of poems *Les Fleurs du Mal* was declared obscene in 1857?

Team 2

1 In which present-day country is the ancient city of Ephesus?
2 To within five years, when was the first *Radio Times* published?
3 What does the third quarter, azure, a harp or stringed argent, represent on the Royal Arms?
4 Which rank is below a group captain and above a squadron leader in the Royal Air Force?
5 Who was Jean-Baptiste Poquelin better known as?

Round 5   Individual questions for Team 1
TV and radio
Name the radio doctor who became chairman of the Independent
Television Authority and then chairman of the governors of the BBC.
Ships
What was the name of the world's first atomic-powered merchant ship
launched in 1959?
Geography
Which is the southernmost state of the USA?
Classical music
Name Prokofiev's orchestral piece in which a narrator tells a fairy tale.
Kings and queens
Overthrown by Alexander the Great, Darius III was king of which country?

Round 6
Team 2

1   Who was hanged for the so-
called A6 murder of 1961?

2   Which French footballer and
philosopher declared, 'When the
seagulls follow the trawler, it is
because they think sardines will
be thrown into the sea'?

3   Which species of fox is most
common in Europe?

4   What is the feminine of gaffer?

5   What nationality was Alfred
Sisley, the artist?

Team 1

1   What other profession did
publican Albert Pierrepoint
follow?

2   Which French philosopher was
of the opinion that 'hell is other
people'?

3   Which is the largest deer native
to Britain?

4   What is the feminine of votary?

5   What nationality was the painter
Jackson Pollock?

Round 7
Team 2

1 In which fictional borough is Coronation Street?
2 Which gulf extends along the coast of France from the Spanish border to Toulon?
3 Which famous photographer brought Jean Shrimpton to the fore as a model?
4 Who abandoned the cinema in 1938 but wrote *Lulu* in Hollywood in 1982?

5 Which star won an Oscar for playing the title role in the film *Hamlet*?

Team 1

1 In which thinly disguised British city is *Casualty* set?
2 Of which country are the Chatham Islands a part?
3 Which Italian designer was murdered in Miami in 1997?
4 Which top American mobster was deported by both the USA and Cuba, before finding sanctuary in Naples?
5 Which actress won an Oscar for her part in the film *On Golden Pond*?

Round 8
Team 2

1 Which of the four gospels is thought to be based on eye-witness information?
2 Of what was Pan the god?
3 In the placings on a cricket field, what position stands between cover point and mid-off?
4 What was the trade of George Ravenscroft?
5 What does *stet* mean?

Team 1

1 Who slayed the Cyclops?

2 Who was the father of Pan?
3 What is the home ground of Surrey County Cricket Club?

4 What was the trade of Peter Carl Fabergé?
5 What does FD stand for?

Round 9

Team 2

1 On which river is the city of Chester?
2 Who was the governor of the Bahamas during the Second World War?
3 Where in the USA are there four busts of presidents carved on the face of a mountain?
4 Which character in *Red Dwarf* is preoccupied with fashion?
5 What was the venue for the 1948 Olympics and for the Live Aid concert of 1985?

Team 1

1 What port is at the mouth of the Scottish Dee?
2 Which British prime minister worked as a research chemist in industry?
3 Name the four presidents carved on Mount Rushmore.
4 Which character in *Red Dwarf* is a hologram?
5 What great sporting event took place at Squaw Valley in 1985?

Round 10   Individual questions for Team 2

TV and radio

Why are soap operas so called?

Ships

Which German battleship was outmanoeuvered by three British cruisers and finally scuttled in the river Plate in 1939?

Geography

Which kingdom of North Africa has a Mediterranean coastline?

Classical music

Who composed the opera *La Clemenza di Tito*?

Kings and queens

Which country did Casimir III rule over?

Drinks round

Team 1

1 Who played the male lead in the film *The Graduate*?
2 What is a gaur?
3 Name the three Cromwells who played a prominent part in English religious and political life in the 16th and 17th centuries.
4 Who is the highest legal ranking officer in England and Wales?
5 Who wrote the novel *Hard Times*?
6 Where are the Lofoten Islands?
7 Which singer was christened Annie Mae Bullock?
8 Which number doubled, exceeds its half by nine?
9 What penal system for young offenders was named after a village near Rochester in Kent?
10 What colour is the gemstone lapis lazuli?

Team 2

1 What part did Anne Bancroft play in *The Graduate*?
2 What is a wheatear?
3 What religious office did the Benedictine Lanfranc hold in England from 1070 to 1089?
4 Who is the second highest legal ranking officer in England and Wales?
5 Who wrote *The Naked and the Dead*?
6 What is the second largest city in Poland?
7 Which rock artist was christened William Perks?
8 Two numbers add up to 19. One is twice the other plus one. What are they?
9 What was the real name of the Boston Strangler?
10 What is another word for plumbago or black lead?

Reserve questions

1 Which dog is the main character of the *Peanuts* cartoon?
2 In which activity might you perform a Bob Major or Grandsire Triple?
3 Who died instantly when she saw Sir Lancelot on horseback?

Pub League Quiz 28

The individual questions are in Rounds 5 and 10 and are on history and warfare, law, pot luck, literature and words.

Round 1

Team 1

1 What name is usually given to the wild rose of the English countryside?
2 The shanny is the most common British species of what sort of fish?
3 Who in religion was born in Mecca?
4 Name the famous mausoleum at Agra.
5 Where was home to Yogi Bear?

Team 2

1 What sort of fruits are Ashton Crosses, Bedford Giants and Fantasies?
2 Which arborial marsupial feeds off eucalyptus leaves?
3 In which city is the tomb of Mohammed?
4 In which city is Carnegie Hall?
5 Which cartoonist created Bogart, the cat?

Round 2

Team 1

1 Who starred with Jeanette Macdonald in the 1940 film musical *Bitter Sweet*?
2 Which Italian poet was famous for the *Divine Comedy*?
3 Which great waterway opened on 16 November 1869?
4 In mythology, which youth fell in love with his own reflection?
5 Who is fourth in line of succession to the British throne?

Team 2

1 Which American actress starred in the films *Jezebel* and *All About Eve*?
2 Who wrote the series of poems *Idylls of the King*?
3 Which waterway links Loch Linnhie with the Moray Firth?
4 Who in mythology were supposed to have hatched from an egg?
5 What relation is the Duke of Kent to HM the Queen?

149

Round 3

Team 1

1 Name the branch of medicine that deals with childbirth, antenatal and post-natal care.
2 Where are the Diamond Sculls competed for?
3 Who wrote the opera *The Magic Flute*?
4 Who discovered penicillin?

5 What does BChD stand for?

Team 2

1 What is the study of family origins and descendants called?

2 What is the country of origin of taekwondo?
3 Who wrote the opera *The Barber of Seville*?
4 Who introduced mercury thermometers?
5 What does BCL stand for?

Round 4

Team 1

1 Who played Alf Garnett's son-in-law in *Till Death Us Do Part*?

2 From what are marshmallows prepared?
3 What would you find at the parallel of latitude 23.58 north of the equator?
4 Who created Brer Rabbit?

5 Who assassinated Abraham Lincoln?

Team 2

1 Which actress played Alf Garnett's wife in *Till Death Us Do Part*?

2 What sort of plant blooms every two years?
3 What connects the Kabul river with Peshawar in Pakistan?

4 Who wrote *The Return of the Native*?
5 To whom did General Robert E. Lee surrender in the American Civil War?

Round 5   Individual questions for Team 1

History and warfare
Where was the so-called Battle of the Nations in 1813?
Law
What in law is easement?
Pot luck
What was a Lee-Enfield?
Literature
Which playwright, author of *Tamburlaine the Great*, was killed in a tavern brawl?
Words
Which word means an assembly of witches?

Round 6

Team 2

1 What unit weighs 200 milligrams?
2 Which boxer was nicknamed the 'Brown Bomber'?
3 Who is on public record as saying of the presentation of debutantes at court, 'We had to stop them. Every tart in London was being presented'?
4 In which English county is Sleap aerodrome?
5 In which parish is Dawn French a TV vicar?

Team 1

1 What is equivalent to 1,852 metres?
2 Who was Pearl White?
3 Which statesman is supposed to have said, 'This is the sort of English up with which I will not put'?
4 What is the most southerly point of England?
5 In which series of TV comedies does Baldrick appear?

Round 7

Team 2

1 Who wrote *Sword Blades and Poppy Seed*?
2 What is a pangolin?
3 Where was the first Test Match in England held?
4 What has been located at Llantrisant, Wales, since 1968?
5 What is the second city and chief port of the Netherlands?

Team 1

1 Who wrote *The Four Zoas*?
2 What is a merganser?
3 In which country did Grand Prix racing begin?
4 What was the trade of Thomas Minton, who died in 1836?
5 Which two rivers meet at Duisburg, one of the largest inland ports in Europe?

Round 8

Team 2

1 Name two of the nine Muses in Greek mythology.
2 To within 10 years, when was the first game of rugby played?
3 Which English king was nicknamed 'Rufus'?
4 What in pottery is biscuitware?
5 What date was the siege of Ladysmith (months and year)?

Team 1

1 Name four of the Muses' arts.
2 To within 10 years, when was the Rugby Union formed?
3 Which English king was nicknamed 'Lionheart'?
4 What is celadon glaze?
5 What date was the siege of La Rochelle (year)?

Round 9

Team 2

1 Who wrote, 'The Holy Roman Empire was neither holy, nor Roman, nor an empire'?
2 What does hepatitis infect?
3 Julius Caesar had a son called Caesarion. Who was his mother?
4 Where is Nelson buried?

5 In which film did Charlie Chaplin first speak?

Team 1

1 Who said, 'No man but a blockhead ever wrote, except for money'?
2 What does gingivitis infect?
3 Who was the husband of Roxana?
4 When was Thomas à Becket murdered?
5 In which film did Ronald Reagan appear as General George Custer?

Round 10   Individual questions for Team 2

History and warfare

A meeting took place between Churchill, Stalin and Roosevelt during the Second World War to decide the fate of Europe after the fall of Hitler's Germany. Where was this held?

Law

What were the criminal courts held four times a year by legal justices of the peace in England and Wales called?

Pot luck

The Jewish patriarch Abraham was born at Ur of the Chaldees. In which modern country is Ur?

Literature

Who according to Shakespeare in *King Lear* is 'the prince of darkness'?

Words

What name is given to the study or collection of coins, tokens and medals?

Drinks round

Team 1

1 Whom did Ffion Jenkins marry in 1997?
2 What year was Earl Mountbatten murdered by the IRA?
3 Who in the 17th Century wrote the dictum which translates to English as, 'The heart has its reasons which reason knows nothing of'?
4 What was the metal frame called that women used to wear to make their dresses stand out?
5 What is the capital of Minorca?
6 Who wrote *Separate Tables*?
7 What was the composer Bizet's Christian name?
8 What does HMSO stand for?
9 What is an egret?
10 What is either a red precious stone or a skin infection worse than a boil?

Team 2

1 Who married Brooke Shields in 1997?
2 Who was vice-president of the USA in 1978?
3 Who in 1558 published a pamphlet entitled *The First Blast of the Trumpet Against the Monstrous Regiment of Women*?
4 What is the Scottish woollen cap with a crease down the crown called?
5 Of which country is Mogadishu the capital?
6 Who wrote *Murder in the Cathedral*?
7 What was the Swiss composer Honegger's given name?
8 What does ASLEF stand for?
9 What is a teal?
10 Where in your body are both your alveoli and pleura?

Reserve questions

1 Why is the Trinity site, near Alamogordo, New Mexico, historically important?
2 Which cocktail is made of gin, Cointreau and lemon juice?
3 How should a series of notes be played that are marked *staccato*?

Pub League Quiz 29

The individual questions are in Rounds 5 and 10 and are on history, entertainment, animals, literature and aircraft.

Round 1

Team 1

1 Where is the highest airport in the world?
2 The Ligurian Sea indents the north-western coast of which country?
3 Which cathedral has a steeple known as Old Steve?
4 Which king died after being thrown against his horse's pommel?
5 How old was Joan of Arc when she was burnt at the stake?

Team 2

1 What do the initials QANTAS represent?
2 Where is the Massabielle grotto?

3 Name the cathedral in Venice.

4 In what language did King George I and his ministers converse?
5 How old was the Emperor Nero when he committed suicide?

Round 2

Team 1

1 In which town did the Wars of the Roses begin?

2 How did Billy Connolly spell his Number 1 UK hit of 1975?
3 The plays *Dear Brutus* and *Mary Rose* were written by whom?
4 Who composed *Die Fledermaus*?

5 Which word means a place for sporting activity in England but a school of the highest grade in Germany?

Team 2

1 Which moor was the scene of a decisive battle in the English Civil War on 2 July 1644?
2 Who recorded 'YMCA' in 1978?

3 What is J. M. Barrie's most famous work?
4 What is the English translation of *Die Fledermaus*?
5 Modern pentathlon consists of cross-country riding and running, epée fencing, swimming and which other sport?

Round 3

Team 1

1 What does IBM stand for?
2 Name the two British hostages incarcerated with Terry Waite in Beirut before being finally released in August 1991.
3 What is the libretto of an opera?

4 What nationality was Rubens?
5 Whose victims were Mary Nichols, Elizabeth Stride, Catharine Eddowes, Mary Kelly and Eliza Chapman?

Team 2

1 What does NASDAQ stand for?
2 Which great composer's first musical experience came when he was appointed bandmaster for the staff of a lunatic asylum?
3 When is an opera a grand opera?
4 What nationality was Whistler?
5 What London address is infamous for the crimes of John Christie and Timothy Evans?

Round 4

Team 1

1 Which religious body was founded by George Fox in the 17th century?
2 Who played Lawrence of Arabia in the film of the same name?

3 Where are the Aberdare range of mountains?
4 What is the name given to a solution of opium in alcohol that used to be given as a tranquilliser?
5 Where were the Nazi war crimes trials, 1945–46 held?

Team 2

1 What name is given to the Japanese school of Buddhism?

2 Which actor won an Oscar for his role in *One Flew Over the Cuckoo's Nest*?
3 Where is the volcano Mauna Loa?
4 What drug derived from the peyote cactus of Texas and northern Mexico was a forerunner of LSD?
5 Which embroidery depicts the Norman conquest of England?

Round 5 Individual questions for Team 1

History
Who was the first king of the House of Windsor?
Entertainment
On which Shakespeare play is the 1938 musical *The Boys from Syracuse* based?
Animals
What sort of creature is a dragonet?
Literature
What is the more usual name for the ancient Egyptian Book of Coming Forth by Day?
Aircraft
The earliest jet engine to be run on test, in April 1937, was designed by whom?

Round 6

Team 2

1 In tennis, what is the women's equivalent of the Davis Cup?

2 Which city was known in Roman times as Byzantium?
3 Name four of Henry VIII's wives.
4 What is the plural of genus?
5 How did a clepsydra measure time?

Team 1

1 The Preakness and Belmont Stakes are two of the three legs of the American Triple Crown for thoroughbreds. What is the third?
2 Which city was known in Roman times as Mediolanum?
3 Which one of Henry VIII's wives survived him?
4 What is the plural of genesis?
5 What is an Archimedes screw used for?

Round 7

Team 2

1 Who had a hit with 'The Carnival is Over', in 1965?
2 In military terms, what does RHA stand for?
3 Which soccer club plays at Highfield Road?
4 What does the 'W' stand for in F. W. Woolworth?
5 Who painted a tin of Campbell's soup?

Team 1

1 Who had a hit with 'It's Now or Never' in 1960?
2 In military terms, what does REME stand for?
3 Which soccer club plays at Deepdale Road?
4 Name the first large department store to open in Britain.
5 Who was the girl in Peter Sellers' soup, in the film?

Round 8

Team 2

1 What is a bean weevil?

2 Who wrote the novel *The Four Just Men* and the play *The Squeaker*?
3 Which river flows through the capital of Afghanistan?
4 Who caused the Trojan War by abducting Helen?
5 What is removed in a meniscectomy?

Team 1

1 Which insect makes a ticking sound and tunnels through wood, especially in old buildings?
2 Who wrote the novel *Mary Barton* and a life of Charlotte Brontë?
3 In which African country is the city Kananga?
4 To house which creature was the labyrinth in Crete built?
5 What would be removed in a mastectomy?

Round 9

Team 2

1 What did John Peake Knight invent that were used unsuccessfully in 1866, and then not again for over half a century?

2 Which two actors teamed up in *The Streets of San Francisco* on TV?

3 Which famous clergyman 'had a dream'?

4 What is the main spice used in Hungarian goulash?

5 Who composed the music for the French national anthem?

Team 1

1 Who invented dynamite?

2 What was the name of the leading character in *Hawaii Five-O*?

3 Which country violated the Locarno Pact in 1936?

4 From what is the spice mace obtained?

5 The words of which country's national anthem are the oldest?

Round 10   Individual questions for Team 2

History

What nationality was the prince known as Henry the Navigator?

Entertainment

Name the two stars of the film *Midnight Cowboy*.

Animals

Which is the largest British wild bird?

Literature

Name one of the volumes comprising J. R .R. Tolkein's *Lord of the Rings*.

Aircraft

To the nearest Mach number, how fast did Concorde cruise?

Just for fun

What was the 'wicked bible'?

This was the name give to an edition of the Holy Scriptures published in 1661. The problem arose over the printed text for Exodus, Chapter 20 where the word 'not' was omitted from the Seventh Commandment, which read: 'Thou shalt commit adultery.'

Drinks round

Team 1

1 In which of Sheridan's plays do Sir Lucius O'Trigger and Sir Anthony Absolute appear?

2 Who played the title role in the 1964 film *Seven Faces of Dr Lao*?

3 What do Mackenzie, Nelson, Peace and Churchill have in common?

4 Which American actress announced in 1998 that she had become pregnant by artificial insemination from a secret donor?

5 What is the 'city' in the Bay City Rollers?

6 Which is Britain's smallest national park?

7 Name the two stars of TV's *Never The Twain*.

8 Who became editor of *Woman* in 1893 and later wrote successful novels about Burslem and district?

9 What name used to be given to an East Indian seaman, derived from the Persian for army or camp?

10 What name is given to teeth used for grinding?

Team 2

1 Which poet of Huguenot descent wrote *Songs of Childhood* under the pseudonym Walter Ramal?

2 Which actor became a star in the 1931 film *The Public Enemy*?

3 What did Flamsteed, Bradley, Bliss, Halley and Maskelyne have in common?

4 Who starred in the film of *Bad Timing* and later married its director, Nicholas Roeg?

5 What was Sting's profession before he took to singing?

6 Which is Britian's largest national park?

7 Which TV show featured the Campbells and the Tates?

8 What was the nickname of Australian aviator Donald Bennett?

9 Who would you be likely to see using water for panning?

10 What name is given to teeth used for tearing?

Reserve questions

1 What is the Greek word for 'the anointed one' of Judaism?
2 To whom was James Boswell biographer?
3 What word describes a social system in which a woman is the wife of several men simultaneously?

Pub League Quiz 30

The individual questions are in Rounds 5 and 10 and are on pop music, children's books, classical music, pot luck and history.

Round 1

Team 1

1 Who played Benny Hawkins in *Crossroads*?
2 What sporting event has taken place at Sebring, Riverside, Watkins Glen and Phoenix?
3 What is the square root of a million?
4 Within 50 years, when did Edward, the Black Prince, die?
5 A true cockney is born within the sound of which bells?

Team 2

1 In which fictional village was the *Crossroads* motel?
2 What major event is played on the Augusta National course?
3 What is a score squared?
4 Where is the ruby known as the Black Prince Ruby to be found today?
5 In which thoroughfare is St Mary-le-Bow?

Round 2

Team 1

1 Which two countries occupy the Scandinavian peninsula?
2 What is a berceuse?
3 What is a stockmarket share price called that is halfway between that at which a dealer will sell and at which he/she will buy?
4 'The Visit to the Quack Doctor' is a part of what series of paintings by Hogarth?
5 In the West, what date is Michaelmas?

Team 2

1 What is the capital of Norway?
2 What is an ayah?
3 In mercantile matters, the price of an article may be quoted as inclusive of c.i.f. What do these letters stand for?
4 Which artist was born in Malaga in 1881 and died at Mougins in 1973?
5 What is celebrated at Michaelmas?

Round 3

Team 1

1 Where in London can you find the Monument?

2 Who wrote *Paradise Lost*?

3 Who played Sue Ellen in *Dallas*?

4 Milk of magnesia is a suspension in water of which chemical?

5 What is a marsupial?

Team 2

1 Why was the Monument built?

2 What was the sequel to *Paradise Lost*?

3 Who played Bobby in *Dallas*?

4 Which group of drugs is called 'uppers'?

5 Which present-day animal most resembles the mastodon?

Round 4

Team 1

1 To where did the prophet Mohammed and his followers flee in 622?

2 What was Burt Lancaster's profession before he became an actor?

3 Whose autobiography was called *Upwardly Mobile*?

4 Which Pacific island is famous for its curious hieroglyphs and formidable stone-carved statues?

5 What are Wyandotte, Buff Orpington and Rhode Island Red?

Team 2

1 What name is given to the person who calls Muslims to prayer?

2 In which film did Peter Fonda and Dennis Hopper star as motorcyclists?

3 Which British institution's motto is 'In Utmost Good Faith'?

4 Under whose jurisdiction does Norfolk Island come?

5 What are Romney Marsh, Suffolk, Clun Forest and Swaledale?

Round 5   Individual questions for Team 1

Pop music

Name the one British member of the American group The Monkees.

Children's books

Who began a famous book, 'One thing is certain, that the white kitten had nothing to do with it...'?

Classical music

Die Lustige Witwe is the title of an opera by which composer?

Pot luck

What is one nautical mile per hour usually called?

History

Who was the first tsar of all Russia?

Round 6

Team 2

1 Whose last novel was *Resurrection*?
2 How is information received that is *sub rosa*?
3 Where in Liverpool did the Beatles perform 292 times?

4 What does AIM stand for?
5 In which country would you find the Murchison river?

Team 1

1 Who wrote the verse novel *Eugene Onegin*?
2 What does the Latin *Dei gratia* mean?
3 Which pop group took its name from a school in south Manchester?
4 What is HOLMES?
5 In which country would you find the Murchison Falls?

Round 7

Team 2

1 What name is given to a word that reads the same forwards and backwards?
2 What building housed the Great Exhibition of 1851?
3 What nationality was Trude Mostue, the star of TV's *Vets in Practice*?
4 Of which country is Maputo the capital?
5 Who wrote the play *Venus Observed*?

Team 1

1 What is a dimeter?

2 Who opened the Great Exhibition of 1851?
3 What is the Christian name of the Queen of Norway?

4 Of which country is Paramaribo the capital?
5 Who wrote the play *Forty Years On*?

Round 8

Team 2

1 Who painted the frescoes in the Vatican, 'The School of Athens' and 'Disputa'?
2 In Norse mythology, where did slain heroes go?
3 Which football team plays at Somerton Road?
4 What was the name of the butler in *Upstairs, Downstairs*?
5 What does FRSA stand for?

Team 1

1 Who painted frescoes showing scenes from Genesis, on the ceiling of the Sistine Chapel?
2 In Roman mythology, who was the supreme god?
3 Which football team plays at the Hawthorns?
4 Which actress starred in *Butterflies*?
5 What does FRCM stand for?

Round 9

Team 2

1 Which plant, often seen in rock gardens, is also known as sea-pink?

2 In which country would you find the Eucumbene dam?

3 Who wrote the novel *Of Human Bondage*?

4 Who followed Benjamin Disraeli as prime minister?

5 What is the monetary unit of Panama?

Team 1

1 Which trailing purple-flowered plant, widely planted in rock gardens, is also known as purple rock cress?

2 In which American state is the Hoover dam?

3 Who wrote the novel *Of Mice and Men*?

4 Who followed A. J. Balfour as prime minister?

5 What is the monetary unit of the Czech Republic?

Round 10   Individual questions for Team 2

Pop music

Name three of the five kinds of spice originally on offer from the Spice Girls.

Children's books

In *Stalky & Co.* by Rudyard Kipling, which two boys comprise the 'Co.'?

Classical music

George II established the custom, still followed today, of the audience standing for which piece of music?

Pot luck

The stigma of a flower is the receptacle for which minute grains, essential for reproduction?

History

Name the daughter of Oedipus by his mother Jocasta.

Drinks round

Team 1

1 What is represented by G in scientific texts?
2 Name the Roman road that connects Exeter, Bath and Lincoln.
3 In which country are the Taurus mountains?
4 Who composed *Pictures at an Exhibition*?
5 Which *Coronation Street* character was shot dead in a wages snatch?
6 Who wrote *Lady Chatterley's Lover*?
7 What does EFTA stand for?
8 Who were known as the 'little princes in the Tower'?
9 Who co-starred with Celia Johnson in *Brief Encounter*?
10 Who in the nursery rhyme had 'rings on her fingers and bells on her toes'?

Team 2

1 What is the SI unit of work and energy?
2 Which Roman road left London by what is now the Edgware Road?
3 What is British Honduras now called?
4 Who composed the music for the opera *Parsifal*?
5 In *Coronation Street*, whose first wife was killed in a car crash?
6 Who wrote *The Day of the Jackal*?
7 What does LNER stand for?
8 When Napoleon abdicated in 1814, who became king of France?
9 Who played Solitaire in the James Bond film *Live and Let Die*?
10 In the nursery rhyme, who did Simple Simon meet?

Reserve questions

1 What, according to the proverb, does an old ox make?
2 What large, carnivorous, wolf-like marsupial became extinct in the 1930s?
3 Pertussis is which infectious disease?

Pub League Quiz 31

The individual questions are in Rounds 5 and 10 and are on sport, soap operas, England, science and art.

Round 1

Team 1

1 Who wrote *Rebecca*?
2 Who composed the Austrian national anthem?
3 What is the capital of Zambia?
4 What is the shape of a pillar known as a caryatid?
5 What was Stewart Granger's real name?

Team 2

1 Who wrote *Cannery Row*?
2 Whose oratorios included *The Dream of Gerontius*?
3 Which port is the capital of Oman?
4 What is nacre also known as?
5 What was James Stewart's real name?

Round 2

Team 1

1 Who was the maker of the world famous Mosquito aircraft?
2 What are farfalle, fettuccine and rigatoni?
3 Women in Britain were first enfranchised in 1918. How old did they have to be to vote?
4 Joseph Priestley discovered it and called it dephlogisticated air. What do we call it now?
5 Who wrote the novels *Farewell My Lovely* and *The Long Goodbye*?

Team 2

1 Who was the maker of the Second World War Lightning aircraft?
2 Which vegetables are usually used in ratatouille?
3 What famous building burned down in London in 1936?
4 What stands between a whole gale and a hurricane on the Beaufort scale of wind force?
5 Who, in 1912, wrote the novel *The Lost World*?

Round 3

Team 1

1 In TV's *Hi-De-Hi!* who played Gladys Pugh?
2 Who won five swimming gold medals, plus a silver and a bronze, at the Seoul Olympics?
3 Who wrote the line, 'A little learning is a dang'rous thing'?
4 What hit TV programme was launched on New Year's Day 1964 from a converted church hall in Manchester?
5 What word, originally the name of a fort captured by David, is a synonym for Jerusalem?

Team 2

1 In *Coronation Street*, who played Minnie Caldwell?
2 At what team sport did Britain win a gold medal at the Seoul Olympics?
3 Who said, 'A radical is a man with both feet firmly planted in the air'?
4 Elvis Presley stood on British soil only once – on 2 March 1960. Where?
5 In which modern country is the town of Tarsus where St Paul was born?

Round 4

Team 1

1 Who is the patron saint of goldsmiths?
2 What type of creature is a cockchafer?
3 What does NFT stand for?
4 Which member of the royal family wrote a best-selling book for children entitled *The Old Man of Lochnagar*?
5 Who lost the French presidency to François Mitterrand in 1981?

Team 2

1 Who is the patron saint of sailors?
2 What type of creature is an anaconda?
3 What does FT stand for?
4 What is the date of HM the Queen's official birthday?

5 Which British prime minister's last words were said to be, 'Die, my dear Doctor, that's the last thing I shall do'?

Round 5   Individual questions for Team 1

Sport
Epée and foil are two forms of fencing competition. Name the third.

Soap operas
In which state was *Dynasty* set?

England
Which city did Matthew Arnold describe as 'home of lost causes and forsaken beliefs'?

Science
Which Greek scientist lost his life to a Roman soldier in Syracuse at the age of 75 in 212BCE?

Art
Which Spanish artist became court painter to Philip IV when he was only 25?

Round 6
Team 2

1 Which country lost to Italy in the World Cup final in 1982?
2 Who won an Oscar for his role as an alcoholic in the 1945 film *The Lost Weekend*?
3 Which South African state was known as Basutoland until 1966?

4 Which Canadian newspaper magnate held high government office in England during both world wars?

5 What kind of creatures are portrayed in the book *Watership Down*?

Team 1

1 What type of sportsman would participate in barrel jumping?
2 Which actor won Oscars in both 1937 and 1938?

3 Zimbabwe used to be the British colony of Southern Rhodesia. What is Northern Rhodesia now called?

4 Which leader of the Russian revolution became Commissar for War but was expelled from the party in 1927 and assassinated in Mexico in 1940?
5 What was the name of the castaway sailor whose adventures led to Daniel Defoe writing *Robinson Crusoe*?

Round 7
Team 2

1 What sort of creature is a laughing jackass?
2 What is a mignonette?
3 What, according to the legal saying, do hard cases make?
4 Which of the T. S. Eliot/ Lloyd Webber cats is named after a book of the Bible?
5 In which country is cricket's Sheffield Shield competed for?

Team 1

1 What is an oryx?
2 What variety of plum, yellow, dark purple or blue to black, has small, oval fruit?
3 What fictional barrister was played by John Thaw?
4 What is the last book of the Bible?
5 Name two of the famous 1950 Alfa Romeo team.

Round 8
Team 2
1 Which architect designed the layout of Regent's Park and Regent Street?
2 Who was the student leader who died in police custody in South Africa in 1977?
3 Which disgraced TV presenter used to present *Strike It Lucky*?
4 Who wrote the comedy *The Government Inspector*?
5 What famous university is located at Ithaca, New York?

Team 1
1 Which architect designed the Guggenheim museum?
2 Which film by Richard Attenborough tells the story of Steve Biko's life?
3 Which comedian's catchphrase was 'You lucky people?'?
4 Who wrote the play *Inadmissible Evidence*?
5 What is the state capital of North Dakota?

Round 9
Team 2
1 Which Wimbledon champion married and was then known as Mrs Court?
2 What was Nelson's rank at Trafalgar?
3 In which city did the assassination of Martin Luther King take place?
4 Where in Scotland is Queen Street railway station?
5 Which American film-maker made many epics on biblical themes including *Samson and Delilah* and *The Ten Commandments*?

Team 1
1 Who in sport is known as 'the Whirlwind'?
2 What was Captain Bligh's rank at the time of the mutiny on the Bounty?
3 What was the name of the governor of Texas who was riding in the car with John F. Kennedy when he was assassinated?
4 Which city has the railway stations Snow Hill and New Street?
5 Which American film director directed John Wayne's *Stagecoach* and *The Man who Shot Liberty Valance*?

Round 10 Individual questions for Team 2

Sport
Which sport is associated with the Federation Cup?

Soap operas
In *Twin Peaks,* what was the name of the first murder victim?

England
Which London street is associated with the film industry?

Science
What theory states that nothing can be measured or observed without disturbing it?

Art
Which artist painted the well-known 'Bubbles'?

Drinks round

Team 1

1 From which Gilbert and Sullivan work comes 'I can't help it, I was born sneering'?

2 Who in 1978 made the record 'Take a Chance on Me'?

3 What is another Christian name for Pentecost?

4 What begins with the vernal equinox?

5 Give the more common name for the plant Convollaria majolis, sometimes used to make perfume.

6 Suez lies at one end of the Suez Canal; which city lies at the other?

7 Who wrote published poems to Maud Gonne, though she finally refused to marry him?

8 Which country manufactured DAF cars?

9 Which actor progressed from *Pennies from Heaven* to *The Long Good Friday*?

10 Who was the founder of Rome?

Team 2

1 From which Gilbert and Sullivan work comes 'I'm very good at integral and differential calculus'?

2 Who in 1978 made the record 'Talking in Your Sleep'?

3 Why was Jesus of Nazareth a thaumaturgist?

4 In Scandinavian countries, what are supposed to roam on Walpurgis Night?

5 Give the more common name for the low-growing Myosotis plant, which has blue, pink or white flowers.

6 Between which two of North America's great lakes do the Niagara Falls lie?

7 Who wrote *The Postman Always Rings Twice*?

8 Where does Limburger cheese come from?

9 Which musical, later made into a film, transferred the Gospel of St Matthew to a community of hippies in New York?

10 Which Roman road ran from Rome to Brindisi?

Reserve questions

1 To within 20 years, when did Britain adopt the Gregorian calendar?
2 What blood messengers are the product of the endocrine glands?
3 What was the family relationship of US presidents William Henry Harrison and Benjamin Harrison?

Pub League Quiz 32

The individual questions are in Rounds 5 and 10 and are on television, classical music, law, general knowledge and nicknames.

Round 1

Team 1

1 Which 1959 film was awarded 11 Oscars?
2 Who was the first Labour Prime Minister with an independent majority?
3 Which capital city stands on the Manzanares river?
4 In which English county would you find the Cheddar Gorge?
5 What type of creature is a nutcracker?

Team 2

1 Which actress won four Oscars between 1932 and 1981?
2 Name the Liberal politician who was succeeded by Jeremy Thorpe as Liberal leader in 1967.
3 Which capital city stands on the Potomac river?
4 What is another name for Shropshire county?
5 To which animal family do martens belong?

Round 2

Team 1

1 Who is sometimes known as the godfather of soul?
2 What is measured with an anemometer?
3 Which poem about a monster did Lewis Carroll's Alice read?
4 What in music is an interval?
5 Who was responsible for the reform of the Carmelite order and died in 1582?

Team 2

1 Which female soul singer issued the album *Young, Gifted and Black* in 1972?
2 What does polyphonic mean?
3 In *Jabberwocky*, what did gyre and gimble in the wabe?
4 What is the smallest interval on a piano called?
5 Who is the patron saint of Spain, a virgin martyr whose emblem is a lamb?

Round 3

Team 1

1 From which film starring Jane Fonda did pop group Duran Duran get their name?
2 What is the home of a hare called?
3 The Opium Wars in the Far East were mainly between which two countries?
4 Who was *The Merchant of Venice* in Shakespeare's play of that name?
5 What is the state capital of Hawaii?

Team 2

1 What was Elvis Presley's first film?
2 What is the home of an eagle called?
3 Which country declared war on Britain on 18 June 1812?
4 Who was the *Moor of Venice* in Shakespeare's play?
5 What is the state capital of California?

Round 4

Team 1

1 Whom did Jimmy Carter succeed as president of the USA?
2 Who wrote Nancy Reagan's unauthorised biography in 1991?
3 How much is a sawbuck in American slang?
4 Who gave Victoria Falls their name?

5 What date is St Swithin's Day?

Team 2

1 Whom did Margaret Thatcher succeed as prime minister?
2 Who wrote the celebrated book *Diana: Her True Story*?
3 What is gambling slang for £500 or $500?
4 Columbus discovered the West Indies by mistake. Where did he originally set sail for?
5 In what month does the Chelsea Flower Show normally take place?

Round 5   Individual questions for Team 1

Television
In which quiz series did the Princess Royal participate?
Classical music
Which work by Vivaldi did Nigel Kennedy make a hit?
Law
Name two of the divisions of the legal year known as sittings.
General knowledge
Which publisher became chairman of Derby County Football Club?
Nicknames
What was General Joseph Stilwell's nickname?

Round 6

Team 2

1 Dundalk is the county town of Ireland's smallest county. What is the county?
2 Who first recorded the song 'I've Got You Babe'?
3 What name was given to Cromwell's troopers in the Civil War?
4 What do onomasticians study?
5 What is the oldest known alcoholic beverage?

Team 1

1 In which Irish county would you find both the Curragh and much of the Bog of Allen?
2 Which zither player provided *The Third Man* theme?
3 By what name are the yeoman warders of the Tower of London better known?
4 What is monotheism?
5 What is a jeroboam?

Round 7

Team 2

1 What planet has the satellite Nereid?
2 What is the name of the ghost ship that reputedly haunts the Cape of Good Hope?
3 Which is the first of *The Canterbury Tales*?
4 What is the distinctive feature of the proboscis monkey?
5 In which county is Stansted airport?

Team 1

1 Triton is a satellite of which planet?
2 What is the name of the wizard who reputedly lived in a cave in Tintagel, Cornwall?
3 Which is the last of *The Canterbury Tales*?
4 Where in the world would you find budgerigars in their natural habitat?
5 What is the name of the home of the Chelsea Pensioners in London?

Round 8

Team 2

1 What do Americans call what we call corn?
2 Who was the Greek god of time?
3 Who wrote the musical *Oliver!*?
4 Who wrote *The Agony and the Ecstacy*?
5 Narcolepsy is the medical term for what?

Team 1

1 What do Americans call coriander?
2 Who was the Roman god of time?
3 From which musical does 'They Call The Wind Maria' come?
4 Who created Dr Fu Manchu?
5 What is acetylsalicylic acid better known as?

Round 9

Team 2

1 Which famous British warship was sunk by the German battleship *Bismarck* in May 1941?

2 Where is The Scotsman newspaper printed?

3 Who was the first king of the Belgians?

4 Who fired blank shots at HM the Queen at the Trooping of the Colour ceremony in July 1981?

5 What make of car was advertised with the slogan 'Vorsprung durch technik'?

Team 1

1 What happened to the transatlantic liner *Lusitania*?

2 What daily newspaper was formerly the *Daily Worker*?

3 Who was the first Stuart king of Scotland?

4 Whom did Mehmet Ali Agca try to assassinate on 13 May 1981?

5 Which model and actress wore a notorious 'safety-pin' dress?

Round 10   Individual questions for Team 2

Television

Which character was the oldest member of *Dad's Army*?

Classical music

Who composed the opera *Ruslan and Ludmilla*?

Law

What word means the 'philosophy of the law'?

General knowledge

What city is known to its residents as the Big Apple?

Nicknames

Which great Florentine artist is known to history by his nickname meaning 'little barrel'?

Drinks round

Team 1

1 Which country has sovereignty over the three Juan Fernandez islands?
2 Prunella Scales has appeared in *Coronation Street*. True or false?
3 For what was Sir Noel Murless noted?
4 Which liqueur bears the letters D. O. M. on the bottle label?
5 What ruined Cistercian abbey is eight miles north of Harrogate?
6 A name for Tommy Handley's radio series was *I.T.M.A*. What did this stand for?
7 Whom did Rocky Marciano defeat to become heavyweight champion of the world?
8 Who was Uncle Mac?
9 In which county is Flodden Field?
10 What is Margaret Thatcher's middle name?

Team 2

1 What is Old Faithful in Yellowstone National Park, Wyoming?
2 *Pardon the Expression* is the only spin-off TV series of *Coronation Street*. True or false?
3 In which sport was Beryl Burton a prolific title holder?
4 What kind of drink is a negus?
5 Which famous zoo would you find near Dunstable?
6 Which British comedian portrayed the incompetent schoolmaster of St Michael's on stage and screen?
7 Which famous singer from Rochdale spent most of her later life on the island of Capri?
8 Who was the Forces' Sweetheart?
9 In which county are the Quantock Hills?
10 The first Lord Stockton died in 1986. By what name will he be most remembered?

Reserve questions

1 Who are the only two commoners in English history to be honoured with a state funeral?
2 Which national flag has vertical stripes of gold and blue, with a black trident in the centre?
3 Which Hollywood film-maker developed the concept of the silly symphony?

Pub League Quiz 33

The individual questions are in Rounds 5 and 10 and are on in common, name the year, pop music, religion and pot luck.

Round 1

Team 1

1 What word meaning literally 'our father' describes the Lord's Prayer recited in Latin?
2 In which country are the Vosges mountains?
3 In which year did *Luna 9* make a soft landing on the moon, Malawi become a republic, talks on Rhodesia on board HMS *Tiger* begin, and was Dr Verwoerd of South Africa assassinated?
4 What was the initial occupation of the Italian dictator Benito Mussolini?
5 How many balls are there on the table at the start of a game of snooker?

Team 2

1 How many beads are there on a rosary?
2 Mount Aconcagua in South America is over 23,000 ft high. In which country is it situated?
3 Which British monarch did John Francis attempt to assassinate?
4 For which profession was Mahatma Gandhi qualified in England before practising in South Africa?
5 What is the name of the game that resembles billiards and is played with numbered cups instead of pockets?

Round 2

Team 1

1 Name one of the two events celebrated by the flying of the Union Flag on government buildings each year on 10 March.
2 Which band had a hit album called *Definitely Maybe*?
3 Which bird has 'eyes' in its tail?
4 Who was the first Duke of Marlborough?
5 In what game are the Bermuda Bowl and the Venice Trophy major competitions?

Team 2

1 Name the three children of the Prince of Monaco.
2 Which comedy duo had a Number 1 hit in 1991 with 'The Stonk'?
3 Which fabulous bird arose from its own ashes?
4 At which battle of 1704 did he defeat the French and Bavarians?
5 K1, K2, C1 and C2 are classes of competition in which sport?

175

Round 3

Team 1

1 Two numbers add up to 54 and there is 12 between them. What are they?
2 Name one of the islands off the coast of Malta.

3 Who was the first man to swim the English Channel?

4 Which team were the first ever winners of the Football League Cup?

5 Who crushed Monmouth's rebellion in 1685?

Team 2

1 If one number is three times another and their difference is 10, what are they?
2 Which country has common borders with Argentina, Bolivia and Brazil?
3 Which sport originated in India and is played on the largest pitch of any ball game in the world?
4 Name two of the three clubs Graham Souness played for before he became player-manager of Glasgow Rangers.
5 What dynasty of kings descended from Pepin the Short?

Round 4

Team 1

1 What does *in toto* mean?
2 Who was the first Director-General of the BBC during 1927–38?
3 On what river does York stand?

4 What was the special skill of the biblical Ishmael, son of Abraham?
5 LOT is the national airline of which country?

Team 2

1 What does *id est* mean?
2 Which West Indian cricketer became a governor of the BBC?
3 On what river does Harrogate stand?
4 What sign of the zodiac is represented by an archer?
5 Which country puts Magyar Posta on its stamps?

Round 5   Individual questions for Team 1

In common
What did James Madison, John Quincy Adams, James Polk and Ulysses S. Grant have in common?
Name the year
In which year did Israel become independent?
Pop music
Who had five successive Number 1 hit singles in the USA, beginning with 'Visions of Love'?
Religion
What is another word for carol singing?
Pot luck
Give the full title of the Bishop of Bath.

Round 6
Team 2
1 How does the male cricket chirp?
2 In the world of international alliances, what is the OAU?
3 In which county is Arundel Castle?

4 What name is given to the sign of conferring a knighthood where the sovereign touches the knight with the flat of the sword?

5 What is a slowworm?

Team 1
1 How does a humming bird hum?
2 What does NFU stand for?

3 Which stately home, with designs by Holbein and Inigo Jones, is the seat of the earls of Pembroke?

4 Name the famous theatre in Dublin founded in 1904, for plays written by Irish playwrights and performed by Irish actors.

5 What name is given to animals that suckle their young?

Round 7
Team 2
1 What part does the Honourable Susan Nicholls play in *Coronation Street*?
2 What in heraldry is a broad, horizontal strip across the middle of a shield?
3 Who wrote *The Count of Monte Cristo*?
4 Name the main Moscow news agency.
5 What school did Billy Bunter attend?

Team 1
1 In *Soap*, what was the name of the Tates' original butler?
2 What is the heraldic term for full-faced?
3 Who wrote the novel *The Moon and Sixpence*?
4 What was the capital of unoccupied France in 1940?
5 Who was the storyteller in the tales of Brer Rabbit?

Round 8
Team 2
1 On which river do the cities of Quebec and Montreal stand?
2 What kind of birds are rock, cushat and stock?
3 Who was the second US president?
4 By what creature was the Greek god Adonis killed?
5 What is the state capital of Tasmania?

Team 1
1 In which US state is the Grand Canyon?
2 Name the Australian wild dog.
3 Who was the first US president?
4 Which queen is supposed to have founded Carthage?
5 Which capital city stands on the Dambovita river?

Round 9

Team 2	Team 1
1 Who was Poet Laureate from 1843 to 1850?	1 Who was Poet Laureate from 1930 to 1967?
2 In which battle of 1346 did the English defeat the French though outnumbered by at least two to one?	2 Which English king was the leader of the Third Crusade with Philip II of France?
3 What was written by the finger of God on two tablets of stone on Mount Sinai?	3 What is the general name for the first four books of the New Testament?
4 What is tapioca made from?	4 What is semolina derived from?
5 What name is given to any substance that speeds up a chemical reaction, but itself remains unchanged?	5 Name the colourless inert gas isolated by Daniel Rutherford in 1772 that has the symbol N.

Round 10   Individual questions for Team 2

In common

Entrechat, glissade, pas seul and fouetté are all terms in which art?

Name the year

Name the year in which George Brown resigned as foreign secretary, Yuri Gagarin was killed and Martin Luther King was assassinated.

Pop music

Which pop singer became Yusuf Islam?

Religion

Name the most sacred of all holy places in the Jewish religion.

Pot luck

Who was the playwright whose first play was *Widowers' Houses*, who won the 1925 Nobel Prize for literature and who declined a peerage?

Drinks round

Team 1

1 From which musical does the song 'Luck Be A Lady' come?

2 By what other names are the constellations *Corona Australis* and *Corona Borealis* better known?

3 Who murdered Martin Luther King?

4 What on a boat are scuppers?

5 When it is 12 noon GMT on New Year's Day in London, what is the time in Paris?

6 Which German artist at the age of 13 drew the first self-portrait in European history, using a mirror?

7 What colour is a moonstone?

8 What does omniscient mean?

9 In which month did the Romans celebrate the feast of Saturnalia?

10 Who was the Oscar-winning star in *Gandhi*?

Team 2

1 From which musical does the song 'My Funny Valentine' come?

2 In which direction does a comet's tail always point?

3 Who murdered Mahatma Gandhi?

4 What on a boat is the taffrail?

5 When it is 12 noon GMT on New Year's Day in London, what is the time in New York?

6 Which artist worked for the Elector of Saxony and is still famous for his woodcuts and copperplates?

7 Give another name for a bloodstone.

8 What is an acronym?

9 The Emperor Claudius had his wife executed for entering a bigamous marriage. What was her name?

10 Who was the Oscar-winning star in *Cabaret*?

Reserve questions

1 Enrico Caruso was regarded as the greatest singer of his day. Was he a tenor, baritone or bass?

2 *Borstal Boy* is the autobiography of which Irish playwright?

3 Which Italian striker joined Middlesbrough for £7 million in July 1996?

Pub League Quiz 34

The individual questions are in Rounds 5 and 10 and are on films, plants and wildlife, dates, sport and general knowledge.

Round 1

Team 1

1 What is the name of the police station in *The Bill*?
2 In which European country is the parliament called the Eduskunta?

3 Who wrote *The Hitchhiker's Guide to the Galaxy*?
4 What does RAAF stand for?

5 Which great city used to be called New Amsterdam?

Team 2

1 What is the name of the town defended by *Dad's Army*?
2 Name the Irish nationalist with whom Gladstone came to terms and introduced the Home Rule Bill in 1886.

3 *Stamp Album* is a book by which actor?
4 What does CGS stand for in the armed forces?
5 What was the name of Volgograd from 1925 to 1961?

Round 2

Team 1

1 In which film did the director's father co-star with Humphrey Bogart?
2 What relation was Henry II of England to Henry I?

3 Which film star's legs were insured for a million dollars by Twentieth Century Fox?

4 What has the atomic number 1?
5 What was the food of the Greek gods?

Team 2

1 Peter Sellers starred in the film *What's New Pussycat?*. Who wrote the script?
2 Which of William the Conqueror's sons became kings of England?
3 Who said, suggesting a well-known phrase, 'a sex symbol becomes an object. I hate being an object'?
4 What has the atomic number 2?
5 What was the drink of the Greek gods?

Round 3

Team 1

1 Who became secretary-general of NATO in 1984?
2 What is sauerkraut?
3 Name The Who's rock opera.
4 What was the heroine's name in the book *A Room with a View*?
5 In the board game, what does the word Ludo mean?

Team 2

1 Who was chancellor of the exchequer in 1974?
2 What is the singular of scampi?
3 Who wrote the music to which 'I vow to thee my country' is set?
4 What did the owl and the pussycat eat with a runcible spoon?
5 How many murder weapons are there in the game of Cluedo?

Round 4

Team 1

1 Name three of the four great estuaries of England.
2 In which country was Bonnie Tyler lost?
3 Who baptised Jesus?
4 What was known as the 'royal disease'?
5 What tropical mammal related to the cat has a perfume gland in the groin?

Team 2

1 Name the highest peaks of England, Scotland, Wales and Ireland (three of the four required).
2 Which state was on Ray Charles's mind?
3 In which river was Jesus baptised?
4 What is the common name for the disease trypanosomiasis?
5 The chihuahua is a native of which country?

Round 5   Individual questions for Team 1

Films
Which was Roger Moore's first Bond film?
Plants and wildlife
What is esparto?
Dates
Of the years 1800, 1900 and 2000, which is a leap year?
Sport
Which French boxer was national champion in every weight and division before becoming light heavyweight champion of the world in 1920?
General knowledge
What is the adult leader of a Brownie pack called?

Round 6
Team 2

1 Which two books by Charles Dickens were written in the first person?
2 How many sides does a nonagon have?
3 What is agoraphobia?
4 Who was quoted as saying, 'My advice if you insist on slimming: eat as much as you like – just don't swallow it'?
5 In which fictional village was *Peak Practice* set?

Team 1

1 Which two characters from *The Army Game* had a comedy series of their own?
2 In which science would you find the concept of final or marginal utility?
3 What is megalomania?
4 Who was quoted as saying, 'If all the young ladies attending [the Yale Prom] were laid end to end, I wouldn't be at all surprised'?
5 Who stars opposite Richard Wilson in *One Foot in the Grave*?

Round 7
Team 2

1 Which country's flag is a blue cross on a white background?
2 What have Leighton Rees, Keith Deller, Bob Anderson and Phil Taylor all won?
3 What is the chemical symbol for phosphorus?
4 In which film did Marilyn Monroe co-star with Laurence Olivier?
5 In which group of Scottish islands is the Old Man of Hoy?

Team 1

1 In which country can you salute a national flag that is different on one side from the other?
2 Who succeeded John Francome as National Hunt champion jockey?
3 What is the most common natural ore of aluminium in the world?
4 In which 1962 film did Alec Guinness portray King Faisal?
5 On which Scottish island is Stornoway?

Round 8
Team 2

1 In which year was Prince Charles born?
2 Which city is the home of the Hallé Orchestra?
3 Who was the first black boxer to win the world heavyweight title?
4 From which poem is the line, 'The curfew tolls the knell of parting day'?
5 Which countries are divided by the 38th parallel?

Team 1

1 What did Albert, Duke of York become?
2 What craft is the town of Cluny in France famous for?
3 To whom did Henry Cooper lose his British heavyweight title in 1971?
4 From which poem is the line, 'Great wits are sure to madness near allied'?
5 Which countries are divided by the 49th parallel?

Round 9

Team 2

1 Who was executed before the Banqueting Hall in Whitehall on 30 January 1649?
2 Who recorded the 1959 hit record 'Living Doll'?
3 What was the book by James Hilton about the life of a schoolmaster, later made into a film?
4 Where did the German fleet mutiny in October 1918?

5 How many points is the letter 'B' worth in Scrabble?

Team 1

1 Which children's book character was always saying, 'Off with his head'?
2 Who wrote 'Living Doll'?

3 Muriel Spark wrote a book about a headstrong schoolmistress, which was made into a film. What was it called?
4 What battle, in May 1942, saved Australia from invasion by the Japanese?

5 If a bingo caller shouts 'Two fat ladies', what number has been drawn?

Round 10   Individual questions for Team 2

Films
Who directed the film *E.T.: The Extra-Terrestrial*?
Plants and wildlife
Which crop is susceptible to the Colorado beetle?
Dates
What heavenly body determines the date of Easter?
Sport
Where were the first Commonwealth Games held?
General knowledge
What, is it said, did President Santa Anna of Mexico keep in his hacienda from 1838 until its ceremonial burial in 1842?

Drinks round

Team 1

1 Whose husbands were Louis VII of France and Henry II of England?

2 On which estuary is the town of Chatham?

3 In which country is the mountain range Sierra Madre?

4 What can be grown in fan, standard, cordon and espalier forms?.

5 Who wrote the plays *Uncle Vanya* and *The Three Sisters*?

6 How does the Bishop of Rochester sign himself?

7 UNITA was dedicated to gaining the independence of which Portuguese colony?

8 Which broadcaster famously threw a glass of wine over Jonathan Aitken?

9 Where was Napoleon Bonaparte born?

10 Which river flows through Hamburg and Dresden?

Team 2

1 What monarch was the son of Mary, Queen of Scots and Lord Darnley?

2 Of which range of chalk hills is Haddington Hill, near Wendover, a part?

3 In which country is the mountain range Sierra Morena?

4 What are made in the form of fly, chain, feather and whipping?

5 Which Verdi opera was based on Victor Hugo's play *Le Roi s'amuse*?

6 How does the Bishop of Carlisle sign himself?

7 In what part of the world is Quechua still spoken?

8 On which factual TV programme did the late Jill Dando and Nick Ross form a team?

9 Where in Italy was Leonardo da Vinci born?

10 Which country beginning with the letter 'A' does not end with that letter?

Reserve questions

1 What part of the body may be affected by nephritis?

2 Pandit Nehru and his daugher Indira were the first and third prime ministers of independent India. Who was the second?

3 Which bandleader had the signature tune 'One o'Clock Jump'?

Pub League Quiz 35

The individual questions are in Rounds 5 and 10 and are on sport, art and artists, nobel prize winners, composers and English monarchs.

Round 1

Team 1

1 In what year did the series of modern Olympic Games begin?

2 What recent invention is generally credited to Martin Cooper?

3 To which book did Alexander Ripley write an authorised sequel?

4 Who, in an act of bravery, walked out of Scott's tent?

5 Which girl were Simon and Garfunkel singing about with the line, 'You're shaking my confidence daily'?

Team 2

1 Which city hosted the first Winter Olympics to be held in Asia?

2 What invention of Jacob Schick could be said to have changed the face of man when it appeared in 1931?

3 Which author disappeared after *The Murder of Roger Ackroyd*?

4 To which movement did the heroes and heroines of the Second World War's Maquis belong?

5 Who sang about Lily the Pink's invention of medicinal compound?

Round 2

Team 1

1 Practically all of the Kalahari Desert is in which country?

2 Who was awarded a 4lb gold soccer ball after scoring his 1,000th goal?

3 Which chemical has the symbol Mg?

4 Which six-letter English word means to stick fast as well as meaning the complete opposite?

5 On which continent did early man first develop, according to most scientists?

Team 2

1 Which two countries lie either side of the Thar Desert?

2 In which ball game did Geoffrey B. Hunt of Australia rise to become world champion?

3 Ra are the letters that represent which element?

4 There is only one genuine English word which ends in the letters 'amt'. What is it?

5 In which African country is Lake Turkana, famous for its remains of early man?

Round 3

Team 1

1 Who wrote *The Alchemist*?
2 In transport, what does APT stand for?
3 What did Heinrich Dreser introduce into medicine in 1893?
4 How many gallons are there in a bushel?
5 In which country is Biskra?

Team 2

1 Who wrote *The Mill on the Floss*?
2 What does BAOR stand for?
3 What did shop proprietor James Ritty patent in 1879?
4 How many gallons are there in a peck?
5 In which country is Beisan?

Round 4

Team 1

1 What is a ruminant?
2 Which of the boulevards in Paris links the Arc de Triomphe and Place de la Concorde?
3 What do Robert Hayes, James Hines and Armin Hary have in common?
4 What is Robin Goodfellow known as in *A Midsummer Night's Dream*?
5 Who played Ma Boswell in *Bread*?

Team 2

1 What is a mendicant?
2 In which American thoroughfare is the White House?
3 In what sphere of athletic sport was Sergey Litvinov a champion?
4 Which of Shakespeare's heroines speaks the lines, 'O brave new world, that has such people in it'?
5 Which entertainer's real name is Cherilyn Sarkisian?

Round 5   Individual questions for Team 1

Sport
What game would you be playing if you were competing for the Swaythling Cup?

Art and artists
What was Rubens' first name?

Nobel Prize winners
Who declined the Nobel Peace Prize shared with Henry Kissinger in 1973?

Composers
Who wrote the 'Sea Symphony'?

English monarchs
Who became king when Henry VI was overthrown in 1461?

Round 6

Team 2

1 From which country do Walloons come?
2 In what liquid does a cook coddle eggs?
3 How many stars make up Orion's belt?
4 In which present-day country was Erasmus born?
5 Which Peter Shaffer play is about a boy who blinds horses?

Team 1

1 In which country will you find the Swiss Guard?
2 Where are a flatfish's eyes?
3 Which of the planets is nearest to the sun?
4 In which country was Albert Einstein born?
5 In which play is Lydia Languish courted by Jack Absolute?

Round 7

Team 2

1 Which South American country had an inflation rate of over 8,000 per cent in 1985?
2 Which was the first country to host both the Summer and the Winter Olympics in the same year?
3 The fry of which fish is served up as whitebait?
4 Which particular art form did Alexander Calder invent and exhibit in the 1930s?
5 Which reality talent show did Paul Potts win?

Team 1

1 In which South American city was Simon Bolivar born?
2 Which British athlete won a gold medal in that year (1924), in the Summer Olympics 400 metres event?
3 Which fish, olive brown with black spots, has a distinctive barbel at each side of its mouth?
4 A group of American landscape painters that included Samuel Morse was named after a river. Which was it?
5 Which secret society was dedicated to driving European settlers out of Kenya?

Round 8
Team 2

1 Which TV series featured Corporal Rocco Barbella?

2 Anne, Dick, George and Julian were four of Enid Blyton's 'Famous Five'. Who was the fifth?

3 Who signed an autograph for his killer shortly before he was assassinated in New York?

4 Who wrote the play *Hedda Gabler*?

5 Which is the oldest of the Bowl games played in American college football?

Team 1

1 Which British TV series inspired the American series *All in the Family*?

2 Name the knighted actor who had children named Hayley, Jonathan and Juliet.

3 In which city was Mrs 'Cory' Aquino's husband assassinated?

4 Who wrote the autobiographical play *Long Day's Journey into Night*?

5 In which stadium do the Miami Dolphins play their home games?

Round 9
Team 2

1 What did John Hawkins start selling to New World settlers in 1562?

2 Which author won the Pulitzer Prize for fiction in 1952 for *The Caine Mutiny*?

3 Who ended Bjorn Borg's run of five successive Wimbledon singles titles?

4 Who discovered radio waves in 1887?

5 What was the name of the hypnotising musician in Gerald du Maurier's *Trilby*?

Team 1

1 Which country was the first to have universal suffrage?

2 Which author won the Pulitzer Prize for fiction in 1953 for *The Old Man and the Sea*?

3 How many players are there on each side in Australian Rules football?

4 Which Briton patented car disc brakes in 1902?

5 Name the film starring Ingrid Bergman which was adapted from the book *The Small Woman*.

Round 10   Individual questions for Team 2
Sport
What do the Sheffield Steelers play?
Art and artists
Which artist had the forenames Joseph Mallord William?
Nobel Prize winners
Which organisation won the Nobel Peace Prize in 1965?
Composers
Which composer's first opera was *Orfeo*?
English monarchs
Who was king before Edward the Confessor?

Drinks round

Team 1

1 Which show from the City Varieties in Leeds was screened for over 30 years?
2 Which trio had a hit with 'Baby Love'?
3 What race in England is over a distance of four miles, one furlong and 180 yards?
4 Where is the setting for John le Carre's *A Small Town in Germany*?
5 Which country is the home of the sweet wine called Tokay?
6 Which planet did *Viking 1* land on?
7 Which animal in Aesop's fable assumed the grapes he couldn't reach were sour anyway?
8 What name is given to an enthusiast of all things French?
9 What was the name of the horse made a consul by Emperor Caligula?
10 Who created the imaginary language Newspeak?

Team 2

1 What TV show was broadcast for the first time at 6.30 a.m. on 17 January 1983?
2 Which UK duo had a hit with 'I Know Him So Well'?
3 What is a good mudder likely to win in the US?
4 Which country provides the setting for the novel *Summer of the 17th Doll*?
5 What is the technical term for new wine, or grape juice, before fermentation is complete?
6 Which planet did the *Mariner 2, 9* and *10* spacecraft explore?
7 How did Apollo punish the prophetess Cassandra?
8 What is phagophobia?
9 What is the name of Clint Eastwood's orangutan film co-star?
10 Who created the imaginary place Blefuscu?

Reserve questions

1 What is the unit of currency in Pakistan?
2 What vaccine preceded Sabin vaccine in the fight against polio?
3 Which Greek philosopher founded his own Academy at Athens?

Pub League Quiz 36

The individual questions are in Rounds 5 and 10 and are on famous people, films, wars, the ancients and plant life.

Round 1

Team 1

1 Which is the world's largest gulf?

2 In the nursery rhyme, what was the only tune that Tom, the piper's son, could play?

3 Which press tycoon did Marion Davies keep company with for over 30 years?

4 What was Jeeves' given name?

5 To which parts of the human body does the word 'volar' relate?

Team 2

1 What region covers Norway, Sweden, Finland and Russia within the Arctic Circle?

2 In the nursery rhyme 'Pease Porridge Hot', how old was the porridge?

3 Which Christine nearly brought down the British government in the Profumo scandal of 1963?

4 Who wrote about Mr Polly and Mr Britling?

5 What is the hardest substance in the human body?

Round 2

Team 1

1 Which country is named after the line of latitude that runs through it?

2 Which film had Mia Farrow and John Cassavetes facing the prospects of bringing up a little devil?

3 Don and Phil were brothers who made up which singing duo?

4 Who was England's first official Poet Laureate?

5 How long is a tennis court from baseline to baseline?

Team 2

1 Which South American country took its name from the Latin for silvery?

2 Which film booted *Singin' in the Rain* back into cinema in 1971?

3 Ray and Dave Davis were brothers in which pop group?

4 From which poem are these lines, 'Know then thyself, presume not God to scan'?

5 How high is the net on a tennis court, at the centre?

Round 3

Team 1

1 Which religion was founded by Guru Nanak?
2 What was the name of P. T. Barnum's famous elephant?
3 What is removal of tissue from a living body for diagnostic purposes called?
4 What does the word Esperanto actually mean?
5 How is 2,000 written in Roman numerals?

Team 2

1 What is the principal religion of the island of Bali?
2 Which US army horse survived after Custer's last stand?
3 What word describes the region of earth, air and water inhabited by living organisms?
4 What does the word kamikaze mean?
5 What number cannot be represented by Roman numerals?

Round 4

Team 1

1 What is the correct title of the daughter of an earl, marquis or duke?
2 In which country are the ruins of Troy?
3 From where does the Kirov Ballet come?
4 What are the highest odds paid by a casino in a roulette game?
5 What is the most sacred river in India?

Team 2

1 What is the correct title of the wife of a knight or baronet?
2 Where in China are the famous terracotta soldiers?
3 Who founded what is now the Royal Ballet?
4 What is the highest score possible from a single stroke at billiards?
5 By what name is the former colony of the Belgian Congo now known?

Round 5   Individual questions for Team 1

Famous people
In which field of the arts did Jacob Epstein achieve fame?
Films
Who directed the film *Apocalypse Now*?
Wars
Which war did the Potsdam Conference follow?
The Ancients
Who was chained to a mountain where an eagle tore at his liver every day?
Plant life
What plant, with a stem of up to a foot, and droopy, pale green flowers, has a stinking variety?

Round 6

Team 2

1 Which is the world's highest navigable lake?

2 Who won an Oscar as best actor in *Coming Home*?

3 In which country was the Boxer Rebellion?

4 Who is the subject of Irving Stone's *Lust for Life*?

5 What caused over 20 million deaths worldwide, in the years 1918 and 1919?

Team 1

1 What port, Israel's only outlet to the Red Sea, stands at the head of the Gulf of Aqaba?

2 Who won an Oscar as best actress, in *Coming Home*?

3 In which country did the Battle of Waterloo take place?

4 Which Hermann Hesse book gave its name to a rock group?

5 Worldwide, which is the most common blood group?

Round 7

Team 2

1 What is the usual diameter of a golf hole?

2 What is another name for a concertina?

3 What is the surname of the Bee Gees?

4 Who wrote *The Alexandria Quartet*?

5 What colour is a Remy Martin bottle?

Team 1

1 In golf, what name is given to an intended stroke where the player misses the ball altogether?

2 How was a dulcimer played?

3 What is the surname of the Beach Boys?

4 Whose first novel was *This Sporting Life*?

5 What makes up a Black Velvet?

Just for fun

What was the original Hobson's choice?

Hobson's choice is a proverbial phrase meaning no choice at all. It arose from the somewhat dictatorial trade practices of an innkeeper of Cambridge named Hobson who hired out horses. The horses were rested in strict rota and Hobson required each potential patron to take the horses nearest the stable door. The choice was clear-cut: 'either that or none'.

Round 8

Team 2

1 Who moved from Radio Luxembourg to Radio 1, where his breakfast show was a great success from 1972 to 1977?
2 Which Carthaginian general had both a brother and a brother-in-law named Hasdrubal?
3 Where is Waikiki beach?

4 Where in North Carolina did the first powered flight by the Wright brothers take place?

5 Which sport features a movement called a veronica?

Team 1

1 What replaced Roy Hattersley when he failed to turn up for his scheduled TV appearance on *Have I Got News For You?*
2 Whom did the Athenians defeat at the Battle of Marathon?
3 Which fictional character was born Jimmy Gatz and had a mansion on Long Island?
4 Who piloted the Hughes H4 Hercules, the largest aeroplane ever flown, when it made its one flight in 1947?
5 In which sport is the goal called a hail?

Round 9

Team 2

1 Which Mediterranean island was celebrated in antiquity for its copper mines?
2 Name the lead singer with Guns 'n Roses.
3 What event is celebrated on 14 July in France?

4 What soap was initially entitled *Dynasty II?*
5 What puts the fizz in soda water?

Team 1

1 Which group of islands carries the Danish name that means 'sheep' in English?
2 Who was the original lead singer with the Pogues?
3 What feast, held on 6 January, celebrates the manifestation of Christ's divinity to the Magi?
4 In *Cheers*, what is Sam Malone's nickname?
5 How many grams make a pound (within five grams)?

Round 10   Individual questions for Team 2

Famous people

Who organised the Transglobe expedition of 1979–82 that traced the Greenwich meridian crossing both Poles?

Films

Which 1973 film was based on a bestseller by the novelist William Peter Blatty?

Wars

Which war ended the Austrian-Hungarian monarchy?

The ancients

Which ancient civilisation believed that an eclipse was caused by a dragon trying to eat the sun?

Plant life

Which fungus has a crown, spores, gills and a stalk?

Drinks round

Team 1

1   Which Australian prime minister disappeared while swimming, in 1967?

2   Who changed groups from the Faces to the Rolling Stones?

3   What nationality is the 100 metres sprint star Donovan Bailey?

4   What cocktail is made from vodka, Galliano and orange juice?

5   What were Babe Ruth's given names?

6   In the Bible, how long did Jonah spend in the belly of the whale?

7   From which language do we get the words catamaran and curry?

8   How many properties are there on a Monopoly board?

9   What fell on 15 February 1942?

10   Who played Captain Kirk in *Star Trek* on TV?

Team 2

1   Which Australian starred in the film *Grease*?

2   Whose first hit was 'Your Song'?

3   Who was disqualified from the Olympic 100 metres final of 1996 after two false starts?

4   Vodka and lime juice are two of the main ingredients of a Moscow Mule. What is the third?

5   What were Jack Hobbs' given names?

6   What ancient book recounts Jewish folklore and the exploits of national heroes?

7   From which language do we get the words gingham and sarong?

8   How many cards does each player have at the start of a game of pinochle?

9   What burned on 27 February 1933?

10   Who, on TV, played the leading role in *I Claudius*?

Reserve questions

1 On which bay does the French resort of Biarritz lie?
2 In what mental illness does the sufferer believe, wrongly, that they are being persecuted by others, and may have delusions of grandeur?
3 What does an ammeter measure?

Pub League Quiz 37

The individual questions are in Rounds 5 and 10 and are on characters, international affairs, disasters, horses and courses and inventions.

Round 1

Team 1

1 What is the largest island in Greece?
2 *Pelléus et Mélisande* is which composer's only opera?

3 Who played the part of *Batman* in the 1966 film?
4 Which species of gull, found on British coasts, spits foul-smelling oil onto its nest to protect it?
5 In what sport are rings a class of competition?

Team 2

1 Which is the largest island of Europe?
2 Which Verdi opera is based on the story of *The Lady of the Camellias*?
3 Who played the part of Joker in the *Batman* film of 1966?
4 What is most common domestic bird in the world?

5 In international boxing, what is now the lightest weight division?

Round 2

Team 1

1 In which American state, according to an early Bee Gees hit, did the lights go out?

2 Who played the part of a gunslinging robot in *Futureworld*?
3 How many nights are there in the *Arabian Nights*?
4 What is a pennyroyal?

5 Which snooker player carried the Olympic torch at the 1956 Olympics?

Team 2

1 Who in a recording of 1963, asked Long-distance Information about someone in Memphis, Tennessee?
2 Who starred in both *Trainspotting* and *The Full Monty*?
3 How many people took refuge in Noah's Ark?
4 What is the more usual name of the carnivorous plant also called a wake-robin or lords-and-ladies?
5 In 1965, for the first time in the 20th Century, two brothers played in the same England soccer team. Who were they?

Round 3

Team 1

1 Whom did Peeping Tom peep at?
2 'Red-Green Gardens', first exhibited in 1921, was the work of which Swiss painter?
3 What is the world's most common compound?

4 In what field of sport is Chris Boardman a star performer?
5 Which country has the most land frontiers?

Team 2

1 According to ancient legends, who holds up the sky?
2 Which Spanish artist is said to have promised to eat his wife after her death?
3 By what fraction of its volume does water expand when it freezes? Is it $\frac{1}{5}$, $\frac{1}{7}$, $\frac{1}{8}$, $\frac{1}{11}$ or $\frac{1}{15}$?
4 At what game was Mike Russell a champion?
5 Which European frontier is only 1.5km long?

Round 4

Team 1

1 Who created the detective Albert Campion?
2 Who wrote the lyrics for the film *Carmen Jones*?
3 Which J. M. Barrie character said, 'To die will be an awfully big adventure'?

4 Which of the five senses develops first?
5 Which is the largest city in Latin America?

Team 2

1 Who played private investigator Hetty Wainthropp on TV?
2 Who wrote the music for *Porgy and Bess*?
3 Who wrote, 'If you can keep your head when all about you are losing theirs ... you'll be a man, my son'?
4 Where is the human skin least sensitive?
5 What is the smallest Latin American country?

Round 5   Individual questions for Team 1

Characters

Who was landlady to Sherlock Holmes?

International affairs

What did America buy for $7.2 million in 1867?

Disasters

Where did two jumbo jets collide in 1977, killing 574 people?

Horses and courses

Which horse won the Grand National in 1973, 1974 and 1977 and came second in 1975 and 1976?

Inventions

What form of camera did Edwin Land invent?

Round 6

Team 2

1 In which American state is Michigan City?
2 Who was a policeman in Kansas before becoming a lawman in Tombstone, Arizona?
3 From what German coin does the dollar get its name?
4 What is 70 per cent of 70?

5 What is a shark's skeleton made of?

Team 1

1 Of which country is Jakarta the capital?
2 Which Hollywood actor was the most decorated soldier in US history?
3 What is the Chinese word for tea?
4 How many years make up a vicennial period?
5 What does a whale shark feed on?

Round 7

Team 2

1 If a dish is described as parmentier, which vegetable will be part of it?
2 Which London museum was founded in 1753 and opened to the public in 1759?
3 Name one of the two artists with whom Barbra Streisand had Number 1 hits?
4 What is the subject of the famous book written by English sage and astrologer Nicholas Culpeper?
5 *The Prisoner* declared in the cult TV series, 'I am not a number, I am a free man.' What number had he been assigned?

Team 1

1 Which fish is traditionally eaten by Poles on Christmas Eve?

2 Who was kept in the Bastille from 1698 until his death in 1703?

3 Which father and daughter had a Number 1 hit in 2003?

4 Which annual first appeared in 1697 and has been published every year since?

5 What was the name of the priceless painting in *'Allo, 'Allo*?

Round 8
Team 2

1 Who played Marlon Brando's elder brother in *On the Waterfront*?
2 Which member of the cat family is unable to retract its claws?

3 In *Les Misérables*, what was Jean Valjean's first crime?
4 Name the supertanker that ran aground off the coast of Brittany in March 1978.
5 Which of Puccini's heroines is a famous singer?

Team 1

1 Which actor led the expedition in the film *Journey to the Centre of the Earth*?
2 Which American mammal is distinguished by a black face mark?

3 What was the name of the *Jew of Malta* in Marlowe's play?
4 Which organisation won the Nobel Peace Prize in 1977?

5 Who wrote symphonies called the *Surprise*, the *Military*, the *Clock*, the *Drum-roll*, the *London* and the *Oxford*?

Round 9
Team 2

1 What form of transport is a felucca?
2 Which Englishman was both knighted and canonised, and was executed in 1535?
3 Which Prime Minister was also president of the MCC?
4 Who wrote a poem which begins, 'Remember me when I am gone away'?
5 Which country's parliament is called the Folketing?

Team 1

1 Who was the first person to reach a speed of 600mph on land?
2 Which US president introduced prohibition?

3 Where is Sabina Park cricket ground?
4 Which bird is referred to in the line, 'Thou was't not born for death, immortal Bird!'?
5 To which branch of Protestantism do the religious majority in Finland belong?

Round 10   Individual questions for Team 2
Characters
What army did Shaw's *Major Barbara* serve in?
International affairs
Which incident prompted the installation of the 'hot line'?
Disasters
Which Australian city was devastated by Cyclone Tracy on Christmas Day 1974?
Horses and courses
Over what distance is the 2000 Guineas at Newmarket run?
Inventions
What household object did Percy LeBaron Spencer invent in 1945?

Drinks round

Team 1

1 In which seaway are the Thousand Islands?
2 Which cricket side has as its emblem six martlets?
3 Who seized power from King Idris after a coup in 1969?
4 In which film did Spencer Tracy play a one-armed stranger?
5 Who wrote *Portrait of the Artist as a Young Man*?
6 In a bottle of wine what is the ullage?
7 What was Max Bygraves' real forename?
8 Which former car factory worker earned a living at the post office in Emmerdale?
9 In which country is there a province called Luxembourg?
10 What is the smallest British mammal?

Team 2

1 Which strait lies between Iceland and Greenland?
2 Who was bowling when Gary Sobers hit his famous six sixes?
3 Who succeeded Khruschev as USSR premier in 1964?
4 In which Hitchcock film does Paul Newman play a scientist?
5 Who wrote *Portrait of the Artist as a Young Dog*?
6 What is the sediment at the bottom of a cask of wine called?
7 Which comedian's real name is Charles Springall?
8 Which *Coronation Street* barmaid's first marriage lasted only a few days before she found solace in the arms of Des Barnes?
9 Where is the island of Rum?
10 Which shrew-like marsupial is native to Australia, Tasmania and New Guinea?

Reserve questions

1 What is HCl?
2 Who was the famous pupil of Anne Sullivan?
3 What did Lloyd George describe as Mr Balfour's poodle?

Pub League Quiz 38

The individual questions are in Rounds 5 and 10 and are on abbreviations, mythology, sport, news of the 1980s and United Kingdom.

Round 1

Team 1

1 Which food product did Gail Borden give to the world in 1858?
2 Who achieved fame in 1920 by the publication of a collection of stories called *Bliss*?
3 On TV, who played Lt Skinner in *In the Heat of the Night*?
4 Which country's heroes are celebrated in Luis de Camoens' poem *The Lusiads*?
5 In a standard pack of cards, if 17 red cards have been played, how many red cards are left?

Team 2

1 What was Johann Gutenberg the first European to invent?
2 Who wrote the poem *Not Waving but Drowning*?
3 In which TV serial did Ian Hendry and Wanda Ventham co-star?
4 Who helped her father rescue shipwreck survivors off the Fame Island in September 1838?
5 Add together the number of players in a Rugby Union side and the number in a Rugby League side. What is the total?

Round 2

Team 1

1 Which two pop stars recorded 'Don't Go Breaking My Heart' in 1976.
2 What nationality was the first explorer to sight the Grand Canyon?
3 Who was George IV's last Prime Minister?
4 Which comic actor starred as Headmaster in the 1985 film *Clockwise*?
5 Which is the most commonly used punctuation mark in the English language?

Team 2

1 Which pop singer recorded the album *Silverbird* in 1973?
2 With the deserts of which continent are the names Charles Sturt and Robert O'Hara Burke associated?
3 Who was Queen Victoria's first Prime Minister?
4 Which 1986 film told the story of rock 'n' roll singer Richie Valens?
5 Which letter in the English alphabet went by the name izzard?

Round 3

Team 1

1 What is Mons Meg?

2 Which mountain can you see from a train called *The Bullet*?

3 Who wrote the novel *Phantom of the Opera* in 1911?

4 Which military conflict forms the background for Shakespeare's *Troilus and Cressida*?

5 Which Second World War leader was killed with his mistress Clara Petacci?

Team 2

1 Where can Mons Meg be seen today?

2 What did the B&O Railroad's initials stand for?

3 What are the surnames of The Two Ronnies?

4 What is the 'sack' of which Sir John Falstaff is so fond in Shakespeare's *Henry IV*?

5 How do we usually contract *Gehime Staatspolizei*?

Round 4

Team 1

1 Which country left the Commonwealth in 1961?

2 What is a homonym?

3 Which novel by Stephen Crane won him immediate recognition when it was published?

4 What nationality was the artist Paul Klee?

5 What is the home of a fox called?

Team 2

1 Which country left the Commonwealth in 1972?

2 What is hyperbole?

3 Which 18th-century novelist wrote *Roderick Random*, *Peregrine Pickle* and *Humphry Clinker*?

4 What nationality was the artist Wassily Kandinsky?

5 What is the home of a beaver called?

Round 5 Individual questions for Team 1

Abbreviations

What does the abbreviation SPCK stand for?

Mythology

The God Anubis was represented by the Egyptians as having a man's body and the head of what?

Sport

How many hoops are used in a game of croquet?

News of the 1980s

In July 1984, lightning was blamed for a fire which badly damaged which famous British cathedral?

United Kingdom

Where is the head office of the Premium Savings Bonds?

Round 6

Team 2

1 Which American playwright achieved a start on Broadway with *Come Blow Your Horn*?
2 What does Toc H stand for?
3 In which year did the half crown cease to be legal tender?
4 Which animal is often known as Brock?
5 Name the character played by Jamie Farr in TV's *M.A.S.H.*

Team 1

1 Which playwright wrote the 1958 play *The Hostage*?
2 Who founded Toc H?
3 In which year did Great Britain get commercial TV?
4 What kind of creature is a red-bellied tamarin?
5 Name the shop assistant portrayed by Wendy Richard in *Are You Being Served*?

Round 7

Team 2

1 What night precedes May Day?
2 How many grains go into a scruple?
3 Who was originally known as Giovanni Bernardone?
4 In 1989, who was sentenced to a three-day prison term for slapping a policeman?
5 What is the correct heraldic name for the colour blue?

Team 1

1 When is Labour Day?
2 How many yards in a chain?
3 Which Basque Jesuit missionary was known as The Apostle of the Indies?
4 Which Sunday newspaper made its first appearance in September 1989?
5 What is the correct heraldic name for the colour black?

Round 8

Team 2

1 Which bank shares went on sale to the public for the first time in October 1986?
2 Who played the original *Liver Birds*?
3 What is the meaning of the phrase 'Caviare to the General'?
4 Which English composer, in 1923, wrote a piece for speaker and chamber orchestra called *Façade*?
5 What replaced the Royal Army Service Corps in 1965?

Team 1

1 During the 1980s, which British industry claimed 'We're getting there' in an advertising slogan?
2 Which comedian was known for his 'odd odes'?
3 What was meant by the saying, 'He was with the colours'?
4 Which Norwegian composer wrote the incidental music for Ibsen's drama, *Peer Gynt*?
5 Which branch of the British Army is known as The Gunners?

Round 9

Team 2

1 What is the maximum number of overs each side is allowed to bowl in a Benson & Hedges Cup match?

2 What type of aircraft did Spain's Juan de la Cierva invent?

3 The lek is the currency of which country?

4 Which sport is known in France as 'Le jeu de paume'?

5 Which American tennis player was nicknamed 'Supermac'?

Team 1

1 How many counties contest the County Championship in cricket, from 1992?

2 What nickname was given to the first Soviet supersonic airliner?

3 The baht is the currency of which country?

4 Which sport does the PRCA represent?

5 Who was the jockey featured in the film *Champions*?

Round 10 Individual questions for Team 2

Abbreviations

What does FRSL stand for?

Mythology

In Greek mythology, King Minos of Crete demanded a payment every nine years. What form did this take?

Sport

Which two players are allowed to score in a game of netball?

News of the 1980s

Who won the Greenwich by-election for the SDP in February 1987?

United Kingdom

Which city lies at the mouth of the river Lagan?

Drinks round

Team 1

1 Into which sea does the Danube flow?
2 Which member of Cream was a Yardbird?
3 Who was responsible for nationalising the Suez Canal?
4 Whose three sons were Shem, Ham and Japheth?
5 Which orange liqueur is based on fine cognac?
6 Which bird is the national symbol of France?
7 Which National Park did Yogi Bear call home?
8 Which volcano buried the city of Pompeii in 79CE?
9 Who painted *The Garden of Earthly Delights*?
10 In which sport are the terms raiders, antis and cant used?

Team 2

1 Of which ocean is the Sargasso Sea part?
2 Who was the lead singer with The Who?
3 Of which country was the House of Hapsburg the ruling dynasty?
4 To which town does *A Town Like Alice* refer?
5 What flavour is the liqueur Framboise?
6 The Hibiscus is the state flower of which American state?
7 Which Disney cartoon saw two animals eating spaghetti at Tony's Restaurant?
8 Who was Roman Procurator of Judea from 26CE to 36CE?
9 What does the painting *The Battle of Gettysburg* claim to be?
10 What mechanical system for marksmen did George Ligowsky invent in 1880?

Reserve questions

1 Which was the world's largest airline in the 1980s?
2 Who had a hit with 'I'm the Urban Spaceman'?
3 Who wrote the *Overture Roman Carnival*?

Pub League Quiz 39

The individual questions are in Rounds 5 and 10 and are on television, sport, plants, religion and words.

Round 1

Team 1

1 What was the name of the first ship to be propelled by steam turbines?
2 Which author created the detective Sergeant Cluff?
3 On TV, in which fictional town was *Crown Court* set?
4 In which country is the volcano Cotopaxi?
5 Who has won both the Nobel Peace Prize and the Nobel Prize for Chemistry?

Team 2

1 What was the name of the first vessel designed by Nansen to winter in the polar ice?
2 Which author created the detective Van der Valk?
3 In which town is *The Little House on the Prairie* set?
4 In which country is the mountain Nanda Devi?
5 A new Nobel Prize was introduced in 1969; what discipline does it cover?

Round 2

Team 1

1 Who first sang about a 'Lady in Red'?
2 Which writer created *Mary Poppins*?
3 What is the monetary unit of Sierra Leone?
4 Which tennis champion of the 1920s and '30s was nicknamed 'Big Bill'?
5 Which UK entrant sang 'Jack-In-A-Box' in the Eurovision Song Contest?

Team 2

1 Who sang the theme song to the movie *Fame*?
2 Who created Mowgli?
3 What s the monetary unit of Kuwait?
4 Which Boxer was nicknamed 'The Sepia Slayer?
5 Who had his first hit album with *The 12-Year-Old Genius*?

Round 3

Team 1

1 Which Florentine statesman wrote *The Prince*?
2 Chaim Weizmann was the President of which country?
3 Who played *Robin Hood* in the first British TV series?
4 Who was the first Democrat President of the USA?
5 In which sport would you find coppers, corners and landlords?

Team 2

1 Which British statesman wrote *Coningsby*?
2 Marshal Pilsudski was head of state of which country?
3 In which film did Humphrey Bogart play a vampire?
4 Which American President was assassinated in 1901?
5 In which sport is the Iroquois Cup awarded?

Round 4

Team 1

1 Which city is graced by Michelangelo's 'David'?

2 Which fictional mad medical man grafted animals and people together to make man-beasts?
3 What is the correct chemical name for saltpetre?
4 Which member of the Royal Family took part in the radio programme *The Archers*?
5 Which actor had a British hit in 1971 with 'The Way You Look Tonight'?

Team 2

1 Name the Florentine sculptor and goldsmith whose auto-biography was not published until more than 150 years after his death.

2 Which fictional medical man took his family to Siberia during the Russian revolution?
3 What is the correct chemical name for Epsom salts?
4 Which member of the Royal Family opened the new Falkland Island's airport in 1985?
5 Which actor had a hit in 1968 with 'MacArthur Park'?

Round 5 Individual questions for Team 1

Television

Which TV series contained the line, 'I am not a number; I am a free man'?

Sport

What sporting body was founded at the Star & Garter Coffee House in Pall Mall in 1750?

Plants

What is the common name for the digitalis plant?

Religion

In which religion do Vishnu and Siva play a major role?

Words

What is dendrochronology?

Round 6

Team 2

1 What was the 1984 sequel to *2001: A Space Odyssey*?
2 Which town in South Australia became the home of the Long Range Weapons Establishment in 1946?
3 Who wrote plays called *The Circle* and *The Constant Wife*?
4 Who wrote *The Old Wives' Tale*?
5 Which actor starred in both the stage and film productions of *Cabaret*?

Team 1

1 Which film released in 1986 was the sequel to *Romancing the Stone*?
2 What large flat area of Australia has a name that comes from the Latin for 'no tree'?
3 Who wrote the play in blank verse, *Tamburlaine the Great*?
4 Who wrote *Children of The New Forest*?
5 Which actress starred with Woody Allen in both the stage and film versions of *Play It Again, Sam*?

Round 7

Team 2

1 Which Italian landmark has nearly 300 steps?
2 From which ballet does 'The Dying Swan' come?
3 What year did Concorde make its first scheduled supersonic flight?
4 Which artist painted *Mrs Pelham Feeding Chickens*?
5 What does 'aardvark' mean in English?

Team 1

1 Which French palace has a famous Hall of Mirrors?
2 What was unusual about Stravinsky's *Circus Polka* ballet?
3 What year did man first walk on the moon?
4 Which Venetian artist is noted for his paintings of London?
5 What does *pterodactyl* mean in English?

Round 8

Team 2

1 How many dice are used in poker dice?
2 Which African country takes its name from the lion?
3 Which 1963 film told the story of the defence of Rorke's Drift?
4 From which plant family does natural vanilla flavouring come?
5 After which US President is New Hampshire's highest mountain named?

Team 1

1 To what number do the opposite sides of a die always add up?
2 Which is the largest town in Alaska?
3 Who starred opposite Jane Fonda in the film *Klute*?
4 What kind of fruit is a kumquat?
5 On which peak did Noah's Ark come to rest?

Round 9

Team 2

1 Which TV series featured novice trail boss Rowdy Yates?
2 Where, in Britain, are the Elgin Marbles?
3 Who wrote *No Highway*?
4 What does T.T.D. mean on a doctor's prescription?
5 What is the positive square root of 676?

Team 1

1 Who played the title role in TV's *Bronco*?
2 Who was the Flanders Mare?
3 Who wrote *Waverley*?
4 What does ECG stand for?
5 What is the positive square root of 529?

Round 10 Individual questions for Team 2

Television
What were the forenames of *The Likely Lads*?
Sport
In which year did Aldaniti win the Grand National?
Plants
Which plant was featured on the reverse side of the three-penny piece minted between 1937 and 1967?
Religion
What is St Patrick said to have used to explain the Trinity?
Words
What would a Scotsman do with a spurtle?

Just for fun

Which British birds lay only a single egg during the nesting season?
Just two: the fulmar and the guillemot. The fulmar is a grey-white seabird of the petrel family that is found in the extreme northerly islands of Scotland. The guillemot is much more common and nests in cliffs all around the coasts of Britain. It is one of the auk group of duck-like birds.

Drinks round

Team 1

1 Where in Britain was King Alfred buried?
2 Who murdered Thomas à Becket?
3 For his part in which film did Bob Hoskins won Best Actor award at the 1986 Cannes Film Festival?
4 In 1866, a decoration was instituted for gallantry in saving life at sea or on land. What is it called?
5 Where in the human body would you find the metatarsals?
6 How much of the Earth's surface is covered with water?
7 What is the name of the PM in *Yes Prime Minister*?
8 Where is the annual dog sled championship race held?
9 By what name is Bernadette Soubirous now known?
10 In which country would you find the Gersoppa Falls?

Team 2

1 Where in Britain would you find Bolton Abbey?
2 Who murdered William the Silent, Prince of Orange?
3 Which 1985 film was all about the kidnapping of a pig?
4 Which decoration, intended for civilians and instituted in 1940, is worn before all others except the VC?
5 Where in the body would you find the carpals?
6 Which is the smallest of the Earth's oceans?
7 Whom did Michael Parkinson replace as host of *Give Us A Clue*?
8 What did Dr Vivian Fuchs achieve in 99 days in 1957/58?
9 What name did the ballerina Lilian Alicia Marks adopt?
10 In which country would you find the Staubbach Falls?

Reserve questions

1 Who is the patron saint of Russia?
2 To which saint is Coventry Cathedral dedicated?
3 Which Shipping Forecast lies immediately to the south of Fisher?

Pub League Quiz 40

The individual questions are in Rounds 5 and 10 and are on Films, which year?, scandal, capitals and science.

Round 1

Team 1

1 In which Alpine resort did France's Jean-Claude Killy win three Olympic golds in 1968?
2 Which scientific instrument did Hans and Zacharias Janssen invent in 1590?
3 Which Gilbert and Sullivan operetta has the subtitle *The Peer and the Peri*?
4 Which European border reopened in February 1985 after 16 years?
5 Which hero said, 'England expects every man will do his duty'?

Team 2

1 In which French resort were the first World Nordic Ski Championships held, in 1924?
2 Which plastic material did John Wesley Hyatt develop in 1870?
3 Which Gilbert and Sullivan operetta has the subtitle *The King of Barataria*?
4 In January 1986, George Younger succeeded Michael Heseltine in which Cabinet post?
5 Who galloped towards Lexington in April 1755 to warn that the British were coming?

Round 2

Team 1

1 In the TV series, where did Dr Finlay live?
2 Where is the Gobi Desert?
3 Which sport would you expect to see in a velodrome?
4 What is 88 in Roman numerals?
5 What did Mencken describe as, 'The theory that common people know what they want, and deserve to get it good and hard'?

Team 2

1 In which city did TV's Mike Hammer work?
2 On which side of the Andes does the Atacama Desert lie?
3 From which sport does the phrase 'to win hands down' come?
4 In Roman numerals, what is MMM minus MD?
5 What did Mencken describe as, 'The ransom that the happy pay to the devil'?

Round 3

Team 1

1 Which Italian cruise ship was hijacked by a PLO group in 1985?
2 Which popular musician played Alias in the film, *Pat Garrett and Billy the Kid*?
3 Who created the cartoon character Blondie?
4 Which country's national sport is hurling?
5 Who was Donalbain's father in *Macbeth*?

Team 2

1 Which Greenpeace campaign ship was sunk in Auckland in 1985?
2 Whose first hit single was 'Mandy' in 1974?
3 Which comic strip superhero did C. C. Beck create?
4 Which country dominated Olympic hockey from 1928 until 1960?
5 Who agreed to marry Benedick at the end of *Much Ado About Nothing*?

Round 4

Team 1

1 Which TV comedy series takes place in a London barber's shop?
2 Which palace was founded on the site of King James' mulberry orchard?
3 In which European country is the famous Jungfraujoch railway station?
4 Which British woman tennis star was five times runner-up in the World Table Tennis Championships?
5 In which year did the old sixpenny coin cease to be legal tender in Britain?

Team 2

1 Who played Colonel Hall in TV's *Bilko*?
2 Where was the original site of Marble Arch?
3 Which European country has a fast train known by the initials TGV?
4 Who won the 1991 New York Women's Marathon?
5 The 900th Anniversary of which book was celebrated in 1986?

Round 5 Individual questions for Team 1

Films
In which musical film will you hear the song 'Always true to you in my fashion'?
Which year?
In which year did Fidel Castro come to power in Cuba?
Scandal
Which English king illegally married Mrs Fitzherbert?
Capitals
What is the Capital of Malta?
Science
What do you call the positive-charged particle that is a constituent of the nucleus of an atom?

Round 6

Team 2

1 Which character did Mrs Danny DeVito play in TV's *Cheers*?
2 Which Stone provided the key to translating Egyptian hieroglyphics?
3 Which country declared war on the Allies in June 1940 and Germany in October 1943?
4 Which nation won football's World Cup in 1982?
5 In 1984, which Indian city was the scene of the chemical works tragedy in which thousands died?

Team 1

1 What is Mrs DeVito's stage name?
2 Which fossil remains, found in 1908, were shown to be a forgery in 1955?
3 Who betrayed Norway to the Nazis in the Second World War?
4 Who were the English league football Champions 1984/5 and 1986/7?
5 In which year was the first 'Hands across Britain' demonstration against unemployment?

Round 7

Team 2

1 What is the meaning of the cooking term 'farci'?
2 What is the name of George Knightley's home in Jane Austin's novel *Emma*?
3 Which actress played Sid James' wife in TV's *Bless This House*?
4 Of which country was Olof Palme Prime Minister?
5 Which Beaufort number relates to 'Moderate breeze'?

Team 1

1 From which animal does prosciutto come?
2 In which novel did Emile Zola depict life in a French mining community?
3 Who hosted The *$64,000 Question* on British TV?
4 Of which country was Adolphe Thiers the President?
5 Which Beaufort number relates to 'Calm'?

Round 8

Team 2

1 Of which sport has Izaak Walton been called the father?
2 What colour is the gem stone amethyst?
3 Who was Mozart's great rival in *Amadeus*?
4 What is 19 squared?
5 Name Frankie Goes To Hollywood's 1984 album.

Team 1

1 For which sport is the *Wisden Annual* published?
2 What colour is the gemstone garnet?
3 Who wrote *Schindler's Ark*?
4 What is the positive square root of 484?
5 Name Helen Reddy's 1972 hit album.

Round 9

Team 2

1 In what year did Greece join the EEC, France abolish capital punishment and the Newcastle metro open?

2 Which American artist painted 'The Biglen Brothers Racing'?

3 Who became British Shadow Foreign Secretary in July 1987?

4 Which composer described his *The Dream of Gerontius* as 'The best of me'?

5 Who was Starsky and Hutch's informant?

Team 1

1 In which year did Donald Campbell die, the Torrey Canyon disaster take place and China explode its first H-bomb?

2 Which female American Impressionist artist was famous for her mother and child paintings?

3 Who became Britain's Secretary of State for Energy in June 1987?

4 What was Puccini's first opera?

5 Terry Gilliam provided the animation for which TV comedy team?

Round 10 Individual questions for Team 2

Films

What is the name of the 1986 British musical based on teenagers' lives in the 1950s?

Which year?

In which year did Great Britain get its first Labour Government?

Scandal

In the 1988 film, *Scandal*, which real-life person was played by Bridget Fonda?

Capitals

What is the capital of Sri Lanka?

Science

What is the coil of an electric motor or dynamo called?

Drinks round

Team 1

1 What sport contests the Leonard Trophy?
2 Where did the League of Nations establish its Permanent Court of International Justice?
3 Who was the Nymph who changed into a laurel bush?
4 In musical terms what does *lento* mean?
5 On which river does the town of Plock stand?
6 In nautical terms, what is a grapnel?
7 For whose household did Mr Hudson and Mrs Bridges work?
8 Which King of England was called the Hammer of the Scots?
9 Where was the Derby run during the Second World War?
10 In which year did it become compulsory in Britain to wear front seat belts in cars?

Team 2

1 What unusual thing happened in the 1877 Boat Race?
2 Which international organisation was established in Addis Ababa in 1963?
3 Who was King of Sparta and husband of Helen of Troy?
4 In musical terms what does *presto* mean?
5 On which river is Yonkers?
6 In nautical terms, what is a hawser?
7 For which school was Mr Potter the caretaker?
8 Which King of England had the nickname 'Longshanks'?
9 The Eclipse Stakes is normally run where?
10 In which year was Prince Henry of Wales born?

Reserve questions

1 Who invented the radio valve in 1904?
2 Which Second World War bomber was nicknamed 'the Wimpey'?
3 To which group of plants does the Christmas Rose belong?

Pub League Quiz 41

The individual questions are in Rounds 5 and 10 and are on general knowledge, counties, space travel, British Prime Ministers and abbreviations.

Round 1

Team 1

1 Who wrote the music for the ballet *Coppelia*?
2 Who became Archbishop of York in 1956 and Archbishop of Canterbury in 1961?
3 What are dulse and carrageen?
4 Who wrote *Auf Wiedersehen Pet*?

5 Who was wooed by Freddy Eynsford Hill in *Pygmalion*?

Team 2

1 Who composed the orchestral suite *Karelia*?
2 What was the name of the black militant nationalist who was shot dead in New York City in 1965?
3 What is pumpernickel?
4 What was unusual about Barry's best man in *Auf Wiedersehen Pet*?
5 How was N. S. Norway better known?

Round 2

Team 1

1 In sporting terms, what is a 'flying mare'?
2 Where are the Drakensberg Mountains?
3 Which actress starred opposite Humphrey Bogart in *The Maltese Falcon*?
4 Who was the first Labour Premier to form a government?

5 Which British bird builds the smallest nest?

Team 2

1 What name is given to the playing objects in curling?
2 Where are the Eastern and Western Ghats?
3 Which actress starred opposite Charlie Chaplin in *Limelight*?
4 Who was the Aztec Emperor when the Spanish invaded Mexico?
5 Which is the largest British amphibian?

Round 3

Team 1

1 What was the first of Paul Simon's ways to leave your lover?

2 Which successful London Lord Mayor, entrepreneur and philanthropist married Alice Fitzwarren?

3 In J. M. Barrie's play, who was the resourceful butler to Lord Loam?

4 What is the name of Rene's wife in 'Allo 'Allo?

5 With which type of whisky is a mint julep made?

Team 2

1 Who was born John Henry Deutschendorf, Jr, and married Annie Martell?

2 Whose trial, on a charge of libelling Oscar Wilde, was to lead to Wilde going to prison himself?

3 Who married Edgar Linton in *Wuthering Heights*?

4 To whom was Tom married in *The Good Life*?

5 What are the two alcoholic ingredients of a Sidecar cocktail?

Round 4

Team 1

1 Of which secret society did Nathan B. Forrest become the first leader in 1866?

2 For which country did Maharajah Ranjitsinhji play Test Cricket?

3 In which Hitchcock film did James Stewart play a detective with a fear of heights?

4 What would you get if you mixed saltpetre, charcoal and sulphur?

5 What colour is a wild canary?

Team 2

1 What was the nickname given to the special force of police deployed in Ireland in 1920?

2 Name the Canadian variation of lacrosse that has six players in a team.

3 In *What Ever Happened to Baby Jane?*, who was served a rat for lunch by Bette Davis?

4 Which metal is obtained from the ore cinnabar?

5 What does a bird use to grind its food?

Round 5   Individual questions for Team 1

General knowledge

At sea, if you took the first dog watch, what time would you start?

Counties

Of which English county is Bristol the administrative headquarters?

Space travel

What was the name of the space station launched by the Americans on 25 May 1973?

British Prime Ministers

To which political party did Prime Minister Herbert Asquith belong?

Abbreviations

In shipping, what does P&O stand for?

Round 6
Team 2

1 What is dredging in culinary terms?

2 Who had a Christmas hit in 1969 with 'Two little Boys'?

3 Which historic locomotive was featured in a 1927 Buster Keaton film?

4 Which Verdi opera contains 'The Chorus of The Hebrew Slaves' ('Va Pensiero')?

5 Who co-hosted *Strictly Come Dancing* with Bruce Forsyth?

Team 1

1 Within 4° Celsius, at what temperature does the pasteurisation of milk take place?

2 Who had a Christmas hit in 1976 with 'When a Child is Born'?

3 Which opera singer had a private waiting room at Craig-y-Nos railway station?

4 Which Saint Saens opera is set in Palestine?

5 Name the character who was leader of TV's *Fairly Secret Army*.

Round 7
Team 2

1 In bowls, what does Jack high mean?

2 If an American recipe tells you to broil a dish, how should you cook it?

3 Who was the Flag Captain of HMS *Victory* at Trafalgar?

4 Who was killed in a plane crash in 1967, along with most of his backing group the Bar-Kays?

5 In which year did Amy Johnson make her solo flight from London to Australia?

Team 1

1 In which sport do you find a tin, a service box and a telltale?

2 In corned beef, what does corned mean?

3 Who was Sir John Gielgud's famous actress great-aunt?

4 Which member of the Byrds was killed by a truck in 1973?

5 In which year did Sheila Scott become the First British woman to fly solo around the world?

Round 8
Team 2

1 Which bumbling TV detective does Peter Falk play?

2 Where in South America is Welsh spoken?

3 What was Paul Muni a *Fugitive* from, in the 1932 film?

4 Which creature has the largest eyes?

5 What or who shrieked and squeaked in 50 different sharps and flats?

Team 1

1 Which TV Western centred on the Cartwright family?

2 In which city would you find a store called GUM?

3 What was the name of *Goldfinger's* bodyguard in the film?

4 Which small bird can fly backwards?

5 Who lived in a forest and tried to trap a Heffalump?

Round 9

Team 2

1 Who succeeded Georges Pompidou as French President?
2 How many dancers perform 'The dance of the Cygnets' in the ballet, *Swan Lake*?
3 Which British building celebrated its 900th anniversary in 1965?
4 In which TV soap opera did Ryan O'Neal and Mia Farrow star?
5 Which Stravinsky ballet caused a riot at its first performance in 1913?

Team 1

1 Who was the fourth man in the Burgess, Maclean, Philby scandal?
2 Which Hungarian-born composer and pianist took holy orders in 1865?
3 What was introduced in Britain on 1 April 1973?
4 Which TV series was a saga about the Seaton family in the north-east during the Depression?
5 As what did Gustav Hoist describe Saturn?

Round 10   Individual questions for Team 2

General knowledge

Who told Ptolemy I that there was no royal road to geometry?

Counties

What is the smallest English county?

Space travel

Yuri Gagarin was the first man in space. What was his spacecraft called?

British Prime Ministers

Whom did John Bellingham assassinate in 1812?

Abbreviations

What does FRAM stand for?

Drinks round

Team 1

1 Which is the only South American country with both Pacific and Caribbean coastlines?

2 Who won the 2006 soccer World Cup?

3 Whose quater-centenary was celebrated in Britain on 23 April 1964?

4 'The Fly' was a 1991 hit for which group?

5 In which film did Jack Nicholson play the caretaker of *The Overlook Hotel*?

6 What was the name of 'She Who Must Be Obeyed' in Rider Haggard's book *She*?

7 What is the traditional Thanksgiving dessert in the USA?

8 What is the official language of Andorra?

9 The Royal Engineers are known as Sappers. What did to sap originally mean?

10 What was the name of the motel in *Psycho*?

Team 2

1 What is the name of the region of the southern oceans where strong prevailing westerlies blow?

2 Which British ice dancers won the World, Olympic and European titles in 1984?

3 Which British city was affected by a typhoid outbreak in May 1964?

4 'Everything I do' was top of the charts in 1991 for whom?

5 In which *Dirty Harry* film did Tyne Daly co-star with Clint Eastwood?

6 Which legal character refers to his wife as 'She Who Must Be Obeyed'?

7 Which cake is named after a legendary girl from Bath?

8 What is the actual translation of terracotta?

9 Roman gladiators took their name from the gladius. What type of weapon was a gladius?

10 What was Elvis Presley's first film called?

Reserve questions

1 Which tree is sacred to the Druids?

2 What does Koh-i-noor, the name given to the famous diamond, mean?

3 What is the name of Postman Pat's black and white cat?

Pub League Quiz 42

The individual questions are in Rounds 5 and 10 and are on the Bible, words, literature, history and sport.

Round 1

Team 1

1 Who had a hit in 1967 with 'This is my Song'?
2 In which poem by Robert Browning would you find the lines 'God's in his heaven – All's right with the world'?
3 In which country would you find the river Vistula?
4 George Peppard played which insurance investigator on TV?
5 The oldest known living tree was named after which Biblical character?

Team 2

1 Who had a hit in 1969 with 'In the Year 2525'?
2 In which poem by W. H. Davies would you find the lines 'What is this life if full of care'?
3 In which country would you find the Clutha river?
4 Which actor played private eye Frank Cannon on TV?
5 Which Cherokee Indian leader gave his name to a tree?

Round 2

Team 1

1 Which ancient city had the famous Lion Gate?
2 Who was Old Bald Peg?
3 Which country's air force was destroyed on the ground in June 1967?
4 Which song from the film *Lovers and Other Strangers* was awarded an Oscar in 1970?
5 On which island country would you find Adam's Peak?

Team 2

1 Which was the oldest of the Greek orders of architecture?
2 What was Sandra Primo's sport?
3 Who challenged President Truman's conduct of the Korean War and was fired for it?
4 Which song from the film *Thank God it's Friday* was awarded an Oscar in 1978?
5 In which country is Mount Hekla an active volcano?

Round 3

Team 1

1 How wide is the goal in polo?

2 In a church or cathedral, where would you find a reredos?

3 What was the remarkable venue for the meeting of Napoleon and the Czar of Russia in Tilsit, July 1807?

4 In which city is the Jacques Cartier Bridge, opened in 1930?

5 'The Raft of Medusa' and 'The Epsom Derby' are among the works of which artist?

Team 2

1 In baseball, what is a switch hitter?

2 In which country of the world did the Coptic Church originate?

3 On which two islands was Napoleon imprisoned in 1814 and 1815 respectively?

4 Where are the Aleutian Islands?

5 'The Murdered Marat in his Bath' and 'The Coronation of Napoleon' are among the works of which artist?

Round 4

Team 1

1 Which American state's song is 'Yankee Doodle Dandy'?

2 Which opera by Benjamin Britten includes characters known as Swallow, Hobson and Auntie?

3 In a university building, what is the SCR?

4 What type of animal is a markhor?

5 Which international TV quiz was hosted by Henry Kelly?

Team 2

1 Which American state's song is 'Home on the Range'?

2 Name the cellist and conductor who founded the Barcelona Orchestra.

3 With reference to records, what did EP mean?

4 What type of animal is a papillon?

5 In which TV competition are contestants given the option to 'phone a friend'?

Round 5   Individual questions for Team 1

The Bible

Which Old Testament book follows Psalms?

Words

Balm, dill and sorrel are all what?

Literature

Whose first novel was *This Sporting Life*?

History

Who was Mary Queen of Scots' first husband?

Sport

Name the youngest-ever World Heavyweight Champion.

Round 6
Team 2

1 On which Canadian river is London, Ontario?
2 In the 1960s, who was the London osteopath who committed suicide at the height of the Christine Keeler affair?
3 Which pop group was originally called High Numbers?

4 Who played the female lead in the 1963 film *The Birds*?
5 In the *Forsyte Saga*, who was Irene's second husband?

Team 2

1 Cairo and Memphis are on which American river?
2 In the 1960s, whose Report had a far-reaching effect on British travel?

3 Which heavy metal group starred in the film *The Song Remains the Same*?
4 Who were the stars of the 1937 film *Lost Horizon*?
5 Who was *The Merchant of Venice*?

Round 7
Team 2

1 In which country is Kvass a traditional drink?
2 Which English city was called Luguvalium by the Romans?
3 What was the moderate socialist party in Russia whose name meant Minority Members and that was suppressed in 1922?
4 What is the main town on the Isle of Sheppey?

5 In which year did the Boston Tea Party take place?

Team 1

1 In which country is the Barossa Valley Vineyard?
2 Which English city was called Durovernum by the Romans?
3 Of which tribe was Boadicea the Queen?

4 Which thoroughfare on Manhattan Island is the centre of New York advertising?
5 In which year did RMS *Queen Elizabeth* make her first commercial voyage?

Round 8
Team 2

1 Which oratorio by Elgar takes a poem by Cardinal Newman as its text?
2 In the 1960s, in which country was Ben Bella overthrown?
3 What does it mean when a drink is served frappé?
4 In which year were the first Winter Olympic Games held?
5 In what sport was Larry Mahan All Round Champion from 1966 to 1970, and again in 1973?

Team 1

1 Which nickname links a Beethoven piano concerto and a Strauss waltz?
2 In the 1960s, what way of detection was first used by Scotland Yard?
3 What do Americans call jam?
4 On which Saint's Day was the Battle of Agincourt fought?
5 Who was Britain's lead-off man in Tokyo in 1991 when they won the 4 x 400m relay world title?

Round 9
Team 2

1 In which language is *Stern* magazine published?
2 Of what was Edward Kennedy convicted in the Chappaquiddick incident?
3 Which island group used to be called the Spice Islands?
4 Who was nicknamed 'the Liberator'?
5 What instrument did Franz Liszt play?

Team 1

1 Which country's alphabet has the most letters?
2 Who is the only American President to have been impeached?
3 Which ancient city, abandoned in 1434, was the capital of the Khmer Empire?
4 Who was nicknamed 'K of K'?
5 What instrument did Sarasate play?

Round 10   Individual questions for Team 2
The Bible
Which city in Turkey was the birth place of St Paul?
Words
If you were studying coleopteran, what would you be examining?
Literature
Who won the Booker Prize in 1981 for *Midnight's Children*?
History
In Mediaeval times there were three kinds of guild. Crafts and religious were two; what was the third?
Sport
Who won the Amateur Grand Slam of Tennis in 1962 and the Open Grand Slam in 1969?

Drinks round

Team 1

1 In the Second World War, what were paravanes used for?
2 Who was the first leader and vocalist of the Crickets?
3 Name one of Chekhov's *Three Sisters*.
4 At which American university were four students shot dead by National Guardsmen in May 1970?
5 By what name is the island group formerly called the New Hebrides now known?
6 Which international Rugby Union side is nicknamed 'The Pumas'?
7 What was the surname of the TV Western hero *Cheyenne*?
8 Of which opera is Captain Macheath the hero?
9 Name the British airship which crashed in France on its first flight to India killing 48 people.
10 Which country country is indicated by the international car registration letters RA?

Team 2

1 What name is given to the knife of the Gurkha soldiers?
2 Who first sang about a dedicated follower of fashion?
3 In *Vanity Fair*, who marries Rawdon Crawley?
4 In the late 1970s, the country house of Lord Rosebery was sold. What was it called?
5 Which West Indian island is occupied by the Dominican Republic and Haiti?
6 Which international Rugby Union side is nicknamed 'The Eagles'?
7 In which 1950s TV series did Broderick Crawford say, 'Ten Four'?
8 In which Puccini opera is the hero shot, the villain stabbed and the heroine commits suicide?
9 Who designed the R100 airship?
10 For which country is T the international car registration letter?

Reserve questions

1 What is Nine Men's Morris?
2 According to legend, which Greek playwright died after being hit on the head by a tortoise dropped by an eagle?
3 Which animal's fur is called nutria?

Pub League Quiz 43

The individual questions are in Rounds 5 and 10 and are on sport, French phrases, opera, literature and which year?

Round 1

Team 1

1 What is the width of a hockey goal?
2 What is a Gloucester Old Spot?
3 St Helena was converted to Christianity by her son. Who was he?
4 From which book was the musical *Half a Sixpence* adapted?
5 Which is the largest island of the West Indies?

Team 2

1 What is the diameter of a basketball ring?
2 What is a scaup?
3 Who is the patron saint of cripples and lepers?
4 From which book was the musical *Hello Dolly* adapted?
5 Which is the largest of the Mediterranean islands?

Round 2

Team 1

1 What is the product of the rattan palm used in furniture?
2 Who played Grasshopper in TV's *Kung Fu*?
3 Who was Secretary General of the UN during the Cuban Missile Crisis?
4 What do Americans call the game of draughts?
5 How many masts does a sloop have?

Team 2

1 Is the bathroom loofah animal, vegetable or mineral?
2 Who starred opposite Victoria Tennant in the TV epic *The Winds of War*?
3 Who was the first Secretary General of the UN?
4 In Monopoly, what is the colour of Bond Street?
5 What colour light is displayed on the starboard side of a ship?

Round 3

Team 1

1 What do Glastonbury, ladderback and fauteuil have in common?
2 By what other name is the constellation Pyxis known?
3 Which well-known tune from Bach's Suite No. 3 in D was transcribed for the lowest string on the violin?
4 Which Italian sauce is made with basil, garlic oil and pine kernels?
5 In which TV play by Alan Bennett did Coral Browne play herself?

Team 2

1 What do St Gotthard, Lotschberg, Cascade and Moffat have in common?
2 In which constellation is the Pole Star?
3 What is the popular name of Chopin's Prelude No. 15 in D Flat, Opus 28?
4 Borsch is a soup from Russian and Poland. From what it is made?
5 Who was the first presenter of *Monitor*, who went on to become Director-General of the BBC?

Round 4

Team 1

1 What significance did the number 49 have for James Knox Polk?
2 What name is given to the smallest of the mosses?
3 In which 18th-century book do we first meet the Yahoos?
4 How is the American Tennis player Hazel Hotchkiss now remembered?
5 In the Old Testament, to whom did Esau sell his birthright?

Team 2

1 On what kind of plane was Lyndon Johnson sworn in?
2 What is the largest agricultural crop by weight of the USA?
3 Which Hemingway novel is set in the Spanish Civil War?
4 Which horse racing institution was founded in 1916 by Colonel Hall-Walker, later Lord Wavertree?
5 In which village did Jesus turn water into wine?

Round 5   Individual questions for Team 1

Sport
In cricket, they are called extras in Britain, but what do the Australians call them?
French phrases
What does *tout de suite* mean?
Opera
Which Italian composer wrote the opera *Turandot*?
Literature
Who wrote *Morte d'Arthur*, printed by Caxton in 1485?
Which year?
In which year did Richard Nixon resign as President of the USA?

Round 6

Team 2

1 Which American dancer died when her scarf caught in the rear wheel of a friend's car in Nice in 1927?
2 Which architect was engaged by James I to design scenery for masques and plays?
3 Which Lloyd Webber show followed *Jesus Christ Superstar*?
4 To the nearest degree, what is absolute zero in the Celsius scale?
5 Who wrote the words of 'Jerusalem'?

Team 1

1 Which British author died of typhoid in Paris in 1931, after drinking the local water to show that it was safe?
2 Who designed the Brighton Pavilion?
3 Which 1971 musical saw David Essex as Jesus Christ?
4 What unit of heat will raise the temperature of 1 gram of water by one degree Celsius?
5 Who wrote the words of 'Auld Lang Syne'?

Round 7

Team 2

1 What is the date of 12th Night?
2 In which country is Tobruk, the scene of heavy fighting during the Second World War?
3 In 1963, which American island prison closed?
4 In which 1959 film did Peter Sellers play a militant shop steward?
5 Who wrote the play *The Second Mrs Tanqueray*?

Team 1

1 What is the date of St David's Day?
2 In which country was Lidice, the village destroyed by Nazis in 1942?
3 What was banned from British TV screens in August 1965?
4 In which 1938 Hitchcock film does Miss Froy write her name on a steamed-up train window?
5 Who wrote the play *An Inspector Calls*?

Round 8

Team 2

1 Where in Britain would you find the Wallace Monument?

2 Who composed *The Walk to the Paradise Garden*?
3 For which country is N the civil aircraft marking?
4 In which TV series did Paul Shane play a family butler?

5 Of which present day country was Gnaeus Julius Agricola governor in the 1st Century CE?

Team 1

1 Where in Britain would you find the Monument marking where Prince Charles Edward raised his standard in August 1745?
2 Who composed *Clair de Lune*?

3 For which country is OO the civil aircraft marking?
4 In which TV series did Ian McShane play a shady antiques dealer?

5 Who was the first Christian Roman Emperor?

Round 9

Team 2

1 Which character in *The Jungle Book* film owed his voice to Phil Harris?
2 Which animal has earned the nickname 'Glutton'?

3 Which group had a hit in 1967 with 'Seven Rooms of Gloom'?
4 Who were the victims of the St Bartholomew's Day Massacre of 1572?
5 Who, in a poem, wrote 'Come friendly bombs and fall on Slough'?

Team 1

1 Who was Roger Rabbit's wife?

2 Which present-day animal is thought to be the closest living relative of the extinct quagga?

3 What was the Village People's only number one hit in Britain?
4 What name was given to the anti-Catholic riots of 1780?

5 Who wrote, in 1948, the novel *The Loved One*, which satirised Hollywood funeral customs?

Round 10   Individual questions for Team 2

Sport
In Equestrian events, what is the literal meaning of dressage?
French phrases
What does *entre nous* mean?
Opera
Which Italian composer wrote the opera *Aida*?
Literature
In *A Tale of Two Cities*, who kept a knitted tally of the names of her aristocratic victims?
Which year?
In which year was the Battle of Waterloo?

Drinks round

Team 1

1 In which European country did Ayatollah Khomeni spend his years of exile before returning to Iran?
2 As whom is Vincent Furnier better known in rock circles?
3 What was the name of the block of flats that collapsed in London in May 1968?
4 Which famous contralto worked as a switchboard operator before her rise to fame?
5 In 'The Ballard of John Axon', what kind of accident was commemorated?
6 Judge Jeffreys presided over the trials in 1685 following which rebellion?
7 What is the modern name for the ancient city of Edo?
8 Who in 1965 became the first foreigner in 45 years to win the American Open Golf title?
9 Who wrote *The Country Diary of an Edwardian Lady*?

10 In musical terms, what does *vivace* mean?

Team 2

1 Who was India's first Prime Minister?
2 Who sang about 'The green green grass of home'?
3 Where, in Wales, was the scene of the mining tip disaster of October 1966?
4 Which English tune is mentioned twice in *The Merry Wives of Windsor*?
5 Which London railway had the first driverless electric trains?
6 Who was the world's first qualified woman pilot?
7 Which island is linked to Brooklyn by the Verrazano Narrows Bridge in New York?
8 What is the only major golf tournament that Arnold Palmer never won?
9 Which renowned English author had been a Polish sailor in the French and British Merchant Service?
10 In musical terms, what does *andante* mean?

Reserve questions

1 Who was President Ford's Vice-President?
2 How many bits are there in a byte?
3 What is O_3?

Pub League Quiz 44

The individual questions are in Rounds 5 and 10 and are on television, mythology, literature, words and sport.

Round 1

Team 1

1 What does RADA stand for?
2 To what animal does the adjective vulpine refer?
3 The Rijks Museum in Amsterdam exhibits Rembrandt's painting 'The Night Watch'. What was revealed when it was cleaned?
4 In the Bible, who was the grandfather of Noah, and who, according to Genesis, lived to the age of 969 years?
5 John George Haigh was hanged for murder in 1949. What method did he use to get rid of the bodies?

Team 2

1 What does PLA stand for?
2 To which animals does the adjective porcine refer?
3 Sir John Suckling was a poet and wit at the Court of Charles I. What did he invent?
4 Simon, called Peter, with his brother were both disciples and followers of Christ. What was Simon's brother's name?
5 According to tradition, who murdered several wives in turn because they showed undue curiosity about a locked room?

Round 2

Team 1

1 Which musical was originally due to be entitled *Welcome to Britain*?
2 In Troy weight, how many grains make a pennyweight?
3 In 1431, which English king was crowned King of Paris?
4 Which baseball fielding position is behind home plate?
5 In which cathedral did French kings used to be crowned?

Team 2

1 Which Hitchcock film of 1934 did he remake in 1956?
2 What would a Dines tilting syphon measure?
3 In the play by Christopher Marlowe, which English king was murdered with a red-hot poker?
4 Which sport do you associate with the Talbot and the Waterloo Handicaps?
5 What is the city now called, that the Romans called Lutetia?

231

Round 3

Team 1

1 Which couple recorded 'At the Drop of a Hat'?
2 Who wrote the novel *The Bridges at Toko-Ri*?
3 In which country are the Swabian Alps?
4 To which flower family does the pimpernel belong?
5 Who wrote the music for *Les Sylphides*?

Team 2

1 Who has played Phil Archer on radio for over 40 years?
2 Who wrote *Kes*?
3 In which country are the Cantabrian Mountains?
4 Which plant is also called elephant's ears?
5 Who composed *Sinfonia Antarctica* in 1953?

Round 4

Team 1

1 What is the collective word for a group of larks?
2 In which English county is Goole?
3 Which poet was MP for Hull for 20 years, and wrote *To His Coy Mistress*?
4 What do you measure with a hygrometer?
5 With whom did Michael Jackson sing on the single 'State of Shock'?

Team 2

1 What is the collective term for a group of magpies?
2 In which English county is Guisborough?
3 Who wrote the poem *Rape of the Lock*?
4 What do you measure with a nolometer?
5 Who sang with Michael Jackson on 'The Girl is Mine'?

Round 5   Individual questions for Team 1

Television

On which programme did the Beatles make their first TV appearance in 1962?

Mythology

According to Greek mythology, what was Charon's employment?

Literature

What author created characters Gabriel Oak, Jude Fawley and Angel Clare?

Words

What was a tocsin?

Sport

Who resigned as manager of Liverpool F.C. in February 1991?

Round 6

Team 2

1 Which city does Haneda International airport serve?
2 Which actress was known as the 'Queen of the Swashbucklers'?
3 In Greek mythology, who is both sister and wife to Zeus?
4 Which European capital city stands on an Island called Zealand?
5 At what boxing weight was Archie Moore World Champion?

Team 1

1 Which American city does McCarran airport serve?
2 What was 'Skip' Homeier's given name?
3 Who was the Roman Goddess who equated with the Greek Hera?
4 Which European capital city's name means 'Danish town'?
5 At which two weights was Terry McGovern world boxing champion?

Round 7

Team 2

1 Which book of the Old Testament precedes Deuteronomy?
2 Peter the Hermit lived between 1050 and 1115. For what was he known historically?
3 Who is the patron saint of spinsters?
4 What sort of creature is a sandpiper?
5 Which great cricketer equalled the world record for the long jump?

Team 1

1 Which book of the New Testament precedes 1 Corinthians?
2 Who was the Italian secretary of Mary Queen of Scots, who was assassinated in front of the Queen in 1566?
3 Which Quarter Day was known as Pack-rag Day?
4 What sort of creature is a cayman?
5 Which great cricketer crossed the Alps accompanied by elephants?

Round 8

Team 2

1 Brontophobia is a fear of what?
2 Which river, 68 miles in length, is the longest wholly within Wales?
3 In which country is the Bay of Pigs?
4 What does a petrologist study?
5 Which soccer team plays home matches at Ewood Park?

Team 1

1 Clinophobia is a fear of what?
2 Stirling is sited on which river?
3 In which country is Monopoli?
4 What does a pedologist study?
5 Which soccer team plays home matches at Portman Road?

Round 9

Team 2

1 Which knight and actor provides the voice of Paddington Bear?

2 Which bird is called a mavis?

3 Whose first novel was *Hatter's Castle* and first play *Jupiter Laughs*?

4 From which roots is the Brazilian spirit Tiquira made?

5 Who, helped by his sons, made the famous violins of Cremona?

Team 1

1 Who played the headmaster of a failing school in the TV drama *Chalk*?

2 Every dog has his day, every man his – what?

3 Whose first novel was *The Loving Spirit* and autobiography *Growing Pains*?

4 From what is rum distilled?

5 Who wrote the *Hammerklavier Sonata*?

Round 10   Individual questions for Team 2

Television

The finals of which boardgame world championship were shown on TV in November 1991?

Mythology

In mythology, what was the only animal that could kill a basilisk?

Literature

Who wrote *Lucky Jim*?

Words

What is a pedagogue?

Sport

Who was the first woman in the 1989 London Marathon?

Drinks round

Team 1

1 In which state of the USA is the Liberty Bell to be seen?
2 In 1976, who was the author of *Ross: story of a shared life*?
3 Which Egyptian caused the Great Pyramid of Cheops to be built?
4 What bone has the medical name sternum?
5 Which County Cricket Club's badge depicts a daffodil?
6 Who had a hit with 'You Spin me Round' in 1985?
7 Who were Mrs Ford and Mrs Page?
8 Which country has sovereignty over Bouvet Island in the South Atlantic?
9 If you were anosmic, what would be wrong with you?
10 Which comedian presented *It's A Square World* on TV?

Team 2

1 Famed in the song, in which state of the USA is Tulsa?
2 Who was the author of *William McGonagal, The Truth At Last*?
3 Which Egyptian King was ousted in 1952?
4 How many fused bones form the coccyx?
5 Which county did Bob Willis play for?
6 Who had a hit with 'Goody Two Shoes'?
7 Which legendary king's sister was Morgan le Fay?
8 In which Bay are the Belcher Islands?
9 What does a funambulist do?
10 Who used to ask the questions in *The Sky's The Limit*?

Reserve questions

1 Which TV company's base was nicknamed 'Eggcup Towers'?
2 Name the Penlee lifeboat lost with all hands just before Christmas 1981.
3 Who wrote the six *Sun Quartets*, so called from the first publisher's trade mark?

Pub League Quiz 45

The individual questions are in Rounds 5 and 10 and are on quotations, plants, poetry, ships and the sea, and television.

Round 1

Team 1

1 Against which King did Hereward the Wake rebel?

2 What sort of creature is a sewin?

3 How long is a standard Olympic rowing course?

4 Which country in South America was called Banda Oriental before independence?

5 Who won her first Oscar for the film *Klute*, in 1971?

Team 2

1 Against which King was a plot hatched by George Brooke and Lord Cobham, his brother?

2 What type of creature is a brandling?

3 In which year did the first (recorded) women's cricket match take place?

4 In which country is the Anti-Lebanon mountain range?

5 Which former TV cop won an Oscar for *Chariots of Fire*?

Round 2

Team 1

1 Which instrument does the hardangerfele closely resemble?

2 Who wrote *Crime and Punishment*?

3 Which artist did a series of etchings called *The Disasters of War*?

4 What would a myologist study?

5 What was Che Guevara's given name?

Team 2

1 Which long-necked, Indian musical instrument has seven strings?

2 Who wrote of a doctor's rise to Harley Street in *The Citadel*?

3 Which artist painted 'The Fighting Temeraire'?

4 What does a somatologist study?

5 Which country was once ruled by Boleslaw the Generous?

Round 3

Team 1

1 According to the saying, was is a swarm of bees in June worth?
2 Of what is nyctophobia the fear?
3 Of which country is Manama the capital?
4 What would you put in a Canterbury?
5 Who wrote the play *John Bull's Other Island*?

Team 2

1 According to the saying, 'Button to the chin 'til' – what?
2 Of what is gymnophobia the fear?
3 Of which country is Harare the capital?
4 For what is a Davenport intended?
5 Who wrote the play *The Lady's not for Burning*?

Round 4

Team 1

1 In apothecaries' weight, how many grains make a scruple?
2 What in the Second World War were talboys and grand slams?
3 Which is the only case in British history of a husband and wife ruling jointly as King and Queen?
4 Who made the 1964 top-selling record, 'I Love You Because'?
5 What is 505 in Roman numerals?

Team 2

1 According to Tennyson, the Light Brigade charged for half a league. How far is a league?
2 What kind of aircraft was the Second World War Horsa?
3 Which French King did Joan of Arc assist to defeat the English?
4 Whose first number one hit was 'Release Me'?
5 Which year uses all the Roman numerals in descending order?

Round 5   Individual questions for Team 1

Quotations
Who wrote, 'Cauliflower is nothing but cabbage with a college education'?
Plants
What flower is sometimes known as the Lent lily?
Poetry
Which Scottish poet was known as the Ettrick Shepherd?
Ships and the Sea
What in shipping terms is a VLCC?
Television
In the TV play *Squaring the Circle*, which political leader was played by Bernard Hill?

Round 6

Team 2

1 How many players are there in a netball team?
2 According to the old saying, which fruit is it unlucky to eat in October?
3 In which king's reign did the Pensionary Parliament assemble?
4 What sort of music did Ira D. Sankey compose?
5 Who wrote *The Hollow Men*?

Team 1

1 How high is the netball net from the ground?
2 Edible, hazel and squirrel-tailed are kinds of what?
3 Which king won the Battle of the Spurs?
4 For singing what type of music was Mahalia Jackson renowned?
5 Who wrote *Fitz-Boodle's Confessions and Professions*?

Round 7

Team 2

1 Which periodical was first published in 1902 and edited by Bruce Richmond?
2 In the 1960s, who had a hit with 'Mellow Yellow'?
3 How many square metres are there in a hectare?
4 What is a layer of oysters called?

5 Which Italian city's symbol is the winged lion of St Mark?

Team 1

1 Which former editor of *The Times* became chairman of the Arts Council?
2 Who had a hit in 1968 with 'Tiptoe Through the Tulips'?
3 What is the minimum number of whole degrees in a reflex angle?
4 Which seaport in Kent has been noted for its oysters since pre-Roman times?
5 In which city is the Palace of the Nations?

Round 8

Team 2

1 Who wrote the book *One Hundred and One Dalmatians*?
2 In which sport would you use the terms spike, dump, dig pass and penetration?
3 What would you have if you had a Dandie Dinmont?
4 In the history of the British Regiments, for what did KOSB stand for?
5 Which Biblical character in the book of Samuel was born in Gath?

Team 1

1 Who wrote the stories about Thomas the Tank Engine?
2 What, in sport, is a karateka?

3 Who or what is a blue-faced booby?
4 What do the initials TAVR stand for?
5 What collective name is given to the three wise men of the East?

Round 9

Team 2

1 Where in your body would you find your adenoids?
2 What is the lowest prime number?
3 In Hindu mythology, what is an avatar?
4 'The Impossible Dream' comes from which musical?
5 In which TV series did Joe Lynch and John Bluthal star together?

Team 1

1 Lentigines is the medical term for what?
2 What is the lowest perfect number?
3 Who was the Greek God of fault finding?
4 Which musical is a fantasy about a dead man returning after 15 years to help his family?
5 In which year was the *Cheers* bar established.

Round 10   Individual questions for Team 2

Quotations

Who wrote, 'If in doubt, win the trick'?

Plants

By what name are the flower trusses of the hazel and willow trees known?

Poetry

Who had an 'ancient, trusty, drouthy, crony' named Souter Johnny?

Ships and the Sea

Name the legendary spectral ship condemned to sail the seas forever, trying to reach Table Bay?

Television

What does ORACLE stand for (exactly)?

Drinks round

Team 1

1 Who wrote the song 'Camptown Races'?
2 In which country is Nagoya?
3 In which year did the Great Train Robbery take place?
4 Systolic and diastolic are the upper and lower values of what?
5 What was the codename for the Battle of Alamein?
6 The Prime Minister lives at 10 Downing Street, the Chancellor at 11; who lives at 12?
7 On which river is Caldron Snout on the Durham/Cumbria border?
8 Who played the part of *Spider-Man* on film opposite Kirsten Dunst?
9 Which sport is played at Cowdray Park?
10 Tocophobia is a fear of what?

Team 2

1 Who wrote the hymn 'Abide with Me'?
2 In which country is Pau?
3 In which year was the first human heart transplant?
4 Name the tubes connecting the nose and ears?
5 What was the codename for the German invasion of The Soviet Union in 1941?
6 Which Prime Minister was nicknamed 'Pam'?
7 By what name is the Thames known as it flows through Oxford?
8 Which actor did his own stunts when playing the lead in the film *Condorman*?
9 Major Ernst Killander is known as the father of which sport?
10 Sitophobia is a fear of what?

Reserve questions

1 Where is the Headquarters of OPEC?
2 Who produced the Camargue car?
3 In which Shipping Forecast Area is Bell Rock Lighthouse?

Pub League Quiz 46

The individual questions are in Rounds 5 and 10 and are on animals, USA, science, television and plays.

Round 1

Team 1

1 In which European country are the Cantabrian Mountains?
2 Who was the husband of Boadicea?
3 What was Mickey Mouse's original name?
4 Which famous African battle took place in 1898?
5 Who wrote 'The Bab Ballads'?

Team 2

1 In which African country are the Aberdare Mountains?
2 Who was the husband of Philippa of Hainault?
3 What is Princess Aurora's better-known name?
4 Which famous English battle took place in 1644?
5 Who wrote the *Piers Plowman* poems?

Round 2

Team 1

1 What is alliteration?
2 What did the Education Act of 1944 do?
3 In which country would you use the currency balboa?
4 Who was British Prime Minister between 1916 and 1922?
5 What shape were the 'boxes' on the *Blockbusters* board?

Team 2

1 What is litotes?
2 What did the Toleration Act of 1689 do?
3 In which country would you use the currency gourde?
4 Who first became Prime Minister in 1868?
5 Which game show was derived from *Hollywood Squares*?

Round 3
Team 1

1 For which blind English composer did Eric Fenby write down the music?
2 Tabasco is a kind of sauce, but in which country is Tabasco?
3 What type of native British amphibians are the crested and the palmated?
4 Which 1963 film starring Tom Courtenay, featured the undertakers, Shadrack & Duxbury?
5 Which island did Britain cede to Germany in 1890?

Team 2

1 What pseudonym was used by the English composer Philip Heseltine?
2 In which counry is Weymouth?
3 Which fish is known as the river Wolf?
4 John Wayne won an Oscar for playing which one-eyed marshal?
5 What did Britain get in exchange for this ceded island?

Round 4
Team 1

1 What has been called the Universal Solvent?
2 Which English poet, born in 1793, became insane in 1837 and died in an asylum in 1864?
3 Which two South American countries do not border Brazil?
4 Who was the creator of TV's *Potty Time*?
5 What is the common term for the tympanic membrane?

Team 2

1 Diamond is one of the crystalline forms of carbon. What is the other?
2 Which American poet entitled a poem, 'Happiness makes up in height for what it lacks in length'?
3 Which two countries have permanent settlements on Spitsbergen?
4 Who was 5C's teacher in *Please Sir*?
5 What is a dactylogram?

Round 5   Individual questions for Team 1
Animals
If an animal is described as pinniped, what does it have?
USA
Which became the 49th state of the USA on 3 January 1959?
Science
Which acid is called vitriol?
Television
For which department did TV cop *Bergerac* work?
Plays
What is the theme of a Passion Play?

Round 6

Team 2

1 Where would you find a crossjack, a spanner and a royal?
2 In 1958, who had a number one hit with his own song, 'Diana'?
3 If you cook pasta *al dente* what does it mean?
4 What is the name of the warship which sank on its maiden voyage in 1628 and is now restored in Stockholm?
5 Which actress starred opposite Humphrey Bogart in *To Have and Have Not*?

Team 1

1 What is a skua?
2 In 1967, who had their first British chart entry with 'New York Mining Disaster 1941'?
3 Which blue-veined cheese is named after a small town near Milan?
4 What were the *Clermont* and the *Comet*?
5 Which actress starred opposite Humphrey Bogart in *Sabrina*?

Round 7

Team 2

1 Who won the 1984 Booker Prize for *Hotel du Lac*?
2 Who owned the 1981 Derby winner?
3 Of which country are Meshed, Tabriz and Abadan are among the chief towns?
4 In which TV series did a female, ex-senior partner expire in the lift shaft?
5 Byzantine, Baroque and Brutalism are all what?

Team 1

1 Who won the 1980 Booker Prize for *Rites of Passage*?
2 Who owned the 1968 Greyhound Derby winner Camira Flash?
3 Of which country are Elbasan, Tirane and Shkoder the chief towns?
4 Who, in a TV series, was the investigator attached to a west country radio station?
5 Indian Runner, Muscovy and Khaki Campbell are all what?

Round 8
Team 2

1 Who was the British author of the survey, *London Labour and the London Poor*?
2 In the 1987 film *Business as Usual*, in which kind of business does the story unfold?
3 Who wrote, 'Woman wants monogamy; Man delights in novelty'?
4 Which is the most northerly capital in the world?
5 What event in May 1987 was a demonstration against unemployment?

Team 1

1 Which playwright's first volume of autobiography was entitled *A Better Class of Person*?
2 Which 1987 film told a story of Britain during the Second World War, as seen by a nine-year-old boy?
3 Who was the English political leader, who asked to be painted, 'warts and everything'?
4 Of which country is Belmopen the capital?
5 In September 1986, who was enthroned as Archbishop of Capetown?

Round 9
Team 2

1 What is French for 30?
2 Of which duchy was Charles the Bold the ruler?
3 In the publishing world, what do the abbreviations CUP stand for?
4 What is the word for a person who sells ribbons, buttons, hooks, tape, etc?
5 When did pound notes first come into circulation in England?

Team 1

1 What is Italian for 40?
2 Of which country was Philip Augustus the ruler?
3 What does the abbreviation OUDS stand for?
4 What is the word for a person who studies elections and voting patterns?
5 In which year was the *Lusitania* sunk?

Round 10   Individual questions for Team 2
Animals
What is the correct name for a kangeroo's pouch?
USA
Which American Vice-President resigned in 1973, in the face of criminal charges?
Science
What is made by infusing carbonic acid gas into water under pressure?
Television
Which actor played Rodney Trotter in *Only Fools and Horses*?
Plays
Which play by Ben Jonson has the alternative title *The Fox*?

Drinks round

Team 1

1 Which comedian used the catch phrase 'Katanga'?

2 What is the common name for Scriveners' Palsy?

3 Which poem ends 'Fled is that music: Do I wake or sleep'?

4 Of whom did Lloyd George say, 'He saw foreign policy through the wrong end of a municipal drainpipe'?

5 What is the most southerly city ever to hold the Olympic Games?

6 Which music accompanied Hamlet cigar TV ads?

7 The film *The Choirboys* was about which body of men?

8 In Greek mythology, who killed Ladon, the dragon of a hundred heads?

9 Which bird in days of old was known as the laverock?

10 Which soccer team is nicknamed the 'Gulls'?

Team 2

1 Which comedian used to reminisce about 'The day war broke out'?

2 Which part of your body does the tragus protect?

3 Who wrote the patriotic poem *Drake's Drum*?

4 Who said of Viscount Montgomery, 'In defeat unbeatable; in victory unbearable'?

5 What is the most northerly city ever to hold the Olympic Games?

6 What classical theme accompanied the Hovis TV ads?

7 In which film does Laurence Olivier torture Dustin Hoffman by drilling into his teeth?

8 In Indian mythology, what is the earth supported by?

9 What is Britain's heaviest breeding bird?

10 Which soccer team is nicknamed the 'Potters'?

Reserve questions

1 Which European city does the airport of Tempelhof serve?

2 What was the name of Henry VIII's fool?

3 Why are 'bonfires' so called?

Pub League Quiz 47

The individual questions are in Rounds 5 and 10 and are on sport, geography, literature, pop music and art.

Round 1

Team 1

1 In which mountain range is Lake Tahoe?
2 What colours are on the flag of the United Nations?
3 Who wrote the play *Mourning becomes Electra*?
4 In 2009, who played Lady Dedlock on TV in *Bleak House*?
5 'On the Street Where You Live' comes from which musical?

Team 2

1 Which sea is between China and Korea?
2 What colour is a palomino horse?
3 Who wrote *The Playboy of the Western World*?
4 Who played the lead in TV's crime series *Target*?
5 Which musical is based on *The Matchmaker*?

Round 2

Team 1

1 Who murdered James I of Scotland?
2 In which country is the Orange river?
3 What are feather, fly, running and herring bone?
4 Who defeated the Russians at the Battle of Tannenburg?
5 From which country does racing driver Nelson Piquet come?

Team 2

1 Who caused the murder of Edward II of England?
2 In which country is the Liffey river?
3 What is a rigadoon?
4 Whose fleet was defeated at the battle of Lepanto?
5 From which country does racing driver Keke Rosberg come?

Round 3

Team 1

1 Of which country was Cetewayo once the ruler?
2 Which country manufactures the Saab motor car?
3 Which poison was given to Socrates?
4 Who portrayed *Edna the Inebriate Woman* on TV in 1971?
5 Victor Barna was 15 times a world champion in which sport?

Team 2

1 Of which country was Henri Christophe once the ruler?
2 Which country manufactures the Buick motor car?
3 Who was Ivanhoe's wife?
4 Who did Peter Ustinov portray in *Quo Vadis*??
5 With which sport is Ann Moore associated?

Round 4

Team 1

1 In which county is Orford Castle?
2 Which King of England was nicknamed 'The Martyr'?
3 In the Bible, who were the Jebusites?
4 Which plant's name comes from the Greek for crane?
5 Who wrote the opera *Elektra*?

Team 2

1 In which county is St Mawes Castle?
2 Of which country was Henry the Navigator a prince?
3 In the Bible, what were the Scribes?
4 Which flower's name means flesh colour?
5 In which opera by Puccini do Ping, Pang and Pong appear?

Round 5   Individual questions for Team 1

Sport
In which game might you use a cleek?
Geography
To which country do the Azores belong?
Literature
Who wrote *An Ideal Husband*?
Pop music
For which singer was 'I am what I am' a 1990s hit?
Art
Who painted 'The Potato Eaters' and 'Starry Night'?

Round 6
Team 2
1 To which organ of the body does astigmatism relate?
2 Which saint was a tax collector before becoming a disciple?
3 What nationality was the artist Juan Gris?
4 Which soccer team is nicknamed 'The Cottagers'?
5 Name the town featured in TV's *In the Heat of the Night*.

Team 1
1 To which organ of the body does cystitis relate?
2 Which saint was a disciple and a physician?
3 What nationality was the artist Henry Fuseli?
4 Of which soccer team is Gay Meadow the home?
5 Who wrote the title music for TV's *In the Heat of the Night*?

Round 7
Team 2
1 In which country is the Great Slave Lake?
2 In 1833, Prince Otto of Bavaria became the first king of which country?
3 What were Mrs Beeton's given names?
4 Where is your occipital artery?
5 Which numbers flank 11 on a dartboard?

Team 1
1 In which country is Lake Torrens?
2 Which country did King Prakrama rule?
3 What was Nell Gwyn's given name?
4 Which is the largest nerve in the human body?
5 Which numbers flank 18 on a dartboard?

Round 8
Team 2
1 Who wrote *Jude the Obscure*?
2 Which planet did Holst call 'The Mystic'?
3 On which race track was Jim Clark killed in 1967?
4 In which English city was Charles Dickens born?
5 Who starred in the 1971 film *Kotch*?

Team 1
1 Who wrote *The Girls of Slender Means*?
2 Who composed the Manfred Symphony in 1885?
3 Who won the 1984 Monaco Grand Prix?
4 In which city did the Peterloo Massacre of 1819 occur?
5 Which actor starred as the submarine commander in *Operation Petticoat*?

Round 9

Team 2

1 Who was *Pot Black* 1991 Champion?
2 In which Canadian province is Gander airport?
3 Which political party ruled India for the first 30 years of independence?
4 Who deals with Top Cat's misdemeanours?
5 Emperor and rockhopper are types of what?

Team 1

1 Who held the Snooker World Championship for 20 years?
2 Which American city is served by Logan International airport?
3 Which French politician was called 'The Tiger'?
4 Name the witch in *Willo the Wisp*.
5 What type of creature is a cottonmouth?

Round 10   Individual questions for Team 2

Sport
By what name is the game mintonette now known?
Geography
In which Gulf is Anticosti Island?
Literature
Who wrote the novel *A Kind of Loving*?
Pop music
Who recorded 'Candy' in 2009?
Art
Who painted 'Two Tahitian Women'?

Just for fun

Why did Napoleon insist on being crowned with an iron crown?
The crown used at the enthronement of Napoleon as Emperor of the French was supposed to be hinged with one of the nails from Christ's cross. It had belonged to the ancient kings of Lombardy and in 1717 was venerated by the Roman Church's Congregation of Relics. It came to France via Germany and was returned to Italy in 1866. The Iron Crown of Lombardy, as it is called, is now in the cathedral at Monza.

Drinks round

Team 1

1 What relation was Lot to Abraham?
2 In Greek mythology, what did Charybdis form?
3 Who founded the British Union of Fascists?
4 Who starred in the 1975 film *Dog Day Afternoon*?
5 In the poem by Kipling, what was Gunga Din's job?

6 In which sport might you perform a mohawk turn?
7 Which English county town used to be known as Dubris?
8 Who wrote the music for the show *Carousel*?
9 Who reputedly haunts Hever Castle?
10 In which TV series did Bombadier Beaumont appear?

Team 2

1 Which prophet denounced Ahab and Jezebel?
2 In Greek mythology, how many eyes had the giant Argus?
3 Who founded the Zoological Society?
4 Who was the male star of the 1966 film *Two For The Road*?
5 In 1892, Gentlemen Jim Corbett knocked out John L. Sullivan. What was remarkable about the fight?

6 In which sport could you be given a mulligan?
7 In which English county are the Quantocks?
8 Who wrote the music for the show *West Side Story*?
9 Which Queen is said to haunt Borthwick Castle?
10 In the original TV series starring Leonard Rossiter, for which company did Reginald Perrin work?

Reserve questions

1 What is hydrogen's atomic number?
2 How many pence today would a crown be worth?
3 Who sings the theme song in the Bond film *Goldfinger*?

Pub League Quiz 48

The individual questions are in Rounds 5 and 10 and are on geography, animal world, poetry, world of plants and television.

Round 1
Team 1
1 Which British city is served by Aldergrove airport?
2 What would be kept using a metronome?
3 In which sport is a piton used?

4 The Yalu and Tumen rivers mark the boundary between which two countries?
5 Who composed the song 'Falling in love with love'?

Team 2
1 Which American city is served by O'Hare airport?
2 What is a rheostat?
3 In which sport would you use a spoon and a niblick?
4 In which country is the river Xingu?
5 Who composed the song 'Over There'?

Round 2
Team 1
1 What instrument did Sidonie Goossens play?
2 Name the two major Baseball leagues in the USA.
3 Which radio series made Arthur Askey's name in the late 1930s?
4 In which country is Quimper?
5 In the field of medicine, what do the letters UCH stand for?

Team 2
1 What instrument did Leon Goossens play?
2 Which club won the 1987 Rugby League Cup Final?
3 Who was radio's Diddy David?

4 In which country is Quatre Bras?
5 In the field of law, what do the letters L. J. stand for?

Round 3

Team 1

1 What is the name for the heraldic colour red?
2 Who was The Doors' keyboard player?

3 Which poem begins with the line, 'April is the cruellest month'?
4 In which Welsh county is the Isle of Anglesey?
5 What does the phrase 'playing to the gallery' mean?

Team 2

1 In heraldry, what is a pale?
2 Who played the part of The Doors' keyboard player in the film *The Doors*?
3 Who wrote the poem *The Waste Land*?
4 In which Welsh county is Brecknock?
5 What does the phrase 'drawing the long bow' mean?

Round 4

Team 1

1 Who won the Silver Medal for the men's 800 metres in the 1984 Olympics?
2 Cholecystitis relates to which part of the body?
3 Who was the first Christian martyr?
4 What is the S.I. unit of measurement for frequency?

5 What nationality was Nobel Peace Prize Winner Lester B. Pearson?

Team 2

1 How many times did Sebastian Coe win the Olympic 1,500 metre race?
2 Mastoiditis relates to which part of the body?
3 Which Pope had the longest reign?
4 What is the S.I. unit of measurement for electrical resistance?
5 What nationality was Nobel Chemistry Prize Winner Frederick Sanger?

Round 5   Individual questions for Team 1

Geography
Of which European city is Piraeus the port?
Animal world
What kind of animal is a skink?
Poetry
If Tuesday's child is full of grace, what is Monday's child?
World of plants
What is the common name for belladonna?
Television
Who was the third *Dr Who*?

Round 6
Team 2
1 What is the capital of Morocco?
2 Spell ANAESTHETIC.
3 At the end of which book does Sydney Carton die?
4 Which pop group's single backed 'Knowing Me, Knowing You' with 'Happy Hawaii'?
5 In which country is Habsburg Castle?

Team 1
1 What is the capital of Zaire?
2 Spell CRUSTACEAN.
3 In which book does Maggie Tulliver feature?
4 Which pop group had a hit with 'Honky Tonk Women'?
5 In which country is Canossa Castle?

Round 7
Team 2
1 What is the common name for *Canis Lupus*?
2 Which English King suffered mental derangement in 1453?
3 The lack of which vitamin causes beriberi?
4 What is Viv Richard's first given name?
5 When Sherlock Holmes retired, what did he become?

Team 1
1 What is the common name for *Pongo pygmaeus*?
2 Which Queen was called Gloriana?
3 Which vitamin deficiency causes scurvy?
4 What was Colin Cowdrey's first given name?
5 What was the name of Sherlock Holmes's brother?

Round 8
Team 2
1 Which actor's real name was William Mitchell?
2 At which battle did the Black Prince win his spurs?
3 To what family does the jackdaw belong?
4 Who wrote the play *The Little Foxes*?
5 What is Cher's real name?

Team 1
1 Which actresses' real name was Ruby Stevens?
2 At which battle did Henry V fight in 1403 at the age 15?
3 What is an ormer?
4 Who wrote the play *The Cocktail Party*?
5 What was Sonny's real name?

Round 9

Team 2

1 In which country is the Maranon river?
2 In the Bible, what was a publican's job?
3 Which footballer was with three World Cup winning teams?
4 Who preceded Creon as King of Thebes?
5 Which musical note is known as double-croche in France?

Team 1

1 In which country is the Menderes river?
2 Which prophet's Lamentations are a book of the Old Testament?
3 Which athlete won three gold medals in the 1952 Olympics?
4 Which Libyan King did Colonel Gaddafi overthrow in 1969?
5 Which note is four times the length of a crotchet?

Round 10   Individual questions for Team 2

Geography

What is the capital of Puerto Rico?

Animal world

During its life, what creature takes the forms of parr, smolt and grilse?

Poetry

Which poet wrote the line 'You're a better man than I am, Gunga Din'?

World of Plants

Which wild fruit is also known as the whortleberry or whimberry?

Television

What was the first product advertised on TV in 1955?

Just for fun

What plant takes 70 years to mature and has a flower head six metres high?

The agave or American aloe. It dies very quickly after reaching full growth. In Mexico, its sap is collected for brewing the strong spirit, mescal, and a single plant can yield a 1,000 litres of sap. It is also known as the century plant, because of its great age.

Drinks round

Team 1

1 Who composed the *Death and the Maiden Quartet*?
2 Who was the husband of Mary II of England, Scotland and Ireland?
3 In which country is Meerut?
4 On 1 January, if the time in London is 12.00 noon, what time is it in Delhi?
5 In which sport is the Hospitals' Cup contested?
6 Who played the title role in the 1972 film *Young Winston*?
7 What is a canvas back?
8 Name Shirley Williams' literary mother.
9 Which American state is known as the Hoosier state?
10 Where does the American football team The Rams come from?

Team 2

1 Who composed the *Tristesse Etude*?
2 Who was the husband of Berengaria of Navarre?
3 In which state of the USA is Bretton Woods?
4 On 1 January, if the time in London is 12.00 noon, what time is it in Tokyo?
5 In karate, what does tamashiwara mean?
6 Who played the title role in the 1974 film *Big Bad Mama*?
7 What is a zander?
8 Who was the leader of the Labour Party prior to Harold Wilson?
9 Which American state is known as the Old Dominion?
10 Where does the American football team the Oilers come from?

Reserve questions

1 In which year did the Post Office introduce Christmas stamps?
2 Who composed the opera *Lohengrin*?
3 Who said 'Let me die with the Philistines'?

Pub League Quiz 49

The individual questions are in Rounds 5 and 10 and are on places, politics, science, words and books.

Round 1

Team 1

1 Who was nicknamed 'Toom Tabard'?
2 What country is known in its native language as Hellas?
3 What is the first section in an international ice-skating competition?
4 In which novel does Lord Marchmain appear?
5 Which Mafioso gangster was called 'Lucky'?

Team 2

1 Who was nicknamed 'Prinny'?
2 Its inhabitants call it Kerkira; what do Britons call it?
3 Which ice-skating event was first added to the 1976 Olympics?
4 In which novel does Alfred Jingle appear?
5 Which gangster was called 'Machine Gun'?

Round 2

Team 1

1 Who painted 'Rape of the Sabines' and 'The Felt Hat'?
2 In which city in the British Isles would you find Phoenix Park?
3 Who wrote more than 400 concertos for Venetian music schools for orphaned girls?
4 How far apart are the goal posts in polo?
5 On what date is Oakapple Day?

Team 2

1 Which English portrait painter's subjects included Dr Johnson and Mrs Siddons?
2 In which city in the British Isles would you find Cathay Park?
3 Which Spanish composer died in 1916, on board the torpedoed Sussex?
4 How far is it between consecutive baseball bases?
5 On what date is Holy Innocents' Day?

Round 3

Team 1

1 Which group had a hit with 'Blackberry Way'?
2 Who wrote, 'Candy is dandy, but liquor is quicker'?
3 Who was the doubter among the apostles?
4 In geology, what is a moraine?
5 Of which American state is Carson City the capital?

Team 2

1 Which group had a hit with 'Blockbuster'?
2 Who wrote, 'He who can, does. He who cannot, teaches'?
3 What was Jesus's first miracle?
4 In geology, what is loess?
5 In which American state is New Orleans?

Round 4

Team 1

1 On which racecourse is the Cesarewitch run?
2 Who wrote *The Black Tulip*?
3 What instrument did Evelyn Rothwell play?
4 Who was the last English King to have a Queen called Catherine?
5 Which actress ran TV's B*agdad Café*?

Team 2

1 Which racecourse crosses the Melling Road?
2 Who wrote the novel *Cousin Bette*?
3 To which conductor was Evelyn Rothwell married?
4 Who was the first English King to obtain a divorce?
5 What is the name of the cab company in TV's *Taxi*?

Round 5   Individual questions for team 7

Places
For what is the town of Meissen in Germany famous?

Politics
Which country's Parliament is known as the Knesset?

Science
With what is the science of cryogenics concerned?

Words
Who or what are norns?

Books
What would you find in *Debrett*?

Round 6

Team 2
1 What nationality was Erasmus?
2 What instrument did Madame Suggia play?
3 Who was the winning Commander at the battle of Tel-el-Kebir?
4 How are showjumpers David Broome and Liz Edgar related?
5 What is the state flower of California?

Team 1
1 What nationality was Caractacus?
2 What instrument did George Thalben-Ball play?
3 Who was the winning Commander at the naval battle of Camperdown?
4 Jill Parker was an English international on 413 occasions. What was her sport?
5 What is the state flower of Florida?

Round 7

Team 2
1 Which civil war took place between 1936 and 1939?
2 In which country is Cape Wrath?
3 Who wrote the operetta *The Grand Duke*?
4 In which Shakespeare play does a statue 'come to life'?
5 The first long-distance race was from Antwerp to London in 1819. Which sport?

Team 1
1 Which mutiny took place in 1857 and 1858?
2 Where is Cape Finisterre?
3 Who wrote the operetta that includes 'The Nuns' Chorus'?
4 In which Shakespeare play does Rosalind disguise herself as Ganymede?
5 In which sport did Claire Tomlinson attain a handicap of five in 1986?

Round 8

Team 2
1 Who is the patron saint of Paris?
2 Which King had the nickname 'Lackland'?
3 What was the Latin name for Paris in Roman times?
4 Which S.I. unit is used to measure energy and quantity of heat?
5 Which group did Tom Rapp lead before going solo?

Team 1
1 Who is the patron saint of Madrid?
2 Which King had the nickname 'Beauclerck'?
3 What was the Latin name for Cadiz in Roman times?
4 Which S.I. unit is used to measure quantity of electricity?
5 Which group was known as 'A.W.B.' for short?

Round 9

Team 2

1 What does the French *hors de combat* mean?

2 In which castle was King Edward the Martyr murdered in 978CE?

3 Which authoress also writes as Barbara McCorquodale?

4 What is ogham?

5 From which show did David Essex's hit song 'Oh What a Circus' come?

Team 1

1 What does the Latin *in loco parentis* mean?

2 Where was the first Prince of Wales proclaimed in 1301?

3 What was the name of Iran before it was called Persia?

4 What is treen?

5 Who was at number 5 in the first British Top Ten, with 'High Noon'?

Round 10   Individual questions for Team 2

Places

Sing Sing is located on the Hudson river. What is it?

Politics

In which country was the political party known as the 'Falangists'?

Science

What is deuterium oxide popularly called?

Words

What occupation does a coper have?

Books

Who wrote 'cautionary tales'?

Just for fun

What literary figure was known as 'Namby-Pamby'?

The English poet Ambrose Philips (c. 1675–1749). This derogatory nickname was coined by Henry Carey, who may have penned 'God Save the King'. Carey was echoing the general view of a collection of Philips's pastoral poems that they were excessively emotional and riddled with affectation. 'Namby-Pamby' passed into the language to mean sugary and sentimental or someone who is a bit of a softy.

Drinks round

Team 1

1 Which motorway links the M25 to Folkestone?
2 In which country are the Ox Mountains?
3 Who ordered Lady Jane Grey to be executed?
4 Who did Karol Wojtyla become?
5 Which cartoonist sent her characters to Tresoddit in Cornwall?
6 To what type of animal does leoprine refer?
7 Who sang 'I'd Like to Teach the World to Sing'?
8 In which country is the region of Andalusia?
9 Which city is the home of the Ajax club?
10 Who designed the Mosquito fighter-bomber?

Team 2

1 Which motorway links the M25 to Cambridge?
2 In which country are the Adirondack Mountains?
3 Which English Queen did the Prince of Saxe-Coburg-Gotha marry?
4 Who is Lord of the Isles?
5 In which newspaper would you find Posy Simmond's cartoons?
6 What type of creature is a water moccasin?
7 Who sang 'I'm into Something Good'?
8 In which country are the Pontine Marshes?
9 Which city is the home of the Benfica club?
10 Who designed the Spitfire?

Reserve questions

1 In which book would you find the 'Slough of Despond'?
2 When is St Sylvester's night?
3 What is the sum total of all the trebles on a dart board?

Pub League Quiz 50

The individual questions are in Rounds 5 and 10 and are on sport, composers, history, art and poems.

Round 1

Team 1

1 What, in the field of computers, does ASCII stand for?
2 Who wrote the novel *Fame is the Spur*?
3 Who was Cain's eldest son?
4 Whose second symphony was known as *The Little Russian*?
5 To which creature were the eyes of Argus transferred by Hera?

Team 2

1 For what, in the field of aviation, do the letters VTOL stand?
2 Who wrote the novel *Scruples*?
3 What was Abel's occupation?
4 Who wrote the *Raindrop Prelude*?
5 What did the Greeks call 'The Pillars of Hercules'?

Round 2

Team 1

1 Where in the British Isles would you find the House of Keys?
2 Where were the 1952 Summer Olympics held?
3 Who sang 'I heard it through the Grapevine'?
4 Which film ends with 'Rosebud' burning?
5 On which river does Leicester stand?

Team 2

1 Where is the world's largest fish and chip shop?
2 Where were the 1968 Winter Olympics held?
3 Who sang 'King of the Road'?
4 In which film was Flubber invented?
5 The Wirral lies between the Mersey and which other river?

Round 3

Team 1

1 Of which country is Asuncion the capital city?
2 Where do the international car registration letters FL come from?
3 Which horse won the Derby, the 2000 Guineas and the St Leger in 1970?
4 Who wrote *The Woodlanders*?
5 Of which flower is lady's slipper a variety?

Team 2

1 What is the capital of the South American country Guyana?
2 Where do the international car registration letters SK come from?
3 Name the race-track where the Kentucky Derby is run.
4 Who wrote *Therese Raquin*?
5 Tobacco is made from the leaves of which family of plants?

Round 4

Team 1

1 Who played 'Gloria' in *It Ain't Half Hot Mum*?
2 In which country is Latakia, famous for its tobacco?
3 Who would wear an orphrey, a morse and a cope?
4 Who or what is a cassowary?
5 Where did Lee surrender to Grant in 1865?

Team 2

1 Who is American TV's equivalent of Alf Garnett?
2 In which group of islands is Corfu?
3 What articles of clothing are domino, cardinal and mantle?
4 Who or what is a dragee?
5 The February Revolution led to the overthrow of which Republic of France?

Round 5   Individual questions for Team 1

Sport
Which horse races for colts form the English Triple Crown?
Composers
Who composed *Eine Alpen-symphonie*?
History
What did the Volstead Act in the USA seek to control?
Arts
Which painting by Millais shows the sea wall at Budleigh Salterton, Devon?
Poems
'White founts falling in the courts of the sun' is the first line of which poem?

Round 6

Team 2

1 Who wrote the thriller *The Five Red Herrings*?
2 Which King was buried at Westminster Abbey a few days after it was consecrated?
3 On which Island are the former British colonies of Sarawak and Brunei?
4 Where in your body is the bone called the trapezium?
5 In which sport is the Thomas Cup awarded?

Team 1

1 Who wrote the book *The Wizard of Oz*?
2 Who was the last English King to be killed in battle?
3 To which European country do the Island groups of Cyclades and Dodecanese belong?
4 Where is your sartorius muscle?
5 From which country does snooker player Dene O'Kane come?

Round 7

Team 2

1 What is eight in binary?
2 Which country did the League of Nations expel in December 1939 for attacking Finland?
3 In the Bible, who was the father of Ishmael?
4 Which abstract impressionist became famous for his drip painting?
5 Which soccer team plays its home games at Hampden Park?

Team 1

1 What is four in binary?
2 Which warship was scuttled near Montevideo in December 1939?
3 Who was Moses father-in-law?
4 Who designed the Albert Memorial?
5 Which is the longest Olympic track race?

Round 8

Team 2

1 Crown Prince Felipe is heir to which European throne?
2 On radio, Kenneth Williams was Sandy; who was Hugh Paddick?
3 What was Joe Gargery's trade in *Great Expectations*?
4 In which country could you spend the Cruzeiro?
5 Which famous battle took place in 1415?

Team 1

1 Crown Prince Frederick is heir to which European throne?
2 'Barwick Green' is the signature tune of which serial?
3 What was Silas Marner's trade, in the George Eliot novel?
4 In which country could you spend the Kwacha?
5 Which famous English battle took place in 1264?

Round 9

Team 2

1 Who wrote, 'Marriage has many pains, but celibacy has no pleasures'?

2 Of where did Queen Margrethe II became the first female sovereign for over 500 years?

3 Of which sport is FIM is the administering body?

4 What was the sequel to the 1933 film *King Kong*?

5 Almaviva was the original name of which Rossini opera?

Team 1

1 Whose last words, on the scaffold, were 'Such is life'?

2 Of which country was Eric Bloodaxe king?

3 How much clearance does a croquet ball have, on passing through a hoop?

4 What was the sequel to the film *Bedtime for Bonzo*?

5 Which Italian composer completed Puccini's opera *Turandot*?

Round 10   Individual questions for Team 2

Sport
Which twins played cricket for Surrey in the 1950s?
Composers
Which composer pianist wrote the opera *Manru* in 1901?
History
Who was the husband of Madame de Maintenon?
Art
Who painted 'Diana Surprised by Actaeon' in 1559?
Poems
Who wrote the poem beginning 'Half a league, half a league'?

Drinks round

Team 1

1 What was the earlier name of Tuvalu?
2 Whose first starring role was in the film *The Invisible Man* in 1933?
3 What is the positive square root of 289?
4 Which American President was architect of the Virginia State Capitol?
5 Who created the imaginary place Narnia?
6 Whose mistress was reputedly the model for Britannia?
7 What is the capital of Lithuania?
8 What sort of bird is a tercel?

9 In which sport do women compete for the Marcel Corbillon Trophy?
10 Who was Antigone's father?

Team 2

1 What was the earlier name of Zambia?
2 Who starred in *Modern Times* in 1936?
3 What is the positive square root of 441 ?
4 Who painted the 'Rokeby Venus'?
5 Who wrote *Elmer Gantry*?
6 Who succeeded Henry VIII and at what age?
7 Where is Kharg Island?
8 To which family of birds does the dabchick belong?
9 Which football club was founded, in 1895, as Thames Ironworks?
10 Who was Eurydice's husband?

Reserve questions

1 Which Scottish Term Day is on 1 August?
2 Who said, 'Life imitates art far more than art imitates life'?
3 Who had a hit record with 'Happiness'?

Pub League Quiz 51

The individual questions are in Rounds 5 and 10 and are on television, famous people, pop music, history and animals.

Round 1

Team 1

1 Who composed 'Jesu, Joy of Man's Desiring?

2 In the First World War, what were 'Little Willies' and 'Big Willies'?

3 In which country did Joanna the Mad reign in the 16th century?

4 'Earth has not anything to show more fair' is from which poem?

5 Name the retirement home in TV's *Waiting for God*.

Team 2

1 Who composed 'Country Gardens' and 'Handel in the Strand'?

2 Which German was given the unique rank of Reichsmarschall in the Second World World War?

3 Of which country was Charles the Bold ruler in 1433–77?

4 'Deep in the shady sadness of a vale' is from which poem?

5 Name one of the actors caught up in the TV's *Time Tunnel*.

Round 2

Team 1

1 Who wrote the song 'Daisy Bell'?

2 What are the dimensions of a snooker table?

3 In which year was the census introduced in Britain?

4 Who recorded 'Below the Salt'?

5 On pencils, what does BBB mean?

Team 2

1 Who wrote the song 'Days of Wine and Roses'?

2 What are the dimensions of a table tennis table?

3 In which year was the two-tier postal system introduced in Britain?

4 Who sang 'Bad Moon Rising'?

5 On pencils, what does HB mean?

Round 3

Team 1

1 Who were the two rival groups in the Battle of Blood river?
2 Who, in Greek mythology, turned Arachne into a spider?

3 In which year did John Curry complete ice-skating's triple crown?
4 Who viewed all of the Promised Land from Mount Nebo?
5 Of which country is Maseru the capital?

Team 2

1 Between which two cities were the Punic Wars fought?
2 In Greek mythology, Deucalion was the equivalent of whom in the Bible?
3 In which year did Cassius Clay first win the world heavyweight title?
4 Who was Zipporah's husband?

5 Of which country is Niamey the capital?

Round 4

Team 1

1 In Greek mythology, what was the Chimera?
2 Who wrote the opera *Mozart and Salieri* in 1898?
3 Who painted 'The Naked Maja'?

4 Who was the Portuguese discoverer of Brazil?

5 What are the two lifts used in Olympic weightlifting?

Team 2

1 In Norse mythology, who wielded Mjolnir?
2 Who wrote the opera *The Saint of Bleecker Street*?
3 In the painting, who was 'The Naked Maja'?
4 Who was the European discoverer of the Mississippi river?
5 Which sports are combined in an Olympic biathlon?

Round 5   Individual questions for Team 1

Television
In which London district is TV's *Only Fools and Horses* set?
Famous People
For what is Francis Scott Key best remembered?
Pop music
Whose hit album was called *Dark Side of the Moon*?
History
Which king is it thought that Walter Tyrell killed in the year 1100?
Animals
What is a guanaco?

Round 6

Team 2

1 In science, what does RNA stand for?
2 Who was the last Ottoman sultan?
3 Where is Cape Comorin?
4 Who wrote *Staying On*?
5 What was Beethoven's only oratorio?

Team 1

1 In science, what does DNA stand for?
2 Who was the first Bourbon king of France?
3 Where is Queen Maud Land?
4 Who wrote *The Battle of the Books*?
5 Who wrote the coronation anthem 'Zadok the Priest'?

Round 7

Team 2

1 Which film made Rudolph Valentino a star?
2 For whom was the Taj Mahal built?
3 Who, in 1882, discovered the tuberculosis bacterium?
4 Which Rugby League player kicked 22 goals in a cup tie?
5 What does Tokyo mean?

Team 1

1 In which film did Fred Astaire sing 'Night and Day'?
2 For whom is Big Ben named?
3 Who discovered radioactivity?
4 Who was the oldest man to play Test Cricket?
5 What was the former name of Tokyo?

Round 8

Team 2

1 Name the two TV *Birds of a Feather*.
2 Where is the Denmark Strait?
3 Whose novels were set and around Brummidge?
4 Who composed the music to 'God Bless the Prince of Wales'?
5 Where in the human body is the brachial artery?

Team 1

1 Name the leading character in TV's *So You Think You've Got Troubles*.
2 Where is the Bay of Fundy?
3 Who created the detective C. Auguste Dupin?
4 Who composed the music to 'Deutschland Uber Alles'?
5 Where in the human body is the pineal gland?

Round 9

Team 2

1 In computer terminology, what does PROM mean?
2 What 'first' reached Britain in July 1586?
3 Who wrote *A Day in the Death of Joe Egg*?
4 Who painted the 'Madonna with the Long Neck'?
5 Who won both the UK and World Professional Billiards Championships in 1987?

Team 1

1 In computer terminology, for what is BASIC an acronym?
2 What 'first' was introduced in Glasgow in October 1865?
3 Who wrote *All Quiet on the Western Front*?
4 Who painted 'Whaam'?
5 Which team won the Super Bowl in 1989?

Round 10   Individual questions for Team 2

Television

Who played Haskins in *The Sweeney*?

Famous People

What was Emperor Haile Selassie's original name?

Pop music

Who had a hit with 'I Feel for You' in 1985?

History

Which Ostrogoth was King of Italy from 493 to 526CE?

Animals

What is a kissing gourami?

Just for fun

Who was England's Queen for nine days?

Lady Jane Grey. On the death of the young Protestant King Edward VI in 1553, the Regency council, headed by the Duke of Northumberland, sought to avoid the succession of Mary Tudor, the next in line to the throne and a Catholic. In a desperate coup, the next legitimate Protestant claimant, Jane Grey, was proclaimed Queen. Mary, with the support of the people, overthrew the coup and the unfortunate Jane's reign ended after just nine days. She was later beheaded in the Tower of London.

Drinks round

Team 1

1 Which countries fought the Chaco War?
2 What is a henry?
3 What is the capital of Qatar?
4 Who starred in the film *She'll be Wearing Pink Pyjamas*?
5 What is a collection of crows called?
6 In Norse mythology, who caused Balder's death?
7 Which musician was portrayed in the film *The Magic Bow*?
8 In which country is the Grande Dixence Dam?
9 Who originally compèred *The Krypton Factor*?
10 Who wrote the poems 'Songs for St Cecilia's Day?

Team 2

1 Who fought whom at Taranaki in 1860?
2 What is a lux?
3 What is the capital of Namibia?
4 Which actor starred in the melodrama *The Bells*?
5 What is the collective term for bears?
6 In Greek mythology, who tried to fly to heaven on Pegasus?
7 Which composer was portrayed in the film *A Song to Remember*?
8 In which country are the Guayra Falls?
9 Who played Darling in TV's *Blackadder*?
10 Who wrote the poem *Metroland*?

Reserve questions

1 In which city was Yehudi Menuhin born?
2 Of which American state is 'North to the Future' the motto?
3 What does the G of G8 stand for?

PART 2

Quick-fire Questions

Rules of the Game

The questions in this section are perfectly straightforward. There are five complete quizzes, each made up of 10 subject categories. There are 20 questions in each category, graded into three levels: *Fairly easy, Not so easy* and *Hard*. One or more rounds of 10 sections constitute a game, depending on the number of players and the time available. If you want to do half a quiz, use only the easy questions, or select, say, five categories for your game. You can agree this before you start.

The questions are in the following basic sections: pot pourri; history; the United Kingdom; music and entertainment; science and nature; definitions; sport and games; the animal kingdom; geography and travel; art and literature.

Within each section, questions 1 to 7 are *Fairly easy*, 8 to 14 are *Not so easy*, and 15 to 20 are *Hard*.

One person acts as quizmaster, and there can be up to six players, in which case each player takes turns to answer first one *Fairly easy* question, then one *Not so easy question*, and finally one *Hard* question. To obtain a question, the players simply call out a number to the quizmaster. If they answer correctly, they score one point for *Fairly easy*, two points for *Not so easy* and three points for *Hard*. If the question is answered incorrectly, it can be answered by the first player to raise his or her hand after the question has been thrown open.

The player with the highest points total at the end of a session of 10 categories is the winner. The score sheet at the end of the section can be copied for home use.

As a variant, a player can elect to take one question only, a *Hard* one, for which four points are awarded for a correct answer. This all-or-nothing option will appeal to gamblers who prefer not to try for the six-point maximum by having to get three questions right in a row.

If you are doing the quiz alone, the following scale is a fair measure of how you have done on any section.

32 points or more:	brilliant
31–23 points:	very good
22–15 points:	good
14–7 points:	average
6 points or below:	don't despair – at least you are learning something!

Quick-fire Quiz Score Sheet

Quiz Number:

Player Category and question	1 Score	2 Score	3 Score	4 Score	5 Score	6 Score
Totals						

Quick-fire Quiz 1

POT POURRI 1

Fairly easy

1 What is Esperanto?
2 Give the name for a written statement, sworn on oath to be true, usually in the presence of a lawyer.
3 From which part of a pig does ham come?
4 What is meant by a fortified wine?
5 According to the old rhyme, the child of which day of the week 'has far to go'?
6 When is Hallowe'en?
7 What are members of the Church of Jesus Christ of Latter-day Saints called?

Not so easy

8 How does a funicular railway operate?
9 In heraldry, what colour is gules?
10 What oath sworn by graduates in medicine regulates their future professional conduct?
11 Who fled Hilldrop Crescent, Islington in 1910 and was later arrested on a ship to Canada in the company of Ethel le Neve?
12 What substitute for silver was developed in the 1740s by Thomas Bolsover of Sheffield?
13 The Day of Atonement is a day of fasting and prayer for Jews. By what Hebrew name is it better known?
14 What is the meaning of the Latin phrase *ad hoc*?

Hard

15 Where would you find an ox-bow lake?
16 What is the stock exchange term for South African mining shares?
17 What is Prattware?
18 In which oriental language are two systems of writing used concurrently?
19 What is the family name of the ruling dynasty of Monaco?
20 In primitive societies, what are shamans?

HISTORY 1

Fairly easy

1   What was drawn up in 1787, adopted in 1789 and has seven articles and 26 amendments?
2   What event brought the United States into the Second World War?
3   What was the family name of the rulers of Russia from the 17th Century to the Revolution in 1917?
4   In which country did the Easter Rising take place in 1916?
5   What ran for over 3,200km (2,000 miles) between Lashio, Burma and Chungking, China, and was the means by which the Allies supplied the forces of Chiang Kai-Shek in the first years of the Second World War?
6   Princess Alexandra's father was George, Duke of Kent. Who was her mother?
7   In which port did Sir Francis Drake 'singe the King of Spain's beard'?

Not so easy

8   What title did William Richard Morris take after building up one of Britain's most successful businesses?
9   Which French engineer built the Suez Canal, but failed to build the Panama Canal?
10   What was the nickname was François Duvalier, dictator of Haiti until 1971?
11   A mace is a symbol of authority in bodies such as the House of Commons, but what was its original purpose?
12   Which 20th-century British queen had a horror of telephones?
13   What was the name given to the statement of policy made by a President of the United States in 1823 that declared that the Americas were not to be a field for colonisation or any political interference by European powers?
14   Which island was awarded the George Cross in April 1942?

Hard

15   Who collaborated with Karl Marx to produce *The Communist Manifesto* in 1848?
16   Which dung beetle was honoured by the ancient Egyptians?
17   The Duke of Marlborough defeated the French at the Battle of Ramillies in 1706. Where is Ramillies?
18   What did the United States purchase from Russia in 1867 for $7,200,000?
19   What was the Atlantic Star?
20   Which British queen is buried in Peterborough Cathedral?

THE UNITED KINGDOM 1
Fairly easy
1 Whom did Margaret Thatcher succeed as leader of the Conservative Party in 1975?
2 In the RAF, which is the higher rank: Group Captain or Wing Commander?
3 Where in Britain is the Strangers' Gallery?
4 Which Scottish river is spanned by the Erskine Bridge?
5 What is the name of the governing body of the Church of England?
6 Where is the garden of England?
7 According to Dr Johnson, if you are tired of London, of what else are you tired?

Not so easy
8 Where is the Battle of Flowers held in August of each year?
9 In which English city is Armley jail?
10 Name the seaside resort that forms the southern part of the city of Portsmouth.
11 Is the maximum depth of Loch Ness 229, 273 or 311 metres (754, 897 or 1,021 feet)?
12 Of which British territory are GBM the international car registration letters?
13 What museum is to be found in Lambeth Road, London SE1?
14 In which English city is Deansgate a major thoroughfare: Birmingham, Manchester or Newcastle?

Hard
15 Which British institution was set up by royal charter in 1927?
16 What does Oxfam stand for?
17 Which great historic building in London was built by Inigo Jones for King James I?
18 In which Essex town is the Old Siege House?
19 What is the county town of Dunbartonshire in Scotland?
20 Which former London prison stood opposite the Old Bailey?

MUSIC AND ENTERTAINMENT 1

Fairly easy

1   Who replaced Sue Lawley as host of *Desert Island Discs*?
2   What is the name of the famous London-based society for conjurors and magicians?
3   Who was Brigitte Bardot's first husband?
4   Which Hollywood vamp is reported to have said: 'When I'm good I'm very good, but when I'm bad I'm better'?
5   Who is the wife and magic partner of Paul Daniels?
6   Which TV soap is set in Walford?
7   What musical composition was written for a. royal picnic on the river in the early 18th Century?

Not so easy

8   The National Theatre Company was formed in 1963 with Sir Laurence Olivier as its head. Who took over as Director in 1973?
9   The original TV game show *Take Your Pick* ran for nearly 20 years. Who was its quiz master?
10 Which is the odd one out from a chaconne, a rigadoon, apassepied and a virginal?
11 Andrew Lloyd Webber wrote a musical based on a collection of children's stories by which poet?
12 Which well-known Jamaican reggae artist died of cancer in May 1981?
13 With which Hollywood hit film do you associate the song 'Moon River'?
14 What instrument is often called the 'clown of the orchestra' by musicians?

Hard

15 Which director's film includes the running gag of the appearance of the words 'See you next Wednesday'?
16 Which British actor played *Hamlet* in 1964 in what at the time the most commercially successful Shakespeare production ever staged on Broadway?
17 What musical instruction means 'becoming gradually softer'?
18 Which jazz genre was started by Dizzy Gillespie?
19 What did composers Beethoven, Brahms, Chopin, Handel, Liszt, Ravel and Schubert all have in common?
20 Which *Blue Peter* dog was honoured with a bronze bust at the entrance to the BBC?

SCIENCE AND NATURE 1

Fairly easy

1   Which planet in our solar system appears to have canals?
2   What is FORTRAN?
3   Give the name for radio waves having wavelengths between one and ten metres.
4   What are the tiny blood vessels called that connect the smallest arteries and veins in the human body? .
5   The powdered root of the white Florentine iris smells of violets and is used in the manufacture of perfumes and of some medicines. What is its name?
6   Which alloy is composed of copper and zinc?
7   What part of the body is served by the acoustic nerve?

Not so easy

8   To convert degrees Celsius to degrees Fahrenheit, you must first multiply by 9, then divide by 5. How do you complete the calculation?
9   From what kinds of tree is turpentine obtained?
10 What is the botanical term for the process by which green plants manufacture food for themselves from atmospheric carbon dioxide and water with the aid of sunlight?
11 What is the trade name for the pain-killing drug acetylsalicyclic acid?
12 Which protein, widely used in foods, is made from the horns, bones and hooves of animals?
13 Which pale yellowish-green gas has the chemical symbol F?
14 To what everyday use is chloride of lime put?

Hard

15 What are China 14, Raduga 14 and Himawari 3?
16 Why is a sunflower so called?
17 In geological time, what name is given to the secondary era, the age of the reptiles and dinosaurs, which lasted for at least 135 million years?
18 What is the condition of the eye that causes round objects to appear as though they were oval?
19 In geology, what is meant by magma?
20 What do astronomers call the redness of the sky just before sunrise?

DEFINITIONS 1

From the five alternatives, choose the word or words *closest* in meaning to
the word given word.

Fairly easy

1   **Interrogate** a) browbeat b) scrutinise c) question d) make demands
     upon e) imprison
2   **Incubate** a) breed b) feed artificially c) sustain growth d) hatch out
     e) keep alive
3   **Rational** a) reasonable b) statement of principles c) thoughtful d) wise
     e) perspicacious
4   **Remote** a) shy b) far-reaching c) lacking in comprehension d) distant
     e) inaccessible
5   **Intimidate** a) prey on the mind b) force c) make afraid d) appal
     e) discourage
6   **Deviate** a) modify b) steer clear of c) deflect d) warped e) change
     course
7   **Approximate** a) alongside b) sufficient c) calculate d) very near
     e) deputise

Not so easy

8   **Contiguous** a) of lasting duration b) separate c) coincidental
     d) adjacent e) argumentative
9   **Belligerent** a) chivalrous b) offensive c) war-like d) undergoing an
     ordeal e) controversial
10   **Incandescent** a) untruthful b) combustible material c) starry
     d) glowing e) luminary
11   **Stalwart** a) adamant b) sturdy c) spirited d) able-bodied e) dynamic
12   **Hapless** a) sad b) prone to failure c) humiliated d) disastrous e) unlucky
13   **Mercurial** a) volatile b) elemental c) fantastic d) eloquent
     e) compassionate
14   **Salutary** a) greeting b) beneficial c) welcoming d) helpful person
     e) beckoning

Hard

15   **Mendicant** a) priest b) medicinal compound c) untruthful d) beggar
     e) claimant
16   **Venial** a) sinful b) justifiable c) relating to wine d) allowable
     e) forgivable
17   **Magnificat** a) canticle b) splendid object c) grandee d) expansion
     e) praise
18   **Exequies** a) dignified withdrawal b) church rituals c) fulsome praise
     d) pertaining to a will e) funeral rites
19   **Setaceous** a) knotty b) bristly c) prickly d) on edge e) unkempt
20   **Saturnine** a) cynical b) serious c) pessimistic d) poisonous e) gloomy

SPORT AND GAMES 1

Fairly easy

1 Which team won the Football League and FA Cup double in the 1993-94 soccer season?

2 Sir Gordon Richards rode only one Epsom Derby winner during his career. Which horse gave him his victory in the 1953 race?

3 Which runner was a simultaneous world record holder at 1,500 metres, 2,000 metres, 3,000 metres and 5,000 metres?

4 In what indoor game is it necessary to finish on a double?

5 What sport combines cross-country running with map-reading?

6 Which cricketer scored over 28,000 runs at an average of 95.14 and made 117 centuries in the first-class game?

7 Catch-as-catch-can is a particular style in what sport?

Not so easy

8 Who was transferred from Fiorentina to Juventus in 1990 for £7.7 million?

9 Name the odd one out from the Washington Redskins, New York Yankees, Seattle Seahawks and Pittsburgh Steelers.

10 What is the premier event in rifle shooting?

11 Who was the first test cricketer to be made a life peer?

12 Morphy, Capablanca and Alekhine were all leading exponents of what game?

13 Which course is the home of the Honourable Company of Edinburgh Golfers?

14 In Rugby Union, which three famous clubs constitute the Exiles?

Hard

15 In which sport does the Lady Paramount act as an official?

16 Which American tennis champion of the 1920s and 1930s was nicknamed Big Bill?

17 If a boxer weighed in at 52 kilograms (8st 3lb), in what weight division would he be fighting?

18 What is the most northerly racecourse in Great Britain?

19 Watsonians are a rugby union club. In which city are they based?

20 In cricket, body-line was a development of what earlier system of bowling and field placement?

ANIMAL KINGDOM 1

Fairly easy

1   Which insects, common in Britain, are red with black spots, black with red spots or yellow with black spots?
2   What large mammal has a tail so powerful that it can actually stand on it and take its hind legs off the ground?
3   Give the name for the tiny plants and animals that float near the surface of fresh or salt water and provide the only source of food for many kinds of fish.
4   The bat is the only mammal that can fly in a true sense. True or false?
5   What are the males of the honeybee called that do no work in the hive and are the only members of a colony that can mate the queen?
6   Which Australian animal feeds exclusively on the leaves of the eucalyptus tree?
7   What is the largest extant bird?

Not so easy

8   How many cavities has the stomach of a cow?
9   If a bird is said to be raptorial, what kind is it?
10   The South African impala, the Indian blackbuck and the North American pronghorn are all types of which animal?
11   What is a more scientific name for the shell of a tortoise?
12   The phoenix is a bird native to the Rocky Mountains of North America. True or false?
13   What kind of dog is a griffon?
14   Field mice are very common in Britain, but are they of the long-tailed or striped variety?

Hard

15   What relative of the modern elephant was hunted by prehistoric man and died out less than 10,000 years ago?
16   Quadruped and biped are familiar terms, but what is a palmiped?
17   What is a Mexican hairless?
18   If an animal is described as feral, what does this tell you about it?
19   What sort of animals are the native British breeds Large White, Wessex Saddleback and Landrace?
20   What beast of prey is sometimes called a glutton?

, *Blucher* and *Puffing Billy*?

t Viceroy of India?

explorer was murdered by natives in Hawaii?

as given to an unknown substance sought by early

at was supposed to change metals into gold?

r was the present Duke of York born?

ich war was the 38th parallel the focal point of diplomatic

ary activity?

h city was John Paul II archbishop before he became Pope?

sy

o would have used the lamp invented by Sir Humphry Davy in

15?

hat did Manstein, Keitel and Model have in common?

Which American physicist was Director of the Los Alamos Laboratory, New Mexico (1943–45), which produced the first atomic bomb?

How did Alexander the Great solve the puzzle set by the Gordian knot?

12 Who was the first king to reign over both England and Scotland?

13 What was the name of the auxiliary police force used by the British to crush the Irish Republicans in the years 1920–21?

14 By what title was Arthur Wellesley better known?

Hard

15 What were the full Christian names of Sir Winston Churchill?

16 Which Apostle was chosen to take the place of Judas Iscariot after the latter's betrayal of Jesus?

17 In medieval England, what was the name of the tax based on one-tenth of a person's possessions?

18 What is the modern name for Van Diemen's Land?

19 Name the British Crown colony in the Malay Peninsula, composed of Malacca, Penang, Singapore and dependencies, which was dissolved in 1946?

20 Which English king is reputed to have died of a surfeit of lampreys?

GEOGRAPHY AND TRAVEL 1

Fairly easy

1 Of which country is KLM the state airline?

2 What are private social clubs for male students in US colleges called?

3 In which royal palace in France is the Hall of Mirrors?

4 Name the official language of Pakistan.

5 What are Cree, Creek and Crow?

6 Give the name for the cold, dry northerly wind that blows in the Mediterranean provinces of France.

7 In which European capital is the boulevard known as 'the Ring'?

Not so easy

8 Of which sea is the Gulf of Riga is an inlet?

9 Mount Redoubt is an active volcano in which American state?

10 An atoll is a type of coral reef found in the tropical waters of the Western and Central Pacific. What is its peculiar shape?

11 What name is given to a language, usually a hybrid one, which is used as a means of communication between different peoples?

12 In the USA, what is a G-man?

13 Which subregion of Aquitaine in south-west France is famous for its brandy?

14 What is the Russian word for the fortress area in old Russian cities, the most famous of which is in Moscow?

Hard

15 What former Arab port is now part of Tel Aviv in Israel?

16 In the USA who are WASPs?

17 For which industry is the town of Delft in South Holland famous?

18 Of which territory in the Caribbean Sea is Beef Island a part?

19 What is the minimum age of the President of the United States?

20 In Russia, what is a samovar?

ART AND LITERATURE 1

Fairly easy

1 Which early 20th-century school of painting was noted for its concentration on geometrical figures?

2 What is the popular title for the collection of stories translated by Sir Richard Burton as *The Thousand Nights and a Night*?

3 Who won the Booker Prize for his novel *The Famished Road*?

4 What is a poem written in memory of someone who has died called?

5 Hannah Massey, Maggie Rowan and Tilly Trotter are all heroines created by which successful novelist?

6 Which English artist's dumb shows such as *Marriage à la Mode* were so widely copied that he became instrumental in the passing of the Copyright Act of 1735?

7 Give the term for someone wholly or partly responsible for a piece of writing published under another person's name.

Not so easy

8 Who wrote a series of science fiction novels about the doomed planet Dune?

9 Thomas Girtin was an English landscape painter of the 18th Century. In what medium did he excel?

10 In Greek mythology, which goddess was the avenger of crime and the dispenser of justice?

11 What French Protestant reformer published his theology in the Institutes of the Christian Religion?

12 Which American author wrote the animal story *Black Beauty*?

13 In Shakespeare's *King Lear*, the King has three daughters. Regan and Cordelia are two: who is the third?

14 Which French novelist wrote nearly a hundred books to which he gave the overall title *La Comedie Humaine*?

Hard

15 Name the black American writer whose works include *Another Country* and *Go Tell It on the Mountain*.

16 What is the term for the literary device involving a sudden descent from the sublime to the ridiculous used to create a deliberate anticlimax?

17 Who in the 1820s wrote essays for the *London Magazine* under the nom-de-plume 'Elia'?

18 Which French impressionist painter, developer of the broken colour technique, painted 'The Girl with a Blue Ribbon'?

19 Which US economist and diplomat wrote a brilliant book of popular economics entitled *The Affluent Society*?

20 In his line 'Thou still unravish'd bride of quietness!' to what was John Keats referring?

Quick-fire Q

POT POURRI 2

Fairly easy

1 Of which reli

2 Of what is dem

3 In economics, wh

4 Libra is a sign of the

5 In knitting one basic sti

6 Who in the Bible lived for

7 What is a Sally Lunn?

Not so easy

8 What is special about the British Guian magenta, of 1856?

9 Which blue-veined French cheese, similar to ewes' milk?

10 Give the name for a bishop with no cathedral of his works as an assistant to the bishop of a diocese.

11 What is a cicatrice?

12 Which iron-bearing clay whose name means literally 'cooked used by sculptors for busts and by pottery factories in the prod of decorative ware?

13 Where would you expect to find an aileron?

14 What is Benedictine?

Hard

15 Give the name for a cotton cloth with a twill weave and a short nap, usually dyed dark.

16 A map that shows altitude, either by the use of colours or shading or by actual 3-D shapes, has a special name. What is it?

17 Which Austrian psychologist and psychiatrist evolved the concept of the 'inferiority complex'?

18 What name is given to the period approximately between early July and mid-August when Sirius rises and sets with the sun, usually characterised by hot, stifling weather?

19 In architecture, segmental, primitive, doucine and elliptical are all different types of what construction?

20 What is the term for the secondary ring of tissue of a plant stem that may turn into bark?

QUICK-FIRE QUIZ 2

HISTORY 2
Fairly easy
1 What were Rocke
2 Who was the la
3 Which British
4 What name
alchemists
In what ye
During
and mili
Of whi

Not so ea
8 Wh
18
9
10
11

UNITED KINGDOM 2

Fairly easy

1   What are the Six Counties?
2   In which British city is the *Sunday Mail* published?
3   Name the Scottish island famous for the production of a distinctive style of jersey said to have derived from survivors of the Spanish Armada?
4   Which English county's name is sometimes abbreviated to Salop?
5   Which river does the Clifton Suspension Bridge span?
6   The ancestral home of the Dukes of Devonshire is in Derbyshire. What is it called?
7   In which Scottish shire does the Eglinton Hunt take place?

Not so easy

8   What is housed at Hertford House in the West End of London?
9   In what English institution are there four pursuivants?
10 Which city is served by Dyce airport?
11 What are the Whitstable Natives?
12 The Shambles is a famous thoroughfare in which English town?
13 The North Foreland is a chalk headland at the extreme eastern end of which English county?
14 What do the Scots call a servant who acts as a hunting and fishing guide?

Hard

15 What is the name of the local government workers' union formerly called NALGO?
16 On what familiar everyday object would you find the words *plodiol wye i'm gwlad*?
17 Where in England is the deep cave called Wookey Hole?
18 What is the popular name for the statue, designed in 1893, that is a famous London landmark and which was originally entitled *The Angel of Christian Charity*?
19 Who designed the Cenotaph in Whitehall?
20 Which cathedral in Britain has the tallest spire?

MUSIC AND ENTERTAINMENT 2

Fairly easy

1   Which actor plays Sergeant Lewis in *Inspector Morse*?
2   In which country did the dance called a mazurka originate?
3   Which Newcastle rock group of the 1960s had a number one hit on both sides of the Atlantic with 'House of the Rising Sun'?
4   Peter Fluck and Roger Law were responsible for which satirical TV show?
5   Which Cockney dance band leader used to greet his audiences with the cry, 'Wakey-Wakey!'?
6   Name the Englishman who first produced the Gilbert and Sullivan comic operas.
7   What musical instrument was featured in the theme music for the 1949 film of *The Third Man*?

Not so easy

8   In what field of the arts was George Balanchine pre-eminent?
9   What was the Christian name of *Roseanne*'s husband in the hit American comedy show?
10   Who sang 'Makin' Whoopee' in *The Fabulous Baker Boys*?
11   What is Fats Domino's real forename name?
12   The goings-on on HMS *Troutbridge* were the subject of which hugely successful radio programme?
13   In what city was the film actress Elizabeth Taylor born? Was it Baltimore, London, Montreal or Paris?
14   Which American Shakespearean actor and film director died in 1985 after ending his career playing in commercials?

Hard

15   Which programme originally billed as 'a daily programme of music, advice and entertainment for the home' had its 50th anniversary in 1996?
16   Who was the English composer who became Master of the Queen's Music in 1953?
17   What famous film actor never won an Oscar for a part in a film, but was given a special Oscar for his 'unique mastery of the art of screen acting'?
18   What is the difference between Scottish and Northumbrian pipes?
19   Name the famous *fin de siecle* French actress who ended her career on one leg.
20   Who or what was the adversary in *Blake's Seven*?

SCIENCE AND NATURE 2

Fairly easy

1 What colour are the flowers of the laburnum tree?
2 How deep is a fathom?
3 What is the scientific term for a substance that influences a chemical reaction without undergoing any permanent change itself?
4 Light amplification by stimulated emission of radiation produces a high-energy monochromatic beam of light. What is the usual name for such a light beam?
5 In astronomy what is a more popular name for the constellation Ursa Minor?
6 Give another name for the breastbone.
7 What are tides with the lowest high waters and the highest low waters called?

Not so easy

8 To within 12 hours, how long does it take for the Moon to orbit the Earth?
9 What is the geometrical term for a solid shape having six faces?
10 Which element has the chemical symbol Ag?
11 How many equinoxes occur during a calendar year?
12 In an electric light bulb which element is most commonly used to make the filament?
13 What is a Blenheim orange?
14 In avoirdupois weight, what is equivalent to 1016.5kg?

Hard

15 A moulin occurs in high mountainous regions. What is it?
16 What name is given to the process by which salt is removed from sea water to make it suitable for drinking or agricultural purposes?
17 Can you give a more popular name for the plant that grows in swamps and is sometimes called a kingcup?
18 Which gas is formed when a hydrogen bomb is detonated?
19 Over how many degrees of longitude do the imaginary bands across the Earth's surface known as time zones stretch?
20 The Cassegranian, Gregorian and Schmidt are all types of what?

DEFINITIONS 2

Choose from the five alternatives the word or words *closest* in meaning to the word given first in bold type.

Fairly easy

1   **Ferocious** a) implacable b) likely to attack c) savage d) carnivorous
     e) angry
2   **Anomaly** a) difference b) confusion c) aberration d) irregularity
     e) discord
3   **Gratis** a) free b) economical c) inexpensive d) complimentary
     e) charitable
4   **Scant** a) petty b) paltry c) insufficient d) diminutive e) modest
5   **Myopic** a) blind b) dim c) invisible d) blurred e) short-sighted
6   **Conundrum** a) ambiguity b) riddle c) trick d) quibble e) diversion
7   **Sceptical** a) discerning b) narrow-minded c) argumentative
     d) disbelieving e) worldly

Not so easy

8   **Bailey** a) castle keep b) parapet c) trench d) castle enclosure e) buttress
9   **Germinate** a) sprout b) reproduce c) conceive d) ferment e) infect
10   **Sequester** a) abduct b) confiscate c) extort d) take by storm e) disinherit
11   **Effervesce** a) vaporise b) flower c) sparkle d) bubble e) foam
12   **Basilica** a) monastery b) auditorium c) church d) mansion e) terrace
13   **Nihilism** a) mutiny b) revolutionary ideas c) impiety d) rejection of
     accepted beliefs e) blasphemy
14   **Eviscerate** a) disembowel b) secrete c) disgorge d) let blood e) vomit

Hard

15   **Hydropathy** a) aversion to water b) measurement of water c) water
     cure d) tendency to turn to moisture e) craving for water
16   **Piscine** a) water-bed b) fish-eating c) bathing-pool d) fish-pond
     e) pea-shaped
17   **Declivity** a) gully b) zig-zag c) precipice d) intersection e) slope
18   **Chromatic** a) brightly coloured b) illuminated c) luminous d) prismatic
     e) relating to chromium
19   **Traduce** a) be contemptuous of b) make a fool of c) speak ill of
     d) disapprove of e) make light of
20   **Uxorious** a) maritally contented b) infatuated c) seductive d) adorable
     e) fond of one's wife

SPORT AND GAMES 2

Fairly easy

1 Who was the first professional footballer to be knighted?
2 The 'eastern cut-off', the 'western roll' and the 'straddle' were all techniques used at different times in what athletics event?
3 In what commercially marketed game do the players act as detectives?
4 Who in golf is nicknamed 'Great White Shark'?
5 Battledore and Shuttlecock is the old form of which modern game?
6 The University Boat Race begins at Putney. Where does it end?
7 At what major sporting event are the Diamond Challenge Sculls competed for?

Not so easy

8 Which horse race has been won by Urban Sea, Carnegie and Lammtarra?
9 In which sport 'Babe' Ruth was pre-eminent?
10 What annual work of reference may be regarded as the cricketers' bible?
11 In a famous victory at Earl's Court in July 1951, Randolph Turpin became World Middleweight Champion. Whom did he beat?
12 In what game is three of a kind called a 'Pung' and four of a kind a 'Kong'?
13 How many horsemen constitute a polo team?
14 Which soccer club play at Pittodrie Park?

Hard

15 What is the name of the American Motorcycle Association's most important road race for professional motorcyclists, held annually in Florida?
16 In cricket, what name is given to a ball bowled by a left-arm bowler that breaks from the off to the leg side?
17 Name the rugby union side that won the County Championship seven times in eight years from 1958.
18 In what sport is a pommel horse used?
19 What name is given to a hold in which a wrestler gets both arms under those of his opponent from behind and clasps his hands behind the neck?
20 What nationality is the champion ice skater Elvis Stojko?

ANIMAL KINGDOM 2

Fairly easy

1   When fishmongers sell dogfish in Britain, what do they incorrectly call it?
2   Which is the larger by weight, a typical African or Indian elephant?
3   Where in Gloucestershire is the Wildfowl Trust?
4   Roe, fallow and sika are all kinds of what animal?
5   What is the maximum life span of a wild rabbit? Is it 10, 15 or 20 years?
6   Which mammals emit squeaks at high frequencies as part of their echo-sounding location system?
7   What sea creature resembles a knight in chess?

Not so easy

8   Which sort of mouse is a legally protected species in Britain?
9   What is a Flemish giant?
10   Which large, rough-coated dog gets its name from a Yorkshire valley?
11   In France, which domestic animal is specially trained to smell out truffles?
12   What sort of creature is a Komodo dragon?
13   Which carnivorous mammal about 60cm (2ft) long and having brown and black fur and white head markings is rare in England but quite common in parts of Wales and Scotland?
14   What is a herbivore?

Hard

15   Which wild pig is found only in north-east and southern Africa?
16   Jacobson's organ is found in the mouths of certain creatures and enables them to follow scent trails. What sort of creatures are they?
17   Can you name one British example of the mammals known as insectivores?
18   Why is the missel thrush so called?
19   What animals make up the *suidae* family?
20   Which wild mountain sheep lives only in Corsica and Sardinia?

GEOGRAPHY AND TRAVEL 2
Fairly easy
1   In which Eastern city is the great thoroughfare known as the Ginza?
2   What body in the United States is divided into the Senate and the House of Representatives?
3   In the Far East, what is the sacred building called which is in the shape of a tapered tower with many stories, each with an upward, projecting roof?
4   Name the French river famous for the many chateaux situated in its middle and lower valleys.
5   Beverly Hills is a suburb of which major American city?
6   In which city is the great library called the Bibliotheque Nationale?
7   Which volcano does the ruined ancient city of Pompeii stands close to?

Not so easy
8   In Italy there are four kinds of train: *rapidissimo*, *diretto*, *accellerato* and *rapido*. Which is the slowest?
9   Moslems must fast by day during the ninth month of the Islamic year. What is it called?
10   What do Australians call a long, narrow lake?
11   Name the wine that is particularly associated with the river Douro.
12   The skiing resort of Zermatt in Valais, Switzerland, is situated below which mountain?
13   In which state of the USA is Death Valley?
14   What is the word, derived from Malay, for rice when its grains are still in their husks?

Hard
15   What is the colourless plum brandy called that is made in several Balkan countries?
16   Give the name of a people of mixed Negro and Arab blood who mostly live in the region of the Nile river.
17   Which group of small Danish islands in the North Atlantic are about half way between the Shetlands and Iceland?
18   Name the major seaport that serves Mexico City.
19   What is the British name for the synthetic material called Dacron in the United States?
20   One of the greatest cod-fishing grounds in the world is a vast extension of the continental shelf in the Atlantic, south-east of Newfoundland. What is it called?

ART AND LITERATURE 2
Fairly easy
1   In the Uncle Remus stories of Joel Chandler Harris, who is the principal adversary of Brer Rabbit?
2   In Greek drama, what was the name for a group of actors who commented in unison on the action of a play?
3   Which novel describes events in Dublin on 16 June 1904?
4   Name the artist, basically an anatomist, who was the most celebrated English painter of horses.
5   Which Victorian lady wrote a famous book about cooking and household management?
6   What work tells of a spiritual journey from the City of Destruction to the Celestial City?
7   In American literature, who was the wealthy bootlegger of the Jazz Age?

Not so easy
8   Pollok Country Park, Glasgow, is the home of which major art collection?
9   In Shakespeare, what do Antony, Romeo and Othello have in common?
10 In which novel are Ralph, Jack and Peterkin three castaways?
11 Who were Currer, Ellis and Acton Bell?
12 Marc Chagall, often regarded as the forerunner of surrealism, spent his life in France, but what was his country of origin?
13 What form of writing with wedge-shaped letters was used by the ancient Babylonians, Persians and Hittites?
14 The writers W. Somerset Maugham, A. J. Cronin and Richard Gordon have something in common. What is it?

Hard
15 Which Elizabethan dramatist wrote *The Spanish Tragedy*?
16 Name the German artist and engraver who became court painter to Henry VIII of England.
17 Who was known as 'the peasant poet'?
18 Which famous science fiction novel begins: 'Behind every man now alive stand thirty ghosts, for that is the ratio by which the dead outnumber the living'?
19 The destruction of which town during the Spanish Civil War, allegedly by German bombing, inspired a great painting by Picasso?
20 What novel by Thomas Mann is a life of the German composer Adrian Leverkuhn 'as told by a friend'?

Quick-fire Quiz 3

POT POURRI 3

Fairly easy

1   What colour is gunmetal?
2   Give the official title of an ambassador of the Pope.
3   According to the proverb, what cannot be made out of a sow's ear?
4   Name the Mexican dish that is made up of chopped meat in a stew with kidney beans and red chillies.
5   What is the most usual use of white beet?
6   In the traffic light sequence, which colour follows amber?
7   What kind of wear are 'oxfords' when they are not very wide trousers?

Not so easy

8   Give the term for a word like 'deified' that reads the same backwards as forwards.
9   Do you know a more familiar name for the national flag sometimes called 'Old Glory'?
10 What is the Montessori system?
11 Which instruction given to a printer means 'let the original stand'?
12 What is the name of the final battle between God and Satan, foretold in the Bible?
13 In cookery, there is a special term meaning to heat in a liquid until partially cooked. What is it?
14 What does a gardener mean by a 'spit'?

Hard

15 Which order of priests base their religious life on the *Spiritual Exercises* of their founder?
16 What law prevents a woman from succeeding to a throne?
17 Name the cut of beef taken from over the bone of the rump.
18 In the world of finance, what distinguishes equities from debentures and preference shares?
19 Who would employ the Rorschach test?
20 What name is given to a commission that promotes an officer in the services to a higher nominal rank than that for which he is paid?

HISTORY 3
Fairly easy
1 In which ancient land did the Ptolemy dynasty rule?
2 The VI flying bomb used by the Germans against London and southern England in 1944 was given a more popular name by the British people. What was it?
3 Who became President of the United States in 1963 after the assassination of John F. Kennedy?
4 Which Islamic Republic was declared on 1 April 1979?
5 What did Saigon become in 1976?
6 According to Sir Winston Churchill, who was 'that bloodthirsty guttersnipe'?
7 Whose fleet was defeated by the British under Nelson at the naval Battle of Copenhagen in 1801?

Not so easy
8 Which nuclear-powered US submarine passed under the ice at the North Pole in 1958?
9 What Greek runner of the 5th Century BCE is said to have run 241km (150 miles) in 48 hours to summon help for Athens?
10 The English translation of the Old and New Testaments made by command of James I, first published in 1611, is sometimes called the King James's Bible. By which title is it more usually known?
11 By what name is the religious teacher Guatama Siddhartha, who died about 480BCE, more commonly known?
12 Which American general took the unconditional surrender of Japan to the Allies on board the battleship *Missouri* in Tokyo Bay on 2 September 1945?
13 Expo '67 was held in which city?
14 The Renaissance was a period in European history from about the middle of the 14th to the end of the 16th Century, but what is the precise meaning of renaissance?

Hard
15 What relation was Prince Philip to Princess Elizabeth before their marriage in 1947?
16 Where in Virginia did General Robert E. Lee surrender to the Union army in 1865, thus ending the American Civil War?
17 Which organisation, founded in 1875, aims to promote international collaboration in postal services?
18 What is the only medieval religious order of English origin?
19 In what famous sea battle was Mark Antony defeated by Octavian in 31BCE?
20 What is the name given to a 'near-man', probably of the genus *pithecanthropus*, whose remains were found in China in the late 1920s?

UNITED KINGDOM 3

Fairly easy

1   Do you know which British decoration is awarded 'For Valour'?
2   What in Scotland is a ceilidh?
3   Name the official London residence of the Archbishop of Canterbury.
4   The Lutine Bell is sounded in which British institution?
5   What British coin ceased to be currency in January 1961?
6   Which Roman road runs from London to Wroxeter in Shropshire via St Albans?
7   The population of Wales is closer to two than three million. True or false?

Not so easy

8   Which festival city has a volcanic plug called 'Arthur's Seat' on its outskirts?
9   If you were travelling by rail from London to Brighton, from what station would you normally leave?
10   Which Yorkshire valley is famous for its cheese?
11   Where did the National Trust present General Eisenhower with a suite of rooms for his personal use in appreciation of his services as Supreme Commander of Allied Forces in Europe?
12   Name the large sandbank in the centre of the Thames estuary that marks the mouth of the river.
13   Where in Scotland is Dunvegan Castle?
14   Which English city was called *Aquae Sulis* by the Romans?

Hard

15   The Giant's Causeway in Northern Ireland consists of about 40,000 columns of which rock?
16   In which English city is the wooden 'Mathematicians' Bridge', said to have been constructed without nails?
17   Where in Britain are two bird sanctuaries with Scandinavian names, Skomer and Skokholm?
18   What is unusual about Loch Faskally near Pitlochry in Perthshire?
19   The former royal residence White Lodge, Richmond Park is now occupied by which royal school?
20   In the West Country of England, what are mops?

MUSIC AND ENTERTAINMENT 3
Fairly easy

1   At which London theatre did actor Brian Rix score numerous successful farce hits in the 1950s and 1960s?
2   In which TV series did Mulder and Scully appear?
3   The world famous pianist Clara Wieck was married to an equally famous German composer. Who?
4   Strathspey is the middle part of the wooded valley of the river Spey, but what else in Scotland is a strathspey?
5   How many TV *Thunderbirds* were there?
6   Who composed *The Blue Danube* waltz?
7   Reginald Dwight is the real name of which British pop singer?

Not so easy

8   What was the name of the British heats for Eurovision's popular show *Jeux Sans Frontieres*?
9   Who played the male lead in the film classic *The Four Horsemen of the Apocalypse*?
10   Which opera company had its 50th anniversary in 1996?
11   By what name is Richard Starkey better known in the entertainment world?
12   Which ballerina was the daughter of a British father and a Brazilian-Irish mother and was christened Peggy Hookham?
13   The size of a television set is measured in inches. How, exactly?
14   *The Knightsbridge March* by Eric Coates was the theme tune of which long-running, topical radio programme?

Hard

15   What female historical figure is a central character in Benjamin Britten's opera *Gloriana*?
16   Dmitri Shostakovich's Symphony No. 7 is a musical tribute to which Second World War battle?
17   Who played American private eye Warshawski on film?
18   In film-making, what name is given to the soundproof cover over a camera that obscures its noise?
19   According to the poet Alexander Pope, which great 18th-century actor, 'never had his equal and never will have a rival'?
20   What is the title of the Welsh national anthem?

SCIENCE AND NATURE 3

Fairly easy

1   From which plant is linseed oil produced?
2   What is the transparent water jelly called that surrounds the yoke of a bird's egg?
3   Give another name for oil of vitriol.
4   What colour are the flowers of speedwell?
5   A tar-like substance is obtained from petroleum. What is it?
6   Give the unit of measurement for an explosive power equal to that of a million tons of TNT.
7   What colour does an alkali turn litmus?

Not so easy

8   Relative density is the density of a substance relative to what?
9   Where would you expect to find a percussion cap?
10   What name is given to the mixture of acids that is able to dissolve gold?
11   When scientists speak of the hydrosphere, to what are they referring?
12   The hereditary disease haemophilia affects only one of the sexes. Which?
13   Where are the Sea of Nectar, the Sea of Showers and the Sea of Clouds?
14   Which gas causes the bubbles in soda water when the pressure on it is released?

Hard

15   What colour does gold leaf appear when held up to the light?
16   Where in the human body would you find the medulla oblongata?
17   In mechanics, what is the mass of an object multiplied by its speed?
18   Which acid, found in wood sorrel, rhubarb leaves and other plants, is used in dyeing and bleaching?
19   With what does the Hubble classification deal?
20   Name the device, originally invented in Holland, used for storing static electricity and that is the oldest type of capacitor.

DEFINITIONS 3

Choose from the five alternatives the word or words *closest* in meaning to the word given first in bold type.

Fairly easy

1   **Exhale** a) sigh b) gasp c) breathe one's last d) eject e) respire
2   **Stanza** a) lyric b) blank verse c) metre d) section of a poem e) ballad
3   **Garish** a) gorgeous b) dashing c) gaudy d) pretentious e) bright
4   **Glacial** a) icy b) snow-clad c) alpine d) mountainous e) extremely cold
5   **Antipathy** a) reluctance b) nausea c) dislike d) disgust e) opposite
6   **Burlesque** a) plagiarism b) satire c) forgery d) parody e) comedy
7   **Venerate** a) have faith in b) revere c) praise d) show courtesy towards
     e) of great age

Not so easy

8   **Convoluted** a) rotating b) spiral c) twisted d) undulatory e) agitated
9   **Dilettante** a) virtuoso b) poseur c) dabbler d) savant e) pundit
10   **Nonpareil** a) up to standard b) superior c) select d) praiseworthy
     e) unequalled
11   **Exculpate** a) reprieve b) exonerate c) condone d) make allowances for
     e) extenuate
12   **Nomenclature** a) technical term b) description c) designation
     d) title-deed e) system of names
13   **Hawser** a) girder b) steel cable c) steel chain d) halyard e) harness
14   **Supine** a) lying face downward b) lying face upward c) backwards
     d) at ground level e) sprawling

Hard

15   **Recondite** a) indefinable b) obscure c) vague d) paradoxical
     e) insoluble
16   **Doctrinaire** a) wrangler b) high-brow c) philosophical d) pedantic
     e) man of letters
17   **Lacuna** a) hiatus b) separation c) void d) interruption e) fracture
18   **Simony** a) abandonment of faith b) breaking of ecclesiastical law
     c) holding excessive number of church offices d) trade in church offices
     e) preaching of heretical doctrines
19   **Sybaritic** a) luxury-loving b) worshipping material things
     c) self-indulgent d) debauched e) sensual
20   **Exigent** a) peremptory b) obdurate c) exacting d) arbitrary
     e) imperative

SPORT AND GAMES 3

Fairly easy

1   At what sport did Mick the Miller excel?
2   In 1971, which cricketer became the first English batsman to average over 100 runs per innings for a complete season and in 1977 scored his 100th 100 in first class matches?
3   From what material are the poles of modern vaulting poles made?
4   What position do fencing opponents adopt when preparing to fence?
5   What is the distance of the longest freestyle event in international swimming?
6   Which sport do the Worthing Bears play?
7   What device was used at Wimbledon for the first time in 2009?

Not so easy

8   In racing slang, how much is a pony?
9   At what sport did Jill Parker play for England a record number of 413 times between 1967 and 1983?
10 Which player scored a hat trick at Wembley in the World Cup Final of 1966?
11 What is medal play in golf?
12 Wing attack and wing defence are playing positions in which game?
13 At Scrabble, what bonus does a player receive for laying down all his or her letters at a single turn?
14 In cycling, what is a derailleur?

Hard

15 Which famous New Zealand Rugby Union player was nicknamed 'the Boot'?
16 What county cricket side has as its emblem a horse rearing above the word *invicta*?
17 When Trevor Francis moved to Nottingham Forest in September 1979, he became the first British footballer to be transferred for £1 million. Which club did he leave?
18 At international level in lacrosse, the game is 10-a-side for men. How many make up a team in the women's game at the same level?
19 At what sport are barani, rudolph and randolph familiar techniques?
20 Which celebrated heavyweight boxer won a gold medal as a light heavyweight at the 1960 Rome Olympics before turning professional?

ANIMAL KINGDOM 3

Fairly easy

1   According to an old legend, which native British bird never uses its voice until it is dying?
2   What is the collective name for a group of lions?
3   Name the ferocious fish shaped like a torpedo that is found in warm seas and is closely related to the sea-perch.
4   What is the title of the ruling body of the competitive dog world in Britain?
5   What type of fish is a shubunkin?
6   Which plant does the Colorado beetle most often attack?
7   What is a young cow called that has not borne any young?

Not so easy

8   Only two mammals lay eggs. One is the spiny anteater: what is the other?
9   Which reptiles, native to tropical America, are very similar in appearance to alligators, except they have bony plates on their bellies instead of scales?
10   In which creature is the direction of hair growth on the body from belly backwards, the opposite way to other mammals, so that rain water runs down without soaking it when hanging upside-down in trees?
11   What name is given to the last stage in the life of a butterfly before it becomes fully adult?
12   How many legs has a flea?
13   A fantail is a fish. True or false?
14   What is the British equivalent of the North American screech owl is called?

Hard

15   What types of European mammal have a pair of dew-claws on each foot?
16   Do pelagic fish live near the top of the sea, near the bottom or in the middle?
17   Porcupines are native to warm regions of Africa and Asia, but where in Europe are they to be found?
18   The main diet of the swift is insects, but what is unusual about the way it catches them?
19   Which burrowing animal of South Africa is closely related to the hyena and feeds on carrion, small mammals and insects?
20   What is a redthread?

GEOGRAPHY AND TRAVEL 3

Fairly easy

1   Give the popular name for the inlet of the Bosporus that constitutes the harbour of Istanbul.
2   In Paris what is the *Bourse*?
3   What do sailors call the stormy belt of ocean between latitudes 40° and 50° south of the Equator?
4   In which Indian city is the Taj Mahal?
5   On what kind of building would you find a tower known as a minaret?
6   Which mountain range forms the backbone of Italy?
7   What is the French-speaking section of the population called who live in the southern part of Belgium?

Not so easy

8   In the USA, what kind of drink is applejack?
9   During its history, the capital of Turkey has had several names. Constantinople and Istanbul are two. What is the third common one?
10   Where in Germany is there a replica of America's Liberty Bell?
11   What do the Spaniards call a bullfight?
12   What were the Federated States of Micronesia formerly called?
13   In Japan, what is the name for the theatre of the townsmen of the 18th and 19th Centuries that is still a popular form of drama?
14   Which European capital is situated at the point where Lake Malar joins the Baltic Sea?

Hard

15   What name is given to the valley of the upper Inn in Switzerland, with a mild, dry climate, famous for its resorts?
16   In Japan, what annual festival is called *oshugatsu*?
17   Give the present name of the seaport on the Adriatic coast formerly called Ragusa.
18   What is the legislature of the Netherlands called?
19   Which straits connect the Persian Gulf with the Arabian Sea?
20   At 7,035 metres (23,081 feet), Aconcagua is the highest mountain in the Andes. In which country is it?

ART AND LITERATURE 3

Fairly easy

1 In which Ayrshire village was Robert Burns born?
2 Who is the male detective in the stories of Dorothy L. Sayers?
3 In Coleridge's *The Rime of the Ancient Mariner,* what does the Ancient Mariner shoot, thus making the sailors believe he has changed their luck?
4 What general name is given to the three books by Olivia Manning, *The Great Fortune*, *The Spoilt City* and *Friends and Heroes*?
5 Which ancient writer wrote a fable entitled *The Dog in the Manger*?
6 What do Samuel Pepys, Francis Kilvert and John Evelyn have in common?
7 Name the great poetic work, written around 1387, that has about 17,000 lines in heroic couplets.

Not so easy

8 What was the pen name of the American writer Samuel Langhorne Clemens?
9 Which English illustrator is best remembered for his work in Oscar Wilde's *Salome* and in *The Yellow Book*?
10 'And gentlemen in England now a-bed shall think themselves accurs'd they were not here. . .'. To what was Shakespeare's *Henry V* referring?
11 In Greek mythology, who were the race of giants with one eye in the centre of their foreheads?
12 What is the literary term for a deliberately exaggerated statement?
13 Lewis Eliot is the hero and narrator of a sequence of novels by which British novelist?
14 Who was the imaginary English country gentleman about whom Joseph Addison and Richard Steele wrote articles in the *Spectator*?

Hard

15 Which Roman poet was the author of at least a dozen books of *Epigrams*?
16 *Les Fauves* was a name given to a group of artists that included Matisse. What does *fauves* mean?
17 Which famous novel begins, 'There was no possibility of taking a walk that day.'?
18 Which 19th Century English novelist had a long and undistinguished career in the postal service?
19 What is a line of poetry called that regularly contains six iambic feet, that is 12 syllables, with a pause after the third foot?
20 Name the Evelyn Waugh hero who is a Catholic gentleman of private means and joins the Halberdiers as a subaltern.

Quick-fire Quiz 4

POT POURRI 4
Fairly easy

1 What is the art of cutting shrubs into ornamental shapes called?
2 Which confection is made from almonds, eggs and sugar?
3 What does the road sign of a circle showing a red car alongside a black car convey?
4 In the book of Genesis, what was the intention in building the Tower of Babel?
5 Give the name for the ceremonial head-dress of a bishop, worn as a symbol of office.
6 How many parts of alloy has 18-carat gold?
7 What is the language of the gipsies?

Not so easy

8 For what purpose would a gardener use BHC or benzene hexachloride?
9 What is the name for a cover used to protect the back of a chair or sofa from dirty marks and literally from hair oil?
10 A mixture of cement, sand and lime is applied to outside walls to form a hard surface. What is it called?
11 Who is protected by the Swiss Guard?
12 What are ornaments of fine gold, silver or copper wire twisted into patterns called?
13 Name the short, pointed tool used for making holes in leather by a shoemaker.
14 In photography what is meant by an SLR camera?

Hard

15 Sedilia are seats in the south side of the chancel of a church for the use of clergy. How many seats usually make up a sedilia?
16 On what liquids is the film of shining scales known as beeswing found?
17 The alphabet of the Russian language is written in a particular kind of script. What word is used to describe it?
18 In the Anglican church, what is the latest time of day a marriage may be celebrated?
19 What embroidery stitch is made by winding thread round the needle and then pushing the needle back through the material at the point where it was originally drawn through?
20 In which pastime is tête-bêche a familiar term?

HISTORY 4

Fairly easy

1 Which British spy died in Moscow in March 1983?
2 Which Nobel Peace Prize winner was sent into exile in the city of Gorky in 1980?
3 Who was Governor of the Bahamas from 1940 to 1945?
4 Name the German battleship scuttled by its own crew in 1939 after the Battle of the River Plate.
5 For what is Matthew Webb famous?
6 Which infamous prison was stormed on 14 July 1789?
7 On how many hills was the ancient city of Rome built?

Not so easy

8 What were Thermidor, Vendemiaire and Brumaire?
9 Before 1879, what did a man accept from a recruiting sergeant that legally bound him to serve as an enlisted soldier?
10 Which is the only country to have had a concert pianist as head of government?
11 Who was shot in 1918 in the city which is now called Sverdlovsk?
12 Which British industry was nationalised on 1 January 1948?
13 Who was the second man to set foot on the moon?
14 Which European sovereign abdicated in 1980?

Hard

15 What was the name given to Edward, eldest son of Edward III of England?
16 The Thugs were suppressed by the British in India in the 19th Century. Who or what were they?
17 What hoisting apparatus used in construction work and in oil drilling gets its name from a London hangman?
18 The Peloponnesian War was fought between Athens and which other state?
19 Wenceslas of the Christmas carol was king of which German country?
20 Nowadays, Charles Edward Stuart is remembered as 'Bonnie Prince Charlie', but what name was he given by the men of his time?

UNITED KINGDOM 4

Fairly easy

1 What is the official name for the court known as the Old Bailey?
2 Who is third in line to the British throne?
3 Where does an Orcadian live?
4 Name the shifting sandbanks off the east coast of Kent, infamous as a danger to shipping.
5 What is the highest order of knighthood in the British Peerage?
6 What did Sir Jack Cohen found?
7 By what collective title are the English seaports of Dover, Hastings, Hythe, Romney and Sandwich known?

Not so easy

8 What is the official name for the British court to which foreign ambassadors are formally accredited?
9 In which English county does the river Thames rise?
10 What coin, with a nominal value of 25p, was specially minted for the 1977 Silver Jubilee?
11 Where in Wales is there a rack railway?
12 Which English hereditary title ranks immediately below that of duke?
13 Name the valley which runs between the Marlborough Downs and Salisbury Plain in Wiltshire.
14 Spell the Scottish town pronounced locally as 'Kercoobrie'.

Hard

15 What sort of British craftsman would use a jigger, a buzz, a flagging iron, a round shaver, an adze and a mallet?
16 Where is the ancient forest called the Burnham Beeches?
17 'The Maiden' is on view at the National Museum of Antiquities in Edinburgh. What is it?
18 What is the official name of Kew Gardens?
19 Give the title of the chief legal officer of the Crown in Scotland.
20 Where in Britain is the mountain peak Snaefell?

MUSIC AND ENTERTAINMENT 4

Fairly easy

1   In the 1962 film *The Music Man*, how many trombones led the big parade?
2   Which actor played *Rumpole of the Bailey*?
3   The *Flowers of the Forest* is a famous lament of which country?
4   Which cult TV show was about the search for the killer of cheerleader Laura Palmer?
5   Which pop group had hits with 'Message in a Bottle', 'Walking on the Moon' and 'Don't Stand So Close'?
6   Who was Grock?
7   Which jazz singer's life was immortalised in the film *Lady Sings the Blues*?

Not so easy

8   Of which musical instrument is the console is a part?
9   Of what legendary dancing troupe was Margaret Kelly the founder?
10   Who sang 'They Call Me Wicked Lola' on film?
11   Which ballet dancer had his greatest triumphs with Diaghilev's Russian Ballet in *L'Après-midi d'un Faune* and *Le Spectre de la Rose*?
12   What were 'platters'?
13   Graeme Garden and Bill Oddie were two of the Goodies. Who was the third?
14   In early pantomime, who was the lover of Columbine?

Hard

15   What do actors Reginald Tate, John Robinson, Andre Morrell and Sir John Mills have in common?
16   Give the musical term used to indicate a chord in which the notes are played one after another and not together.
17   What was the name taken by the great French actor and comic playwright of the 17th Century born Jean-Baptiste Poquelin?
18   *The Summoning of Everyman* is the greatest example of what medieval art form?
19   Name the American actress who won an Oscar in 1944 for her part in the film *None but the Lonely Heart* in which she played Cary Grant's mother.
20   Which American musician, composer and bandleader originated 'progressive' jazz?

SCIENCE AND NATURE 4

Fairly easy

1   What instrument is used for the detection of alpha, beta and gamma rays?
2   Name the chemical substances, now extensively used in medicine, produced from moulds or fungi.
3   Which ocean has the greatest depth?
4   What is the colour of the gem stone amethyst?
5   Where would you expect to find a retro-rocket?
6   What contains 92.5 parts of silver and 7.5 parts of copper?
7   What sort of fruit is a nectarine?

Not so easy

8   For what purpose are mercury vapour and sodium vapour lamps widely used?
9   Is the begonia an annual, a biennial or a perennial plant?
10   The oil of which tree is used in the production of gin?
11   What is another name for solid carbon dioxide?
12   In astronomy, what is the general name for the minor planets?
13   What great work by Sir Isaac Newton states the laws of motion and gravitation?
14   What is the industrial use of acetylene when burnt in oxygen?

Hard

15   What name is given to the spore-bearing leaf of a fern?
16   What is theoretically produced during nuclear reactions when the positive charges for protons and the negative charges for electrons are reversed?
17   Give the term that describes any two colours that together produce white light.
18   Which aquatic carnivorous plant, native to Britain, traps insects by means of pouches on its leaves?
19   What is the lightest known metal?
20   What kind of instrument might be described as plano-convex?

DEFINITIONS 4

Choose from the five alternatives the word or words *closest* in meaning to the word given first in bold type.

Fairly easy

1   **Discrepancy** a) repugnance b) contradiction c) inconsistency
    d) discrimination e) modification
2   **Profile** a) contour b) side view c) image d) etching e) head and
    shoulders
3   **Contagion** a) poison b) infirmity c) fever d) infectious disease
    e) inflammation
4   **Longevity** a) durability b) long life c) dotage d) distance east or west
    from a meridian e) great length
5   **Criterion** a) judgement b) symbol c) experiment d) valuation
    e) standard
6   **Leeward** a) to the sheltered side b) alongside c) astern d) to the left
    e) with the wind
7   **Excommunicate** a) expel an evil spirit b) sentence c) abandon d) expel
    from the church e) retire from the world

Not so easy

8   **Mutate** a) merge with b) change c) revert d) tamper with e) discontinue
9   **Invective** a) innuendo b) verbal abuse c) backbiting d) outcry
     e) disparagement
10   **Dialectic** a) scientific experimentation b) relating to local speech
     c) rationalism d) phraseology e) logical discussion
11   **Epicure** a) lover of pleasure b) glutton c) prude d) gourmet e) libertine
12   **Decamp** a) march b) retreat c) leave suddenly d) part company e) leave
     in the lurch
13   **Suffrage** a) body politic b) the vote c) election d) poll e) democracy
14   **Wraith** a) ghost b) heathen god c) fairy d) siren e) fiend

Hard

15   **Vitreous** a) like stone b) acidic c) like glass d) sulphurous e) crystalline
16   **Narcissism** a) self-satisfaction b) self-love c) self-praise d) self-
     sufficiency e) self-indulgence
17   **Episcopacy** a) church government b) the ministry c) Christendom
     d) ecclesiastical courts e) bishops of the church
18   **Simian** a) like a sheep b) like a pig c) like a fox d) like a monkey e) like
     a snake
19   **Welkin** a) the oceans b) the stars c) sky d) creation e) the clouds
20   **Refractory** a) irresistible b) radiant c) reflecting light d) stubborn
     e) caused by heat

SPORT AND GAMES 4
Fairly easy
1   In which sport would players use a broom?
2   In what sport would a player use the spider?
3   In the Tour de France cycle race, how is the current leader distinguished?
4   How many times did Bjorn Borg win the Men's Singles title at Wimbledon?
5   What is the name of the small rubber disc used in ice hockey?
6   In June 1970, who became the first Briton in half a century to win the US Open Golf Championship?
7   If the Hammers played the Gunners in a football match, which two sides would be involved?

Not so easy
8   Which Australian runner broke 11 world records in 1965 yet never won an Olympic gold medal?
9   In what sport is a left-handed scissors forward crossover a manoeuvre?
10   On what cricket ground did Jim Laker take his record-breaking 19 for 90 against Australia in August 1956?
11   Name the card game where a player can score 'one for his nob'.
12   What sport was devised in Canada in 1891 and became an Olympic sport for men in 1936 and for women in 1976?
13   In fencing, what name is given to a stroke made in answer to an opponent's attack that has been parried?
14   In 1961, which club was the first to achieve the Football League Championship and FA Cup double in the 20th century?

Hard
15   In which sport is playing left-handed against the rules?
16   What is Dumbo Crambo?
17   In which sport would a participant use a gaff?
18   In cricket what is the distance between the popping crease and the bowling crease?
19   Which soccer club is nicknamed the Shakers?
20   If someone employed the Ruy Lopez against you, what game would you be playing?

311

ANIMAL KINGDOM 4

Fairly easy

1   Which creature produces gossamer?
2   The python is a poisonous snake. True or false?
3   Which tropical bird with a long neck and legs and a curiously shaped bill is brilliantly coloured in shades from scarlet to coral pink?
4   What is the gait of a horse called that is faster than a trot but slower than a gallop?
5   In England, Wales and Scotland, which is the odd one out: the water vole, the otter or the beaver?
6   To what usually fatal sickness are rabbits most prone?
7   What is *Canis familiaris*?

Not so easy

8   Which bird of East Africa with a familiar relative of the same name in Britain is called 'superb' because of its brilliant plumage of metallic blues and purples?
9   What is an oak beauty?
10   Which animal produces mohair?
11   How many wings has a mayfly?
12   A sacred ibis is native to Africa. What kind of creature is it?
13   How do whale and basking sharks differ from other types of shark?
14   A whippet is used for coursing hares, but can you name the other breed of dog most commonly employed in this type of hunting?

Hard

15   What is a horse called that is a cross between a thoroughbred and an Arab?
16   There are only two wild representatives of the cat family living in Europe. The European wild cat is one: name the other.
17   What kind of poisonous tropical creature is a Portuguese man o' war?
18   Which animal is sometimes said to be 'in velvet'?
19   What is a Southdown?
20   Can you say what name is given to curdled milk from the stomach of an unweaned calf?

GEOGRAPHY AND TRAVEL 4

Fairly easy

1   Name the highest mountain in Greece, the home of the gods in Greek mythology.
2   What is the term of office of a President of the United States?
3   Name the seven continents.
4   What is the Jungfrau?
5   Who has a summer residence at Castel Gandolfo on the shores of Lake Albano in Italy?
6   The Chinese and English in the Far East communicate by what mixed language?
7   To which British meal does the Italian *pranzo* correspond: breakfast, lunch or dinner?

Not so easy

8   What is the longest river in South Africa, flowing 2,091km (1,300 miles) from Basutoland to the Atlantic?
9   Which city has the cathedrals St Patrick's and Christ Church?
10   Name the famous fashionable German spa town in the Black Forest.
11   In what ocean are the Seychelles?
12   Is the Sierra Nevada in Andalusia, Spain or California, USA?
13   Where in Europe might you find red snow?
14   In Paris, what are Franklin D. Roosevelt, Stalingrad and Louis Blanc?

Hard

15   Which French town on the river Creuse, in the *department* of that name, is renowned for tapestry-weaving and carpet-making?
16   What Austrian coin formerly had a value of one-hundredth of a schilling?
17   What is the great mass of stone trees in the Painted Desert, Arizona, USA called?
18   Japan consists of four main islands. Honshu, Hokkaido and Kyushu are three: what is the fourth?
19   Of which country is Bogota the capital?
20   Which of the Great Lakes of North America is the only one wholly in the United States?

ART AND LITERATURE 4
Fairly easy
1　Which author of a series of successful novels in English was born Konrad Korzeniowski?
2　In what town did Robert Browning set his poem about a pied piper?
3　What is the name of the winged horse of Greek legend?
4　Who wrote about Middle Earth?
5　What was 'burning bright in the forests of the night' in a poem by William Blake?
6　Which sculptor's 'St Michael and the Devil' appears on the facade of Coventry Cathedral?
7　Who in literature was the 'knight of the doleful countenance'?

Not so easy
8　What is the type of poster paint made from mixing watercolours with gum arabic called?
9　Which wild and remote area is the setting for Conan Doyle's story *The Hound of the Baskervilles*?
10　Name the Jesuit priest whose poems were only published after his death through the agency of the poet laureate Robert Bridges.
11　In the Old Testament, what is the more usual name for the Decalogue?
12　Which English poet became Dean of St Paul's?
13　Give the term for a word that has the opposite meaning to another, for example good to bad.
14　Which 'poet of empire' wrote the *Barrack Room Ballads*?

Hard
15　In Greek mythology, who created man?
16　Which English novelist died from typhoid in 1931 after drinking a glass of Parisian water to demonstrate that it was safe?
17　Who was the French painter who led the modern French *intimiste* school and who painted 'Dining Room in the Country'?
18　Name the English critic who wrote *The Great Tradition*, a celebrated work on the history of English literature.
19　John Sloan and George Bellows belong to what American school of realist painters?
20　According to Shakespeare, to whom did Julius Caesar bequeath 75 drachmas?

Quick-fire Quiz 5

POT POURRI 5

Fairly easy

1   The emblem of the former French royal family is also the emblem of the boy scouts. What is it?
2   Which unit for measuring liquid is equal to one quarter of an imperial pint?
3   In architecture, what is the rectangular base of a column called?
4   Give the term for the decoration of furniture by inlaying coloured woods in the surface.
5   The meatiest and most expensive kind of chicken is a male bird that has been unsexed and specially fattened. What is it called?
6   Name the principal flavouring of brandy snap.
7   What is copperplate?

Not so easy

8   The Chinese language has a number of dialects. Which dialect is spoken by about 80 per cent of the mainland population?
9   Which prophet of the 9th Century BCE denounced Ahab and Jezebel?
10   What is *koldt bord*?
11   Who is the spiritual head of the Ismaili Moslems?
12   When a food is prepared in a sauce whose top surface is covered with mixture of butter, breadcrumbs and grated cheese, then baked or grilled, how is it said to be cooked?
13   What in economics is the doctrine according to which government avoids controls in economic life?
14   In the Old Testament, from whom did David steal his wife Bathsheba?

Hard

15   What is the name of the non-commissioned officer in the Royal Artillery holding the rank equivalent to a corporal?
16   Give the legal term for goods jettisoned at sea but secured to a buoy so that they may be recovered.
17   The sacred writings of which religion are divided into the *Tripitaka*?
18   What familiar flat, thin cake means literally in French 'twice cooked'?
19   Which type of bridge, named after its inventor, is made of latticed parts that can be easily transported and quickly assembled?
20   Do you know what kind of marriage is polyandry?

HISTORY 5

Fairly easy

1   Which London royal residence was originally called Nottingham House?
2   What was the principal profession of Capability Brown?
3   Which motoring association was founded in 1905?
4   Name the world figure who publicly renounced his divinity in 1946.
5   Name the important European figure who was assassinated at Sarajevo on 28 June 1914.
6   Which nation was ultimately to derive most benefit from the Balfour Declaration of 1917?
7   Who was shot outside the Hilton Hotel in Washington in March 1981?

Not so easy

8   What was the old colonial name of the central African republic now called Zaire?
9   In the 19th Century, who or what was 'the sick man of Europe'?
10   Which English king was unable to speak English with any degree of fluency?
11   Name the royal residence designed by Prince Albert, the consort of Queen Victoria.
12   For which country was Hibernia the Roman name?
13   How many seats did the Spitfire fighter plane have?
14   Which Labour leader went into a general election with the slogan 'You know Labour government works'?

Hard

15   The Battle of Bosworth Field in 1485 was the decisive battle of the Wars of the Roses, but in which English county is Bosworth Field?
16   What name was given to the religious movement, based on an emphasis on High Church ritual, led by John Henry Newman and John Keble?
17   Which British Prime Minister did Churchill describe as 'a modest little man with much to be modest about'?
18   A Greek historian is known as the 'Father of History'. Who was he?
19   What nationality was the post-war statesman John Diefenbaker?
20   Name the palace in Spain built by the Moslem rulers of Granada in the 13th and 14th centuries.

UNITED KINGDOM 5

Fairly easy

1 In England, up to what age may a person be made a ward of the court?
2 Which school's song begins, 'Harrow may be more clever . . .'?
3 In which county is Whipsnade Zoo?
4 In Wales, what is the Cader Idris?
5 In which city is the National Space Centre?
6 Sir John Hawkins, Sir Francis Drake and Sir Walter Raleigh were famous seafaring Elizabethans. In which county were they all born?
7 What in Scotland is the name for a man's cap, Highland in origin, creased from back to front, and worn with small streamers at the back?

Not so easy

8 In which English city would you find the Radcliffe Camera?
9 What feature is peculiar to the postage stamps of Great Britain?
10 Who is the First Lord of the Treasury?
11 Give the collective name for the group of London craft guilds of which the Worshipful Company of Salters is one.
12 Where in Britain is there a maze of alleys full of antique shops referred to as 'The Lanes'?
13 Name the Scottish river which rises on Ben Lui on the border of Perthshire and Argyllshire where it is called the Fillan.
14 What is the BDA?

Hard

15 When Sir Walter Scott wrote of a North Country town, 'half church of God, half castle 'gainst the Scot', to which town was he referring?
16 Where in Britain was the *ultima thule* (farthest region) of the Romans?
17 What town has a coat of arms of railway wheels with six spokes representing the important routes for which it is a junction?
18 Of which trade is Mincing Lane in London the traditional home?
19 What is the name of the sovereign's bodyguard in Scotland?
20 Which Midlands city has a Goose Fair on the first Thursday in October and the two following days?

MUSIC AND ENTERTAINMENT 5

Fairly easy

1   What is the lowest female singing voice?
2   What was the former name of Radio 3?
3   Who wrote the play *Karaoke*, which was presented on television shortly after his death?
4   In which TV sitcom did Linda Robson and Pauline Quirke star?
5   Which pop singer and bandleader, generally regarded as the founder of rock 'n' roll, died in 1982?
6   What clockwork device is used to mark musical time?
7   Which British comic actor played Inspector Clouseau in the 'Pink Panther' films?

Not so easy

8   'Can't act. Slightly bald. Can dance a little.' This was the verdict on which film star's first Hollywood screen test?
9   Of what musical instrument was Arcangelo Corelli?
10   Which British actor was romantically involved with Rachel Roberts and Shirley Ann Field in the film of *Saturday Night and Sunday Morning*?
11   Russia has two outstanding ballet companies. One is the Bolshoi: name the other.
12   Which composer wrote 104 symphonies?
13   From which northern theatre was the TV old-time music hall show *The Good Old Days* transmitted?
14   In which film did Clark Gable speak the famous line, 'Frankly my dear, I don't give a damn'?

Hard

15   What name is given to the form of dramatic entertainment made up of a series of short pieces, often highly sensational in character?
16   Who, according to an Elton John song, lived her life 'like a candle in the wind'?
17   On whose original novel was the film *Jaws* based?
18   Which Austrian composer was shot in 1945 at Mittersill, near Salzburg, by an American military policeman for breaking the curfew imposed by the allied forces of occupation?
19   Who were the Lord Chamberlain's Men?
20   Czech composer Smetana wrote a set of six orchestral tone poems entitled *Ma Vlast*. What does *Ma Vlast* mean?

SCIENCE AND NATURE 5

Fairly easy

1   What plant is a cross between a blackberry and a raspberry?
2   What poisonous gas is found in the exhaust fumes of car engines?
3   What is the principal constituent of amalgam as used in dentistry?
4   Name the type of leather made from dried untanned skins that is nowadays used for binding books of very fine quality.
5   With what is the science of seismology concerned?
6   Cirrus, cirrocumulus and cirrostratus are cloud forms. Are they, high, medium or low?
7   What is Universal Time more frequently called?

Not so easy

8   Which technique uses a radioactive isotope for dating archaeological findings?
9   On the Fahrenheit scale, is the boiling point of water 212°, 216° or 222°?
10 From which natural ore is aluminium most frequently obtained?
11 The process of heating rubber with chemicals, principally sulphur, by which it is made strong and durable, has a scientific name. What is it?
12 Name the largest planet in the solar system.
13 Which plane figure forms the basis of trigonometry?
14 To what part of the body do the two carotid arteries carry blood?

Hard

15 Which rare gas is sometimes called 'heavy hydrogen' and is present in natural water as an oxide when it is known as 'heavy water'?
16 What group of mostly alpine, perennial herbs whose name means literally 'stone-breaker', are so called because their roots break up rocks by growing into cracks?
17 Name the milky fluid from rubber trees that yields natural rubber on coagulation.
18 For which flower is cranesbill another name?
19 How many moons has the planet Mercury?
20 Where would you expect to find a graphite moderator?

DEFINITIONS 5

Choose from the five alternatives the word or words *closest* in meaning to the word given first in bold type.

Fairly easy

1   **Contraband** a) smuggled goods b) booty c) gun-running d) ill-gotten gains e) embargo
2   **Listless** a) bemused b) half-hearted c) lazy d) languid e) slow-moving
3   **Peruse** a) glean b) learn by heart c) enquire d) read carefully e) refer to
4   **Enunciate** a) take a stand b) lay stress on c) insist d) state clearly e) specify
5   **Impasse** a) stoppage b) opposition c) thoroughfare d) blind alley e) stumbling block
6   **Puerile** a) youthful b) brainless c) childish d) paltry e) irrational
7   **Firmament** a) the heavens b) universe c) globe d) nature e) constellation

Not so easy

8   **Presage** a) foresee b) predict c) usher in d) hold out hope e) foreshadow
9   **Nascent** a) introductory b) starting afresh c) primeval d) entering in e) being born
10   **Assiduous** a) diligent b) agile c) blunt d) sharp e) meddlesome
11   **Geocentric** a) relating to the centre of the earth b) relating to the earth's crust c) having the earth as the centre d) relating to the pivot of the earth e) formed of regular curves, lines and angles
12   **Ingenuous** a) clever b) artless c) foolish d) impractical e) matter of fact
13   **Grandiloquent** a) magnificent in scale b) flamboyant c) musically loud d) having great power e) pompous in speech
14   **Missive** a) correspondent b) letter c) bulletin d) thesis e) bill

Hard

15   **Eclectic** a) clear-cut b) derived from various sources c) optional d) neutral e) presenting several alternatives
16   **Sorrel** a) charcoal b) chestnut c) indigo d) chalky e) crimson
17   **Monotheism** a) doctrine that there is only one god b) orthodoxy c) doctrine that there is only one true church d) religion inspired by divine revelation e) belief in the unity of God as opposed to the doctrine of the Trinity
18   **Logistics** a) science of quantity b) science of reasoning c) science of troop deployment d) science of weaponry e) science of rocketry
19   **Etiolate** a) strangle b) terrify c) render unconscious d) make pale e) incapacitate
20   **Sacerdotal** a) monastic b) apostolic c) hierarchical d) diocesan e) priestly

SPORT AND GAMES 5

Fairly easy

1   Of which race course is Becher's Brook is a feature?
2   What is the show-jumping event called where horses have to jump only especially high and wide fences?
3   Which game was the immediate forerunner of contract bridge?
4   Which is the odd one out from Jimmy Connors, Boris Becker, Ilie Nastase and John Newcombe?
5   In athletics, what is another name for the triple jump?
6   With which sport do you associate Smith's Lawn?
7   In which sport do contestants travel from Paris to Dakar?

Not so easy

8   Who made a maximum 147 break in the World Snooker Championship of 1983?
9   All racehorses have the same official birthday. What is it?
10   Ian Botham's fame rests on his prowess as a test cricketer, but for which English played soccer club did he play?
11   In Monopoly, what colour group are Bow Street, Marlborough Street and Vine Street?
12   Who was the first swimmer to break the minute for 100 metres and the five-minute barrier for 400 metres and later became a Hollywood *Tarzan*?
13   In what sport are you required to ride, fence, shoot, swim and run?
14   Which county achieved a hat trick of wins in the County Cricket Championship in 1966, 1967 and 1968?

Hard

15   In what sport may contestants compete at open weight?
16   1984 saw the first whitewash in a five-test cricket series in England when West Indies trounced the home country. Who captained the West Indies?
17   In what sport were Babe Zaharias, Louise Suggs and Patty Berg the 'Big Three' in the post-war years?
18   Which Salford kicker scored a world record of 221 goals in a rugby league season in 1971–72?
19   In which gambling game is transversale a term?
20   What is the name of the most important North American ice hockey trophy?

ANIMAL KINGDOM 5

Fairly easy

1 The West African gorilla is carnivorous. True or false?
2 What South American burrowing rodent, grey and white in colour, is much sought after for its fur?
3 The roe of which fish is made into caviar?
4 The black rat and brown rat are both found in Britain. Which is the larger?
5 Is the leatherback a snake, a turtle or a kind of fish?
6 What is a cabbage white?
7 How many arms has a starfish?

Not so easy

8 What are fallows, lutinos and opalines?
9 Which mammal's breathing apparatus is called a blowhole?
10 What is the scientific name for the trunk of an elephant?
11 The emu is one flightless bird of Australia: name another?
12 What word describes a white and brown or a white and red horse?
13 Which wild European bird can be taught to talk?
14 Give another name for the Russian wolfhound.

Hard

15 To which part of the world is the highly poisonous Russell's viper native?
16 Name the grey, short-haired terrier that takes its name from a village in Northumberland.
17 What is a scut?
18 Which family of carnivorous fishes that are found in warm seas attach themselves by a sucking disk to sharks, other large fish and ships?
19 What is the part of a horse's foot called that corresponds to the ankle in humans?
20 The name of which ape is derived from a Malay word meaning 'man of the woods'?

GEOGRAPHY AND TRAVEL 5

Fairly easy

1　In which city is the Ponte Vecchio?
2　What do the Greeks call Greece?
3　Name the national emblem of Canada.
4　Give the English name for Afrikaans-speaking South Africans of mainly Dutch descent.
5　In which American state is Harvard University?
6　Which European language is the official language of Brazil?
7　Of which country is Puerto Rico a territory?

Not so easy

8　On which Caribbean island is Montego Bay a tourist attraction?
9　What is the English name for the lake in the Alps the Germans call the Bodensee?
10　The total area of which European country is about 10 per cent lakes?
11　The southern part of a marsh plain in the Rhone delta, south-east France, is a zoological and botanical reserve. What is it called?
12　What is the short, stabbing spear carried by Zulus called?
13　Which hot, south wind blows on the European coast of the Mediterranean?
14　The Macgillycuddy's Reeks are in County Kerry, Eire. What are they?

Hard

15　Name the high-level road along the French Riviera between Nice and Menton with magnificent views of land and sea.
16　What do sailors call a phantom ship of evil omen that according to legend can appear in the waters off the Cape of Good Hope?
17　Where are the Thousand Islands?
18　At the heart of Paris there are two islands. One is the Île de la Cité: what is the other?
19　In which European country is the Romansch language spoken?
20　What name is given to low-pressure areas near the Equator where the weather is usually hot and sultry?

ART AND LITERATURE 5
Fairly easy
1   At what age did Adrian Mole write his secret diary?
2   What 16th-century Italian sculptor, engraver and goldsmith wrote a celebrated autobiography?
3   In the story by Washington Irving, for how long did Rip Van Winkle sleep?
4   Which English artist of the 18th Century painted portraits of the aristocracy, including 'The Blue Boy'?
5   Who was the British scholar and soldier who described his adventures in the Middle East in *The Seven Pillars of Wisdom*?
6   Which former royal jockey became a best-selling writers of thrillers about horse racing?
7   In the novel of Jules Verne how, long did Phileas Fogg take to get round the world?

Not so easy
8   In what type of painting did celebrated Scottish artist Sir Henry Raeburn specialise?
9   Was *The Count of Monte Cristo* written by Alexandre Dumas, *pere* or Alexandre Dumas, *fils*?
10 Who assembled at The Tabard Inn, Southwark?
11 Which Linton marries Heathcliff in Emily Bronte's *Wuthering Heights*?
12 In one of his poems, W. H. Auden wrote of 'a low dishonest decade'. To what decade was he referring?
13 Which English poet wrote 'Of Man's First Disobedience'?
14 In Arthurian legend, what was the sword called that the king received from the Lady of the Lake?

Hard
15 What German movement in modern art was divided into two groups, the 'Blue Rider' and the 'Bridge'?
16 Name the French post impressionist painter who developed the technique known as pointillism.
17 Which classic French novelist's real name was Marie Henri Beyle?
18 Which Charles Dickens novel is centred on Marshalsea Prison in London?
19 How precisely did American writer and adventurer Ernest Hemingway die?
20 By what collective name are the first five books of the Old Testament sometimes known?

Pub League
Quiz Answers

Pub League Quiz 1 – Answers

Round 1
Team 1
1 Nicosia
2 Robert Redford
3 Primo Carnera
4 1948
5 Tom Cruise

Team 2
1 Abuja
2 Paul Newman
3 Mike Tyson
4 1970
5 Vivien Leigh

Round 2
Team 1
1 George IV
2 The Korean War
3 Royal Navy Reserve

4 *Kim*
5 The river Aire

Team 2
1 George I
2 The Hundred Years War
3 Royal National Institute for the Blind
4 *The Old Curiosity Shop*
5 Taw

Round 3
Team 1
1 Kew Gardens
2 Ballistics
3 Leo Hendrick Baekeland
4 Jacques Offenbach
5 Alto saxophone

Team 2
1 Lambeth Palace, South Bank
2 Ecology
3 Jean-Christophe Denner
4 Richard Wagner
5 Trumpet

Round 4
Team 1
1 Paris
2 Abyssinia
3 November
4 A sheep
5 Ash Wednesday

Team 2
1 Icarus
2 Addis Ababa
3 January
4 A Himalayan goat
5 Easter

Round 5
Sport: Giacomo Agostini
Classical music: Maurice Ravel
TV and radio: Vulcan
Science: A gas
Law: Lincoln's Inn, Inner Temple, Middle Temple, Gray's Inn

Round 6

Team 2
1 Ambridge
2 James Thomas Brudenell, 7th Earl of Cardigan
3 Daniel Defoe
4 On the Zambezi river, on the Zimbabwe/Zambia border
5 Lawn Tennis Association

Team 1
1 Liverpool
2 General Neguib
3 James Joyce
4 Fermanagh
5 Marylebone Cricket Club

Round 7

Team 2
1 Edward VII
2 An edible shellfish
3 Christopher Wren
4 Francis Bacon
5 Abbott and Costello

Team 1
1 George III
2 A tropical tree
3 John Vanbrugh
4 Sir Stanley Spencer
5 Douglas Fairbanks Jnr

Round 8

Team 2
1 Lord Aberdeen
2 Canterbury Cathedral
3 Pierre Abeland
4 Acrophobia
5 Carpets

Team 1
1 The Easter Rising
2 Runnymede
3 Franz Kafka
4 Beauty
5 Lace

Round 9

Team 2
1 Approval given by the British Sovereign to a bill agreed by parliament
2 Lake Chad
3 The Colorado
4 Palermo
5 Baking soda

Team 1
1 Nancy Witcher Astor
2 Lake Superior
3 The Nile
4 Palma
5 Salt

Round 10

Sport: 1872
Classical music: *Turandot*
TV and radio: *NYPD Blue*
Science: Absolute zero
Law: Their funeral expenses

Drinks round

Team 1

1 Oasis
2 Milan
3 W. C. Fields
4 Anne of Cleves
5 Umberto Eco
6 25 March
7 Gamma
8 Accra
9 International Monetary Fund

10 Gustave Flaubert

Team 2

1 Queen
2 New York
3 Vivien Leigh
4 Anne Boleyn
5 George Orwell
6 1 March
7 Omega
8 Rabat
9 International Standard Book Number

10 James Fenimore Cooper

Reserve questions

1 Martin Peters
2 A baboon
3 *Olympic*

Pub League Quiz 2 – Answers

Round 1

Team 1
1 1 November
2 London Bridge
3 Mosaic
4 *True Grit*
5 June 1944

Team 2
1 2 November
2 Westminster Bridge
3 Collage
4 Marion Morrison
5 8 May 1945

Round 2

Team 1
1 Nikolai Rimsky-Korsakov
2 *Torrey Canyon*
3 Dr Hook
4 Titania
5 Shark

Team 2
1 Aram Khachaturian
2 *Mary Rose*
3 Diana Ross
4 Oberon
5 Its hooves

Round 3

Team 1
1 Eight
2 Alabama
3 William Hogarth
4 Mary Queen of Scots
5 Mrs Goggins

Team 2
1 Seven
2 Florida
3 Igor Stravinsky
4 King Edgar
5 Elmer Fudd

Round 4

Team 1
1 Ferdinand Porsche
2 Madrid
3 Men's 200 metres
4 Stethoscope
5 Oscar Wilde

Team 2
1 Adolf Hitler
2 Louis XIV
3 High jump
4 Fire, water, earth and air
5 Robert Louis Stevenson

Round 5

Animals: A hunting dog
Pop music: Racing Cars
Transport: Penzance
Kings and queens: Edward VII
Geography: Sardinia

Round 6

Team 2

1 George Fox
2 Hong Kong
3 A mischievous trick
4 Cambodia
5 Lillehammer

Team 1

1 Charles Russell
2 Martin Luther King
3 A hoisting rope
4 Indonesia
5 Ice hockey

Round 7

Team 2

1 Uranus
2 Westminster Abbey
3 Architecture and design
4 Adam Faith

5 The Royal Flying Corps

Team 1

1 William Herschel
2 The Pope
3 Exploration (he discovered Newfoundland)
4 James May
5 1918

Round 8

Team 2

1 A pack of playing cards
2 Nancy Mitford
3 European Space Agency

4 Fratricide
5 Bread sticks

Team 1

1 Dice
2 Stan Barstow
3 National Vocational Qualification

4 High Seas
5 Highly seasoned smoked beef prepared from a shoulder cut

Round 9

Team 2

1 A cooper
2 $4\pi r^2$
3 Six
4 Rocky Marciano
5 *One Man and His Dog*

Team 1

1 A shoemaker
2 ⅜u¹
3 Eamon de Valera
4 Joe Louis
5 Jeremy Paxman

Round 10

Animals: Goldcrest
Pop music: Sheffield
Transport: A light four-wheeled, horse-drawn carriage
Kings and queens: William IV
Geography: Between Sicily and Tunisia

Drinks round

Team 1

1 They cannot pass rabies to humans
2 Second
3 Bob Dylan
4 Cat's eyes
5 The guineapig
6 A derby hat
7 Scorpio
8 In or amongst trees
9 Dennis Skinner
10 *Absolutely Fabulous*

Team 2

1 Scene of the Great Train Robbery
2 A Moslem religious leader
3 Stevie Wonder
4 The hovercraft
5 New Guinea
6 A Jewish skull cap
7 Pisces
8 Ponies
9 Norman Tebbit
10 Betty Turpin

Reserve questions

1 Cuzco
2 Miss Moneypenny
3 Sherlock Holmes

Pub League Quiz 3 – Answers

Round 1

Team 1
1 Charles de Gaulle
2 Fellow of the Royal Astronomical Society
3 Mary Quant
4 Yorkshire
5 Tasman Sea

Team 2
1 The pigs
2 Fellow of the Royal College of Veterinary Surgeons
3 Christian Dior
4 Somerset
5 Cook Strait

Round 2

Team 1
1 March
2 A2
3 Douglas
4 John Fowles
5 July 1776

Team 2
1 September
2 A23
3 Lockheed
4 John Masters
5 11 November 1918

Round 3

Team 1
1 Rio de Janiero
2 1929
3 Albert Finney
4 Two
5 David

Team 2
1 K2 (Mount Godwin Austen)
2 Salem, Massachusetts
3 Stanley Kramer
4 Dromedary
5 Cain and Abel

Round 4

Team 1
1 Leonard Bernstein
2 James Callaghan
3 *Fidelio*
4 Four
5 Marquis of Queensberry

Team 2
1 Stephen Sondheim
2 Michael Foot
3 Aaron Copland
4 Piccolo
5 Reading

Round 5

History: Henry VII
TV and radio: Harold
Science: Trees
Literature and poetry: Faust
Discoverers and explorers: Edward Whymper

Round 6

Team 2
1 Venus
2 Sediment or silt deposited
   by streams
3 A gill
4 A sheep dog
5 Moldau (Czech: Vltava)

Team 1
1 Pluto
2 Igneous
3 Electrical resistance
4 A Scottish hunting terrier
5 Vistula (Polish: Wisla)

Round 7

Team 2
1 Pb
2 Hestia
3 Glenda Jackson
4 USA
5 His policy of systematically
   murdering the Jews

Team 1
1 Al
2 Ares
3 Richard Harris
4 Bayern Munich
5 Lidice

Round 8

Team 2
1 Knight Commander, Order of
   St Michael and St George
2 Edith Nesbit
3 Lake Ontario
4 A card game similar to whist
5 Both Archbishops of Canterbury

Team 1
1 Knight of the Thistle
2 D. H. Lawrence
3 Uganda (Ruwenzori range)
4 Fleet Street, The Strand
5 All neutral in the Second World
   War

Round 9

Team 2
1 Campanology
2 19
3 Mu
4 Lemuel Francis Abbott
5 Sheikh Muhammad Abdullah

Team 1
1 The ear and its diseases
2 21
3 Omicron
4 Thomas Eakins
5 Hannibal

Round 10

History: William of Wykeham
TV and radio: Bill Maynard
Science: A bruise
Literature and poetry: Seamus Heaney
Discoverers and explorers: Father Louis Hennepin

Drinks round

Team 1

1 An American grasshopper

2 Ham
3 Alan Ladd
4 Agincourt
5 Ben Jonson
6 New Zealand
7 Acetic
8 Hypnos
9 Fats Waller
10 Belfast and Dungannon

Team 2

1 16 (four pairs for walking, four pairs for swimming)

2 Aaron
3 Judy Garland
4 Wilhelm II
5 John Osborne
6 Mount McKinley
7 Lactic
8 Dionysus
9 Count Basie
10 Belfast and Ballymena

Reserve questions

1 King Juan Carlos of Spain
2 Clarence Birdseye
3 1876 ('Come here, Watson, I want you.')

Pub League Quiz 4 – Answers

Round 1

Team 1
1 Vanessa Redgrave
2 Italy and Austria
3 Five
4 Callaghan
5 Mary II

Team 2
1 Present the weather
2 Ecuador, Colombia, Brazil
3 Groucho, Chico, Harpo, Zeppo, Gummo
4 Wives of Clint Eastwood
5 George V

Round 2

Team 1
1 Polish
2 18
3 Jules Verne
4 John Huston
5 Jeroboam

Team 2
1 Danish
2 One
3 Nemo
4 Roman Polanski
5 Champagne

Round 3

Team 1
1 A cat
2 Inigo Jones
3 William Holman Hunt
4 Toyland
5 Port-of-Spain

Team 2
1 The Komodo dragon
2 Sir Joseph Paxton
3 Edouard Manet
4 Bedrock
5 Honolulu

Round 4

Team 1
1 Leprosy
2 A34
3 Michael Heseltine
4 George Smiley
5 Kensington

Team 2
1 Lockjaw
2 A40
3 Spiro Agnew
4 Colonel Nicholson
5 Whitehall

Round 5

Classical music: Edward Elgar
Geology: Coral
Inventors: Michael Faraday
Famous men: John Flamsteed
Words: *Negro*

Round 6

Team 2
1 My master
2 Pedro Alvarez Cabral
3 Marlon Brando
4 Cargo vessels built during the Second World War as part of the US war effort
5 Charles Lindbergh

Team 1
1 Anointed or the anointed one
2 Christopher Columbus
3 Greer Garson
4 The Liberty Bell

5 *Spirit of St Louis*

Round 7

Team 2
1 Fleetwood Mac
2 Golda Meir
3 Wilfred Owen
4 An Australian game bird
5 Nine

Team 1
1 The Cure
2 Mata Hari
3 Alfred Noyes
4 A snake
5 Five

Round 8

Team 2
1 Loch Lomond
2 Radius, ulna
3 Neptune
4 Lady Jane Grey
5 Anthea Turner

Team 1
1 Lough Neagh
2 Fibula, tibia
3 Poseidon
4 George V
5 Nick Park

Round 9

Team 2
1 Lime
2 Dhaka
3 Franklin D. Roosevelt and Winston S. Churchill
4 A halo of light painted over a holy figure
5 The Isle of Wight

Team 1
1 Methane
2 Abu Dhabi
3 1941

4 An engraved design cut into a hollow (opposite of cameo)
5 Dorset

Round 10

Classical music: Yehudi Menuhin
Geology: Cannel coal
Inventors: The fountain pen
Famous men: Peter Rachman
Words: The study of spores and pollen

Drinks round

Team 1

1 Irving Berlin

2 *1984*
3 Little Rock
4 Meryl Streep
5 Jennifer Capriati
6 A sleepwalker
7 Duke of Marlborough
8 National Farmers' Union
9 La Paz
10 Cheese

Team 2

1 Alan Jay Lerner and
   Frederick Loewe
2 George Orwell
3 Louisiana
4 Jack Nicholson
5 Marc Rosset
6 A member of a subversive group
7 Duke of Wellington
8 Organisation of African Unity
9 Managua
10 Honey

Reserve questions

1 Charles Dickens
2 Reindeer
3 China clay

Pub League Quiz 5 – Answers

Round 1

Team 1
1 Yellow, green
2 Rugby and Carlisle
3 River Witham
4 *Pygmalion*
5 25 April

Team 2
1 Rose, purple
2 Birmingham and Exeter
3 River Colne
4 Hercule Poirot
5 The first Sunday after Easter

Round 2

Team 1
1 International Atomic Energy Agency
2 Those of the Maundy Money
3 Cape Town
4 Alexander Borodin
5 Admiral's Cup

Team 2
1 Vienna
2 Peter Carl Fabergé
3 Pretoria
4 *Aida*
5 John Ngugi

Round 3

Team 1
1 Nine
2 Sodium and chlorine
3 Small monkeys
4 South Vietnam
5 Mr Bean

Team 2
1 Twelve
2 Chromium
3 Rodents of the squirrel family
4 The While Nile (in the Sudan)
5 Benny Hill

Round 4

Team 1
1 Italian
2 A nun
3 Aldous Huxley
4 Sir Charles Barry
5 Pandora

Team 2
1 Russian
2 Moss Bros
3 Henry James
4 Inigo Jones
5 Hope

Round 5
Pop music: Simply Red
Politics: Empress Dowager Nagako
General knowledge: Northern Line
Words: A Scotsman
Films: *The Miracle Worker*

Round 6

Team 2

1 Oliver Cromwell and his son
  Richard
2 Cantabrigians
3 Tigris and Euphrates
4 Cilla Black
5 Ellery Queen

Team 1

1 Farouk
2 Mancunians
3 Babylonia
4 Austria
5 Sam Spade

Round 7

Team 2

1 A second marriage
2 Stanley Kubrick
3 Isle of Man
4 A jet
5 Corgi

Team 1

1 Marie Antoinette
2 Esther
3 Schipol
4 Willy Messerschmitt
5 They are migrating

Round 8

Team 2

1 Gaza City
2 Asuncion
3 Litmus
4 Ambrosia
5 Patella

Team 1

1 St Louis
2 Quito
3 Nickel and iron
4 Nectar
5 Scapula

Round 9

Team 2

1 Robin Knox-Johnson
2 Greenwich
3 Flute
4 Agnates
5 Charles de Gaulle

Team 1

1 Sir Vivian Fuchs
2 St James's
3 Three
4 Cognates
5 Abraham Lincoln

Round 10

Pop music: Bryan Adams
Politics: Herbert Asquith
General knowledge: 29 September
Words: Strength and grace of movement
Films: *Sunset Boulevard*

Drinks round

Team 1

1 INXS
2 Nyasaland
3 North America
4 Robert Raikes (1780)
5 Salford
6 Peter Maxwell Davies
7 Christ's body
8 Ammonia
9 Billiards
10 Princess Beatrice of York

Team 2

1 Oasis
2 Bechuanaland
3 The finch family
4 Methodism
5 David Hockney
6 Ted Hughes
7 Kings I and II
8 Antifreeze
9 Table tennis
10 Rose

Reserve questions

1 Samuel Beckett
2 World Student
3 St John's

Pub League Quiz 6 – Answers

Round 1

Team 1
1   Dwight D. Eisenhower
2   Graeme Hick
3   Pooh-Bah
4   Bob Hope and Bing Crosby
5   Yuri Gagarin

Team 2
1   Nagasaki
2   Leg-spin
3   William and Arthur
4   Singapore
5   Neil Armstrong

Round 2

Team 1
1   1983
2   July
3   A hobo
4   Garret Fitzgerald
5   Eight weeks

Team 2
1   1980
2   March
3   Potato chips
4   Eamon de Valera
5   Nine weeks

Round 3

Team 1
1   Cardinal Wolsey
2   Robert Clive
3   Pablo Picasso
4   Baldness
5   Karate

Team 2
1   Henry VIII
2   Sir Thomas Stamford Raffles
3   Venice
4   A very small head
5   Jujitsu

Round 4

Team 1
1   Frederick William Lanchester
2   The Garonne
3   *Huit*
4   Jack Lemmon
5   Cricket

Team 2
1   Bicycles
2   The Tigris
3   *Neuf*
4   Sir John Mills
5   1880

Round 5

Law: Lien
Geology: Alabaster
London: Westminster Abbey
Horse racing: 2000 Guineas, St Leger, Derby
TV and radio: *The World at One*

Round 6

Team 2
1   Thor Heyerdahl
2   Dustin Hoffman
3   Nine
4   Madagascar
5   Sardine

Team 1
1   *1984* by George Orwell
2   Bucks Fizz
3   Kenya
4   Melbourne
5   Elver

Round 7

Team 2
1   Geoffrey Boycott
2   Bingo
3   Vitamin Bl (thiamine)
4   The Scarlet Pimpernel
5   Pythagoras

Team 1
1   Lynn Davies
2   One or 11
3   (Middle) ear
4   Python
5   Robert Hawley Ingersoll

Round 8

Team 2
1   Charlie Chaplin's
2   Oliver Cromwell
3   A sow
4   Coalbrookdale, Shropshire
5   Joseph

Team 1
1   Jimi Hendrix
2   The Stone of Scone
3   The kingfisher
4   Mississippi
5   For looking back at the destruction of Sodom

Round 9

Team 2
1   Lebanon
2   Royal Observer Corps
3   Tansu Ciller
4   Arnold Bennett
5   Boxing

Team 1
1   The Cornucopia
2   Royal Army Ordnance Corps
3   Albert Einstein
4   Germaine Greer
5   Cornwall

Round 10

Law: Treason
Geology: A soft coal with a carbon content higher than peat but lower than other coals
London: Threadneedle Street
Horse racing: Grundy
TV and radio: Holmfirth

Drinks round

Team 1

1 *Vostok 1*
2 Madonna
3 Sophocles
4 Resin from coniferous trees
5 Robert Altman

6 *Panorama*
7 Holland
8 Bull
9 Katmandu
10 Burgundy

Team 2

1 *Eagle*
2 David Bowie
3 Henryk Sienkiewicz
4 The Carboniferous period
5 Sir Richard Attenborough (and Sidney Hayers)

6 *Crossroads*
7 Henry III
8 Any hoofed animal
9 Havana
10 Gironde

Reserve questions

1 James Thurber's
2 A small rocky island
3 Ethanol or ethyl alcohol

Pub League Quiz 7 – Answers

Round 1

Team 1
1 Sir Ernest Henry Shackleton
2 Johannes Brahms
3 Madagascar
4 Decca
5 126

Team 2
1 *Endurance*
2 George Frederick Handel
3 A snake
4 Motown
5 210

Round 2

Team 1
1 Paul Eddington
2 William Hogarth
3 *The Jazz Singer* (1927)
4 Lady Emma Hamilton
5 Erskine Caldwell

Team 2
1 Tyne Daly and Sharon Gless
2 Henri Matisse
3 Al Jolson
4 Mary Queen of Scots
5 Kingsley Amis

Round 3

Team 1
1 Atlanta
2 John Dalton (Daltonism)
3 Loki
4 Scott Joplin
5 Cranium

Team 2
1 Adelaide
2 Ernest Rutherford
3 Nike
4 *The Sting*
5 Melanin

Round 4

Team 1
1 Fairyhouse
2 *Mariner 1*
3 Laszlo Biro
4 Majorca, Minorca and Ibiza
5 *Ad interim*, in the meantime

Team 2
1 Bogside
2 *Rangor 7*
3 Linus Yale (full name required)
4 Ecuador
5 *Ad modum*, in the manner of

Round 5

Boxing: Peek-a-boo
Biology: Ectoplasm
Literature: Gabriel Oak, the shepherd
Wars: Battle of Edgehill
Pot luck: (A nickname for) Edinburgh

Round 6

Team 2
1 Points under the sea of equal depth
2 *Lady and the Tramp*
3 London
4 A cutlet
5 Offa's Dyke

Team 1
1 An earthquake or eruption on the sea bed (it is a tidal wave)
2 *Dumbo*
3 Wells Fargo
4 Yellow
5 The Fens

Round 7

Team 2
1 Liguria
2 Laurie Lee
3 Bachelor of Civil Law
4 Edward V
5 Old Street

Team 1
1 *Campania*
2 T. E. Lawrence
3 Bachelor of Laws
4 George VI
5 St Martin's Place

Round 8

Team 2
1 Czech
2 Henry VIII
3 1985
4 Sidney Lumet
5 Liechtenstein

Team 1
1 Terence
2 Prison reform
3 Sony
4 Richard Lester
5 Vaduz

Round 9

Team 2
1 The Olympic Games
2 One
3 1665/6
4 Kingsley Amis
5 Taurus

Team 1
1 1940s (1947)
2 One
3 The Great Fire of London
4 P. L. Travers
5 Libra

Round 10

Boxing: Sonny Liston
Biology: In your hair and nails
Literature: Bella Wilfer
Wars: John Jellicoe
Pot luck: A monsoon wind

Drinks round

Team 1

1 *The Brook*
2 A bird

3 Joe Johnson
4 A wicker basket for holding fish
5 Paul
6 Stockton and Darlington
7 Variations in electrical current
8 Ougadougou
9 Terence Rattigan
10 The Invergordon Mutiny

Team 2

1 Alfred Lord Tennyson
2 A Central American lizard (or a serpent of mythology)
3 Dennis Taylor
4 A secret political group
5 42
6 Paris and Istanbul
7 Earthquakes
8 Uganda
9 Arthur Ransome
10 The New Model Army

Reserve questions

1 Green, white and red
2 The Klondike
3 A supernova

Pub League Quiz 8 – Answers

Round 1

Team 1
1 Gait McDermot
2 Trick cyclist
3 Canadian
4 Venezuela
5 32

Team 2
1 Gerome Ragni and James Rado
2 Keelhaul
3 Germany
4 Peso
5 16

Round 2

Team 1
1 Christian Science
2 Genoa
3 Charles Laughton
4 Robert Edwin Peary
5 Audie Murphy

Team 2
1 Dervishes
2 The Solent
3 Judy Garland
4 Henry Morton Stanley
5 Spencer Tracy

Round 3

Team 1
1 America
2 A Tibetan dog
3 St Mark
4 The Sphinx
5 Leon Uris

Team 2
1 Germany
2 A wild llama
3 Islam
4 Diogenes
5 John Buchan

Round 4

Team 1
1 Holby
2 Rough Quest
3 Billy Wells
4 Wiltshire
5 Vladimir Ilyich

Team 2
1 *The Bill*
2 Imperial Call
3 Jake La Motta
4 Kent
5 Ulyanov

Round 5

Athletics: Four
Geography: Faro
Pot luck: Romance writer and dramatist
Famous women: Catherine of Valois
Britain: Both 'new towns'

Round 6

Team 2
1 Marsh birds
2 Public Enemy
3 Morpheus
4 Optics
5 Sodium

Team 1
1 The grouse
2 Prince
3 Theseus
4 Pathology
5 Zirconium

Round 7

Team 2
1 North Downs
2 A type of non-venomous snake
3 Jack London
4 Anatomy
5 Hanover

Team 1
1 Medway
2 A type of monkey
3 David Niven
4 Anthropology
5 Tudor

Round 8

Team 2
1 One ounce
2 Greta Garbo
3 Karl Marx
4 Islas Malvinas
5 All on the Danube

Team 1
1 $\frac{1}{27}$
2 Veronica Lake
3 Joan of Arc
4 Ethiopia
5 Mekong

Round 9

Team 2
1 Scott Joplin
2 A small sailing ship
3 Architecture
4 Morocco
5 Buddha

Team 1
1 'Moonlight Serenade'
2 A hansom cab
3 Prophecies
4 Europe
5 The Koran

Round 10

Athletics: Bob Beamon
Geography: Iraq
Pot luck: The planet Venus
Famous women: Dame Nellie Melba
Britain: A promontory

Drinks round

Team 1
1 Mr Bumble
2 Aaron
3 Matthew Arnold
4 1961
5 A breed of small rabbit
6 The day before Good Friday
7 A litre
8 The inability to sleep

9 Michael Elphick
10 South-west India

Team 2
1 *Oliver Twist*
2 Jesse
3 John Masefield
4 1956
5 A dog similar to a husky
6 Shrove Tuesday
7 A calorie or therm
8 Let the buyer beware (he should be aware of the bargain he is making)

9 William Shatner
10 Goat Island

Reserve questions

1 Cutting, polishing and engraving of gem stones
2 Tapioca
3 The Mafia

Pub League Quiz 9 – Answers

Round 1
Team 1
1 Westminster Bridge
2 The Battle of Culloden
3 Ivor Novello
4 Ernest Bevin
5 Sweden

Team 2
1 *Me and My Girl*
2 By the Pope in Rome
3 Rodgers and Hammerstein
4 James Kier Hardie
5 Marsala, Sicily

Round 2
Team 1
1 Emperor of India

2 The Public Record Office
3 Simon of Cyrene
4 Silicon
5 It is the Queen's birthday

Team 2
1 The Isle of Man and the
   Channel Islands
2 Captain Scott's (of the Antarctic)
3 Tiberius
4 A metal
5 The Busby

Round 3
Team 1
1 James Hadley Chase
2 By successfully defending his
   title in three successive bouts
3 *Mare Nostrum* (Our Sea)
4 *Herald of Free Enterprise*
5 Belgium

Team 2
1 *Chateau d'If*
2 Golf (to measure the pace of the
   greens)
3 Albion
4 March
5 Norway

Round 4
Team 1
1 Corinthians I
2 John Nettles
3 Groucho Marx
4 David Essex
5 Of the same blood, related by
   birth

Team 2
1 The council of Nicaea
2 Tom Selleck
3 W. C. Fields
4 Grace Kelly
5 Brotherhood

Round 5
Soap operas: Melbourne
Space travel: *Columbia*
Buildings: The Old Vic
Art: The Prado, Madrid
Rugby union: The Calcutta Cup

Round 6

Team 2
1 Abba
2 Panama Canal
3 John Dryden
4 Mary Magdalene
5 Julia Roberts

Team 1
1 In a plane crash
2 King Camp
3 'And I'll not look for wine.'
4 St Michael
5 Huckleberry Finn

Round 7

Team 2
1 Pauntley, Gloucestershire
2 Aries
3 Stefan Edberg
4 General George Patton
5 Thomas Telford

Team 1
1 Alice Fitzwarren
2 Gemini
3 Pele
4 Leopold III
5 Robert Stephenson

Round 8

Team 2
1 Gene Hackman
2 Lima
3 Flense
4 Skopje, Albania
5 1951

Team 1
1 John Osborne
2 Luanda
3 Hibernal
4 Florence
5 1926

Round 9

Team 2
1 Great Soul
2 Niki Lauda
3 Karen Blixen
4 Congressional Medal of Honour
5 Having the same colour

Team 1
1 Destiny or fate
2 Gerhard Berger
3 John Buchan
4 A lieutenant
5 A social outcast, descendent of Ishmael

Round 10

Soap operas: The Swan
Space travel: *Sputnik 1*
Buildings: John Nash
Art: A reddish-brown
Rugby union: Australia

Drinks round

Team 1

1 Winston Churchill
2 Greenwich Village
3 Billy the Kid
4 Graham Greene
5 Kurt Weill
6 Paul Young
7 African National Congress
8 The lynx (cat) family
9 France
10 37°C, 98.6°F

Team 2

1 James Callaghan's
2 Hyde Park, London
3 Buffalo Bill
4 John Galsworthy
5 *The Threepenny Opera*
6 Aerosmith
7 British Film Institute
8 The waterhog (rodent) family
9 USA
10 Seven

Reserve questions

1 Christmas
2 Daffodil
3 The arms of a Greek cross are the same length; on a Latin cross one is longer than the other

Pub League Quiz 10 – Answers

Round 1

Team 1

1 Thor Heyerdahl

2 Edouard Lalo
3 Europe
4 Sir Walter Scott
5 James II and his Stuart descendants

Team 2

1 To prove that reed boats could have crossed the Atlantic Ocean
2 Georges Bizet
3 Africa
4 Alfred, Lord Tennyson
5 Charles I

Round 2

Team 1

1 A crab
2 'Puppet on a String'
3 The eland
4 Inveraray
5 Hanover

Team 2

1 Capricorn
2 H. E. Bates
3 An eel-like fish
4 County Durham
5 Mary, Queen of Scots

Round 3

Team 1

1 Radio detection and ranging

2 Mars
3 Wallace Hume Carothers
4 By right or by lawful right
5 Freddie Mercury

Team 2

1 Organisation de l'Armée Secrète or Organisation of American States
2 Venus
3 John Deere
4 1949
5 Dangerous

Round 4

Team 1

1 Mrs Sirimavo Bandaranaike
2 The collar bone
3 Pat Eddery
4 Ottawa
5 Nicholas Monsarrat

Team 2

1 Charlotte Corday
2 Over your shoulder joint
3 John Naber
4 Adelaide
5 Sir Thomas More

Round 5
Films: *The Taming of the Shrew* (Shakespeare)
Sport: Ty Cobb
Science: The speed of light
Pot luck: Tenor
Geography: Arctic plains or deserts

Round 6

Team 2	Team 1
1 Chlorophyll	1 Wolfram
2 A trout	2 A jack
3 Norman Mailer	3 John le Carré
4 Fine Gael	4 1911
5 St Nicholas	5 St Denis

Round 7

Team 2	Team 2
1 Granddaughter	1 Great-grandson
2 Brian Jones	2 Franz Schubert
3 4,840	3 640
4 Benjamin Franklin	4 Edmund Cartwright
5 Peter Sellers	5 Harry Secombe

Round 8

Team 2	Team 1
1 Arnold Bennett's	1 Thomas Hardy's
2 A diving bird	2 A fish
3 W. A. Mozart	3 Four
4 Olive Oyl	4 Dennis the Menace
5 Five	5 The Trimurti

Round 9

Team 2	Team 1
1 Adolphe Adam	1 *The Hebrides Overture*
2 Golgotha or Calvary	2 Gethsemane
3 W. C. Fields	3 William Claude Dukenfeld
4 Richard Oastler	4 Wat Tyler
5 Stentor	5 Sir Galahad

Round 10
Films: James Cagney (*Yankee Doodle Dandy*)
Sport: Maureen Connolly
Science: Homeopathy
Pot luck: Gilbert White
Geography: Sargasso Sea

Drinks round

Team 1
1 Geoffrey Chaucer
2 Royal Army Pay Corps
3 Manila
4 A peach
5 Michelangelo
6 1948
7 Aretha Franklin
8 Six

9 Random Access Memory
10 Larkspur

Team 2
1 Herman Melville
2 Royal Logistic Corps
3 Caracas
4 Orange
5 Caravaggio
6 George Eastman
7 Fleetwood Mac
8 France, West Germany, the Netherlands, Belgium, Luxembourg and Italy
9 Read Only Memory
10 The tobacco plant

Reserve questions
1 Hercule Poirot
2 Alcatraz
3 Archie Hahn

Pub League Quiz 11 – Answers

Round 1

Team 1
1 Purple or red
2 The cinema organ
3 The franc
4 Green, white and red
5 Sea of Marmora

Team 2
1 Green
2 The trumpet
3 The quetzal
4 Red, white and black
5 Italy

Round 2

Team 1
1 The Magna Carta was signed
2 A musical instrument

3 Wind speed or force

4 One ('The Red Vineyard', sold to Belgian artist Anna Boch)
5 Ernest Hemingway

Team 2
1 St Helena
2 A corruption of Bethlehem (The Bethlehem Hospital, Bishopsgate, London, was converted into a lunatic asylum)
3 An instrument used to measure the velocity of a fluid flow
4 René Magritte

5 Jane Austen

Round 3

Team 1
1 Marvin Gaye
2 They drew after extra time and had to have a replay
3 *Middlemarch*
4 Bangladesh
5 Harold Macmillan

Team 2
1 Cliff Richard
2 Ingemar Johansson

3 *A Clockwork Orange*
4 The Dolomites
5 Winston S. Churchill

Round 4

Team 1
1 The Duke of Medina Sidonia
2 British Airways
3 Longships
4 Man Ray
5 1945

Team 2
1 Lord Howard of Effingham
2 Martini
3 Eddystone
4 Daniel Mytens
5 Stalingrad

Round 5
Films: Olivia de Havilland
The arts: *The Rite of Spring* by Igor Stravinsky
Paris: Pont Neuf
Who said?: David Lloyd George
World leaders: Fitzgerald

Round 6

Team 2	Team 1
1 Legendary giants	1 Beowulf
2 Slowly with broad dignity	2 *Sostenuto*
3 Victoria Tower	3 Cheltenham
4 The Bible	4 Three
5 Australia	5 Italy

Round 7

Team 2	Team 1
1 Denmark	1 Iceland
2 John Milton	2 *The Burial of Sir John Moore After Corunna* (Charles Wolfe)
3 Canada	3 Utah
4 Zwanzig	4 Otto
5 Kenya	5 USA

Round 8

Team 2	Team 1
1 The right to take from wood or wasteland a reasonable portion of wood for use in the home	1 A right of way over land for access only, as in the case of the carriage of minerals from a mine or quarry
2 Ozone	2 The element chromium
3 Diana Rigg	3 Honor Blackman
4 A garden summerhouse	4 Campanile
5 Royal College of Veterinary Surgeons	5 European Free Trade Association

Round 9

Team 2	Team 1
1 Tuberculosis	1 In a motorcycle accident
2 Himself	2 Alexander the Great
3 Greyhounds	3 The Derby is for three-year-olds only
4 The Friendly Islands	4 Vancouver Island
5 Magpie	5 A sunken fence, hedge or wall

Round 10

Films: Raymond Massey
The arts: Horse racing, ballet and women washing
Paris: Montmartre
Who said?: Winston S. Churchill
World leaders: Archbishop Makarios

Drinks round

Team 1

1 Honey and plenty of money wrapped up in a five pound note
2 *Hamlet*
3 God willing
4 The Louvre, Paris
5 Ramadan
6 Argentina
7 General Noriega of Panama
8 A shoulder cape with elongated sides
9 Saxophone
10 Peter Sallis

Team 2

1 On Wednesday he was married
2 Uriah Heep
3 Of sound mind
4 Antwerp
5 Armageddon
6 Greece (Macedonia)
7 Olaf Palme
8 A close-fitting cap
9 Charlie Parker
10 Raymond Burr

Reserve questions

1 James Cook
2 The epicentre
3 Stanley Baldwin

Pub League Quiz 12 – Answers

Round 1

Team 1
1 Irving Berlin
2 C
3 Kings of Siam used to give an elephant to people they disliked since the cost of keeping one was more trouble than it was worth
4 Before the reign of Richard I
5 Clement Attlee

Team 2
1 Bob Geldof and Midge Ure
2 Q
3 Down a mine (it is the miners' name for methane)

4 A year and a day
5 Hugh Gaitskell

Round 2

Team 1
1 An Australian snake
2 Fellow of the Royal Geographical Society
3 Oxford
4 J. M. W. Turner
5 518 feet

Team 2
1 A griffon
2 National Union of Students

3 Bristol
4 Sir Alfred Gilbert
5 984 feet

Round 3

Team 1
1 The Netherlands
2 1984
3 Caves
4 Finland
5 Tristan da Cunha

Team 2
1 Toledo
2 Rowing or sculling
3 A deputy or substitute
4 Poland
5 Willem Barents and Jacob Heemskerk

Round 4

Team 1
1 Uruguay
2 William II
3 Sergei Prokofiev
4 Indian Ocean
5 Culture Beat

Team 2
1 Uruguay
2 The Court of Verderers
3 British
4 Mahé
5 Vince Clarke

Round 5
Pot luck: A plug at the mouth of some wind instruments
History: Captain (later Sir) Henry Morgan
Politics: William Wilberforce
Biology: Eighty beats a minute
Art: Michelangelo

Round 6
Team 2
1 Amen
2 16
3 Arabic, English, French
4 San Francisco
5 Detroit

Team 1
1 Genesis, Exodus and Leviticus
2 18
3 Christian, Muslim, Druse
4 A brand new jersey
5 Red

Round 7
Team 2
1 The storm (or stormy) petrel
2 Eight

3 Edward I
4 Prague
5 Ice hockey

Team 1
1 The missel thrush
2 Noun, pronoun, adjective,
   adverb, verb, preposition,
   conjunction, interjection
3 Edward I
4 Delhi
5 Rowing

Round 8
Team 2
1 Kublai Khan

2 La Manche
3 William Arthur Philip Louis
4 David Janssen
5 Zinc

Team 1
1 *The Ballad of Reading Gaol* (Oscar
   Wilde)
2 The bends
3 Kenya
4 A one-armed man
5 Chromite

Round 9
Team 2
1 La Paz
2 Georgy Porgy
3 Mexico
4 The afghani
5 1983

Team 1
1 Port of Spain
2 The Great Plague 1665–66
3 Staffa, Inner Hebrides
4 The krona
5 Moorgate

Round 10
Pot luck: Calcutta
History: Alfred Dreyfus
Politics: Josip Broz
Biology: Eugenics
Art: Raphael

Drinks round

Team 1
1 Pampas
2 Wilkie Collins
3 Helena
4 Three
5 *Enola Gay*
6 Sweden
7 Mace
8 France
9 Goliath
10 Four points

Team 2
1 The Mistral
2 Nancy Mitford
3 Mont Blanc
4 Sulphuric acid
5 The Duke of Gloucester (1954)
6 Germany
7 Seaweed
8 Sudan
9 Reggae
10 Two points

Reserve questions
1 Norway, Sweden, Finland and Russia
2 Sarajevo
3 Globe, Jerusalem and Chinese

Pub League Quiz 13 – Answers

Round 1

Team 1
1   Clint Eastwood
2   J. Fenimore Cooper
3   Esperanto
4   The TT Races
5   The Italian Republic

Team 2
1   Warren Beatty
2   Iago
3   1887
4   Tourist Trophy
5   The Quai d'Orsay

Round 2

Team 1
1   Ariel
2   *Apollo 11*
3   The hip
4   Fellow of the Institute of Actuaries
5   Detective/police thriller

Team 2
1   Gertrude
2   Laika
3   Clematis
4   Fellow of the Chartered Institute of Bankers
5   *Van der Valk*

Round 3

Team 1
1   A stew of lamb with root vegetables

2   Protestant
3   Benjamin Disraeli
4   Tony Jacklin
5   Joseph

Team 2
1   A dessert made from cream beaten with sugar, wine or cider and often lemon juice
2   Roman Catholic
3   Vivian Grey
4   Tiger country
5   Joshua

Round 4

Team 1
1   David Bowie
2   Israel
3   Five
4   Merlin
5   Gazetteer

Team 2
1   In white satin
2   Romania
3   Ten pence
4   Camelot
5   Mycology

Round 5

Kings and queens: King Louis XVI of France
Famous men: John F. Kennedy
Sport: White
Places: Porcelain
General knowledge: They were built as defences against invasion during the Napoleonic Wars

Round 6

Team 2
1 Mercury or Venus
2 Sarah Catherine Martin
3 The Storting
4 Vincente Minnelli

5 Victor Hugo

Team 1
1 Mercury or Venus
2 Oliver Postgate
3 The University of Paris
4 Tim Rice and Andrew Lloyd Webber
5 Boris Pasternak

Round 7

Team 2
1 Mexico
2 Gopher wood
3 Mounted guns, cannons and artillery
4 John Gay
5 Peru

Team 1
1 Rio Grande
2 The Dead Sea Scrolls
3 Turkey and Egypt

4 The Old Testament
5 *The Scarlet Pimpernel*

Round 8

Team 2
1 Thomas Gray
2 Cleopatra's Needle
3 Jon Pertwee
4 South Africa
5 Road making: macadamising, from which tarmac developed

Team 1
1 Percy Bysshe Shelley
2 1440
3 Una Stubbs
4 Greece
5 The Mini Minor

Round 9

Team 2
1 Its footprint

2 Napoleon I (Bonaparte)
3 The strings
4 Joseph
5 Eire (1938–45)

Team 1
1 The offence of trading in church offices
2 Voltaire
3 A flute
4 Mary Magdalene
5 Spanish

Round 10

Kings and queens: William the Conqueror (William I)
Famous men: He died of a self-inflicted gunshot wound
Sport: 1912
Places: Uxbridge
General knowledge: Anthony Wedgwood (Tony) Benn

Drinks round

Team 1

1. St Mark
2. Thomas à Becket
3. Major-General
4. The sol
5. Stendhal
6. Boris Karloff
7. Burma
8. Five
9. Canada
10. Trevor Eve

Team 2

1. St James (the Greater)
2. Leon Trotsky
3. Commodore
4. The rupee
5. Honoré de Balzac
6. Tony Curtis
7. England
8. Four
9. Wales
10. Jeremy Irons

Reserve questions

1. A dinner jacket
2. Butter
3. Drink from it

Pub League Quiz 14 – Answers

Round 1
Team 1
1 A bird
2 Bobby Moore
3 Montreal
4 Munster
5 Boris Pasternak

Team 2
1 The coyote
2 Gerd Müller
3 Hereford United
4 Clare, Cork, Kerry, Limerick, Tipperary and Waterford
5 Captain Frederick Marryat

Round 2
Team 1
1 Felix Mendelssohn
2 William Bateson
3 Fellow of the Royal College of Surgeons
4 Peter Lorre
5 River Danube

Team 2
1 Seven
2 St Mary's
3 Fellow of the Royal Horticultural Society
4 Hungary
5 Switzerland

Round 3
Team 1
1 A little over 40mph
2 Gladys Knight and the Pips
3 Eric Morecambe
4 A fairy
5 The Yorkshire Ripper

Team 2
1 A little over nine minutes
2 The Kinks
3 Ernie
4 Africa
5 Idi Amin

Round 4
Team 1
1 The cuttlefish
2 Giacomo Matteoti's
3 Custard pies
4 Claudius I
5 John Cleese

Team 2
1 10
2 Prime Minister of South Africa
3 Speedy Gonzales
4 Richard II
5 Prunella Scales

Round 5
Mythology and legend: Temple of Athena
Africa: Togo
Entertainment: Moulin Rouge
People and places: Crete (named after King Minos)
Numbers: A £12, B £20, C £34

Round 6

Team 2

1 Dr Elizabeth Garrett Anderson, 1908
2 Sir Malcolm Sargent
3 The Albert Medal
4 W. Somerset Maugham
5 Leo

Team 1

1 St Augustine
2 She led the women's suffrage movement
3 The Congressional Medal of Honor
4 William Shakespeare
5 Sagittarius

Round 7

Team 2

1 Benjamin Disraeli
2 John XIII
3 The Mountains of Mourne
4 Faith
5 An instrument for measuring specific gravity

Team 1

1 Napoleon Bonaparte
2 John Paul I
3 Slieve Donard
4 Paul Simon
5 An instrument that measures magnetic forces, especially of the earth

Round 8

Team 2

1 Iceland (The Althing, 930CE)
2 Venus
3 John Creasey
4 Ava Gardner
5 10

Team 1

1 German
2 Venus
3 G. K. Chesterton
4 Joan Crawford
5 The triple jump

Round 9

Team 2

1 Hampshire
2 Polo
3 Solomon
4 Cole Porter
5 Richard Dimbleby

Team 1

1 Gloucestershire
2 Show jumping
3 'Thou shalt have no other gods before me'
4 Vaudeville
5 The Light, Home and Third Programmes

Round 10

Mythology and legend: Cupid
Africa: Mali
Entertainment: Lou Ferrigno
People and places: Public opinion polls
Numbers: Seven, nine

Drinks round

Team 1

1 Entrecôte

2 *The Soldier* of Rupert Brooke
3 Water
4 Robert Donat
5 Bright green
6 Three days and nights
7 Tennessee Williams
8 Osbert Lancaster
9 1660
10 Linus

Team 2

1 Cod's roe (sometimes grey mullet's)
2 Empty tomb
3 Nitrogen
4 Ingrid Bergman
5 Yellow
6 Salome
7 Emlyn Williams
8 William Heath Robinson
9 1867
10 Minnie

Reserve questions

1 A song bird
2 Russia
3 Albany

Pub League Quiz 15 – Answers

Round 1
Team 1
1 A shallow ornamental bowl or cup mounted on a base
2 Thomas Edison
3 All of them
4 Nell Dunn
5 Tony Blair

Team 2
1 A large stone used in prehistoric constructions (such as Stonehenge)
2 Georges Clemenceau
3 Falstaff
4 Paul Scott
5 Baroness Thatcher of Kesteven

Round 2
Team 1
1 Quinine
2 Siam
3 Yom Kippur

4 Stanley Baldwin
5 An instrument for producing and photographing a spectrum

Team 2
1 Anaesthetic
2 Oxonian
3 The religious coming of age of a 13-year-old Jewish boy
4 Harry S. Truman
5 An instrument for signalling using the sun or for photographing the sun

Round 3
Team 1
1 The Urals
2 Queen's Park
3 Kaaba
4 Navy, Army and Air Force Institutes
5 Richard Harris

Team 2
1 The Yellow River
2 22 yards
3 Hinduism
4 Organisation of Petroleum Exporting Countries
5 Margaret Lockwood

Round 4
Team 1
1 Edward VI
2 Swastika
3 Robert Burns
4 Richard Ingrams
5 Metro-Goldwyn-Mayer

Team 2
1 95
2 Fascism
3 Ella Wheeler Wilcox
4 John Lennon
5 RKO

Round 5
Classical music: Hector Berlioz
Motoring: 1905
History: John Bellingham
Television: *Callan*
Chance: India and Sri Lanka

Round 6
Team 2
1 Australia
2 Margaret Mitchell
3 Allah
4 Fellow of the Royal Society of Literature
5 Armagnac

Team 1
1 California
2 Evelyn Waugh
3 The head of John the Baptist
4 Naval Officer in Charge
5 A very dry sherry

Round 7
Team 2
1 Greece
2 Karate
3 Clouds
4 John Keats
5 Sir Alec Douglas-Home

Team 1
1 Horatio Nelson
2 Jujitsu (or judo)
3 Dystopia
4 William Wordsworth
5 P. I. Tchaikovsky

Round 8
Team 2
1 Mr Pastry

2 Trinity House
3 Skiing
4 Kitsch
5 Sir Henry Morton Stanley and Dr David Livingstone

Team 1
1 *Help, A Hard Day's Night, Yellow Submarine, Magical Mystery Tour, Let It Be*
2 Portsmouth
3 New South Wales, Australia
4 Grandma Moses
5 Sherlock Holmes and Professor Moriarty

Round 9
Team 2
1 Node
2 Rock Hudson
3 Cervix
4 District of Columbia
5 Charlie Peace

Team 1
1 Taproot
2 Nigel Havers
3 The common cold
4 Airborne Warning and Control System
5 A black hat

Round 10

Classical music: Franz Joseph Haydn
Motoring: Flashing beacon highlighting a pedestrian crossing
History: Anne Boleyn
Television: *What the Papers Say*
Chance: Master of Surgery

Drinks round

Team 1

1 Map making
2 False
3 Castor and Pollux

4 The outer
5 Baseball
6 The Special Theory of Relativity
7 Victor Hugo
8 A light coloured horse (or a pigeon or dove)
9 Garbage In, Garbage Out
10 Skye

Team 2

1 Tonga
2 True
3 Procustes was a monster who killed his victims by stretching them, or cutting off their legs, to fit into his bed
4 The bar
5 Soccer (it is the World Cup)
6 Albert Einstein
7 John Masters
8 A small South American bird

9 Antimony
10 Loch Lomond

Reserve questions

1 David Low
2 Chicago
3 Madonna

Pub League Quiz 16 – Answers

Round 1

Team 1
1 George Pompidou
2 G. K. Chesterton
3 A second
4 Thomas Arne
5 Four

Team 2
1 Andrew Bonar Law
2 Richard Brinsley Sheridan
3 Sulphur
4 George Frederick Handel
5 High jump

Round 2

Team 1
1 Kappa
2 Auguste Rodin
3 *The Lavender Hill Mob*
4 Spain
5 Gibraltar

Team 2
1 Delta
2 Miniatures
3 Rod Steiger
4 The Ottawa river
5 Colonel Thomas Blood

Round 3

Team 1
1 World Council of Churches

2 Graham Greene
3 Malaysia
4 Calculus

5 Cole Porter

Team 2
1 Confederation of British Industry
2 Ernest Hemingway
3 Morgan
4 From the Latin, *salarium*, meaning salt, with which Roman soldiers were paid
5 Jerome Kern

Round 4

Team 1
1 A duck
2 The period directly before Christmas
3 William Kent
4 *Citizen Kane*
5 South Atlantic Ocean

Team 2
1 A lizard
2 The coming
3 John Nash
4 A New York subway train
5 Indian Ocean

Round 5

Holiday and travel: The Isle of Man
Food and drink: Tortilla
Music: Johann Sebastian Bach
The Bible: Zacharias and Elizabeth
History: Son-in-law

Round 6

Team 2
1 Limestone and clay
2 The pancreas
3 The London Marathon
4 David and Ruth Archer (*The Archers*)
5 Mitre

Team 1
1 Bauxite
2 The ear
3 Wigan
4 'Dirty Den' Watts
5 Sarong

Round 7

Team 2
1 A Spanish princess
2 Islamabad
3 D. H. Lawrence
4 Royal Naval Volunteer Reserve
5 Denis Healey

Team 1
1 A Polish dance
2 Halifax
3 David Herbert
4 Royal Canadian Mounted Police
5 Edward Heath

Round 8

Team 2
1 Citrus
2 The Battle of Trafalgar
3 Jersey Joe Walcott
4 The shins
5 The river Itchen

Team 1
1 Sequoia or redwood
2 The Battle of Culloden
3 Bob Fitzsimmons
4 A crusade
5 The Ouse and Trent

Round 9

Team 2
1 Switzerland
2 Edward I
3 They are names of stud poker games
4 Ted Hughes
5 Mexico

Team 1
1 D
2 The Battle of the Boyne
3 78
4 John Masefield
5 Argentina and Chile

Round 10

Holiday and travel: Her Britannic Majesty's Secretary of State
Food and drink: Potatoes
Music: Ludwig van Beethoven
The Bible: The temple at Jerusalem
History: Jefferson Davis

Drinks round

Team 1

1 Nyasaland
2 Andy Capp
3 The Red Cross
4 Absinthe
5 Busby Berkeley
6 Persian or Pushtu
7 Jeffrey Archer
8 Montevideo
9 1972
10 Tom Mix

Team 2

1 India
2 Flash Gordon
3 The Red Crescent
4 Maraschino
5 Gene Kelly
6 Albania
7 Richard Eyre
8 Ulan Bator
9 1983
10 Max Brand

Reserve questions

1 Aintree
2 Eight
3 Charles Macintosh

Pub League Quiz 17 – Answers

Round 1
Team 1
1 Basra
2 Omnivores
3 Ham, Shem and Japheth
4 Lace

5 Josiah Wedgwood

Team 2
1 Oran
2 Invertebrate
3 Rahab
4 A window that tapers to an arched point
5 Thomas Minton

Round 2
Team 1
1 Sir Douglas Fairbanks, Charlie Chaplin, D. W. Griffith and Mary Pickford
2 Oliver Cromwell (and Lord Leven)
3 Kingsley Amis
4 Rocks formed by the cooling and solidifying of molten magmas
5 Lanolin

Team 2
1 Charlie Chaplin

2 Edward I

3 Hans Christian Andersen
4 Lithosphere

5 Ozone

Round 3
Team 1
1 Androcles
2 A famous US jazz singer
3 In your eyes
4 Arthur Ashe
5 Giacomo Puccini

Team 2
1 Daedalus
2 John Dankworth
3 In your nose
4 Four
5 Don Carlos

Round 4
Team 1
1 The planet Pluto
2 Mary Wells
3 Thomas Alva Edison
4 Electrocardiogram
5 Tony Hancock

Team 2
1 A nebula
2 'Eleanor Rigby'
3 James Hargreaves
4 Medical Research Council
5 Una Stubbs

Round 5

Dress and fashion: Christian Dior
Law: Impeachment
Inventors and inventions: Sir James Dewar
Famous men: Sigmund Freud
Words: Intended for teaching or instructing

Round 6

Team 2
1 Durham
2 The ugli
3 Sheffield
4 *The Sleepwalkers*
5 Corsica

Team 1
1 Harvard
2 The loganberry
3 Manchester
4 Budapest
5 Tenerife

Round 7

Team 2
1 King Faisal I
2 Woody Allen and Mia Farrow
3 George Peppard
4 John le Carré
5 'Del Boy'

Team 1
1 Saud
2 Tyne Daly
3 Dirk Benedict
4 R. D. Blackmore
5 He played a mute

Round 8

Team 2
1 Three
2 Pale blue and white
3 London and Bristol
4 Whitney Houston
5 A terrier

Team 1
1 Prostitution
2 'The Star-spangled Banner'
3 1825
4 Glasgow
5 Cardiganshire, Pembrokeshire

Round 9

Team 2
1 The Lake District National Park
2 Tasmania
3 Austrian
4 Old Trafford, Manchester
5 Military Medal

Team 1
1 Octavia Hill, Sir Robert Hunter and Canon Hardwicke Rawnsley
2 Sydney
3 Polish
4 Golf
5 Minimum Lending Rate

Round 10
Dress and fashion: Coco Chanel
Law: Intestate
Inventors and inventions: Charles Babbage
Famous men: Dr Christian Barnard
Words: Longsightedness

Drinks round

Team 1
1 George Meredith
2 A rocking chair
3 New Zealander
4 Large marine fish
5 Jean-François Millet
6 Bobbysoxers
7 Hg
8 Sophomores
9 Malt
10 Nepal, Bhutan

Team 2
1 Beatrix Potter
2 Raymond Baxter
3 1912
4 A leveret
5 'Mona Lisa'
6 The cornet
7 Mg
8 Sophism (sophistry)
9 A type of maize
10 Natal

Reserve questions
1 Over 5,500
2 0.6 seconds
3 Plums

Pub League Quiz 18 – Answers

Round 1

Team 1
1 John Lennon
2 In the fabric of a cathedral
3 Germaine Greer
4 New Zealand
5 Confucius

Team 2
1 *Brothers in Arms*
2 In a castle
3 *Pride and Prejudice*
4 Joan of Arc
5 The Bishop of Salisbury

Round 2

Team 1
1 Red
2 Absent without leave
3 Its prehistoric cave paintings
4 The Penguin
5 The Washington Monument

Team 2
1 Black
2 Son of
3 The horse
4 Krypton
5 The Spanish Steps

Round 3

Team 1
1 Brazil
2 Brown
3 Egypt
4 Operation Barbarossa
5 Natalie Wood

Team 2
1 Martina Navratilova
2 Amtrak
3 Shylock
4 Operation Overlord
5 Jayne Mansfield

Round 4

Team 1
1 Grenada
2 Italian earthenware

3 Aquarius
4 *Women in Love*
5 Paavo Nurmi

Team 2
1 On the Panama Canal
2 Toasted Italian bread with a savoury topping
3 Sirius
4 Sir Walter Scott
5 Jim Thorpe

Round 5

Water life: A calf
Television: Billy Connolly
Organisations: Amnesty International
Games: Contract bridge
Flight: De Havilland

Round 6

Team 2
1 100 years
2 Dorothy
3 Tin
4 The Flying Bedstead
5 The Statue of Liberty

Team 1
1 Willy Wonka
2 Jim Henson
3 Australia
4 The Tin Lizzie
5 The Paris Exhibition of 1889

Round 7

Team 2
1 Middle class
2 *Camelot*
3 The emu
4 *Morning Cloud*
5 Biennially

Team 1
1 The House of Commons
2 *The Rocky Horror Show*
3 Sydney Harbour Bridge
4 Robert E. Peary
5 Cruiserweight

Round 8

Team 2
1 The flag of the UK
2 Ulster Defence Regiment
3 Amelia Earhart
4 Spain
5 Turkey

Team 1
1 The flag of Chile
2 Basketball
3 London (the Reform Club)
4 Lancashire
5 Green

Round 9

Team 2
1 Aquavit
2 *Gentlemen Prefer Blondes*
3 Haile Selassie
4 71 per cent

5 The mosquito

Team 1
1 Gin
2 Earl D. Biggers
3 Nicholas Breakspear
4 In the Arctic Ocean between Alaska and the North Pole
5 German measles

Round 10

Water life: A killer whale
Television: Mia Farrow
Organisations: Khmer Rouge
Games: Five
Flight: Croydon

Drinks round

Team 1
1 A French poodle
2 Tombstone, Arizona
3 Mount Denali
4 Oak apples
5 Barbra Streisand
6 Morocco
7 Poker
8 The caribou or reindeer
9 George Stubbs
10 Wiltshire

Team 2
1 The Uncle Remus books
2 *High Noon*
3 Alaska
4 Yew trees
5 El Cid
6 Lake Victoria
7 Blackjack or pontoon
8 The antelope family
9 John Constable
10 London's British Museum

Reserve questions
1 Three
2 Melbourne
3 Stephen Sondheim

Pub League Quiz 19 – Answers

Round 1
Team 1
1 Nashville
2 George Bernard Shaw
3 Knight, Order of St Patrick
4 Longchamp
5 Gamal Abdel Nasser

Team 2
1 Portland
2 Harold Pinter
3 Member, Royal Victorian Order
4 Prix de L'Arc de Triomphe
5 Mao Tse-tung

Round 2
Team 1
1 Anode
2 Le Mans
3 Marilyn Monroe
4 Loire
5 ZZ Top

Team 2
1 Cathode
2 Mike Hawthorn
3 Norma Jean Baker
4 Africa
5 Wings

Round 3
Team 1
1 Anna Ford
2 Benito Mussolini
3 Anna Karenina
4 A wild ass
5 Four

Team 2
1 Anna Friel
2 Il Duce
3 Fyodor Dostoyevsky
4 A breed of sheep
5 Ramsay MacDonald, Clement Attlee, Harold Wilson and James Callaghan

Round 4
Team 1
1 Staffordshire
2 *Breakfast at Tiffany's*
3 The area of a parallelogram
4 Birds' eggs
5 Alaska

Team 2
1 The Cecils
2 Henry Mancini
3 Force
4 The study of the origin and development of words
5 Pennsylvania

Round 5
Cathedrals: Rheims
Heraldry: A term for colour which is used on a shield or coat of arms
Numbers: Nine
Who said?: Harold Wilson
Soap operas: *Brookside*

Round 6

Team 2
1 Rudyard Kipling
2 Richard Trevithick
3 Normandy

4 Allan-a-Dale

5 Spain

Team 1
1 John Bunyan
2 Worcester
3 Ground almonds, sugar and egg white
4 He helped to carry her off when she was about to be married to an old knight against her will
5 USA (Kansas)

Round 7

Team 2
1 The skin
2 Or
3 Vice-Admiral Sturdee
4 Green Park
5 Native America Indian

Team 1
1 The brain
2 Argent
3 Lord Kitchener
4 Burlington House
5 Italian

Round 8

Team 2
1 Henrik Ibsen
2 Andorra
3 Saltpetre or nitre
4 Aphrodite
5 Thesaurus

Team 1
1 Oscar Wilde
2 The Algarve
3 Nitrous oxide
4 Venus
5 Concordance

Round 9

Team 2
1 Haemoglobin

2 Dinghy
3 Czech
4 Edwin (Buzz) Aldrin
5 Supernova

Team 1
1 A hereditary defect that prevents blood clotting
2 Skiing
3 Maurice Ravel
4 Early Bird
5 Mercury

Round 10

Cathedrals: Aachen
Heraldry: A knight's tunic emblazoned with the arms of the king or with his own coat of arms
Numbers: 18 and 30
Who said?: Abraham Lincoln
Soap operas: Grace Archer

Drinks round

Team 1

1 International Atomic Energy Agency
2 The Netherlands

3 H. Rider Haggard
4 Jack Ruby
5 Alfred the Great
6 Sophia Loren
7 Wellington
8 Silver
9 Fiona 3¾ and Jean 4½
10 Scotland

Team 2

1 International Civil Aviation Organisation
2 Maine, New Hampshire, Vermont, Rhode Island, Connecticut, Massachusetts
3 Charles Kingsley
4 Sirhan Sirhan
5 Macbeth
6 Miranda
7 Luxembourg
8 Roy Rogers
9 Edward 28 and Cyril 52
10 Northern Ireland

Reserve questions

1 Earl
2 12
3 Billiards

Pub League Quiz 20 – Answers

Round 1
Team 1
1 Durham
2 Portugal
3 Baseball
4 A set
5 1947

Team 2
1 Somerset
2 Bulgaria
3 Gymnastics
4 A drey
5 Lord Louis Mountbatten of
Burma

Round 2
Team 1
1 Santiago
2 Georges Bizet
3 Dislike or fear of strangers
4 Prometheus
5 Brian

Team 2
1 Mexico City
2 Johannes Brahms
3 Rabies
4 The Gorgons
5 Ermintrude

Round 3
Team 1
1 Charles Bronson
2 Charles Dickens
3 An Arabian sailing ship
4 70 minutes (2 x 35 minutes)
5 The Searchers

Team 2
1 John Ford
2 Inspector Maigret
3 A large Eskimo canoe
4 Seven
5 Bonnie Tyler

Round 4
Team 1
1 Hymen
2 'Success'
3 China (in the Tibetan Highlands)
4 Philately
5 Smallpox

Team 2
1 Charon
2 Katharine Hepburn
3 Italy
4 Butterfly specimens
5 The liver

Round 5
Films: *Kid Galahad*
The arts: Paul Gauguin
Literature: Anthony Trollope
Sport: Point-to-point
Proverbs: Repent at leisure

Round 6

Team 2
1 Lawrence of Arabia
2 Randy Crawford
3 The Fleur de Lys (the Prince of Wales' feathers)
4 Enid Blyton
5 Albert Finney

Team 1
1 Arthur Miller
2 Diana Ross
3 A lion
4 The *Black Pig*
5 Buster Keaton

Round 7

Team 2
1 A butterfly
2 70
3 Portuguese
4 Six
5 Leeds United

Team 1
1 A British sporting dog
2 A tangent
3 Spanish
4 50
5 Leicester City

Round 8

Team 2
1 12
2 Greece
3 Henri de Toulouse-Lautrec
4 British Dental Association
5 *Juke Box Jury*

Team 1
1 11
2 Belgium
3 Jean Honoré Fragonard
4 Estimated Time of Departure
5 Jack Klugman

Round 9

Team 2
1 The Miners' Union
2 Louis XIV
3 Leeds
4 Nebuchadnezzar
5 Tommy Steele

Team 1
1 Prime Minister of Great Britain
2 Charles II
3 Southend-on-Sea
4 Peter and Philip
5 Cat Stevens

Round 10

Films: *She Done Him Wrong*
The arts: Leonardo da Vinci
Literature: Caesura
Sport: Tottenham Hotspur
Proverbs: Good intentions

Drinks round

Team 1
1 Addis Ababa
2 Hans Christian Andersen
3 *Madame Butterfly*
4 Lead
5 The telephone
6 Canada
7 A mongoose
8 The Torridge
9 The Doors
10 Baseball

Team 2
1 Lerwick
2 George Lucas
3 Gilbert and Sullivan
4 Copper
5 The Chinese
6 Rifle shooting
7 Ants
8 River Nene
9 10CC
10 Billiards

Reserve questions

1 Uranus
2 St Stanilaus
3 Germany

Pub League Quiz 21 – Answers

Round 1

Team 1
1 Forget-me-not
2 In a library (It is a system for classifying books)
3 Ellery Queen
4 Darlington, County Durham
5 Venezuela

Team 2
1 Hyacinth
2 In the sky (it is a star group)
3 William Shakespeare
4 Weymouth
5 Belgium

Round 2

Team 1
1 The Dave Clark Five
2 Dr Johnson
3 26
4 Fair Isle
5 Marie Stopes

Team 2
1 Elvis Costello
2 George Orwell
3 12
4 Triassic
5 Dr Thomas Barnardo

Round 3

Team 1
1 1969
2 Redingote
3 A rock climber
4 The gift of prophecy
5 Master of the Rolls

Team 2
1 1955 (allow one year either way)
2 Gaberdine
3 Tug-of-war
4 Saturday, after Saturn
5 'My Lord'

Round 4

Team 1
1 Tagus
2 Marshal of the Royal Air Force
3 Its Wall Game
4 La Mancha
5 Harry

Team 2
1 The river Moskva
2 Through hardship to the stars
3 Old Kent Road
4 1984
5 Connie Francis

Round 5

Pop music: Fairport Convention
The Olympics: None (the USA boycotted the games, held in Moscow)
The Bible: Daniel
What comes next?: Seven (they are numbers around a dartboard)
Where is it?: North Island, New Zealand

Round 6

Team 2

1 Hydrology
2 In your throat at the back of your mouth
3 William Pitt, first Earl of Chatham
4 Crete
5 *Mansfield Park* by Jane Austen

Team 1

1 Metallurgy
2 The outermost layer of the skin
3 Harold Macmillan
4 Cologne
5 Mary Shelley

Round 7

Team 2

1 Deuteronomy
2 Finland
3 Crabs
4 Columbia Broadcasting System
5 Two over par for a hole

Team 1

1 The feeding of the five thousand
2 The krone
3 A snake
4 Royal Academy of Dramatic Art
5 Nine

Round 8

Team 2

1 35
2 The Queen of Hearts in Alice in Wonderland
3 The British national anthem, 'God Save the King'
4 Oliver
5 Lord Scarman

Team 1

1 Christmas Day
2 *Tess of the d'Urbervilles*
3 George and Ira Gershwin
4 Jefferson
5 Winston S. Churchill

Round 9

Team 2

1 *Macbeth*
2 A hog
3 The bicycle
4 The dollar
5 A bat

Team 1

1 *Twelfth Night*
2 A jenny
3 The Montgolfier brothers
4 The dinar
5 A diving sea duck

Round 10

Pop music: The Scaffold
The Olympics: Jesse Owens
The Bible: Abraham
What comes next?: Richard Nixon
Where is it?: The Louvre, Paris

Drinks round

Team 1

1 George IV
2 Cheese
3 Norwich City
4 John Cabot
5 Caustic soda
6 Peru and Bolivia
7 Argentina
8 The Wurzels
9 Zsa Zsa Gabor
10 Windsor Castle

Team 2

1 James I (VI of Scotland)
2 Oysters
3 Luton Town
4 Dutch
5 Epsom salts
6 Canada
7 Chaim Weizzman
8 T Rex
9 Tony Benn
10 Coventry Cathedral

Reserve questions

1 Pete Townsend
2 Kentucky
3 Angels on horseback

Pub League Quiz 22 – Answers

Round 1

Team 1
1 Damascus
2 Alfred, Lord Tennyson, (*The Charge of The Light Brigade*)
3 British Academy of Film and Television Arts
4 Turpentine
5 Australia

Team 2
1 Ankara
2 George Bernard Shaw
3 National Union of Journalists
4 French polish
5 Tunbridge Wells

Round 2

Team 1
1 Nottinghamshire
2 The eye
3 Beethoven
4 Perth
5 Meat Loaf

Team 2
1 Warwickshire
2 The skin
3 Mendelssohn
4 Armagh
5 Gene Pitney

Round 3

Team 1
1 Mount Olympus
2 Richard I, William II (William Rufus) and Harold II
3 Sylvester Stallone
4 Stanley Spencer
5 Aviation, particularly helicopters

Team 2
1 Helicon
2 Richard II

3 Robert Redford
4 Rembrandt
5 Jet propulsion

Round 4

Team 1
1 Juniper
2 A mast or sail
3 Zinc and copper
4 Johnny Horton
5 The Boer War

Team 2
1 Rum
2 A vessel of hot water in which cooking pans are slowly heated
3 Mercury
4 Kenneth Roberts
5 The Battle of Jutland

Round 5
Entertainment: Lee Strasberg
Words: Fire
Industry: Cotton
Finance: The Dow Jones Index
Music: Glenn Miller

Round 6
Team 2
1 Garrick Street
2 The Swiss Guard
3 Basketball
4 The Taj Mahal
5 Sculpture

Team 1
1 Poste Restante
2 The Quakers
3 Baseball
4 St Paul's Cathedral
5 Opera

Round 7
Team 2
1 Pedro Cabral
2 Venus
3 The development of the atomic bomb in the Second World War
4 Trigonometry
5 The Hollies

Team 1
1 Francisco de Orellana
2 Neptune
3 The fields of Flanders were covered with poppies
4 920
5 Otis Redding

Round 8
Team 2
1 Tunisia
2 Devon
3 Bouvier
4 Turmeric
5 Orthopaedics

Team 1
1 William the Conqueror
2 Telford (Thomas Telford)
3 Marie Antoinette
4 Chicory
5 Spoonerism

Round 9
Team 2
1 Libra
2 Anwar Sadat
3 *Dallas*
4 The 'Pathétique'
5 Melancholy

Team 1
1 Twelve
2 Julius Caesar
3 Stephanie Beacham
4 The 'Choral' Symphony
5 Melanin

Round 10
Entertainment: Atlanta
Words: 'I came, I saw, I conquered'
Industry: Hops
Finance: Gross National Product
Music: Leonard Bernstein

Drinks round

Team 1
1 Catch 22
2 Measuring blood pressure
3 Herbs

4 A kettledrum
5 Anthony Fokker
6 The diaphragm
7 Georges Seurat
8 Franklin D. Roosevelt
9 Little Minch
10 Anthony Eden

Team 2
1 For example
2 Ringing in the ears
3 They are the old names for the fingers and thumb of the hand
4 Gondoliers
5 Wernher von Braun
6 The shoulder blade
7 Andy Warhol
8 Abraham Lincoln
9 Off Anglesey, North Wales
10 Golda Meir

Reserve questions
1 Television
2 The Northwest Passage
3 Irene

Pub League Quiz 23 – Answers

Round 1

Team 1
1 Charles I
2 The Toilet of Venus
3 104
4 James II
5 The eight of diamonds

Team 2
1 Typhoid fever
2 *The Picture of Dorian Gray*
3 94
4 Cavaliers
5 Mahjong

Round 2

Team 1
1 A skylark
2 Tahiti
3 A single horse hair
4 Wonderbra
5 Modest Mussorgsky

Team 2
1 T. S. Eliot
2 Antrim
3 Cronus
4 Pierre Cardin
5 Bela Bartok

Round 3

Team 1
1 Ernest Hemingway
2 The west coast of the USA, centred on San Francisco
3 The edible entrails of a deer or other animal
4 Joe Mercer
5 Inter-Continental Ballistic Missile

Team 2
1 Catherine Cookson
2 Sri Lanka

3 Small dumplings made of potatoes, flour or semolina
4 Stanley Matthews
5 Strategic Arms Limitation Talks

Round 4

Team 1
1 Freetown
2 A bomber
3 Clara Peggotty
4 Wolverhampton
5 Dail Eireann

Team 2
1 Kingston
2 France
3 Peter Mayle
4 Hyde Park
5 Niccolo Machiavelli

Round 5

The Bible: The Acts of the Apostles
Opera: *Don Giovanni*
Mythology: Ra
Trees and plants: Elm
Games and pastimes: Diabolo

Round 6

Team 2
1 Four
2 The one nearest the stern
3 St James's Palace
4 Edward de Bono
5 Zambia

Team 1
1 Duodenum
2 Two
3 A gaol
4 John Flamsteed's
5 Death Valley, California

Round 7

Team 2
1 Benjamin Disraeli
2 Cornwall
3 Ballet
4 1910
5 Apples

Team 1
1 John le Carré
2 Edinburgh
3 Graham Sutherland
4 King John
5 Oranges

Round 8

Team 2
1 20
2 A type of heavy draught horse
3 Six
4 Robin Day
5 A mule

Team 1
1 150
2 The making of dictionaries
3 Pete Sampras
4 Robert Robinson
5 Basenji

Round 9

Team 2
1 Queen Catherine (of Aragon)
2 Cataract
3 Purdah
4 Jonathan Swift
5 1966

Team 1
1 Ophelia's
2 In the neck
3 Jehad
4 Irwin Shaw
5 Gary Kasparov

Round 10

The Bible: Bathsheba
Opera: Yeoman of the Guard
Mythology: Daphne
Trees and plants: Tuber
Games and pastimes: The Queen of Spades

Drinks round

Team 1

1 Harold Macmillan
2 *Middlemarch*
3 Nellie the Elephant
4 The Nile
5 Carrots
6 A small writing desk

7 Patricia Highsmith's
8 Des O'Connor
9 *The Far Pavilions*
10 Action on Health and Smoking

Team 2

1 Benjamin Disraeli
2 Samuel Butler
3 Looby-Loo
4 Morocco
5 Cauliflower
6 A glass container used in distilling

7 Agatha Christie's
8 Rolf Harris
9 *The Wind in the Willows*
10 Extra-sensory perception

Reserve questions

1 *Hard Times*
2 Morphine (Morpheus)
3 One

Pub League Quiz 24 – Answers

Round 1

Team 1
1 The Nuba

2 Northern Australia
3 Dirk Bogarde
4 November
5 Cana of Galilee

Team 2
1 Their height (they are the world's tallest tribe)
2 Gulf of Bothnia
3 Bob Hope
4 23 April
5 A raven

Round 2

Team 1
1 Matchbox labels
2 Deng Xiaoping
3 Mae West
4 Monday
5 A crocodile

Team 2
1 Rodents
2 Chris Patten
3 Shirley MacLaine
4 High-Rise
5 A beetle

Round 3

Team 1
1 Sancho Panza
2 Aurora Borealis

3 Leonardo da Vinci
4 The throat

5 Caramel

Team 2
1 Windmills
2 Jupiter, Saturn, Uranus and Neptune
3 Horses
4 To test colour vision, including the absence of it
5 Mulligatawny

Round 4

Team 1
1 Boeing B29 Superfortress
2 My struggle
3 , Claude Debussy
4 Peso
5 Chile

Team 2
1 Vickers
2 Our thing
3 Frederick Delius
4 Maltese lira
5 The Caucasus

Round 5

Soccer: Arsenal
Famous women: The Princess Royal
Name the year: 1914
Nature: The shamrock
Spelling: Pseudonym

Round 6

Team 2
1 St Mark
2 A (louse) fly
3 Ferdinand and Isabella
4 A clutch
5 Khartoum

Team 1
1 St Christopher
2 A herbaceous plant
3 Spain or Portugal
4 A host
5 Tirana

Round 7

Team 2
1 Australian and New Zealand Army Corps
2 *Mansfield Park*
3 Johnny Cash
4 Tintagel
5 *Are You Being Served?*

Team 1
1 Electronic Random Number Indicator Equipment
2 Mr Rochester
3 Paul McCartney
4 King Arthur
5 *Bread*

Round 8

Team 2
1 Cumberland Gap
2 Joseph Stalin
3 A long-sleeved coat worn loose

4 The Netherlands
5 The Penny Post

Team 1
1 Aiguille Verte
2 Schicklgruber
3 A strip of cloth wound spirally around the leg as protection
4 Catalan
5 Boxing gloves

Round 9

Team 2
1 Chicago
2 Harriet Harman

3 P. I. Tchaikovsky
4 Morris Garages
5 National Aeronautics and Space Administration

Team 1
1 Oregon
2 The Trotter family (*Only Fools and Horses*)

3 Claude Debussy
4 Tachometer
5 European Space Agency

Round 10

Soccer: Bertie Mee
Famous women: Sheila Van Damm
Name the year: 1960
Nature: Rhododendron
Spelling: Pharyngitis

Drinks round

Team 1

1 A cartographer
2 The Bass Strait
3 Georges Braque
4 *Dallas*
5 Blue blooded (veins show blue under very white skin)
6 Ferdinand Magellan
7 Sophia Loren
8 Bobby Sands
9 Testatrix
10 Photography

Team 2

1 An ornithologist
2 New York City
3 Camden Town
4 Miami
5 *El Dorado*

6 The Crimean War
7 Candice Bergen
8 Trevor Lock
9 Ogress
10 Patrick Lichfield

Reserve questions

1 Gigot
2 An apple
3 Hamlet

Pub League Quiz 25 – Answers

Round 1

Team 1
1 Coco the Clown
2 Marmalade sandwiches
3 *Calypso*
4 Black
5 Food and Agricultural Organisation (of the United Nations)

Team 2
1 Jack Benny
2 Cinderella
3 *Mary Rose*
4 Tic-tac-toe
5 Rome

Round 2

Team 1
1 Quentin Crisp
2 Saudi Arabia
3 A salmon
4 A famous encyclopaedia
5 Dinar

Team 2
1 Mia Farrow
2 The Dalai Lama's
3 An (Indian) buffalo
4 *Encyclopaedia Britannica*
5 Spain (eight reales)

Round 3

Team 1
1 Geoffrey Rush
2 Prophesy
3 Louise May Alcott
4 None
5 Crocus

Team 2
1 *A Streetcar Named Desire*
2 The fear of Jehovah
3 *Far from the Madding Crowd*
4 Mars
5 A bouquet garni

Round 4

Team 1
1 Lake Superior
2 *In the Heat of the Night*
3 Italy
4 Henry V, Act III, Scene III
5 Portsmouth harbour

Team 2
1 Chicago
2 *Little Caesar*
3 Operation Barbarossa
4 Verona
5 Buxton

Round 5

Books: Georges Simenon
Also known as: Zorro
Characters: Sir Galahad
Time: 16th Century
Pot luck: The Niger

Round 6

Team 2
1 Ice figure skating (pairs)
2 On the coast of County Antrim, Northern Ireland
3 The colour black
4 The whale shark
5 Letchworth

Team 1
1 Ice figure skating (individual)
2 Liverpool
3 Nelson Mandela
4 Bats and owls
5 Horse Guards

Round 7

Team 2
1 Carbon monoxide
2 Early golf balls
3 Birds
4 The fruit of the poor lemon
5 Bonnie Prince Charlie (Prince Charles Edward Stuart)

Team 1
1 Ne
2 Curling
3 Four
4 Through the streets of London
5 Switzerland

Round 8

Team 2
1 C. S. Lewis
2 Dot
3 St Moritz
4 The English Channel
5 *Madame Butterfly*

Team 1
1 *Peyton Place*
2 Levée
3 Norwegian
4 Monaco
5 *The Magic Flute*

Round 9

Team 2
1 Raymond Chandler
2 The albatross
3 Real Madrid
4 George I
5 Zorba the Greek

Team 1
1 Ian Ogilvy
2 Two
3 Geoff Hurst
4 Benjamin Britten
5 Edgar Allan Poe

Round 10

Books: Alexandre Dumas (fils)
Also known as: Michael Caine
Characters: A flying school
Time: Julius Caesar
Pot luck: Plymouth

Drinks round

Team 1

1 Mexican
2 South China Sea
3 Eric Liddell
4 *Bleak House*
5 *The Trouble with Harry*
6 Lord Lucan
7 'Oh, East is East and West is West'
8 23
9 Franz Beckenbauer
10 Venezuela

Team 2

1 Belgian
2 Madagascar
3 *The Full Monty*
4 *Pride and Prejudice*
5 Sam Goldwyn
6 John Stonehouse
7 James Thurber
8 Never
9 Johan Cruyff
10 Angels Falls (in Venezuela)

Reserve questions

1 Winifred Atwell
2 Dolly
3 A woman scorned

Pub League Quiz 26 – Answers

Round 1
Team 1
1 Herman Wouk
2 30 November
3 *Moby Dick*
4 He invented the flush toilet
5 A computer that beat world champion Garry Kasparov

Team 2
1 Colleen McCullough
2 17 March
3 *Twelfth Night*
4 The Bo or Bodhi tree
5 A swimming pool

Round 2
Team 1
1 Darwin
2 Kismet
3 Demon eyes
4 Sir Terence Conran
5 M69

Team 2
1 A missionary
2 *Four Weddings and a Funeral*
3 The Ombudsman
4 Landscapes and gardens
5 Turin

Round 3
Team 1
1 Sammy Davis Jnr
2 John F. Kennedy

3 A cat
4 Mauritania
5 Roulette

Team 2
1 Bob Hope
2 James Monroe (the capital is Monrovia)
3 Bounce
4 United States
5 15

Round 4
Team 1
1 Lurch
2 Four
3 Zurich
4 Nevil Shute
5 Gioacchino Rossini

Team 2
1 Morocco
2 Syncopate
3 Kentucky
4 G. K. Chesterton
5 Karl Marx

Round 5
Pop music: David Soul
Astronomy: The corona
Drink: A bloody mary
Motor sports: Graham Hill
Land animals: The rattlesnake

Round 6

Team 2
1 All are Welsh born
2 W. A. Mozart
3 The Berlin Wall
4 Graham Greene
5 The ostrich

Team 1
1 The Czech Republic
2 P. I. Tchaikovsky
3 He became Pope
4 Lord Peter Wimsey
5 The kiwi

Round 7

Team 2
1 FIFA
2 Hong Kong
3 *Straw Dogs*
4 The Gettysburg Address
5 Franz Kafka

Team 1
1 Jules Rimet
2 Arnhem
3 *The Graduate*
4 Béla Bartók
5 Thomas Mann

Round 8

Team 2
1 Michael Crawford
2 Georgi Malenkov
3 Chinese
4 Copenhagen (the Olsen Clock in the Town Hall)
5 The Atlantic

Team 1
1 Twiggy
2 Andrew Johnson
3 Spanish
4 Salisbury Cathedral

5 The Maldive Islands

Round 9

Team 2
1 Kublai Khan
2 Robert Wagner
3 Romulus
4 Palaeontology
5 Lake Ontario

Team 1
1 The North-west Passage
2 Jill Esmond
3 Friday (after Frig)
4 Ecology
5 The USA/Mexico border

Round 10

Pop music: The Three Degrees
Astronomy: Pluto
Drink: Dom Pérignon
Motor sport: Jackie Stewart
Land animals: The giraffe

Drinks round

Team 1
1 W. C Fields
2 An alcoholic
3 Gloucestershire
4 Honolulu
5 Alcoholics Anonymous
6 Edward Lear
7 A vacuum
8 Haka
9 India
10 A body

Team 2
1 *A Day at the Races*
2 The liver
3 Sir Donald Bradman
4 Rainer Werner Fassbinder
5 Four
6 Maine
7 As an anaesthetic
8 Cardiff City
9 Tibet
10 Murphy's law

Reserve questions

1 The last king of Albania
2 Blackbird
3 A lettuce

Pub League Quiz 27 – Answers

Round 1

Team 1
1 The Mediterranean
2 Papillon
3 The Curia
4 *Bismarck*
5 Sumo wrestling

Team 2
1 Belgium
2 Voltaire
3 The Pope
4 Malta
5 Stephen Hendry

Round 2

Team 1
1 Edwin Lutyens
2 Night watchman and keeper of the dog pound
3 *Oliver Twist*
4 Pommel
5 Roald Amundsen

Team 2
1 Harewood House
2 Beagle

3 Jack Dawkins
4 Japanese
5 Howard Carter

Round 3

Team 1
1 Kissing hands
2 Frances de la Tour
3 J. R. R. Tolkien
4 Royal National Lifeboat Institution
5 Dwight D. Eisenhower

Team 1
1 Tammany Hall
2 Glynis Barber
3 Emily Brontë
4 North Atlantic Treaty Organisation
5 Nikita Khrushchev

Round 4

Team 1
1 Rome
2 1922 (as the British Broadcasting Company)
3 George V (of the future Edward VIII)
4 Lieutenant-colonel
5 Charles Baudelaire

Team 2
1 Turkey
2 1923

3 Ireland

4 Wing-commander
5 Molière

Round 5

TV and radio: Charles Hill
Ships: Savannah
Geography: Hawaii
Classical music: *Peter and the Wolf*
Kings and queens: Persia

Round 6

Team 2
1 James Hanratty
2 Eric Cantona
3 The red fox
4 Gammer
5 French

Team 1
1 Hangman
2 Jean-Paul Sartre
3 The red deer
4 Votaress
5 American

Round 7

Team 2
1 Weatherfield
2 Gulf of Lions
3 David Bailey
4 Louise Brooks
5 Laurence Olivier

Team 1
1 Bristol
2 New Zealand
3 Gianni Versace
4 Lucky Luciano
5 Katharine Hepburn

Round 8

Team 2
1 Gospel of St Mark
2 Woods and fields, or shepherds and their flocks (either answer acceptable)
3 Deep extra cover
4 Glassmaker
5 Let it stand

Team 1
1 Apollo
2 Hermes or Zeus (either answer acceptable)
3 The Oval
4 Goldsmith and jeweller
5 Defender of the Faith (*Fidei Defensor*)

Round 9

Team 2
1 Dee
2 The Duke of Windsor
3 Mount Rushmore, South Dakota
4 Cat
5 Wembley stadium

Team 1
1 Aberdeen
2 Margaret Thatcher
3 Washington, Jefferson, Lincoln and Theodore Roosevelt
4 Rimmer
5 The Winter Olympics

Round 10

TV and radio: In the 1930s in the USA they were radio serials sponsored by soap manufacturers
Ships: *Graf Spee*
Geography: Morocco
Classical music: W. A. Mozart
Kings and queens: Poland

Drinks round

Team 1
1 Dustin Hoffman
2 An asiatic wild ox
3 Thomas, Oliver and Richard
4 Lord Chancellor
5 Charles Dickens
6 Off the coast of Norway
7 Tina Turner
8 Six
9 Borstal
10 Deep blue

Team 2
1 Mrs Robinson
2 A small bird
3 Archbishop of Canterbury
4 Lord Chief Justice
5 Norman Mailer
6 Lodz
7 Bill Wyman
8 Six and 13
9 Albert Desalvo
10 Graphite

Reserve questions

1 Snoopy
2 Bell ringing
3 The Lady of Shalott

Pub League Quiz 28 – Answers

Round 1

Team 1
1 Dog rose
2 Blenny
3 Mohammed
4 Taj Mahal
5 Jellystone National Park

Team 2
1 Blackberries
2 Koala bear
3 Medina
4 New York
5 Peter Plant

Round 2

Team 1
1 Nelson Eddy
2 Dante Alighieri
3 Suez Canal
4 Narcissus
5 Prince Andrew

Team 2
1 Bette Davis
2 Alfred, Lord Tennyson
3 Caledonian Canal
4 Castor and Pollux
5 Cousin

Round 3

Team 1
1 Obstetrics (do not allow gynaecology)
2 Henley Royal Regatta
3 W. A. Mozart
4 Sir Alexander Fleming
5 Bachelor of Dental Surgery

Team 2
1 Genealogy
2 Korea
3 Gioacchino Rossini
4 Gabriel Fahrenheit
5 Bachelor of Civil Law

Round 4

Team 1
1 Anthony Booth
2 The root of the marshmallow plant
3 The Tropic of Cancer
4 Joel Chandler Harris
5 John Wilkes Booth

Team 2
1 Dandy Nicholls
2 A biennial
3 The Khyber Pass
4 Thomas Hardy
5 Ulysses S. Grant

Round 5

History and warfare: Leipzig
Law: The legal right to use land belonging to another for a particular purpose, such as access or drainage
Pot luck: An army rifle
Literature: Christopher Marlowe
Words: Coven

Round 6

Team 2

1 A carat
2 Joe Louis
3 Princess Margaret
4 Shropshire
5 Dibley

Team 1

1 The international nautical mile
2 An actress of the silent films
3 Winston Churchill
4 The Lizard
5 *Blackadder*

Round 7

Team 2

1 Amy Lowell
2 A scaly anteater
3 The Oval
4 The Royal Mint
5 Rotterdam

Team 1

1 William Blake
2 A duck
3 France (1906)
4 A potter
5 Rhine and Ruhr

Round 8

Team 2

1 Calliope, Clio, Urania, Terpsichore, Thalia, Euterpe, Erato, Melpomene, Polyhymnia

2 1823 (at Rugby School)
3 William II
4 Pottery fired but not glazed

5 November 1899–February 1900

Team 1

1 Epic poetry and eloquence, history, astronomy, choral song and dance, comedy, lyric poetry and music, love poetry and music, tragedy, sacred poetry and music

2 1871
3 Richard I
4 An old Chinese glaze, greyish to blue-green
5 1627–28

Round 9

Team 2

1 Voltaire
2 The liver
3 Cleopatra (VII of Egypt)
4 St Paul's Cathedral
5 *The Great Dictator* (1940)

Team 1

1 Samuel Johnson
2 The gums
3 Alexander the Great
4 1170
5 Santa Fé Trail

Round 10

History and warfare: Yalta in the Crimea
Law: Quarter sessions
Pot luck: Iraq
Literature: 'A gentleman'
Words: Numismatics

Drinks round

Team 1

1 William Hague
2 1979
3 Blaise Pascal
4 A farthingale
5 Mahon
6 Terence Rattigan
7 Georges
8 Her (His) Majesty's Stationery Office
9 A wading bird (a white heron)
10 Carbuncle

Team 2

1 Andre Agassi
2 Walter Mondale
3 John Knox
4 A glengarry
5 Somalia
6 T. S. Eliot
7 Arthur
8 Associated Society of Locomotive Engineers and Firemen
9 A small duck
10 Your lungs

Reserve questions

1 It was the test site for the first atomic bomb
2 A Copenhagen Mary
3 Detached from one another

Pub League Quiz 29 – Answers

Round 1

Team 1
1 Lhasa, Tibet
2 Italy
3 St Stephen, Vienna
4 William the Conqueror
5 19

Team 2
1 Queensland and Northern Territory Airline Service
2 Lourdes
3 St Mark's
4 French
5 31

Round 2

Team 1
1 St Albans
2 'DIVORCE'
3 J. M. Barrie
4 Johann Strauss (the Younger)
5 Gymnasium

Team 1
1 Marston Moor
2 Village People
3 *Peter Pan*
4 The bat
5 Pistol shooting

Round 3

Team 1
1 International Business Machines
2 John McCarthy and Brian Keenan
3 The book or text of the performance
4 Flemish (Belgian)
5 Jack the Ripper

Team 2
1 National Association of Securities Dealers Automated Quotations.
2 Edward Elgar
3 When the whole text is sung
4 American
5 10 Rillington Place

Round 4

Team 1
1 Quakers
2 Peter O'Toole
3 Kenya
4 Laudanum
5 Nuremberg

Team 2
1 Zen
2 Jack Nicholson
3 Hawaii
4 Mescalin
5 The Bayeux tapestry

Round 5
History: George V
Entertainment: *The Comedy of Errors*
Animals: A beautifully coloured fish
Literature: The Book of the Dead
Aircraft: Frank Whittle

Round 6

Team 2
1 Wightman Cup
2 Istanbul
3 Catherine of Aragon, Anne Boleyn, Jane Seymour, Anne of Cleves, Catherine Howard and Catherine Parr
4 Genera
5 By means of flowing water

Team 1
1 Kentucky Derby
2 Milan
3 Catherine Parr

4 Geneses
5 Raising water

Round 7

Team 2
1 The Seekers
2 Royal Horse Artillery
3 Coventry City
4 Winfield
5 Andy Warhol

Team 1
1 Elvis Presley
2 Royal Electrical and Mechanical Engineers
3 Preston North End
4 Selfridges
5 Goldie Hawn

Round 8

Team 2
1 A beetle
2 Edgar Wallace
3 River Kabul
4 Paris
5 Knee cartilage

Team 1
1 Deathwatch beetle
2 Mrs Gaskell
3 Zaire
4 The Minotaur
5 The female breast

Round 9

Team 2
1 Traffic lights
2 Karl Malden and Michael Douglas
3 Martin Luther King
4 Paprika
5 Claude-Joseph Rouget de Lisle

Team 1
1 Alfred Nobel
2 Steve Garrett

3 Germany
4 Nutmeg
5 Japan's

Round 10
History: Portuguese
Entertainment: Dustin Hoffman and John Voight
Animals: The mute swan
Literature: *The Fellowship of the Ring*; *The Two Towers*; *The Return of the King*
Aircraft: Mach 2

Drinks round

Team 1
1 *The Rivals*
2 Tony Randall
3 They are all Canadian rivers
4 Jodie Foster
5 Edinburgh
6 Pembrokeshire coast
7 Donald Sinden and Windsor Davies
8 Arnold Bennett
9 Lascar
10 Molars

Team 2
1 Walter de la Mare
2 James Cagney
3 They were all Astronomers Royal
4 Theresa Russell
5 Schoolmaster
6 The Lake District
7 Soap
8 Pathfinder Bennett
9 A gold prospector
10 Incisors

Reserve questions
1 Christ
2 Dr Samuel Johnson
3 Polyandry

Pub League Quiz 30 – Answers

Round 1
Team 1
1 Paul Henry
2 US Grand Prix
3 1,000
4 1376
5 Bow Bells (St Mary-le-Bow)

Team 2
1 King's Oak
2 US Masters (golf)
3 400
4 Set in the Imperial State Crown
5 Cheapside

Round 2
Team 1
1 Norway and Sweden
2 A lullaby
3 The middle price
4 *Marriage à la Mode*
5 29 September

Team 2
1 Oslo
2 A Hindu nurse or ladies' maid
3 Cost, Insurance, Freight
4 Pablo Picasso
5 The feast of St Michael and All Angels

Round 3
Team 1
1 Pudding Lane (near the north end of London Bridge)
2 John Milton
3 Linda Gray
4 Magnesium hydroxide
5 An animal with a pouch

Team 2
1 To commemorate the Great Fire of London
2 *Paradise Regained*
3 Patrick Duffy
4 Amphetamines
5 The elephant

Round 4
Team 1
1 Medina
2 A circus acrobat
3 Norman Tebbit's
4 Easter Island
5 Breeds of chicken

Team 2
1 Muezzin
2 *Easy Rider*
3 Lloyd's of London
4 Australia's
5 Breeds of sheep

Round 5
Pop music: Davy Jones
Children's books: Lewis Carroll (*Through the Looking-Glass and What Alice Found There*)
Classical music: Franz Lehár (*The Merry Widow*)
Pot luck: A knot
History: Peter I (the Great)

414

Round 6

Team 2
1 Leo Tolstoy
2 In secret
3 The Cavern Club
4 Alternative Investment Market
5 Australia

Team 1
1 Alexander Pushkin
2 By the grace of God
3 The Hollies
4 Home Office Large Major Enquiry System (the police national database of criminal records)
5 Uganda

Round 7

Team 2
1 Palindrome
2 The Crystal Palace
3 Norwegian
4 Mozambique
5 Christopher Fry

Team 1
1 A line of verse of two measures
2 Queen Victoria
3 Sonja
4 Surinam
5 Alan Bennett

Round 8

Team 2
1 Raphael
2 Valhalla
3 Newport County
4 Hudson
5 Fellow of the Royal Society of Arts

Team 1
1 Michelangelo
2 Jupiter (or Jove)
3 West Bromwich Albion
4 Wendy Craig
5 Fellow of the Royal College of Music

Round 9

Team 2
1 Thrift
2 Australia
3 W. Somerset Maugham
4 William Gladstone
5 Balboa

Team 1
1 Aubretia
2 Colorado
3 John Steinbeck
4 Sir Henry Campbell-Bannerman
5 Koruna

Round 10

Pop music: Ginger, Scary, Posh, Baby and Sporty
Children's books: McTurk and Beetle
Classical music: The 'Hallelujah Chorus' from Handel's *Messiah*
Pot luck: Pollen
History: Antigone

Drinks round

Team 1

1 Gravity (that is, usually the constant of gravitation in Newton's Law)
2 The Fosse Way
3 Turkey
4 Modest Mussorgsky
5 Ernie Bishop
6 D. H. Lawrence
7 European Free Trade Association
8 The murdered Edward V and his brother Richard, Duke of York
9 Trevor Howard
10 'A fine lady upon a white horse'

Team 2

1 Joule

2 Watling Street
3 Belize
4 Richard Wagner
5 Alf Roberts
6 Frederick Forsyth
7 London and North Eastern Railway
8 Louis XVIII

9 Jane Seymour
10 A pieman

Reserve questions

1 A straight furrow
2 Tasmanian tiger (thylacine)
3 Whooping cough

Pub League Quiz 31 – Answers

Round 1

Team 1
1 Daphne du Maurier
2 Franz Joseph Haydn
3 Lusaka
4 Like a woman
5 James Stewart

Team 2
1 John Steinbeck
2 Edward Elgar
3 Muscat
4 Mother-of-pearl
5 James Stewart

Round 2

Team 1
1 De Havilland
2 Pasta shapes
3 30
4 Oxygen
5 Raymond Chandler

Team 2
1 Lockheed
2 Peppers, aubergines, courgettes, onions
3 The Crystal Palace
4 A storm
5 Arthur Conan Doyle

Round 3

Team 1
1 Ruth Madoc
2 Matt Biondi
3 Alexander Pope
4 *Top of the Pops*
5 Zion

Team 2
1 Margo Bryant
2 Men's hockey
3 Franklin D. Roosevelt
4 At Prestwick airport
5 Turkey

Round 4

Team 1
1 St Dunstan
2 A beetle
3 National Film Theatre
4 Prince Charles
5 Valéry Giscard d'Estaing

Team 2
1 St Nicholas
2 A snake
3 *Financial Times*
4 14 June
5 Lord Palmerston

Round 5
Sport: Sabre
Soap operas: Colorado
England: Oxford
Science: Archimedes
Art: Velasquez

Round 6

Team 2
1 West Germany
2 Ray Milland
3 Lesotho
4 Lord Beaverbrook
5 Rabbits

Team 1
1 An ice skater
2 Spencer Tracy
3 Zambia
4 Leon Trotsky
5 Alexander Selkirk

Round 7

Team 2
1 An Australian bird (kookaburra)
2 A sweet-scented garden plant
3 Bad law
4 Old Deuteronomy
5 Australia

Team 1
1 A large antelope
2 Damson
3 *Kavanagh QC*
4 Revelations
5 Fangio, Farina and Fagioli

Round 8

Team 2
1 John Nash
2 Steve Biko
3 Michael Barrymore
4 Nikolai Gogol
5 Cornell

Team 1
1 Frank Lloyd Wright
2 *Cry Freedom*
3 Arthur Askey
4 John Osborne
5 Bismarck

Round 9

Team 2
1 Margaret Smith
2 Vice-admiral
3 Memphis, Tennessee
4 Glasgow
5 Cecil B. de Mille

Team 1
1 Jimmy White
2 Lieutenant
3 John Connolly
4 Birmingham
5 John Ford

Round 10

Sport: Women's tennis
Soap operas: Laura Palmer
England: Wardour Street
Science: Quantum theory
Art: John Everett Millais

Drinks round

Team 1
1 *The Mikado*
2 Abba
3 Whit Sunday
4 Spring
5 Lily of the valley
6 Port Said
7 William Butler Yeats
8 Holland
9 Bob Hoskins
10 Romulus

Team 2
1 *The Pirates of Penzance*
2 Crystal Gayle
3 He performed miracles
4 Witches
5 Forget-me-not
6 Lakes Erie and Ontario
7 James Cain
8 Belgium
9 *Godspell*
10 The Appian Way

Reserve questions
1 1752
2 Hormones
3 Grandfather and grandson

Pub League Quiz 32 – Answers

Round 1

Team 1
1 *Ben-Hur*
2 Clement Attlee
3 Madrid
4 Somerset
5 A bird

Team 2
1 Katharine Hepburn
2 Jo Grimond
3 Washington
4 Salop
5 The weasel family

Round 2

Team 1
1 James Brown
2 Wind speed

3 *Jabberwocky*
4 The difference in pitch between two notes
5 St Teresa of Avila

Team 2
1 Aretha Franklin
2 Many voiced, or represented by different sounds
3 The slithy toves
4 A semitone

5 St James (Jaime)

Round 3

Team 1
1 *Barbarella*
2 A form
3 Britain and China
4 Antonio
5 Honolulu

Team 2
1 'Love Me Tender'
2 An eyrie
3 USA
4 Othello
5 Sacramento

Round 4

Team 1
1 Gerald Ford
2 Kitty Kelley
3 $10
4 David Livingstone
5 15 July

Team 2
1 James Callaghan
2 Andrew Morton
3 A monkey
4 India
5 May

Round 5

Television: *A Question of Sport*
Classical music: The Four Seasons
Law: Hilary, Easter, Trinity and Michaelmas
General knowledge: Robert Maxwell
Nicknames: Vinegar Joe

Round 6

Team 2

1 Louth
2 Sonny and Cher
3 Ironsides
4 Proper names
5 Mead

Team 1

1 Kildare
2 Anton Karas
3 Beefeaters
4 Belief in one god
5 A large wine bottle

Round 7

Team 2

1 Neptune
2 *The Flying Dutchman*
3 *The Knight's Tale*
4 A long nose
5 Essex

Team 1

1 Neptune
2 Merlin
3 *The Parson's Tale*
4 Australia
5 The Royal Hospital, Chelsea

Round 8

Team 2

1 Maize
2 Chronus
3 Lionel Bart
4 Irving Stone
5 The inability to stay awake

Team 1

1 Cilantro
2 Saturn
3 *Paint Your Wagon*
4 Sax Rohmer
5 Aspirin

Round 9

Team 2

1 HMS *Hood*

2 Edinburgh
3 Leopold I (1831–65)
4 Marcus Sargeant
5 Audi

Team 1

1 It was sunk by a German submarine
2 *The Morning Star*
3 Robert II (1371–90)
4 Pope John Paul II
5 Liz Hurley

Round 10

Television: Private Godfrey
Classical music: Mikhail Glinka
Law: Jurisprudence
General knowledge: New York
Nicknames: Sandro Botticelli

Drinks round

Team 1

1 Chile
2 True
3 Racehorse training
4 Benedictine

5 Fountains Abbey
6 *It's That Man Again*
7 Jersey Joe Walcott
8 Derek McCulloch
9 Northumberland
10 Hilda

Team 2

1 A geyser
2 True
3 Cycle racing
4 Sweetened spiced wine with hot water

5 Whipsnade Zoo
6 Will Hay
7 Gracie Fields
8 Vera Lynn
9 Somerset
10 Harold Macmillan

Reserve questions

1 The Duke of Wellington and Sir Winston Churchill
2 Barbados
3 Walt Disney (for example, *Fantasia*)

Pub League Quiz 33 – Answers

Round 1

Team 1
1 Paternoster
2 France
3 1966
4 Schoolmaster
5 22

Team 2
1 165
2 Argentina
3 Queen Victoria
4 Lawyer
5 Bagatelle

Round 2

Team 1
1 Commonwealth Day and the birthday of Prince Edward
2 Oasis
3 The peacock
4 John Churchill
5 Contract bridge

Team 2
1 Albert, Caroline and Stephanie
2 Hale and Pace
3 The phoenix
4 Blenheim
5 Canoeing

Round 3

Team 1
1 33 and 21
2 Gozo or Comino
3 Captain Matthew Webb
4 Rotherham United

5 James II

Team 2
1 15 and 5
2 Paraguay
3 Polo
4 Liverpool, Middlesborough, Sampdoria
5 Carolingians

Round 4

Team 1
1 Entirely or completely
2 John Reith
3 Ouse
4 Archery
5 Poland

Team 2
1 That is (ie)
2 Learie Constantine
3 Nid
4 Sagittarius
5 Hungary

Round 5

In common: They were all American presidents
Name the year: 1948
Pop music: Mariah Carey
Religion: Wassailing
Pot luck: The Bishop of Bath and Wells

Round 6

Team 2
1 By rubbing its wing covers together
2 The Organisation of African Unity
3 Sussex
4 Accolade
5 A legless lizard

Team 1
1 By flapping its wings very rapidly
2 National Farmers Union
3 Wilton House
4 The Abbey Theatre
5 Mammals

Round 7

Team 2
1 Audrey Roberts
2 Fesse
3 Alexander Dumas (père)
4 Tass
5 Greyfriars

Team 1
1 Benson
2 Gardant
3 W. Somerset Maugham
4 Vichy
5 Uncle Remus

Round 8

Team 2
1 St Lawrence
2 Pigeons or doves
3 John Adams
4 A boar
5 Hobart

Team 1
1 Arizona
2 Dingo
3 George Washington
4 Dido
5 Bucharest

Round 9

Team 2
1 William Wordsworth
2 The Battle of Crécy

3 The Ten Commandments
4 Cassava roots
5 Catalyst

Team 1
1 John Masefield
2 Richard I (Richard the Lionheart)
3 The Gospels
4 Wheat
5 Nitrogen

Round 10

In common: Ballet
Name the year: 1968
Pop music: Cat Stevens
Religion: The Wailing Wall in Jerusalem
Pot luck: George Bernard Shaw

Drinks round
Team 1
1 *Guys and Dolls*
2 Southern Crown and Northern Crown
3 James Earl Ray
4 Small holes that let water run off the deck
5 13.00 hrs (1pm)
6 Albrecht Dürer
7 Milky-bluish
8 Infinite knowledge, all knowing

9 December
10 Ben Kingsley

Team 2
1 *Pal Joey*
2 It always points away from the sun
3 Nathuram Godse
4 A rail across or round the stern of the boat
5 07.00 hrs (7am)
6 Lucas Cranach
7 Heliotrope
8 A name made up of initial letters (for example, ERNIE)
9 Messalina
10 Liza Minnelli

Reserve questions
1 A tenor
2 Brendan Behan
3 Fabrizio Ravanelli

Pub League Quiz 34 – Answers

Round 1

Team 1
1 Sun Hill
2 Finland
3 Douglas Adams
4 Royal Australian Air Force
5 New York

Team 2
1 Warmington-on-Sea
2 Charles Stewart Parnell
3 Terence Stamp
4 Chief of the General Staff
5 Stalingrad

Round 2

Team 1
1 *The Treasure of Sierra Madre* (Walter Huston)
2 Grandson
3 Betty Grable
4 Hydrogen
5 Ambrosia

Team 2
1 Woody Allen
2 William II and Henry I
3 Marilyn Monroe
4 Helium
5 Nectar

Round 3

Team 1
1 Lord Carrington
2 Pickled cabbage
3 *Tommy*
4 Lucy Honeychurch
5 I play

Team 2
1 Denis Healey
2 Scampo
3 Gustav Holst
4 Mince and slices of quince
5 Six

Round 4

Team 1
1 Humber, Thames, Severn and Mersey
2 France
3 John the Baptist
4 Haemophilia
5 Civet

Team 2
1 Scafell Pike, Ben Nevis, Snowdon and Carrantuohill
2 Georgia
3 River Jordan
4 Sleeping sickness
5 USA

Round 5

Films: *Live and Let Die*
Plants and wildlife: A type of grass
Dates: 2000
Sport: Georges Carpentier
General knowledge: Brown Owl

Round 6

Team 2

1 *David Copperfield* and *Great Expectations*
2 Nine
3 The fear of public or open places
4 Harry Secombe
5 Cardale

Team 1

1 Bootsie and Snudge
2 Economics
3 An all-consuming passion for power
4 Dorothy Parker
5 Annette Crosbie

Round 7

Team 2

1 Finland
2 The world professional darts championship
3 P
4 *The Prince and the Showgirl*
5 Orkney

Team 1

1 Paraguay
2 Peter Scudamore
3 Bauxite
4 *Lawrence of Arabia*
5 Lewis

Round 8

Team 2

1 1948
2 Manchester
3 Jack Johnson
4 *Elegy Written in a Country Churchyard* (Thomas Gray)
5 North and South Korea

Team 1

1 King George VI
2 Lace-making
3 Joe Bugner
4 *Absalom and Achitophel* (John Dryden)
5 USA and Canada

Round 9

Team 2

1 Charles I
2 Cliff Richard
3 *Goodbye Mr Chips*
4 Kiel
5 Three

Team 1

1 The Queen of Hearts
2 Lionel Bart
3 *The Prime of Miss Jean Brodie*
4 *The Battle of the Coral Sea*
5 88

Round 10

Films: Steven Spielberg
Plants and wildlife: The potato
Dates: The moon
Sport: Hamilton, Canada
General knowledge: His amputated leg

Drinks round

Team 1
1 Eleanor of Aquitaine
2 The Medway
3 Mexico
4 Trees
5 Anton Chekov
6 'Roffen'
7 Angola

8 Anna Ford
9 Corsica
10 River Elbe

Team 2
1 James I (of England)
2 The Chilterns
3 Spain
4 Stitches
5 *Rigoletto*
6 Carliol
7 South America (Ecuador and Peru)
8 *Crimewatch UK*
9 Vinci (Tuscany)
10 Afghanistan

Reserve questions
1 The kidneys
2 Lal Bahadour Shastri
3 Count Basie

Pub League Quiz 35 – Answers

Round 1

Team 1
1 1896
2 Mobile phone
3 *Gone with the Wind*
4 Captain Lawrence Oates
5 Cecilia

Team 2
1 Sapporo in Japan
2 The electric razor
3 Agatha Christie
4 The French Resistance
5 The Scaffold

Round 2

Team 1
1 Botswana
2 Pelé
3 Magnesium
4 Cleave
5 Africa

Team 2
1 India and Pakistan
2 Squash
3 Radium
4 Dreamt
5 Kenya

Round 3

Team 1
1 Ben Jonson
2 Advanced Passenger Train
3 Aspirin
4 Eight
5 Algeria

Team 2
1 George Eliot
2 British Army of the Rhine
3 The cash register
4 Two
5 Israel

Round 4

Team 1
1 A hoofed animal that chews the cud (for example, a sheep, cow or goat)
2 The Champs Elysées
3 All Olympic 100 metres champions
4 Puck
5 Jean Boht

Team 2
1 A beggar (or a friar of a begging order)
2 Pennsylvania Avenue
3 Hammer
4 Miranda in *The Tempest*
5 Cher

Round 5

Sport: Table tennis
Art and artists: Peter
Nobel Prize winners: Le Duc Tho (North Vietnam)
Composers: Ralph Vaughan Williams
English monarchs: Edward IV

Round 6

Team 2
1 Belgium
2 Water
3 Three
4 The Netherlands
5 *Equus*

Team 1
1 Italy (Vatican City)
2 Both on one side of its head
3 Mercury
4 Germany
5 *The Rivals*

Round 7

Team 2
1 Bolivia
2 France (1924)
3 Herring or sprats
4 Mobiles
5 *Britain's Got Talent*

Team 1
1 Caracas, Venezuela
2 Eric Liddell
3 Gudgeon
4 Hudson (Hudson River School)
5 Mau Mau

Round 8

Team 2
1 *The Phil Silvers Show*
2 Timmy, the dog
3 John Lennon
4 Henrik Ibsen
5 The Rose Bowl

Team 1
1 *Till Death Us Do Part*
2 John Mills
3 Manila
4 Eugene O'Neill
5 The Orange Bowl

Round 9

Team 2
1 African slaves
2 Herman Wouk
3 John McEnroe
4 Heinrich Hertz
5 Svengali

Team 1
1 New Zealand
2 Ernest Hemingway
3 18
4 Frederick W Lanchester
5 *The Inn of the Sixth Happiness*

Round 10

Sport: Ice hockey
Art and artists: Turner
Nobel Prize winners: UNICEF
Composers: Claudio Monteverdi's
English monarchs: Hardicanute

Drinks round

Team 1

1 *The Good Old Days*
2 The Supremes

3 The Boat Race
4 Bonn
5 Hungary
6 Mars
7 The fox

8 Francophile
9 Incitatus
10 George Orwell (in 1984)

Team 2

1 *Breakfast Time*
2 Elaine Page and Barbara Dickson

3 A horse race in the wet
4 Australia
5 Must
6 Venus
7 By ensuring that her prophecies were not believed
8 The fear of eating
9 Clyde
10 Jonathan Swift (in *Gulliver's Travels*)

Reserve questions

1 Rupee
2 Salk
3 Plato

Pub League Quiz 36 – Answers

Round 1

Team 1
1 The Gulf of Mexico
2 'Over the Hills and Far Away'
3 William Randolph Hearst
4 Reginald
5 The palms of the hands or the soles of the feet

Team 2
1 Lapland
2 Nine days' old
3 Christine Keeler
4 H. G. Wells
5 Tooth enamel

Round 2

Team 1
1 Ecuador
2 *Rosemary's Baby*
3 Everly Brothers
4 John Dryden
5 78 feet

Team 2
1 Argentina
2 *A Clockwork Orange*
3 The Kinks
4 *Essay on Man* (Alexander Pope)
5 Three feet

Round 3

Team 1
1 Sikhism
2 Jumbo
3 Biopsy
4 The hoping or hopeful one
5 MM

Team 2
1 Hinduism
2 Comanche
3 Biosphere
4 Divine wind
5 Zero

Round 4

Team 1
1 Lady
2 Turkey
3 Leningrad (St Petersburg)
4 35 to 1
5 Ganges

Team 2
1 Dame
2 Xi'an
3 Dame Ninette de Valois
4 10
5 Zaire

Round 5

Famous people: Sculpture
Films: Francis Coppola
Wars: The Second World War
The Ancients: Prometheus
Plant life: Hellebore

Round 6

Team 2
1 Lake Titicaca
2 Jon Voight
3 China
4 Vincent Van Gogh
5 Influenza

Team 1
1 Eilat
2 Jane Fonda
3 Belgium
4 Steppenwolf
5 Group O

Round 7

Team 2
1 4¼ inches
2 Melodion
3 Gibb
4 Lawrence Durrell
5 Green

Team 1
1 An air (or fresh air) shot
2 With small wooden hammers
3 Wilson
4 David Storey
5 Champagne and stout

Round 8

Team 2
1 Noel Edmonds
2 Hannibal
3 Hawaii
4 Kitty Hawk
5 Bullfighting

Team 1
1 A tub of lard
2 The Persians
3 Jay Gatsby
4 Howard Hughes himself
5 Shinty

Round 9

Team 2
1 Cyprus
2 Axl Rose (real name William Bailey)
3 The storming of the Bastille
4 *The Colbys*
5 Carbon dioxide

Team 1
1 The Faroe Islands
2 Shane McGowan
3 Epiphany
4 Mayday
5 454

Round 10

Famous people: Ranulph Fiennes
Films: *The Exorcist*
Wars: The First World War
The Ancients: Chinese
Plant life: Mushroom

Drinks round

Team 1

1　Harold Holt
2　Ronnie Wood
3　Canadian
4　A Harvey Wallbanger
5　George Herman
6　Three days and three nights
7　Tamil
8　28
9　Singapore
10　William Shatner

Team 2

1　Olivia Newton-John
2　Elton John
3　Linford Christie
4　Ginger beer
5　John Berry
6　The Haggadah
7　Malay
8　12
9　The Reichstag
10　Derek Jacobi

Reserve questions

1　The Bay of Biscay
2　Paranoia
3　Electric current

Pub League Quiz 37 – Answers

Round 1

Team 1
1 Euboea
2 Claude Debussy
3 Adam West
4 Fulmar
5 Gymnastics

Team 2
1 Great Britain
2 La Traviata
3 Cesar Romero
4 The chicken
5 Straw

Round 2

Team 1
1 Massachusetts
2 Yul Brynner
3 1,001
4 A moorland plant
5 Eddie Charlton

Team 2
1 Chuck Berry
2 Robert Carlyle
3 Eight
4 Cuckoo-pint
5 Jackie and Bobby Charlton

Round 3

Team 1
1 Lady Godiva
2 Paul Klee
3 Water
4 Cycle racing
5 China

Team 2
1 Atlas
2 Salvador Dali
3 $\frac{1}{11}$
4 Billiards
5 Between Spain and Gibraltar

Round 4

Team 1
1 Margery Allingham
2 Oscar Hammerstein II
3 *Peter Pan*
4 Smell
5 Mexico City

Team 2
1 Patricia Routledge
2 George Gershwin
3 Rudyard Kipling
4 The heel
5 El Salvador

Round 5

Characters: Mrs Hudson
International affairs: Alaska
Disasters: Tenerife
Horses and courses: Red Rum
Inventions: The Polaroid camera

Round 6

Team 2
1 Indiana
2 Wyatt Earp
3 Thaler
4 49
5 Cartilage

Team 1
1 Indonesia
2 Audie Murphy
3 Cha
4 20
5 Plankton

Round 7

Team 2
1 The potato
2 The British Museum
3 Neil Diamond or Donna Summer
4 Herbal medicine
5 Six

Team 1
1 Carp
2 *The Man in the Iron Mask*
3 Kelly and Ozzy Osbourne

4 *Old Moore's Almanack*
5 'Fallen Madonna with the Big Boobies'

Round 8

Team 2
1 Rod Steiger
2 The cheetah
3 He stole a loaf of bread
4 Amoco Cadiz
5 Floria Tosca

Team 1
1 James Mason
2 The raccoon
3 Barabas
4 Amnesty International
5 Franz Joseph Haydn

Round 9

Team 2
1 A small ship with sails and/or oars
2 Sir Thomas More
3 Sir Alec Douglas-Home
4 Christina Rossetti

5 Denmark's

Team 1
1 John Cobb

2 Woodrow Wilson
3 Kingston, Jamaica
4 The nightingale (in *Ode to a Nightingale*, by Keats)
5 Lutheranism

Round 10

Characters: The Salvation Army
International affairs: The Cuban missile crisis
Disasters: Darwin
Horses and courses: One mile
Inventions: Microwave oven

Drinks round

Team 1

1 The Saint Lawrence
2 Sussex
3 Colonel Gaddafi
4 *Bad Day at Black Rock*
5 James Joyce
6 The air gap between the cork and the wine
7 Walter
8 Vic Windsor
9 Belgium
10 Pigmy shrewmouse

Team 2

1 The Denmark Strait
2 Malcolm Nash
3 Alexei Kosygin
4 Torn Curtain
5 Dylan Thomas
6 The lees
7 Charlie Drake
8 Sam Failsworth
9 In the Inner Hebrides
10 The bandicoot

Reserve questions

1 Hydrochloric acid
2 Helen Keller
3 The House of Lords

Pub League Quiz 38 – Answers

Round 1
Team 1
1 Condensed milk
2 Kathleen Mansfield
3 Alan Autry
4 Portugal's
5 9

Team 2
1 The printing press
2 Stevie Smith
3 *The Lotus Eaters*
4 Grace Darling
5 28

Round 2
Team 1
1 Elton John and Kiki Dee
2 Spanish
3 The Duke of Wellington
4 John Cleese
5 The comma

Team 2
1 Leo Sayer
2 Australia
3 Viscount Melbourne
4 *La Bamba*
5 Z

Round 3
Team 1
1 An iron cannon (which burst in 1680 when firing a salute to Charles II)
2 Mount Fuji in Japan
3 Gaston Leroux
4 The Trojan War
5 Benito Mussolini

Team 2
1 Edinburgh Castle

2 Baltimore and Ohio
3 Barker and Corbett
4 A type of wine
5 The Gestapo

Round 4
Team 1
1 South Africa
2 A word that sounds the same as another but has a different meaning
3 *The Red Badge of Courage*
4 Swiss
5 Earth

Team 2
1 Pakistan
2 Exaggeration

3 Tobias Smollett
4 Russian
5 Lodge

Round 5
Abbreviations: Society for the Promotion of Christian Knowledge
Mythology: A jackal
Sport: 6
News of the 1980s: York Minster
United Kingdom: Lytham St Annes, Lancashire

Round 6

Team 2
1 Neil Simon
2 TH, for Talbot House
3 1970
4 The badger
5 Corporal Klinger

Team 1
1 Brendan Behan
2 'Tubby' Clayton
3 1955
4 A monkey
5 Miss Brahms

Round 7

Team 2
1 Walpurgis Night
2 20
3 St Francis of Assisi
4 Zsa Zsa Gabon
5 Azure

Team 1
1 1st May
2 22
3 St Francis Xavier
4 *The Sunday Correspondent*
5 Sable

Round 8

Team 2
1 TSB (Trustee Savings Bank)
2 Polly James and Nerys Hughes
3 Above the taste or comprehension of ordinary people
4 Sir William Walton
5 The Royal Corps of Transport

Team 1
1 British Rail
2 Cyril Fletcher
3 On active military service
4 Greig
5 The Royal Artillery

Round 9

Team 2
1 55
2 The autogyro
3 Albania
4 Real tennis
5 John McEnroe

Team 1
1 18
2 Concordski
3 Thailand
4 Rodeo
5 Bob Champion

Round 10

Abbreviations: Fellow of the Royal Society of Literature
Mythology: seven young men and seven young women to feed to the Minotaur
Sport: Goal shooter and goal attack
News of the 1980s: Rosie Barnes
United Kingdom: Belfast

Drinks round

Team 1

1 The Black Sea
2 Eric Clapton
3 Gamel Abdal Nasser
4 Noah's
5 Grand Marnier
6 The cock
7 Jellystone National Park
8 Vesuvius
9 Hieronymus Bosch
10 Kabaddi

Team 2

1 The Atlantic
2 Roger Daltry
3 Austria
4 Alice Springs in Australia
5 Raspberry
6 Hawaii
7 *Lady and the Tramp*
8 Pontius Pilate
9 The world's largest painting
10 The clay pigeon trap

Reserve questions

1 The USSR's Aeroflot
2 The Bonzo Dog Do-dah Band
3 Berlioz

Pub League Quiz 39 – Answers

Round 1

Team 1
1 The *Turbinia*
2 Wilkie Collins
3 Fulchester
4 Ecuador
5 Linus Pauling

Team 2
1 The *Fram*
2 Nicolas Freeling
3 Walnut Grove
4 India
5 Economics

Round 2

Team 1
1 Chris de Burgh
2 P. L. Travers
3 The Leone
4 W. T. Tilden
5 Clodagh Rodgers

Team 2
1 Irene Cara
2 Rudyard Kipling
3 The dinar
4 Henry Armstrong
5 Stevie Wonder

Round 3

Team 1
1 Niccolo Machiavelli

2 Israel
3 Richard Greene
4 Andrew Jackson
5 Skittles

Team 2
1 Benjamin Disraeli (Earl of Beaconsfield)
2 Poland
3 *The Return of Doctor X* (1939)
4 William McKinley
5 Lacrosse

Round 4

Team 1
1 Florence
2 Dr Moreau (*The Island of Dr Moreau*, H. G. Wells)
3 Potassium nitrate
4 Princess Margaret
5 Edward Woodwood

Team 2
1 Benvenuto Cellini
2 Dr Zhivago
3 Magnesium sulphate
4 Prince Andrew
5 Richard Harris

Round 5

Television: *The Prisoner*
Sport: The Jockey Club
Plants: Foxglove
Religion: The Hindu religion
Words: The dating of past events by analysis of tree rings

Round 6

Team 2
1 2010
2 Woomera
3 W. Somerset Maugham
4 Arnold Bennett
5 Joel Grey

Team 1
1 *The Jewel of the Nile*
2 The Nullarbor Plain
3 Christopher Marlowe
4 Frederick Marryat
5 Diane Keaton

Round 7

Team 2
1 The Leaning Tower of Pisa
2 None, it is a solo

3 1976
4 Sir Joshua Reynolds
5 Earth-pig

Team 1
1 The Palace of Versailles
2 It was written for baby elephants
   to perform in a circus ring
3 1969
4 Canaletto
5 Wing finger

Round 8

Team 2
1 5
2 Sierra Leone (Lion Mountain
   Ridge)
3 *Zulu*
4 The orchid
5 George Washington (Mount
   Washington)

Team 1
1 7
2 Anchorage

3 Donald Sutherland
4 A small orange
5 Mount Ararat

Round 9

Team 2
1 *Rawhide*
2 The British Museum
3 Nevil Shute
4 Times a day
5 26

Team 1
1 Ty Hardin
2 Anne of Cleves
3 Sir Walter Scott
4 Electrocardiogram
5 23

Round 10

Television: Terry and Bob
Sport: 1981
Plants: The thrift
Religion: A shamrock
Words: Stir his porridge with it (it is a kitchen utensil)

Drinks round

Team 1

1 Winchester
2 Four knights of Henry II
3 *Mono Lisa*
4 The Albert Medal
5 They are bones in the feet
6 About seven-tenths
7 Jim Hacker
8 Anchorage to Nome, Alaska

9 St Bernadette
10 India

Team 2

1 North Yorkshire (near Skipton)
2 Balthazar Gerard
3 *A Private Function*
4 The George Cross
5 They are bones in the wrist
6 The Arctic
7 Michael Aspel
8 The first surface crossing of the Antarctic

9 Alicia Markova
10 Switzerland

Reserve questions

1 St Andrew
2 St Michael
3 German Bight

Pub League Quiz 40 – Answers

Round 1

Team 1
1 Grenoble
2 The microscope
3 *Iolanthe*
4 That between Gibraltar and Spain
5 Horatio Nelson

Team 2
1 Chamonix
2 Celluloid
3 *The Gondoliers*
4 Defence Secretary
5 Paul Revere

Round 2

Team 1
1 Tannochbrae
2 Mongolia
3 Cycling (or motor racing)
4 LXXXVIII
5 Democracy

Team 2
1 New York
2 The west
3 Horse racing
4 MD (M = 1,000 and D = 500)
5 Alimony

Round 3

Team 1
1 *Achille Lauro*
2 Bob Dylan
3 Chic Young
4 Ireland's
5 Duncan, King of Scotland

Team 2
1 *Rainbow Warrior*
2 Barry Manilow's
3 Captain Marvel
4 India
5 Beatrice

Round 4

Team 1
1 *Desmond's*
2 Buckingham Palace
3 Switzerland
4 Ann Haydon Jones
5 1980

Team 2
1 Paul Ford
2 In front of Buckingham Palace
3 France (*Train Grand Vitesse*)
4 Liz McColgan
5 The Domesday Book

Round 5

Films: *Kiss Me Kate*
Which year: 1959
Scandal: George IV
Capitals: Valletta
Science: A proton

Round 6

Team 2
1 Carla
2 The Rosetta Stone
3 Italy
4 Italy
5 Bhopal

Team 1
1 Rhea Perlman
2 The Piltdown Man
3 Vidkun Quisling
4 Everton
5 1987

Round 7

Team 2
1 Stuffed
2 Donwell Abbey
3 Diana Coupland
4 Sweden
5 4

Team 1
1 The pig (it is a raw smoked ham)
2 *Germinal*
3 Bob Monkhouse
4 France
5 0

Round 8

Team 2
1 Angling
2 Violet
3 Antonio Salieri
4 361
5 'Welcome To The Pleasuredome'

Team 1
1 Cricket
2 Red
3 Thomas Keneally
4 22
5 'I am Woman'

Round 9

Team 2
1 1981
2 Thomas Eakins
3 Gerald Kaufman
4 Edward Elgar
5 Huggy Bear

Team 1
1 1967
2 Mary Cassatto
3 Cecil Parkinson
4 *Le Villi*
5 *Monty Python's Flying Circus*

Round 10

Films: *Absolute Beginners*
Which year?: 1924
Scandal: Mandy Rice-Davies
Capitals: Colombo
Science: An armature

Drinks round

Team 1

1 Bowls

2 The Hague, Netherlands
3 Daphne
4 Slow
5 Vistula
6 A type of anchor
7 The Bellamys'
8 Edward I
9 Newmarket
10 1983

Team 2

1 It was the first and only dead heat

2 Organisation of African Unity
3 Menelaus
4 Fast
5 Hudson
6 A large rope, or a cable
7 Fenn Street
8 Edward I
9 Sandown Park
10 1984

Reserve questions

1 Sir Ambrose Fleming
2 The Wellington
3 Hellebore

Pub League Quiz 41 – Answers

Round 1
Team 1
1 Delibes
2 Dr Ramsey
3 Seaweeds
4 Dick Clement and
   Ian La Frenais
5 Eliza Doolittle

Team 2
1 Sibelius
2 Malcolm X
3 A type of bread
4 He had six

5 Nevil Shute

Round 2
Team 1
1 A throw in wrestling
2 Southern Africa
3 Mary Astor
4 Ramsay MacDonald
5 The Goldcrest

Team 2
1 Stones, or granites
2 Southern India
3 Claire Bloom
4 Montezuma
5 The common toad

Round 3
Team 1
1 Just slip out the back, Jack
2 Dick Whittington
3 *The Admirable Crichton*
4 Edith
5 Bourbon

Team 2
1 John Denver
2 The Marquess of Queensberry's
3 Catherine Earnshaw
4 Barbara
5 Brandy and Cointreau

Round 4
Team 1
1 The Ku Klux Klan
2 England
3 *Vertigo*
4 Gunpowder
5 Green

Team 2
1 The Black and Tans
2 Box lacrosse
3 Joan Crawford
4 Mercury
5 Its gizzard

Round 5
General knowledge: 4pm
Counties: Avon
Space travel: Sky lab 2
British Prime Ministers: The Liberal Party
Abbreviations: Peninsular and Oriental

Round 6

Team 2
1 Sprinkling with flour or other powder
2 Rolf Harris
3 General
4 *Nabucco*
5 Tess Daly

Team 1
1 63° Celsius
2 Johnny Mathis
3 Adelina Patti
4 *Samson and Delilah*
5 Major Harry Truscott

Round 7

Team 2
1 The wood is level with the jack
2 Grill it
3 Captain Hardy
4 Otis Redding
5 1930

Team 1
1 Squash
2 Preserved with salt
3 Ellen Terry
4 Clarence White
5 1966

Round 8

Team 2
1 Colombo
2 Patagonia
3 A chain gang
4 The Atlantic giant squid
5 The rats in *The Pied Piper of Hamelin*

Team 1
1 *Bonanza*
2 Moscow
3 Oddjob
4 The humming bird
5 Winnie-the-Pooh

Round 9

Team 2
1 Valery Giscard D'Estaing
2 Four
3 Westminster Abbey
4 *Peyton Place*
5 *The Rite of Spring*

Team 1
1 Sir Anthony Blunt
2 Liszt
3 VAT
4 *When the Boat Comes In*
5 The Bringer of Old Age

Round 10

General knowledge: Euclid
Counties: Isle of Wight
Space travel: *Vostock I*
British Prime Ministers: Spencer Perceval
Abbreviations: Fellow of the Royal Academy of Music

Drinks round

Team 1

1 Colombia
2 Germany

3 William Shakespeare's
4 U2
5 *The Shining*
6 Ayesha
7 Pumpkin Pie
8 Catalan
9 To make a covered trench, so as to approach a besieged place
10 Bates Motel

Team 2

1 The Roaring Forties
2 Jayne Torvill and Christopher Dean
3 Aberdeen
4 Bryan Adams
5 *The Enforcer*
6 Horace Rumpole
7 Sally Lunn
8 Baked earth
9 A sword

10 *Love Me Tender*

Reserve questions

1 The oak
2 Mountain of Light
3 *Jess*

Pub League Quiz 42 – Answers

Round 1
Team 1
1 Petula Clark
2 Tippa Passes
3 Poland
4 Banacek
5 Methuselah

Team 2
1 Zager and Evans
2 Leisure
3 New Zealand
4 William Conrad
5 Sequoia

Round 2
Team 1
1 Mycenae
2 The earliest mare in the *General Stud Book*
3 Egypt's
4 'For All We Know'
5 Sri Lanka

Team 2
1 Doric
2 Water skiing

3 General Douglas MacArthur
4 'Last Dance'
5 Iceland

Round 3
Team 1
1 Eight yards

2 At the back of the altar or communion table
3 It was on a raft in the middle of a river
4 Montreal

5 Jean Louis Gericault

Team 2
1 A player able to bat right-handed or left-handed
2 Egypt

3 Elba and St Helena

4 West of Alaska, between the Bering Sea and the Pacific Ocean
5 Jacques-Louis David

Round 4
Team 1
1 Connecticut
2 *Peter Grimes*
3 Senior Common Room
4 A large wild goat
5 *Going for Gold*

Team 2
1 Kansas
2 Pablo Casals
3 Extended Play
4 A breed of toy dog
5 *Who Wants to be a Millionaire?*

Round 5
The Bible: Proverbs
Words: Herbs
Literature: David Storey's
History: Francois II, the Dauphin of France
Sport: Mike Tyson

Round 6

Team 2
1 River Thames
2 Stephen Ward
3 The Who
4 Tippi Hedren
5 Young Jolyon (Forsyte)

Team 1
1 The Mississippi
2 Dr Beeching's
3 Led Zeppelin
4 Ronald Colman and Jane Wyatt
5 Antonio

Round 7

Team 2
1 Russia
2 Carlisle
3 The Mensheviks
4 Sheerness
5 1773

Team 1
1 Australia
2 Canterbury
3 The Iceni
4 Madison Avenue
5 1946

Round 8

Team 2
1 *The Dream of Gerontius*
2 Algeria
3 It is cold, iced or chilled
4 1924
5 Rodeo

Team 1
1 Emperor
2 Identikit
3 Jelly
4 St Crispin's Day
5 Roger Black

Round 9

Team 2
1 German

2 Leaving the scene of an accident
3 The Moluccas
4 Daniel O'Connell
5 Piano

Team 1
1 The Cambodian alphabet (72 letters)
2 Andrew Johnson
3 Angkor Thorn
4 Earl Kitchener of Khartoum
5 Violin

Round 10

The Bible: Tarsus
Words: Beetles
Literature: Salman Rushdie
History: Merchant
Sport: Rod Laver

Drinks round

Team 1

1 Severing the mooring cables of sea mines
2 Buddy Holly
3 Olga, Masha and Irina
4 Kent State University, Ohio
5 Vanuaatu
6 Argentina
7 Bodie
8 *The Beggar's Opera*
9 R101
10 Argentina

Team 2

1 The kukri
2 The Kinks
3 Becky Sharp
4 Mentmore Towers
5 *Hispaniola*
6 USA
7 *Highway Patrol*
8 Tosca
9 Barnes Wallis
10 Thailand

Reserve questions

1 A game; an indoor form of quoits
2 Aeschylus
3 The coypu's

Pub League Quiz 43 – Answers

Round 1

Team 1
1 1.8 metres
2 A breed of pig
3 The Emperor Constantine
4 *Kipps* (by H. G. Wells)

5 Cuba

Team 2
1 18 inches
2 A bird (a duck)
3 St Giles
4 *The Matchmaker* (Thornton Wilder)
5 Sicily

Round 2

Team 1
1 Cane
2 David Carradine
3 U Thant
4 Checkers
5 One

Team 2
1 Vegetable
2 Robert Mitchum
3 Trygve Lie
4 Green
5 Green

Round 3

Team 1
1 They are types of chair

2 The Compass
3 *Air on a G String*
4 Pesto
5 *An Englishman Abroad*

Team 2
1 They are some of the world's longest railway tunnels
2 Ursa Minor (the Little Bear)
3 *The Raindrop Prelude*
4 Beetroot
5 Huw Wheldon

Round 4

Team 1
1 As US President, he established the 49th parallel as the Canadian-USA border
2 Pygmy moss
3 *Gulliver's Travels*
4 She was donor of the Wightman Cup (as Mrs Wightman)
5 Jacob, his brother

Team 2
1 A Boeing 707

2 Corn
3 *For Whom the Bell Tolls*
4 The National Stud
5 Cana

Round 5
Sport: Sundries
French phrases: Immediately (as soon as possible or with all possible haste)
Opera: Puccini
Literature: Sir Thomas Malory
Which year?: 1974

Round 6
Team 2
1 Isadora Duncan
2 Inigo Jones
3 *Evita*
4 -273°C
5 William Blake

Team 1
1 Arnold Bennett
2 John Nash
3 *Godspell*
4 One calorie
5 Robert Burns

Round 7
Team 2
1 6th January
2 Libya
3 Alcatraz
4 *I'm All Right Jack*
5 Arthur Wing Pinero

Team 1
1 1st March
2 Czechoslovakia
3 Cigarette adverts
4 *The Lady Vanishes*
5 J. B. Priestley

Round 8
Team 2
1 Stirling
2 Delius
3 USA
4 *You Rang M'Lord?*
5 Britain

Team 1
1 Glenfinnan
2 Debussy
3 Belgium
4 *Lovejoy*
5 Constantine

Round 9
Team 2
1 Baloo the Bear
2 The wolverene
3 The Four Tops
4 The French Protestants
5 John Betjeman

Team 1
1 Jessica Rabbit
2 The zebra
3 'YMCA'
4 The Gordon Riots
5 Evelyn Waugh

Round 10
Sport: Training
French phrases: Between ourselves
Opera: Verdi
Literature: Madame Defarge
Which year?: 1815

Drinks round

Team 1
1 France
2 Alice Cooper
3 Ronan Point
4 Kathleen Ferrier
5 A runaway train (Chapel-en-le-Frith, 1957)
6 The Monmouth Rebellion
7 Tokyo
8 Gary Player
9 Edith Holden
10 Lively

Team 2
1 Pandit Jawaharlal Nehru
2 Tom Jones
3 Aberfan
4 'Greensleeves'
5 The Post Office Railway
6 Elise Deroche
7 Staten Island
8 The PGA
9 Joseph Conrad
10 At walking pace

Reserve questions
1 Nelson Rockefeller
2 8
3 Ozone

Pub League Quiz 44 – Answers

Round 1

Team 1
1 Royal Academy of Dramatic Arts
2 To the fox
3 It was a daytime scene
4 Methuselah
5 An acid bath

Team 2
1 Port of London Authority
2 Pigs
3 Cribbage
4 Andrew
5 Bluebeard

Round 2

Team 1
1 *Cabaret*
2 24
3 Henry VI
4 Catcher
5 Rheims

Team 2
1 *The Man Who Knew Too Much*
2 Rain (it is a rain gauge)
3 Edward II
4 Crown green bowls
5 Paris

Round 3

Team 1
1 Flanders and Swann
2 James Michener
3 Germany
4 The primrose family
5 Chopin

Team 2
1 Norman Painting
2 Barry Hines
3 Spain
4 The begonia
5 Vaughan Williams

Round 4

Team 1
1 An exaltation
2 Humberside
3 Andrew Marvell
4 Humidity
5 Mick Jagger

Team 2
1 A tiding
2 Cleveland
3 Alexander Pope
4 Radiation
5 Paul McCartney

Round 5

Television: *People and Places*
Mythology: He rowed the dead over the River Styx into Hades
Literature: Thomas Hardy
Words: A warning or signal bell
Sport: Kenny Dalglish

Round 6

Team 2
1 Tokyo
2 Maureen O'Hara
3 Hera
4 Copenhagen
5 Light-heavyweight

Team 1
1 Las Vegas
2 George
3 Juno
4 Tallinn
5 Bantamweight and featherweight

Round 7

Team 2
1 Numbers
2 He led a division of Paupers on the First Crusade
3 St Catherine
4 A bird
5 C. B. Fry

Team 1
1 Romans
2 David Rizzio
3 Martinmas
4 It is a reptile like a crocodile
5 Ian Botham

Round 8

Team 2
1 Thunder
2 The river Towy
3 Cuba
4 Rocks
5 Blackburn Rovers

Team 1
1 Going to bed
2 The Forth
3 Italy
4 The science of soils
5 Ipswich Town

Round 9

Team 2
1 Sir Michael Horden
2 The thrush
3 A. J. Cronin
4 Tapioca
5 Antonio Stradivari

Team 1
1 Lenny Henry
2 Hour
3 Daphne du Maurier
4 Sugar cane
5 Beethoven

Round 10

Television: Scrabble
Mythology: Weasel
Literature: Kingsley Amis
Words: A schoolmaster or teacher
Sport: Veronique Marot

Drinks round

Team 1

1 Pennsylvania
2 Norris McWhirter
3 King Cheops (or Khufu)
4 The breast bone
5 Glamorgan's
6 Dead or Alive
7 The Merry Wives of Windsor
8 Norway
9 No sense of smell
10 Michael Bentine

Team 2

1 Oklahoma
2 Spike Milligan
3 King Farouk
4 4
5 Warwickshire
6 Adam and the Ants
7 King Arthur'
8 Hudson Bay
9 Walks a tight-rope
10 Hughie Green

Reserve questions

1 TV AM's, which had giant egg cups on its roof
2 *The Solomon Browne*
3 Haydn

Pub League Quiz 45 – Answers

Round 1

Team 1
1 William I
2 A sea trout
3 2000 metres
4 Uruguay
5 Jane Fonda

Team 2
1 James I
2 A red worm (used as bait)
3 1745
4 In Syria
5 Colin Welland

Round 2

Team 1
1 The violin
2 Dostoyevsky
3 Goya
4 Muscles in the body
5 Ernesto

Team 2
1 The sitar
2 A. J. Cronin
3 Turner
4 The human body
5 Poland

Round 3

Team 1
1 A silver spoon
2 Darkness
3 Bahrain
4 Sheet music
5 George Bernard Shaw

Team 2
1 May be in
2 Nakedness
3 Zimbabwe
4 As a writing desk
5 Christopher Fry

Round 4

Team 1
1 20
2 Large bombs
3 William III and Mary II
4 Jim Reeves
5 DV

Team 2
1 About three miles
2 A glider
3 Charles VII
4 Englebert Humperdinck
5 1666 (MDCLXVI)

Round 5

Quotations: Mark Twain (in *Pudd'nhead Wilson's Calendar*)
Plants: The daffodil
Poetry: James Hogg
Ships and the Sea: Very Large Crude Carrier
Television: Lech Walesa

Round 6
Team 2
1 Seven
2 Blackberries
3 Charles II
4 Religious music, hymns
5 T. S. Elliot

Team 1
1 11 feet
2 Dormouse
3 Henry VIII
4 Gospel music
5 W. M. Thackeray

Round 7
Team 2
1 The *Times Literary Supplement*
2 Donovan
3 10,000
4 A bed
5 Venice's

Team 1
1 Sir William Rees Mogg
2 Tiny Tim
3 181 degrees
4 Whitstable
5 Geneva

Round 8
Team 2
1 Dodie Smith
2 Volleyball
3 A dog
4 King's Own Scottish Borderers
5 Goliath

Team 1
1 Reverend W. Awdry
2 Someone who practises karate
3 A large sea bird
4 Territorial Army Volunteer Reserve
5 The Magi

Round 9
Team 2
1 At the back of the nose and throat
2 Two
3 The descent of a deity to earth in a bodily form
4 *Man of La Mancha*
5 *Never Mind the Quality, Feel the Width*

Team 1
1 Freckles
2 6 (1 + 2 + 3)
3 Momus
4 *Carousel*
5 1895

Round 10
Quotations: Edmond Hoyle (in his 1742 book on whist)
Plants: Catkins
Poetry: Tam O'Shanter (in Burns' poem)
Ships and the Sea: The Flying Dutchman
Television: Optical Reception of Announcements by Coded Line Electronics

Drinks round

Team 1

1 Stephen Foster
2 Japan
3 In 1963
4 Blood pressure
5 Lightfoot
6 The Government Chief Whip
7 The Tees
8 Tobey Maguire
9 Polo
10 Childbirth

Team 2

1 Henry Lyte
2 France
3 In 1967
4 The Eustachian tubes
5 Operation Barbarossa
6 Lord Palmerston
7 Thelsis
8 Michael Crawford
9 Orienteering
10 Food

Reserve questions

1 In Vienna
2 Rolls Royce
3 Forth

Pub League Quiz 46 – Answers

Round 1
Team 1
1 Spain
2 Prasutagus
3 Mortimer
4 The Bade of Omdurman
5 W. S. Gilbert

Team 2
1 Kenya
2 Edward III
3 *Sleeping Beauty*
4 The Battle of Marston Moor
5 William Langland

Round 2
Team 1
1 The use of words that begin with or include the same letters or sounds
2 Introduce secondary education for all
3 Panama
4 David Lloyd George
5 Hexagonal

Team 2
1 An understatement, often ironical
2 Establish freedom of worship
3 Haiti
4 Benjamin Disraeli
5 *Celebrity Squares*

Round 3
Team 1
1 Delius
2 Mexico
3 Newts
4 *Billy Liar*
5 The Island of Heligoland

Team 2
1 Peter Warlock
2 Dorset
3 The Pike
4 *Rooster Cogburn*
5 Zanzibar

Round 4
Team 1
1 Water
2 John Clare
3 Chile and Ecuador
4 Michael Bentine
5 The ear drum

Team 2
1 Graphite
2 Robert Frost
3 Norway and Russia
4 Bernard Hedges
5 A finger print

Round 5
Animals: It has fin feet
USA: Alaska
Science: Sulphuric acid
Television: Bureau des Etrangers
Plays: Christ's suffering and death

Round 6

Team 2
1 On a sailing ship (they are sails)
2 Paul Anka
3 It is firm to the teeth
4 *Wasa* (or *Vasa*)
5 Lauren Bacall

Team 1
1 A sea bird
2 The Bee Gees
3 Gorgonzola
4 Two of the first successful steamships
5 Audrey Hepburn

Round 7

Team 2
1 Anita Brookner
2 The Aga Khan (Shergar)
3 Iran
4 *LA Law*
5 Periods of architecture

Team 1
1 William Golding
2 HRH The Duke of Edinburgh
3 Albania
4 Eddie Shoestring
5 Breeds of ducks

Round 8

Team 2
1 Henry Mayhew
2 Fashion
3 Dorothy Parker
4 Reykjavik
5 Hands across Britain

Team 1
1 John Osborne's
2 *Hope and Glory*
3 Oliver Cromwell
4 Belize
5 Desmond Tutu

Round 9

Team 2
1 Trente
2 Burgundy
3 Cambridge University Press

4 Haberdasher
5 1914

Team 1
1 Quaranta
2 France
3 Oxford University Dramatic Society

4 Psephologist
5 1915

Round 10

Animals: Marsupium
USA: Spiro Agnew
Science: Soda water
Plays: Volpone

Drinks round

Team 1

1 Lenny Henry
2 Writer's cramp

3 *Ode to a Nightingale*
4 Neville Chamberlain
5 Melbourne (1956)
6 Bach's *Air on a G String*
7 The Los Angeles police
8 Hercules
9 The lark
10 Torquay United

Team 2

1 Rob Wilton
2 The inner ear (it is the flap at the entrance to the ear)
3 Sir Henry Newbolt
4 Winston Churchill
5 Helsinki (1952)
6 Dvorak's *New World Symphony*
7 *Marathon Man*
8 Sacred elephants
9 The mute swan
10 Stoke City

Reserve questions

1 Berlin
2 Will Somers
3 Originally bone fires (where bones were burned)

Pub League Quiz 47 – Answers

Round 1
Team 1
1 Sierra Nevada
2 Pale blue and white
3 Eugene O'Neill
4 Gillian Anderson
5 *My Fair Lady*

Team 2
1 The Yellow Sea
2 Cream coloured
3 J. M. Synge
4 Patrick Mower
5 *Hello Dolly*

Round 2
Team 1
1 Sir Robert Graham
2 South Africa
3 Stitches
4 The Germans
5 Brazil

Team 2
1 His wife, Isabella
2 Republic of Ireland
3 A lively dance
4 The Turkish
5 Finland

Round 3
Team 1
1 Zululand
2 Sweden
3 Hemlock
4 Patricia Hayes
5 Table tennis

Team 2
1 Haiti
2 USA
3 Rowena
4 Nero
5 Showjumping

Round 4
Team 1
1 Suffolk
2 Edward (975-979)
3 The original inhabitants of Jerusalem
4 Geranium
5 Richard Strauss

Team 2
1 Cornwall
2 Portugal
3 Teachers of Law
4 The carnation
5 *Turandot*

Round 5
Sport: Golf
Geography: Portugal
Literature: Oscar Wilde
Pop music: Gloria Gaynor
Art: Van Gogh

Round 6

Team 2
1 The eye
2 St Matthew
3 Spanish
4 Fulham
5 Sparta

Team 1
1 The bladder
2 St Luke
3 Anglo-Swiss
4 Shrewsbury
5 Quincy Jones

Round 7

Team 2
1 Canada
2 The Hellenes (Greece)
3 Isabella Mary
4 Behind your ear
5 Eight and 14

Team 1
1 Australia
2 Ceylon (Sri Lanka)
3 Eleanor
4 The sciatic nerve
5 One and four

Round 8

Team 2
1 Thomas Hardy
2 Neptune
3 Hockenheim
4 Portsmouth
5 Walter Matthau

Team 1
1 Muriel Spark
2 Tchaikovsky
3 Alain Prost
4 Manchester
5 Cary Grant

Round 9

Team 2
1 Steve Davis
2 Newfoundland
3 The Congress Party
4 Officer Dibble
5 Penguin

Team 1
1 Joe Davis
2 Boston, Massachusetts
3 Georges Clemenceau
4 Evil Edna
5 A snake

Round 10

Sport: Volleyball
Geography: The Gulf of St Lawrence, Quebec
Literature: Stan Barstow
Pop music: Paulo Nutini
Art: Paul Gauguin

Drinks round

Team 1

1 His nephew
2 A whirlpool
3 Sir Oswald Mosley
4 Al Pacino
5 A water carrier

6 Figure skating

7 Dover
8 Richard Rodgers
9 Anne Boleyn
10 *It Ain't Half Hot Mum*

Team 2

1 Elijah
2 100
3 Sir Thomas Stamford Raffles
4 Albert Finney
5 It was the first championship fight with gloves
6 Golf (it is a free shot in a friendly game)
7 Somerset
8 Leonard Bernstein
9 Mary, Queen of Scots
10 Sunshine Desserts

Reserve questions

1 One
2 25
3 Shirley Bassey

Pub League Quiz 48 – Answers

Round 1

Team 1
1 Belfast
2 Musical time
3 Mountaineering (or rock climbing)
4 China and North Korea
5 Rodgers and Hart

Team 2
1 Chicago
2 A variable electrical resistance
3 Golf
4 Brazil
5 George M. Cohen

Round 2

Team 1
1 The harp
2 National League and American League
3 *Bandwagon*
4 France
5 University College Hospital (London)

Team 2
1 The oboe
2 Halifax
3 David Hamilton
4 Belgium
5 Lord Justice

Round 3

Team 1
1 Gules

2 Ray Manzarek
3 *The Waste Land*
4 Gwynedd
5 Showing off

Team 2
1 A broad stripe running the length of the shield
2 Kyle MacLachlan
3 T. S. Eliot
4 Powys
5 Exaggerating

Round 4

Team 1
1 Sebastian Coe
2 Gall bladder
3 St Stephen
4 Hertz
5 Canadian

Team 2
1 Twice
2 The skull, near the ear
3 Pius IX (1846-78)
4 The Ohm
5 British

Round 5
Geography: Athens
Animal world: A lizard
Poetry: Fair of face
World of plants: Deadly nightshade
Television: Jon Pertwee

Round 6

Team 2
1 Rabat
2 Anaesthetic
3 *A Tale of Two Cities*
4 Abba
5 Switzerland

Team 1
1 Kinshasa
2 Crustacean
3 *The Mill on the Floss*
4 The Rolling Stones
5 Italy

Round 7

Team 2
1 The grey wolf
2 Henry VI
3 Vitamin B1 (thiamine)
4 Isaac
5 A bee-keeper

Team 1
1 The Orangutan
2 Elizabeth I
3 Vitamin C (ascorbic acid)
4 Michael
5 Mycroft

Round 8

Team 2
1 Peter Finch
2 Crecy
3 Crow
4 Lillian Hellman
5 Cherilyn Sakisian

Team 1
1 Barbara Stanwyck
2 Shrewsbury
3 A shell-fish
4 T. S. Eliot
5 Salvatore Bono

Round 9

Team 2
1 Peru
2 He collected taxes
3 Pele
4 Oedipus
5 The semi-quaver

Team 1
1 Turkey
2 Jeremiah's
3 Emil Zatopek
4 King Idris
5 A semibreve

Round 10

Geography: San Juan
Animal world: The salmon
Poetry: Rudyard Kipling
World of plants: The bilberry
Television: Gibbs SR Toothpaste

Drinks round

Team 1

1 Schubert
2 William III (William of Orange)
3 India
4 5.30pm
5 Rugby Union
6 Simon Ward
7 A breed of duck
8 Vera Brittain
9 Indiana
10 Los Angeles, California

Team 2

1 Chopin
2 Richard I
3 New Hampshire
4 10.00pm
5 Wood-breaking
6 Angie Dickinson
7 A fish (like a pike)
8 Hugh Gaitskell
9 Virginia
10 Houston, Texas

Reserve questions

1 1966
2 Wagner
3 Samson

Pub League Quiz 49 – Answers

Round 1
Team 1
1 John de Balliol (Chosen King of Scotland, 1292)
2 Greece
3 Compulsory figures
4 *Brideshead Revisited*
5 Charles Luciano

Team 2
1 George, Prince Regent (later, George IV)
2 Corfu
3 Ice dancing
4 *Pickwick Papers*
5 George Kelly

Round 2
Team 1
1 Rubens
2 Dublin
3 Vivaldi
4 Eight yards
5 29 May

Team 2
1 Sir Joshua Reynolds
2 Cardiff
3 Enrique Granados
4 30 yards
5 28 December

Round 3
Team 1
1 The Move
2 Ogden Nash
3 Thomas
4 The rock and soil debris deposited by a glacier
5 Nevada

Team 2
1 Sweet
2 George Bernard Shaw
3 Changing water into wine
4 Yellowish-grey loam soil
5 Louisiana

Round 4
Team 1
1 Newmarket
2 Alexandre Dumas (the elder)
3 The oboe
4 Charles II
5 Whoopi Goldberg

Team 2
1 Aintree
2 Pushkin
3 Sir John Barbirolli
4 Henry VIII
5 The Sunshine Cab Company

Round 5
Places: Porcelain (or China)
Politics: Israel's
Science: Very low temperatures
Words: The female Fates of Scandinavian mythology
Books: It is a reference book of British nobility

Round 6
Team 2
1 Dutch
2 Cello
3 Lord Wolseley
4 They are brother and sister
5 The golden poppy

Team 1
1 Ancient British
2 Organ
3 Admiral Duncan
4 Table tennis
5 Orange blossom

Round 7
Team 2
1 Spanish Civil War
2 Scotland
3 Gilbert and Sullivan
4 *The Winter's Tale*
5 Pigeon racing

Team 1
1 Indian Mutiny
2 North-west Spain
3 Johann Strauss (the younger)
4 *As You Like It*
5 Polo

Round 8
Team 2
1 Genevieve
2 King John
3 Lutetia
4 The Joule
5 Pearls Before Swine

Team 1
1 Isidore the Labourer
2 Henry I
3 Gades
4 The Coulomb
5 The Average White Band

Round 9
Team 2
1 Out of condition to fight

2 In Corfe Castle, Dorset
3 Barbara Cartland
4 Ancient British and Irish alphabet
5 *Evita*

Team 1
1 In the place of a parent (acting as a guardian)
2 Lincoln
3 Iran
4 An object made of wood
5 Frankie Laine

Round 10
Places: New York State Prison
Politics: Spain
Science: Heavy water
Words: He is a dealer in horses
Books: Hilaire Belloc

Drinks round

Team 1

1 M20
2 Republic of Ireland
3 Mary Tudor, Queen Mary I
4 Pope John Paul II
5 Posy Simmonds
6 A hare
7 The New Seekers
8 Spain
9 Amsterdam
10 Sir Geoffrey de Havilland

Team 2

1 Mil
2 The USA
3 Queen Victoria
4 Prince Charles
5 *The Guardian*
6 A snake
7 Herman and the Hermits
8 Italy
9 Lisbon
10 R. J. Mitchell

Reserve questions

1 *Pilgrim's Progress*
2 31 December
3 630

Pub League Quiz 50 – Answers

Round 1

Team 1
1 Vertical Take Off and Landing
2 Howard Spring
3 Enoch
4 Tchaikovsky
5 The peacock (on to his tail)

Team 2
1 International Civil Aviation Organisation
2 Judith Krantz
3 He was a shepherd
4 Chopin
5 The Straits of Gibraltar

Round 2

Team 1
1 The Isle of Man
2 Helsinki
3 Marvin Gaye
4 *Citizen Kane*
5 The River Soar

Team 2
1 Guiseley, West Yorkshire (Harry Ramsden's)
2 Grenoble, France
3 Roger Miller
4 *The Absent Minded Professor*
5 The Dee

Round 3

Team 1
1 Paraguay
2 Liechtenstein
3 Nijinsky
4 Thomas Hardy
5 The Orchid

Team 2
1 Georgetown
2 Sarawak
3 Churchill Downs (Louisville, Kentucky)
4 Emile Zola
5 Nicotiana

Round 4

Team 1
1 Melvyn Hayes
2 In Syria
3 A member of the clergy
4 A large flightless bird
5 Appomattox

Team 2
1 Archie Bunker
2 The Ionian Islands
3 Cloaks or Capes
4 A chocolate drop (or other sweetmeat)
5 The Second

Round 5

Sport: The Derby, The St Leger and the 2000 Guineas
Composers: Richard Strauss
History: The production and sale of alcoholic drinks
Art: 'The Boyhood of Raleigh'
Poems: *Lepanto* (Chesterton)

Round 6

Team 2
1 Dorothy L. Sayers
2 Edward the Confessor (in 1066)
3 Borneo
4 In the wrist
5 Badminton

Team 1
1 L. Frank Baum
2 Richard III
3 Greece
4 In the thigh
5 New Zealand

Round 7

Team 2
1 1000
2 Russia
3 Abraham
4 Jackson Pollock
5 Queen's Park

Team 1
1 100
2 *The Admiral Graf Spee*
3 Jethro
4 Sir Gilbert Scott
5 10,000 metres

Round 8

Team 2
1 The throne of Spain
2 His friend Julian
3 A blacksmith
4 Brazil
5 The Battle of Agincourt

Team 1
1 The throne of Denmark
2 *The Archers*
3 Linen weaver
4 Zambia
5 The Battle of Lewes

Round 9

Team 2
1 Samuel Johnson
2 Denmark
3 Motorcycling
4 *Son of Kong*
5 *The Barber of Seville*

Team 1
1 Ned Kelly's
2 Norway
3 $\frac{1}{16}$ inch
4 *Bonzo Goes to College*
5 Franco Alfano

Round 10
Sport: Alec and Eric Bedser
Composers: Paderewski
History: Louis XIV
Art: Titian
Poems: Alfred, Lord Tennyson

Drinks round

Team 1
1 The Ellice Islands
2 Claude Rains
3 17
4 Thomas Jefferson
5 C. S. Lewis
6 Charles II
7 Vilnius
8 A male falcon
9 Table tennis
10 Oedipus

Team 2
1 Northern Rhodesia
2 Charlie Chaplin
3 21
4 Velasquez
5 Sinclair Lewis
6 His son Edward VI, aged 10
7 In the Persian Gulf
8 The grebe family
9 West Ham United
10 Orpheus

Reserve questions
1 Lammas
2 Oscar Wilde
3 Ken Dodd

Pub League Quiz 51 – Answers

Round 1

Team 1
1 Bach
2 Tanks
3 Spain
4 *Composed upon Westminster Bridge* (Wordsworth)
5 Bay view

Team 2
1 Percy Grainger
2 Hermann Goering
3 Burgundy
4 *Hyperion* (Keats)
5 James Darren and Robert Colbert

Round 2

Team 1
1 Harry Dacre
2 12ft x 6ft
3 1801
4 Steeleye Span
5 Triple Black

Team 2
1 Henry Mancini
2 10ft x 5ft
3 1968
4 Creedence Clearwater Revival
5 Hard Black

Round 3

Team 1
1 The Boers and the Zulus
2 Athene
3 1976
4 Moses
5 Lesotho

Team 2
1 Carthage and Rome
2 Noah
3 1964
4 Moses
5 Niger

Round 4

Team 1
1 A monster with a lion's head a goat's body and a serpent tail
2 Rimsky-Korsakov
3 Goya
4 Pedro Alvares Cabral
5 The snatch and the clean and jerk

Team 2
1 Thor (it was his hammer)
2 Gian-Carlo Menotti
3 The Duchess of Alva
4 Hernando de Soto
5 Cross-country skiing and shooting

Round 5

Television: Peckham
Famous people: He wrote 'The Star Spangled Banner' (in 1814)
Pop music: Pink Floyd
History: William Rufus
Animals: A wild llama

Round 6

Team 2

1 Ribonucleic acid
2 Mehmed VI
3 At the most southerly point of India
4 Paul Scott
5 *Christ on the Mount of Olives*

Team 1

1 Deoxyribonucleic acid
2 Henry IV
3 Antarctica
4 Jonathan Swift
5 Handel

Round 7

Team 2

1 *The Four Horsemen of the Apocalypse*
2 Mumtaz Mahal (wife of Shah Jahan)
3 Robert Koch
4 Jim Sullivan (in 1925)
5 Eastern Capital

Team 1

1 *The Gay Divorce* (1934)
2 Sir Benjamin Hall
3 Antoine Henri Becquerel
4 Wilfred Rhodes (for England, aged 52 years)
5 Edo

Round 8

Team 2

1 Tracey and Sharon
2 Between Greenland and Iceland
3 David Lodge
4 Brinley Richards
5 The arm

Team 1

1 Ivan Fox
2 Between Nova Scotia and New Brunswick, Canada
3 Edgar Allan Poe
4 Joseph Haydn
5 The brain

Round 9

Team 2

1 Programmable Read Only Memory
2 The potato
3 Peter Nichols
4 Parmigianino (also known as Parmigiano)
5 Norman Dagley

Team 1

1 Beginners All-purpose Symbolic Instruction Code
2 Antiseptic surgery
3 Erich Maria Remarque
4 Roy Lichtenstein
5 The San Francisco 49ers

Round 10

Television: Garfield Morgan
Famous people: Ras Tafari
Pop music: Chaka Khan
History: Theodoric the Great
Animals: A fish

Drinks round

Team 1
1 Bolivia and Paraguay
2 The SI unit of electromagnetic inductance
3 Doha
4 Julie Walters
5 A murder
6 The giant Loki
7 Paganini
8 In Switzerland
9 Gordon Burns
10 John Dryden

Team 2
1 New Zealand colonists
2 The SI unit of illuminance
3 Windhoek
4 Sir Henry Irving
5 A sleuth
6 Bellerophon
7 Chopin
8 In Brazil
9 Tim McInerny
10 Sir John Betjeman

Reserve questions

1 New York
2 Alaska
3 Group of (eight countries)

Quick-fire Quiz Answers

Quick-fire Quiz 1 – Answers

Pot Pourri 1
1 An artificial language
2 Affidavit
3 Hind leg
4 One strengthened with alcohol
5 Thursday
6 31 October
7 Mormons

8 By means of cables
9 Red
10 Hippocratic oath
11 Dr Henry Crippen
12 Sheffield Plate

13 Yom Kippur
14 For this special purpose

15 On a meandering river (it occurs when a river changes course to isolate a hairpin bend and so forms a lake)
16 Kaffirs
17 Pottery (it was produced by Felix Pratt in Staffordshire in about 1780–1820)
18 Japanese
19 Grimaldi
20 Medicine men

History 1
1 The Constitution of the United States
2 The bombing of Pearl Harbor
3 Romanov
4 Ireland
5 The Burma Road
6 Princess Marina
7 Cadiz

8 Viscount Nuffield
9 Ferdinand de Lesseps
10 'Papa Doc'
11 As a weapon used like a club

12 Queen Mary
13 The Monroe Doctrine
14 Malta

15 Friedrich Engels
16 Scarab
17 Belgium
18 Alaska
19 A medal for British servicemen who served in the Atlantic and other seas round Britain during the Second World War
20 Catherine of Aragon

United Kingdom 1

1	Edward Heath	13	Imperial War Museum
2	Group Captain	14	Manchester
3	Houses of Parliament		
4	Clyde	15	British Broadcasting
5	General Synod		Corporation
6	The County of Kent	16	Oxford Committee for Famine
7	Life		Relief
		17	The Banqueting Hall of
8	St Helier, Jersey		Whitehall Palace in London
9	Leeds	18	Colchester
10	Southsea	19	Dumbarton, not Dunbarton
11	229 metres (754 feet)	20	Newgate
12	Isle of Man		

Music and Entertainment 1

1	Kirsty Young	11	T. S. Eliot
2	The Magic Circle	12	Bob Marley
3	Roger Vadim	13	*Breakfast at Tiffany's*
4	Mae West	14	Bassoon
5	Debbie McGee		
6	*EastEnders*	15	John Landis
7	Handel's *Water Music*	16	Richard Burton
		17	Diminuendo
8	Peter Hall	18	Bebop
9	Michael Miles	19	They all remained bachelors
10	Virginal (it is an obsolete	20	Petra
	musical instrument; the others		
	are all kinds of dance)		

Science and Nature 1

1	Mars	12	Gelatine
2	A computer language	13	Fluorine
3	VHF or very high frequency	14	As a bleaching agent
4	Capillaries		
5	Orris	15	Artificial satellites in orbit
6	Brass		around the earth
7	The ear	16	Because when the sun comes
			out its flowers turn to face it
8	Add 32 to the result	17	Mesozoic
9	Most kinds of pine tree	18	Astigmatism
10	Photosynthesis	19	Hot molten rock
11	Aspirin	20	Aurora

Definitions 1

1	c		11	b
2	d		12	e
3	a		13	a
4	d		14	b
5	c			
6	e		15	d
7	d		16	e
			17	a
8	d		18	e
9	c		19	b
10	d		20	e

Sport and Games 1

1	Manchester United		11	Leerie Constantine
2	Pinza		12	Chess
3	Said Aouita		13	Muirfield
4	Darts		14	London Irish, London Scottish and London Welsh
5	Orienteering			
6	Sir Donald Bradman			
7	Wrestling		15	Archery
			16	W. T. Tilden
8	Roberto Baggio		17	Bantamweight
9	New York Yankees (they are a baseball team; the others play American football)		18	Perth
			19	Edinburgh
			20	Leg theory
10	Queen's Prize			

Animal Kingdom 1

1	Ladybirds		12	False (it is a creature of Egyptian mythology)
2	Kangaroo			
3	Plankton		13	Terrier
4	True		14	Only the long-tailed occurs in Britain
5	Drones			
6	Koala			
7	Ostrich		15	Mammoth
			16	Any bird with webbed feet
8	Four		17	A hairless breed of dog
9	Bird of prey		18	A domestic animal gone wild for example, park fallow deer
10	Antelope			
11	Carapace		19	Pig
			20	Wolverine

Geography and Travel 1

1 Netherlands
2 Fraternities
3 Versailles
4 Urdu
5 Tribes of North American Indians
6 Mistral
7 Vienna
8 Baltic
9 Alaska
10 A ring or horseshoe enclosing a lagoon
11 *Lingua franca*
12 A member of the Federal Bureau of Investigation
13 Armagnac
14 Kremlin
15 Jaffa
16 White Anglo-Saxon Protestants
17 Pottery
18 British Virgin Islands
19 35 years of age
20 A type of tea urn

Art and Literature 1

1 Cubist
2 *The Arabian Nights*
3 Ben Okri
4 Elegy
5 Catherine Cookson
6 William Hogarth
7 Ghost writer
8 Frank Herbert
9 Watercolour
10 Nemesis
11 John Calvin
12 Anna Sewell
13 Goneril
14 Honoré de Balzac
15 James Baldwin
16 Bathos
17 Charles Lamb
18 Pierre-Auguste Renoir
19 J. K. Galbraith
20 A Grecian urn

Quick-fire Quiz 2 – Answers

Pot pourri 2

1   Hinduism
2   Population
3   Gross National Product
4   The scales
5   Purl
6   Methuselah
7   A teacake (from Bath where Sally Lunn kept a shop)

8   It is the world's rarest and most valuable stamp
9   Roquefort
10 Suffragan

11 A scar formed after the healing of a wound
12 Terracotta
13 On an aeroplane (it is a lateral-control flap on the tip of a wing)
14 A liqueur

15 Fustian
16 Relief map
17 Alfred Adler
18 The dog days
19 Arch
20 Cortex

History 2

1   Early steam engines
2   Earl Mountbatten of Burma
3   Captain James Cook
4   Philosopher's stone
5   1960
6   Korean War
7   Krakow

8   Coal miners
9   They were all German field-marshals in the Second World War

10 Robert Oppenheimer
11 He simply cut it with a sword
12 James I of England, James VI of Scotland
13 Black and Tans
14 (1st) Duke of Wellington

15 Winston Leonard Spencer
16 Matthias
17 Tithe
18 Tasmania
19 Straits Settlements
20 Henry I

United Kingdom 2

1 The name sometimes given to Northern Ireland
2 Glasgow
3 Fair Isle
4 Shropshire
5 Avon
6 Chatsworth House
7 Ayrshire

8 The Wallace Collection
9 The College of Arms
10 Aberdeen
11 Oysters
12 York
13 Kent
14 Gillie

15 UNISON
16 £1 coin
17 Somerset
18 The statue of Eros in Piccadilly Circus
19 Sir Edwin Lutyens
20 Salisbury

Music and entertainment 2

1 Kevin Whateley
2 Poland
3 The Animals
4 *Spitting Image*
5 Billy Cotton
6 Richard D'Oyly Carte
7 Zither

8 Ballet choreography
9 Dan
10 Michelle Pfeiffer
11 Antoine
12 *The Navy Lark*
13 London
14 Orson Welles

15 *Woman's Hour*
16 Sir Arthur Bliss
17 Cary Grant
18 Scottish inflated by mouth, Northumbrian by arm pressure
19 Sarah Bernhardt (her severely diseased leg was amputated in 1915)
20 The Federation

Science and nature 2

1 Yellow
2 1.82 metres (6 feet)
3 Catalyst
4 Laser
5 Little Bear
6 Sternum
7 Neap tides

8 27 days 7 hours 43 minutes
9 Hexahedron
10 Silver
11 The sun crosses the Equator twice a year
12 Tungsten
13 Eating apple
14 1 ton

15 A nearly vertical shaft in a glacier
16 Desalination
17 Marsh marigold
18 Helium
19 15
20 Telescope

Definitions 2

1	c		11	d
2	d		12	c
3	a		13	d
4	c		14	a
5	e			
6	b		15	c
7	d		16	c
			17	e
8	d		18	a
9	a		19	c
10	b		20	e

Sport and games 2

1	Sir Stanley Matthews		11	Sugar Ray Robinson
2	High jump		12	Mah-jong
3	Cluedo		13	Four
4	Greg Norman		14	Aberdeen
5	Badminton			
6	Mortlake		15	The Daytona 200
7	Henley Regatta		16	Chinaman
			17	Warwickshire
8	Prix de l'Arc de Triomphe		18	Gymnastics
9	Baseball		19	Full Nelson
10	*Wisden's Cricketers' Almanack*		20	Canadian

Animal kingdom 2

1	Rock salmon		12	Lizard
2	African		13	Polecat
3	Slimbridge		14	A plant-eating animal
4	Deer			
5	10 years		15	Warthog
6	Bats		16	Snakes
7	Sea horse		17	Hedgehog, mole or shrew
			18	Because of its liking for mistletoe berries
8	Dormouse			
9	Rabbit		19	Pigs
10	Airedale		20	Moufflon
11	Pig			

Geography and travel 2

1	Tokyo	11	Port
2	The Congress	12	Matterhorn
3	Pagoda	13	California
4	Loire	14	Paddy
5	Los Angeles		
6	Paris	15	Slivovitz
7	Vesuvius	16	Nubians
		17	Faroe Islands
8	Accellerato	18	Veracruz
9	Ramadan	19	Terylene
10	Billabong	20	The Grand Banks

Art and literature 2

1 Brer Fox
2 The chorus
3 *Ulysses* by James Joyce
4 George Stubbs
5 Mrs Isabella Beeton
6 *The Pilgrim's Progress* by John Bunyan
7 The Great (Jay) Gatsby

8 The Burrell Collection
9 They all commit suicide
10 *The Coral Island* by R. M. Ballantyne

11 The Bronte sisters (these were their first pseudonyms)
12 Russia
13 Cuneiform
14 All doctors of medicine

15 Thomas Kyd
16 Hans Holbein
17 John Clare
18 *2001: A Space Odyssey* by Arthur C. Clarke
19 'Guernica'
20 *Doctor Faustus*

Quick-fire Quiz 3 – Answers

Pot Pourri 3

1 Dark grey
2 Nuncio
3 A silk purse
4 Chilli con carne
5 To make sugar
6 Red
7 Walking shoes

8 Palindrome
9 'Stars and Stripes'
10 A method of nursery teaching
11 Stet

12 Armageddon
13 Parboiling
14 A spade-depth of soil in digging

15 Jesuits
16 Salic law
17 Aitchbone
18 Equities, unlike the others, do not pay a fixed rate of interest
19 A psychiatrist or psychologist
20 Brevet

History 3

1 Egypt
2 Doodlebug
3 Lyndon Baines Johnson
4 Iran
5 Ho Chi Minh City
6 Adolf Hitler
7 Denmark's

8 *Nautilus*
9 Pheidippides
10 The Authorised Version

11 Buddha
12 General Douglas MacArthur
13 Montreal, Canada
14 Rebirth

15 Third cousin
16 Appomattox
17 Universal Postal Union
18 Gilbertines
19 Actium
20 Peking man

United Kingdom 3

1	Victoria Cross	11	Culzean Castle, Ayrshire
2	A party with singing and dancing	12	The Nore
		13	Isle of Skye
3	Lambeth Palace	14	Bath
4	The underwriting room at Lloyd's of London	15	Basalt
5	Farthing	16	Cambridge
6	Watling Street	17	Off the Welsh coast, near Milford Haven
7	False (2.9m)	18	It is artificial
8	Edinburgh	19	The Royal Ballet School
9	Victoria	20	Fairs (originally where labour was hired)
10	Wensleydale		

Music and entertainment 3

1	Whitehall Theatre	11	Ringo Starr
2	*The X Files*	12	Dame Margot Fonteyn
3	Robert Schumann	13	Diagonally across the screen
4	A country dance	14	*In Town Tonight*
5	Five		
6	Johann Strauss II	15	Elizabeth I
7	Elton John	16	Leningrad
		17	Kathleen Turner
8	*It's a Knockout*	18	Blimp
9	Rudolph Valentino	19	David Garrick
10	Welsh National Opera	20	'Land of Our Fathers'

Science and nature 3

1	Flax	11	The seas and oceans
2	Albumen	12	Male
3	Sulphuric acid	13	On the moon
4	Blue	14	Carbon dioxide
5	Bitumen		
6	Megaton	15	Green
7	Blue	16	In the brain
		17	Momentum
8	Water	18	Oxalic acid
9	In a firearm	19	Galaxies
10	Aqua regia	20	Leyden jar

Definitions 3

1	e	11	b
2	d	12	e
3	c	13	b
4	a	14	b
5	c		
6	d	15	b
7	b	16	d
		17	a
8	c	18	d
9	c	19	a
10	e	20	c

Sport and games 3

1 Greyhound racing
2 Geoffrey Boycott
3 Fibre glass
4 En garde
5 1,500 metres
6 Basketball
7 The sliding roof over Centre Court

8 £25
9 Table tennis
10 Geoff Hurst
11 Competitions where scoring is by number of strokes not number of holes

12 Netball
13 50 points
14 A type of gear

15 Don Clarke
16 Kent
17 Birmingham City
18 Twelve
19 Trampolining (they are all kinds of somersault)
20 Cassius Clay, later Muhammad Ali

Animal kingdom 3

1 Swan
2 A pride
3 Barracuda
4 The Kennel Club
5 Goldfish
6 Potato
7 Heifer

8 Duck-billed platypus
9 Caimans
10 Slot
11 Pupa or chrysalis

12 Six (it is a true insect)
13 True (it is a type of goldfish)
14 Barn owl

15 Cloven-hoofed mammals
16 Near the surface
17 Only in Southern Italy and Sicily
18 On the wing
19 Aardwolf
20 Seashore worm

Geography and travel 3

1	*The Golden Horn*	11	Corrida
2	The Stock Exchange	12	Caroline Islands
3	Roaring Forties	13	Kabuki
4	Agra	14	Stockholm
5	On a mosque		
6	Apennines	15	Engadine
7	Walloon	16	New Year
		17	Dubrovnik
8	Brandy made from apples	18	States General
9	Byzantium	19	Straits of Hormuz
10	West Berlin	20	Argentina

Art and literature 3

1	Alloway	11	Cyclopes
2	Lord Peter Wimsey	12	Hyperbole
3	An albatross	13	C. P. Snow
4	*The Balkan Trilogy*	14	Sir Roger de Coverley
5	Aesop		
6	They all wrote famous diaries	15	Martial
7	*The Canterbury Tales*	16	Wild animals
		17	*Jane Eyre*
8	Mark Twain	18	Anthony Trollope
9	Aubrey Beardsley	19	Alexandrine
10	Battle of Agincourt	20	Guy Crouchback

Quick-fire Quiz 4 – Answers

Pot pourri 4

1	Topiary	11	The Pope
2	Marzipan	12	Filigree
3	No overtaking	13	Awl
4	It was supposed to reach heaven	14	Single-lens reflex
5	Mitre	15	Three
6	Six	16	Wines
7	Romany	17	Cyrillic
		18	3 p.m.
8	As an insecticide	19	French knot
9	Antimacassar	20	Philately
10	Stucco		

History 4

1	Donald Maclean	11	Tsar Nicholas II and his family
2	Dr Andrei Sakharov	12	Railways
3	Duke of Windsor	13	Edwin E. Aldrin
4	*Graf Spee*	14	Queen Juliana of the Netherlands
5	He was the first man to swim the English Channel		
6	The Bastille	15	The Black Prince
7	Seven	16	Professional robbers and assassins
8	Months of the French Revolutionary calendar	17	Derrick (about 1600)
		18	Sparta
9	The King's (or Queen's) shilling	19	Bohemia
		20	'The Young Pretender'
10	Poland (Ignace Paderewski)		

United Kingdom 4

1   Central Criminal Court
2   HRH Prince Henry of Wales
3   Orkney Islands
4   Goodwin Sands
5   The Most Noble Order of the Garter
6   The Tesco supermarket chain
7   Cinque Ports

8   The Court of St James's
9   Gloucestershire
10   Crown

11   Mount Snowdon
12   Marquis
13   Vale of Pewsey
14   Kirkcudbright

15   Cooper
16   Buckinghamshire
17   A guillotine
18   Royal Botanic Gardens
19   Lord Advocate
20   Isle of Man

Music and entertainment 4

1   76
2   Leo McKern
3   Scotland
4   *Twin Peaks*
5   Police
6   A famous Swiss clown and acrobat
7   Billie Holliday

8   Organ
9   The Bluebell Girls
10   Marlene Dietrich

11   Vaslav Nijinsky
12   78rpm shellac discs
13   Tim Brooke-Taylor
14   Harlequin

15   They have all played Professor Quatermass
16   Arpeggio
17   Molière
18   Morality play
19   Ethel Barry more
20   Stan Kenton

Science and nature 4

1   Geiger counter
2   Antibiotics
3   Pacific 11,515 metres (37,782 feet) at the Mindano Deep
4   Mauve
5   On a spacecraft (it is fired as a brake)
6   Sterling silver
7   Peach

8   In street lighting
9   Perennial

10   Juniper
11   Dry ice
12   Asteroids
13   *Principia Mathematica*
14   For welding or cutting metals

15   Frond
16   Anti-matter
17   Complementary
18   Bladderwort
19   Lithium
20   A lens

Definitions 4

1	c	11	d
2	b	12	c
3	d	13	b
4	b	14	a
5	e		
6	a	15	c
7	d	16	b
		17	e
8	b	18	d
9	b	19	c
10	e	20	d

Sport and games 4

1   Curling
2   Snooker (or billiards)
3   He wears a yellow jersey
4   Five
5   Puck
6   Tony Jacklin
7   West Ham United ('Hammers') and Arsenal ('Gunners')

8   Ron Clarke
9   Ice skating
10 Old Trafford, Manchester

11 Cribbage
12 Basketball
13 Riposte
14 Tottenham Hotspur

15 Polo
16 A kind of charades
17 Angling (it is a strong lifting hook)
18 1.2 metres (4 feet)
19 Bury
20 Chess

Animal kingdom 4

1   Spider
2   False
3   Flamingo
4   Canter
5   Beaver (of the three, it is the only one extinct in Britain)
6   Myxomatosis
7   Domestic dog

8   Superb starling
9   Moth
10 Angora goat
11 Four (true insects have only two)
12 Bird

13 They are not predators but feed on plankton
14 Beagle

15 Anglo-Arab
16 Lynx
17 Jellyfish
18 Deer (velvet is soft skin covering the antlers at a certain period of development)
19 Sheep (it is a hornless breed originally from Sussex or Hampshire)
20 Rennet

Geography and travel 4

1 Olympus
2 Four years
3 Europe, Asia, Antarctica, North America, South America, Africa, Australia
4 Mountain peak
5 The Pope
6 Pidgin English
7 Lunch

8 Orange River
9 Dublin
10 Baden-Baden

11 Indian Ocean
12 Both
13 In alpine regions where snow can be reddened by certain algae
14 Metro stations

15 Aubusson
16 Groschen
17 The Petrified Forest
18 Shikoku
19 Colombia
20 Michigan

Art and literature 4

1 Joseph Conrad
2 Hamelin
3 Pegasus
4 J. R. R. Tolkein
5 *The Tyger*
6 Jacob Epstein
7 *Don Quixote*

8 Gouache
9 Dartmoor
10 Gerard Manley Hopkins

11 The Ten Commandments
12 John Donne
13 Antonym
14 Rudyard Kipling

15 The demigod Prometheus
16 Arnold Bennett
17 Pierre Bonnard
18 F. R. Leavis
19 Ashcan
20 Every Roman citizen

Quick-fire Quiz 5 – Answers

Pot pourri 5

1   Fleur-de-lis
2   Gill
3   Plinth
4   Marquetry
5   Capon
6   Ginger
7   A style of decorative handwriting
8   Mandarin
9   Elijah
10 A Danish and Norwegian meal of cold meat, salad, fish and bread

11 Aga Khan
12 Au gratin
13 Laissez-faire
14 The Hittite warrior Uriah
15 Bombardier
16 Lagan
17 Buddhism
18 Biscuit
19 Bailey bridge
20 Marriage of one woman to several husbands

History 5

1   Kensington Palace
2   Lancelot Brown was a famous 18th-century English landscape gardener
3   Automobile Association
4   Hirohito, Emperor of Japan
5   Archduke Franz Ferdinand of Austria
6   The Jews (it acknowledged their right to a national home in Palestine)
7   President Ronald Reagan
8   Belgian Congo

9   Ottoman Empire
10 George I
11 Balmoral
12 Ireland
13 One
14 Harold Wilson
15 Leicestershire
16 The Oxford movement
17 Clement Attlee
18 Herodotus
19 Canadian
20 The Alhambra

United Kingdom 5

1	Up to the 18th birthday	10	Prime Minister
2	Eton	11	Livery companies
3	Bedfordshire	12	Brighton
4	A mountain	13	Tay
5	Leicester	14	British Dental Association
6	Devon		
7	Glengarry	15	Durham
		16	Shetland Islands
8	Oxford (it is a rotunda that houses part of the Bodleian Library)	17	Crewe
		18	Tea
		19	Royal Company of Archers
9	They do not bear the name of the country, only the head of the sovereign	20	Nottingham

Music and entertainment 5

1	Contralto	12	Franz Haydn
2	The Third Programme	13	Leeds
3	Dennis Potter	14	*Gone with the Wind*
4	*Birds of a Feather*		
5	Bill Haley	15	Grand Guignol
6	Metronome	16	Marilyn Monroe
7	Peter Sellers	17	Peter Benchley
		18	Anton von Webern
8	Fred Astaire	19	A group of 16th-century actors of whom Shakespeare was one
9	Violin		
10	Albert Finney	20	My fatherland
11	The Kirov		

Science and nature 5

1	Loganberry	11	Vulcanisation
2	Carbon monoxide	12	Jupiter
3	Mercury	13	Triangle
4	Vellum	14	The head
5	The study of earthquakes		
6	High	15	Deuterium
7	Greenwich Mean Time (GMT)	16	Saxifrages
		17	Latex
8	Carbon 14 dating	18	Geranium
9	212°	19	None
10	Bauxite	20	In a nuclear reactor

Definitions 5

1	a	11	c
2	d	12	b
3	d	13	e
4	d	14	b
5	d		
6	c	15	b
7	a	16	b
		17	a
8	e	18	c
9	e	19	d
10	a	20	e

Sport and games 5

1	Grand National	10	Scunthorpe United
2	Puissance	11	Orange
3	Auction Bridge	12	Johnny Weissmuller
4	Ilie Nastase (unlike the others, he did not win the Men's Singles Championship at Wimbledon)	13	Modern pentathlon
		14	Yorkshire
		15	Judo
5	Hop, step and jump	16	Clive Lloyd
6	Polo	17	Women's golf
7	Motor rallying	18	David Watkins
		19	Roulette
8	Cliff Thorburn	20	Stanley Cup
9	1 January		

Animal kingdom 5

1	False; gorillas are vegetarians	11	Cassowary
2	Chinchilla	12	Skewbald
3	Sturgeon	13	Jackdaw
4	Brown rat	14	Borzoi
5	Turtle		
6	Butterfly	15	The Indian sub-continent
7	Five	16	Bedlington terrier
		17	Tail of a rabbit, hare or deer
8	Budgerigars	18	Remora
9	Whale	19	Pastern
10	Proboscis	20	Orang-utan

Geography and travel 5

1	Florence	12	Assagai
2	Hellas	13	Sirocco
3	Maple leaf	14	Mountain range
4	Boers		
5	Massachusetts	15	Grande Corniche
6	Portuguese	16	*The Flying Dutchman*
7	USA	17	In the St Lawrence River (USA/Canada)
8	Jamaica	18	Ile St-Louis
9	Lake Constance	19	Switzerland, in the canton of Graubiinden
10	Finland		
11	Camargue	20	The doldrums

Art and literature 5

1	13 per cent	11	Isabella
2	Benvenuto Cellini	12	The 1930s (1 September 1939)
3	20 years	13	John Milton in *Paradise Lost*
4	Thomas Gainsborough	14	Excalibur
5	T. E. Lawrence (of Arabia)		
6	Dick Francis	15	Expressionism
7	80 days	16	Georges Seurat
		17	Stendhal
8	Portraiture	18	*Little Dorrit*
9	Pere	19	He shot himself
10	Chaucer's Canterbury Pilgrims	20	The Pentateuch

Score sheets

FINAL SCORE:

Home Team   Away Team

1st HALF	HOME		AWAY	
ROUND 1	SCORE	BONUS	SCORE	BONUS
Q1				
Q2				
Q3				
Q4				
Q5				
TOTAL				
ROUND 2				
Q1				
Q2				
Q3				
Q4				
Q5				
TOTAL				
ROUND 3				
Q1				
Q2				
Q3				
Q4				
Q5				
TOTAL				
ROUND 4				
Q1				
Q2				
Q3				
Q4				
Q5				
TOTAL				
ROUND 5				
Q1				
Q2				
Q3				
Q4				
Q5				
TOTAL				
1st HALF	HOME		AWAY	
TOTAL				

FINAL SCORE:

Home Team   Away Team

2nd HALF	HOME		AWAY	
ROUND 6	SCORE	BONUS	SCORE	BONUS
Q1				
Q2				
Q3				
Q4				
Q5				
TOTAL				
ROUND 7				
Q1				
Q2				
Q3				
Q4				
Q5				
TOTAL				
ROUND 8				
Q1				
Q2				
Q3				
Q4				
Q5				
TOTAL				
ROUND 9				
Q1				
Q2				
Q3				
Q4				
Q5				
TOTAL				
ROUND 10				
Q1				
Q2				
Q3				
Q4				
Q5				
TOTAL				
2nd HALF	HOME		AWAY	
TOTAL				

FINAL SCORE:

Home Team   Away Team

1st HALF	HOME		AWAY	
ROUND 1	SCORE	BONUS	SCORE	BONUS
Q1				
Q2				
Q3				
Q4				
Q5				
TOTAL				
ROUND 2				
Q1				
Q2				
Q3				
Q4				
Q5				
TOTAL				
ROUND 3				
Q1				
Q2				
Q3				
Q4				
Q5				
TOTAL				
ROUND 4				
Q1				
Q2				
Q3				
Q4				
Q5				
TOTAL				
ROUND 5				
Q1				
Q2				
Q3				
Q4				
Q5				
TOTAL				
1st HALF	HOME		AWAY	
TOTAL				

FINAL SCORE:

Home Team   Away Team

2nd HALF	HOME		AWAY	
ROUND 6	**SCORE**	**BONUS**	**SCORE**	**BONUS**
Q1				
Q2				
Q3				
Q4				
Q5				
TOTAL				
ROUND 7				
Q1				
Q2				
Q3				
Q4				
Q5				
TOTAL				
ROUND 8				
Q1				
Q2				
Q3				
Q4				
Q5				
TOTAL				
ROUND 9				
Q1				
Q2				
Q3				
Q4				
Q5				
TOTAL				
ROUND 10				
Q1				
Q2				
Q3				
Q4				
Q5				
TOTAL				
2nd HALF	**HOME**		**AWAY**	
TOTAL				

FINAL SCORE:

Home Team   Away Team

1st HALF	HOME		AWAY	
ROUND 1	SCORE	BONUS	SCORE	BONUS
Q1				
Q2				
Q3				
Q4				
Q5				
TOTAL				
ROUND 2				
Q1				
Q2				
Q3				
Q4				
Q5				
TOTAL				
ROUND 3				
Q1				
Q2				
Q3				
Q4				
Q5				
TOTAL				
ROUND 4				
Q1				
Q2				
Q3				
Q4				
Q5				
TOTAL				
ROUND 5				
Q1				
Q2				
Q3				
Q4				
Q5				
TOTAL				
1st HALF	**HOME**		**AWAY**	
TOTAL				

FINAL SCORE:

Home Team   Away Team

2nd HALF	HOME		AWAY	
ROUND 6	**SCORE**	**BONUS**	**SCORE**	**BONUS**
Q1				
Q2				
Q3				
Q4				
Q5				
TOTAL				
ROUND 7				
Q1				
Q2				
Q3				
Q4				
Q5				
TOTAL				
ROUND 8				
Q1				
Q2				
Q3				
Q4				
Q5				
TOTAL				
ROUND 9				
Q1				
Q2				
Q3				
Q4				
Q5				
TOTAL				
ROUND 10				
Q1				
Q2				
Q3				
Q4				
Q5				
TOTAL				
2nd HALF	**HOME**		**AWAY**	
TOTAL				

Quick-fire Quiz Score Sheet

Quiz Number:

Player	1	2	3	4	5	6
Category and question	Score	Score	Score	Score	Score	Score
Totals						

Quick-fire Quiz Score Sheet

Quiz Number:

Player Category and question	1 Score	2 Score	3 Score	4 Score	5 Score	6 Score
Totals						